C000219029

How
THE **BEATLES**
Knew

How
THE BEATLES
Knew

A Theory of How They Wrote Their Songs

ILSE NICCOLINI

How The Beatles Knew

Includes Appendices, Reference Notes and Index.

FIRST   EDITION

1. Music criticism
2. Literary criticism
3. Social Sciences
4. Social History—Sixties
5. McCartney, Paul—songwriting analysis
6. Songwriters, British – 20th century

Cover: Mirror Pix/Alamy and PA Images/Alamy

ISBN: 978-1-7365171-2-3
978-1-7365171-3-0 (ebook)

Tonal Publications

Printed and Manufactured in the United States of America

"It seemed to Western youth that The Beatles *knew* – that they had the key to current events and were somehow orchestrating them through their records."

−IAN MACDONALD

To my one and only

Contents

CHAPTER I

Days in Conversation: Paul Moves in With the Ashers

Paul McCartney met Jane Asher in April 1963, and moved into the Asher home on 57 Wimpole Street, London, in November of that year. For Paul, to be welcomed into the center of a close, intellectual, cultured and liberal family such as the Asher's was "like the world opening up." Jane was a talented young actress, her mother Margaret a music teacher who had tutored The Beatles' producer, George Martin. Dr. Richard Asher was a published and respected doctor, and Clare and Peter, Jane's siblings, were in the entertainment business. The Ashers formed a complete family unit, something that Paul had not had enough of before.

Paul was born on June 18th, 1942 in Liverpool, only five months after bombing by the German Luftwaffe had ended. His mother Mary was given a more comfortable room at the hospital to have her baby because she had been nursing sister in charge of the maternity ward. Paul's father worked in the cotton exchange, and was also a musician. The cotton exchange had been closed for the war; after the war the industry would be thrown into chaos, and then slowly dwindle. But as Paul grew up, many babies were being born due to the post-war baby boom, and so Mary, who had trained to be a midwife, was kept busy and became the family's primary breadwinner.[1]

Liverpool had been the largest Atlantic port, one of the busiest shipping hubs in the world; it had boasted an iron overhead railway to transport cargo. Tens of thousands of workers had been employed there. Now the bombed-out port was being surrounded by new "estates" or housing developments on the outskirts of Liverpool, where Paul and several of his relatives lived. On Sundays his extended family of aunts and uncles came over for sing-alongs, his father Jim going through a repertoire at the piano.[2]

Paul was an intelligent boy, but his schoolmasters noted that he did not always put in the effort required. He could be an excellent student if he just applied himself, one wrote.[3] Paul was a brilliant mimic, and at recess a crowd of schoolchildren would gather around him as he acted out scenes from radio shows, taking all the parts.[4]

In 1956, when Paul was fourteen, his mother was diagnosed with cancer. She had surgery, but due to complications she died two weeks later.[5] Jim had bought Paul a trumpet, but Paul traded it in for a guitar, after asking Jim's permission to do so. The guitar came just at the right time.[6] Now, the children gathering round the beautiful Paul McCartney in the schoolyard would be treated to renditions of popular songs, and the "rock 'n' roll" music which Chuck Berry and Elvis Presley had almost invented.[7]

Jim was left to raise Paul and Mike, the younger son, on his own. Jim had written a few songs about which he was modest: all he had done, he said, was to "make them up."[8] Paul began to write some songs; his first composition was, "I Lost My Little Girl." After his mother died, he said later, "I learned to put a shell around me."[9]

Paul was becoming a multi-instrumentalist even as a young teen: he could play piano, learned guitar, and taught himself drums. Although Paul liked to learn, he wanted to pick what he would learn. His teachers noted he was bright, but said that he could achieve so much more if he put his mind to it. A later biographer noted of Paul, "he hated being told what to do."[10]

Paul had passed his 11-Plus exams and his "O" levels with ease; these ruthless portcullises descend at ages eleven and sixteen in the U.K., and largely determine a child's future expectations. Paul's friend John Lennon had failed his "Elevenses," in that he did not qualify for a spot at the Liverpool Institute, which Paul was attending; John was attending the art school adjacent to the Institute, where students had to meet certain requirements in order to advance. John was not set to advance in art school,[11] perhaps because his drawings did not show innate ability. However, he looked the part of an art school student-rock 'n' roller to a T.[12] Dressed in a long "flood" jacket, black boots and tight drainies, his hair greased and styled in a pompadour like his idols Elvis Presley and Little Richard, John radiated street-toughness. Refusing to wear glasses although his eyesight was poor, John could whip out acerbic remarks and seemed to have an impenetrable shell.

Paul had grown to be, if not menacing in appearance, moderately tall at five foot eleven, and had a singular male beauty, just shy of effeminacy. He and John had become friends in 1957, after Paul picked up the guitar;[13] Paul joined John's band, The Quarrymen, its name inspired by a high school anthem.[14]

John and Paul's shared interest was not art school, but songwriting, and the raw, high-energy expression of rock and roll. Sailors passing through the port brought new records with them from such American artists as Elvis Presley, Gene Vincent, and Little Richard. Rock was a medium where John and Paul could scream and shout, and let out all the energy that was in them. Playing covers and some of their own compositions at the Cavern Club and the Casbah in Liverpool and in the seedy strip-bars and dives of Hamburg, Germany, they joined an underground of people who flaunted conventional morality whether out of personal motivations or simply for income. They had a symbiotic partnership: John was the leader of the band, but he was rather lazy in his work habits. To observers in those early days, Paul seemed more driven and perfectionist than John.[15] Along with drummer Pete Best, they added guitarist George Harrison, just turned fifteen, to their line-up. Adding Harrison relegated Paul to bass guitar, although Paul could easily have been the group's guitarist.

The leather-clad, raucous Beatles had amassed a following in Liverpool by October 28th, 1961, when Brian Epstein, aged twenty-seven, saw them perform at the Cavern Club in Liverpool and decided to take them under his wing. Epstein's family owned the well-established North England Music Stores (NEMS) chain. Epstein got the Beatles signed to Parlophone/EMI after firing Pete Best as drummer (Best's mother owned the Casbah music venue) and luring away talented drummer Ringo Starr from Rory Storm (Caldwell)'s band. Paul had dated Caldwell's sister Iris, and Caldwell's band was one of their primary competitors. Their lineup solidified by the time of their first release, the Beatles debuted in October 1962 with a single, "Love Me Do," with a B-side of "P.S. I Love You," both songs Paul had written.

The Beatles formed "a gang," as John later described it, and then a family of sorts with the addition of management and mentorship by Epstein. The Ashers were to be another family, one that would nurture Paul's talent so that it would have unprecedented influence, in ways no one could have foreseen.

By April 1963, the Beatles had released three singles and one album on the Parlophone label. "Please Please Me" was the title of their debut album released in April and of their second single released in January of 1963, with a B-side of "Ask Me Why." Almost half of their first album was cover songs. In April 1963, they released another single, co-written, "From Me To You," with a B-side of "Thank You Girl." Paul and John had reportedly co-written dozens of songs at this point, a few of which they would use on subsequent albums.

That same month, Paul met just-turned seventeen Jane Asher at a television show taping, and subsequently fell in love with her. Jane would inspire some of his most beautiful ballads, among them "Here, There and Everywhere," and "And I Love Her." They made a striking couple, and soon not only would young men copy Paul's hairstyle, but young women and girls would be exhorted to copy Jane's. With her long red hair and womanly yet childish face, Jane was a suitable consort to Paul with his man-boy visage. Besides having a beautiful profile, Paul had delicately arched eyebrows, large eyes and a distinctively shaped head, which the urchin haircut he wore suited to perfection. The Beatles' haircuts had been solidified in Hamburg, before they met Epstein: they were the "Existential" or "Exi" art student's cut[16] worn by youth in Germany and Paris. Epstein took the Beatles out of leather and put them into Saville-Row-tailored suits and the same style of pointed-toe boot, but a more expensive version. Paul's good manners were an asset under Epstein's management and helped his winning Jane.

Paul's biographer Barry Miles in *Many Years From Now* wrote, "in fact, Paul's relationship with the Ashers was ultimately more important than his relationship with Jane."[17] I will argue that the Asher's areas of interests would be a major, if not *the* influence on Paul's songwriting. In this book I will show how the discoveries Paul made living at the Asher home began his artistic process and led the Beatles. Incredibly, within the confines of the Asher household Paul created the synthesis from which he would launch not only the phenomenon of The Beatles, but also create the "culture" of Sixties.

It is almost impossible to date with *utter* certainly when any Beatles song was written. An artist can compose material that is published immediately or is kept in mental storage for many years. Songs are not like literature, paintings or sculpture, artworks that exist in the material world as soon as they are created. Music can be composed and exist solely within the composer's mind. Even if tablature or notes are written down, the arrangement and myriad other details about the music exist only in the composer's head, until the song is performed in front of other people. It is a feeling of power peculiar to musical composers, that they have "an ace up their sleeve." They could have a song in mind that they intuit is good, as Paul felt about "Yesterday," but they will not have corroboration of this until they complete the process of releasing it. To be a songwriting success, and to receive validation of an identity as such, a composer's song must be recorded, released, heard, reviewed, and then, one hopes, bought in vast numbers. While The Beatles were releasing material, they were always credited as co-writers; now with the advent of the internet, there are lists available which state which songs Paul wrote all or mostly on his own, which songs were John's, and which songs were co-written. This book is focusing on Paul and his artistic process; so I will necessarily look at those songs which according to internet sources, Paul wrote all or mostly on his own. But I will also talk about some co-written songs, and John and George's songs, inasmuch as Paul's artistic process affected them.

While acknowledging that composers can release songs out of order, I will assume that Paul wrote songs shortly before they were recorded, unless it is known otherwise.

Beginning with Paul's meeting Jane and the Asher family in April 1963, we see a development in his work. Paul's published output up until then had not been notable for introspection. He had written, on his own, both sides of The Beatles' first single in 1962. Additionally to their first album he had contributed "I Saw Her Standing There," a song he wrote in his teens. That was the extent of Paul's released output as of April 1963, excluding co-writes with John. These songs were simple in lyric content and emotion. Then, suddenly we have a newer Paul, a deeper Paul, if you will, upon his meeting Jane.

His new depth was of course ascribed to normal maturation, and also, to his being a songwriter, falling in love and becoming inspired. I will show it was more than this which enabled Paul to give the world such compelling songs.

At the Asher residence, the Paul who had been exposed to the underbelly of Hamburg would now be a Paul exposed to a cultured, intellectual environment. The entire family had a serious approach to self-improvement through learning, books were valued objects and dinnertimes were forums for discussion and word-games with the dictionary. Both the children and the parents had professional attitudes: each of the children acted,[18] the mother taught at the Guildhall Academy of Music and Drama, and Dr. Asher was president of the

Clinical Section of the Royal Society of Medicine.[19] It was as if Paul was suddenly put into a story beloved in English literature, of the changeling or the pauper switched at birth who becomes a Prince. Paul had grown up in a home that had no clothes washer, and now he was welcomed as a son into a cultured family living in a multi-storied Edwardian home. Richard Asher's bloodline went back to the reign of King James, and Margaret Asher's family had an ancestral seat in the countryside.[20] It must have felt like a new beginning to Paul, or a fairytale. Jane was his fairytale princess, he the young prince.

A poignant melody he wrote soon after he moved in, in fact some date it to the month he moved in, "Yesterday" would be one of his most feeling works. But I suggest that the reason for its eventual completion and widespread success was due to an artistic and emotional process that Paul began while being exposed to influences in the Asher household. "Yesterday" was Paul becoming expert at his artistic process. He grew into it slowly, and this book will chart its development. What I write may shock some readers. It is not the usual story of Paul, and it is one I had no idea I would tell when I first began researching Paul as an artist.

Artists are influencers, but they also are perhaps more receptive to their environment than other people. Of course this changed after the Sixties, when everyone was encouraged (as author Arthur Koestler put it) that "all creatures have the capacity for creative activity."[21] If we admit that artists might be more influenced by their environments than say, those who choose to become doctors, dentists or teachers, than we might come a bit closer to understanding the mentality of Paul. And to Paul, living at the Asher's was an ideal loam for his creative ability to grow and flourish. He later described the home, the Asher family, the warm environment of talk and creativity and professional attitudes, as "it was kind of perfect!"[22] He had left a barren communal Beatle house, a bachelor pad, for this stimulating household. Everything was here, including two musicians, tape recorders, two (later, three) pianos, a doctor who worked in the field of psychology, a music teacher, a beautiful young daughter, three children in the entertainment business, and home-cooked meals.

So Paul would undoubtedly have been influenced to embrace this environment – to really be immersed in all it had to offer. It might seem very strange, what I am about to propose happened with Paul. I could not have imagined it until I had analyzed each and every one of his songs and then faced the fact that Paul was undeniably influenced by the world of psychology which Dr. Asher intersected with, and the world of acting which the children were immersed in. These two worlds Paul used to inform the world he had chosen to enter – that of music.

Paul would synthesize the Asher worlds into his music compositions. He would glean material from both the world of psychology and the topsy-turvy world of acting, where no one is as they seem. In time both these worlds would collide and even collude: psychology in the Sixties would become radicalized through the work of psychiatrist R.D. Laing, and acting would burst its confines to become "street theatre" and Abbie-Hoffman-style resistance to the "status quo."

But Paul, becoming a familiar presence at the Asher home in spring 1963, had no way of foreseeing any of these developments.

Paul was soaking up new material – information. He told biographer Barry Miles in *Many Years From Now* that he was always looking for material: he would go out, he said, "collecting information, *peep peep peep*, antenna out."[23] For songwriting, he thought, he needed the telling detail – "the lonely old person opening her can of catfood and eating it herself"[24] – the little bit that would encapsulate a story for people. These little narrative truths are staples in theatre, where it is important to show as much as tell. In novels as well, a detail can tell much about a person and their circumstances.

But Paul needed more than just mundane details – the can of catfood. He needed to, and wanted to, express emotions. Being a rock and roller was not quite enough. I assert that the Asher household, specifically the doctor's library, would contain the very material that he needed.

Dr. Asher had worked for several years as supervising physician of the mental observation ward at Central Middlesex hospital. One of his duties was to evaluate incoming patients and make an initial diagnosis of who was to enter the mental hospital, and who was to be admitted to the general hospital. He also administered hypnotherapy to those suffering from psychosomatic illness. He was a specialist in blood diseases, and was also regarded as an authority on neuroses, as well as physical conditions whose symptoms mimicked mental illness. Dr. Asher wrote many articles for the prestigious *Lancet* journal, including *Respectable Hypnosis*, and *Munchausen's Syndrome*. He also wrote a book, *Nerves Explained.*[25]

An M.D. with a sense of humor, Asher would lie down on the floor in his office sometimes, so as not to intimidate patients.[26] He also loved to play pranks and make jokes at the dinner table.

Interviewing the mentally ill for therapy and diagnostic purposes had become widespread practice by the early Sixties. Few outside the psychiatric profession read the patient interviews, of which even one patient's transcripts could fill a book. "Talk therapy" for mental patients had reached its apex in the early Sixties. Beginning in the mid-Fifties, such treatments as electroshock and insulin comas were being used much less in favor of talk therapy. The head of McLean mental hospital in Boston had enthusiastically instituted talk therapy even for the most insane,[27] and in the U.K. talk therapy was also being used, with detailed interviews given to patients on their admittance to the hospital.

Dr. Asher diagnosed, treated, and was in contact with the mentally ill every day. He would have regularly reviewed patient interview transcripts, as part of his diagnosis and treatment.

In the course of reading and assessing patient interview transcripts, as well as performing physical examinations, Dr. Asher identified and named Munchausen Syndrome in 1953. Munchausen Syndrome, named for the Baron Munchausen who told fantastical tales of his exploits and travels, is when a person feigns sickness for various reasons including to gain attention, receive drugs, have bed and board at the hospital, or for the joy of deception. Although the persons are acting ill in a convincing manner, they are also compelled to act in this fashion. Many people are compelled (one might argue) by society to act moral, fair, or generally put up a façade; but those with Munchausen Syndrome are choosing to act ill, even injuring themselves, in self-destructive acts. It is a form of acting that is compulsive and counter-intuitive. This begs the question, when does behavior become insanity? Not something a person controls, but something a person can't help doing. When is "acting" outside of one's own control?

It is interesting that during the time Dr. Asher was diagnosing and writing about Munchausen's, all three of his offspring were becoming actors. Margaret Asher was, according to Paul, "a bit of a stage mum."[28] Peter had been a child actor, and youngest sister Clare was a radio actress. Jane, the middle child, was pursuing a career on the stage. She had been acting since age six, and when Paul met her had both stage and screen credits to her name. It could be argued that Paul, too, was very interested in acting. He had grown up wanting to be an actor, "all smooth and in command."[29] Paul had from childhood enjoyed miming and mimicry in the schoolyard. He liked having an audience and now he was acting, in a sense, in The Beatles.

Paul was twenty-one when he moved in with the Ashers, but the Asher family had much to offer him developmentally. Mr. and Mrs. Asher treated him both as a son, and a future son-in-law. Paul was living with people who thought about acting, how to convey feelings, who studied maladaptation to society, and who drew lines between these areas in their professions. The family were keenly interested in music and theatre. Paul might have been drawn to Jane for deep reasons of his own. She might be able to see him, and not the actor in him. Just as Dr. Asher wanted to delineate precisely where a façade left off (of feigning illness for sympathy) and a diagnosable "syndrome" began, perhaps Jane, at age seventeen an experienced actress, would be able to let Paul know a finer line between acting and being real. Any lover usually wants to be understood by the other. But in any event from her Paul could learn much more about the fine points of acting, which he was doing *de facto* as a member in a pop band.

A World Without Love

Important to understanding Paul's emerging songwriting process is a discussion of "A World Without Love." This gentle song, which Paul had written as a teenager, was a Number One hit for Peter and Gordon in 1964. Paul had written the main melody and half the lyrics while living with his family on Forthlin Road.[30] I will argue that Paul gave the song to Jane's brother Peter Asher in friendship, but also that the song was a way for Paul to test something – a metaphorical device, a subtext that would shape his later work.

"A World Without Love" introduces a person who is asking that he be locked away. This is a striking anomaly from Paul's other songs where he was playing the role of swain, out and about in the world, looking at girls. In "World," Paul (the singer) asks, "Please, lock me away/And don't allow the day/Here inside, where I hide with my loneliness/I don't care what they say, I won't stay in a world without love."

John thought the song was "too soft" for the Beatles. Paul shopped it around to other singers, after John's veto: but he had to release this song into the world, because it contains the nugget of Paul's aesthetic, even of the Beatles. This song made use of unusual points of view, without anyone bothering to make a connection. Paul could test in releasing this song certain ideas, and how they could fit into songs. Paul needed metaphors – he needed images to plug into songs. But he could write a really good song because the concept spoke to him. Because this song had a subtext that Paul could write into a well-formed composition, the song had as we call it, "legs." It stuck in people's minds – it could get around. Paul gave it to Peter Asher, Jane's brother, and Peter and Gordon took it to Number One in both the U.K. and the U.S. in 1964.[31]

Let's look a little more closely at this seminal song for Paul, and by one remove, for the Beatles.

Paul had reportedly plenty of songs laying around by mid-1963 that were not deemed good enough to release as Beatles songs: he said he would give away songs that he thought were second-rate to other artists. Why was "A World Without Love" the song he picked from his slush pile to give away? I suggest it was because Paul realized that way he could test a certain subtext, without any risk to the Beatles.

Peter Asher wrote a middle-eight section that qualifies the request to be "locked away" is because of the singer's lack of confidence in finding love.[32] But the main idea of the song, as Paul wrote it, was much more restricted. The only place a person can ask to be locked away in is a mental asylum (a voluntary commitment). It was much more a mental patient's plaint: "Birds sing out of tune, and rain clouds hide the moon/I'm okay, here I'll stay, with my loneliness," Paul wrote. The outside world is perceived as off-key and "not right," compared to the place where he is "locked away" in.

The song's asylum-seeker seeks to hide from the world. A metaphor of the world inside and out as a mental hospital, or psych ward, is incongruous with the music, a sensitive-sounding ballad. Paul then gave the song to Peter Asher to finish, and humorously, the lyrics completed the tale and proposed a nonsensical solution to having no love: to be locked away from the world!

Paul gave this song to Peter shortly after he had moved in with the Ashers. I suggest that this song was Paul's "proof of concept," where he tried the idea of extending a metaphor, using a motif from the world of the mentally ill – the world Dr. Asher diagnosed. I suggest that Paul, finding himself in the midst of patient interviews and related literature in Dr. Asher's library, gave the song to Peter Asher to see if using an asylum metaphor like this would fly. It did – "A World Without Love" went to Number One in the U.K. and the U.S after being released in February 1964. (The B-side was, rather ironically since I am suggesting Peter acted as his proxy, "If I Were You.")

Another novel thing about "A World Without Love" is its circular logic, which we will encounter several times in Beatles songs. The asylum-seeker seeks to hide from the world, and love; in his loneliness, he rejects people. Having a non-solution seem like a solution is typical of nonsense verse. Paul was familiar with nonsense verse through art school and John. Since he had been a young boy, John had been a big fan of writers such as Edward Lear and Lewis Carroll.[33] John displayed a talent, even a preference, for communicating with wordplay, satire and quoting nonsense verse. In mixing absurd circular logic (as well as subtexts from the world of mental patients) with the sensical (the expectations of conventional audiences), Paul could write in a complimentary way to John. They would separately and together write songs that were quite different than the usual fare. "A World Without Love" would prove Paul's idea that both circular logic and the subtext of a mental patient could be fused in a song format, and also that no one would make the connection and see (or if they did, object to) the song's metaphor of a mental asylum.

All My Loving

Paul's first song written after meeting the Ashers has a sense of surrealism, absence and dislocation, and it is a letter-writing song, one of his favorite formats. These motifs would often inform his later songs.

Paul wrote "All My Loving" in May of 1963, a few weeks after meeting Jane. He recorded the song in July of 1963. The song was not intended to be a single. It got so much radio play and audience reaction, however, that it was released in 1964 as the title song of a best-selling EP.[34] The song first appeared on the group's second album, "With The Beatles," released in November of 1963.

On that album, six of the fourteen tracks were covers, including a Chuck Berry song, "Roll Over Beethoven," and the Marvelette's 1961 Motown hit, "Please Mr. Postman." "All My Loving," which originated as a lyric Paul wrote while the Beatles were on tour with Roy Orbison, had hallmarks of what would become Paul's distinctive writing style. It was different from the usual epistolary song.

In 1963 Paul would begin to introduce concepts into songs that I submit were taken from his reading psychiatric literature. However a sense of what I can only call dislocation is also a motif in his songwriting. The fact that this appears in his early songs argues for Paul's having his own personal artistic process, and not one necessarily imposed on him by the Ashers or others. He began a personal songwriting journey which was profoundly influenced and nurtured at the Asher's, but he had written part of a song, "A World Without Love," which connected to this process even before he had met Jane.

Paul's first song written after meeting Jane, "All My Loving" suggests more confidence and had a sense of wordplay that was related to, but not the same, as John's. John favored puns or double meanings, a wink to listeners "in the know." Paul's wordplay would suggest disjuncture, dislocation, or distance (besides a split, which we shall discuss). Even though his voice and writing style were typically smoother than John's, his lyrics were dissonant in a subtle way. For "All My Loving," Paul wrote, "Close your eyes, and I'll kiss you/ Tomorrow I'll miss you/Remember, I'll always be true/And then while I'm away…" In the first verse, there are five images of distance. First, he tells her to close her eyes. Although he is kissing her, he is already thinking of when they will be apart. He asks her to remember this moment, when she is apart from him. He is thinking of what he will do, while he is away—write every day. Then, the chorus—he will send her all his loving. But where is the expression of love in the present? The verse has avoided completely describing the moment of their kiss, or the lovers' presence; the song lyrics are talking about absence.

Most songwriters of that era would write about the moment of a kiss: the rapture, her lips, the feeling of love, and so on. This kiss of Paul's invention is given very little *location*.

Another type of disjuncture, which manages to be both coy and surreal, occurs in the lyric, "I'll pretend/That I'm kissing/The lips I am missing." Of course, one assumes the singer will be missing (kissing) her lips, but the line as written is that he is missing his *own* lips. It's a little joke, a small one, at language's expense. One could even read the lyric as the singer pretending to kiss himself, and that he has no lips with which to do so. It's sort of a strange way to read the lyrics,

I know, but I think this hear-part-of-the-puzzle-oh-wait-here's-the-other-half style of writing kept people listening. Something a little puzzling would be placed into context in the lines following it. This is similar to what he would do in "What You're Doing," where he clarifies the situation as one encountered in a love relationship. However on examination, in both these songs, the puzzlement is still there, just explained somewhat.

As Paul gained ground as a songwriter, he was using motifs of dislocation, along with (increasingly, as I shall show in this book) motifs from the field of psychology. He was also employing dislocation in terms of acting a part, sometimes in a Laingian sense (this reference will become clearer after the discussion in Chapter Three).

Paul would often use an epistolary or letter-writing format in his songs. This format combined with the singer's absence from the present moment increases the sense of disjuncture in "All My Loving" until it verges on surrealism – a lipless kisser. But there is a psychological motif or implication to these lyrics as well, which I ask the reader to consider. The words, allowed to sink in, evoke (very subtly, I admit) the *feeling* of absence, or even of an absent person. The grounding word in the song is "home," which is also emphasized in the music. "I'll write *home* every day/And I'll send all my loving to you." The absent person will write home, every day. He *can* write. Subtle hallmarks of Paul's artistic process are in the song with its motifs of dislocation, absence, and the idea of writing a letter.

She Loves You

Paul presented John with a concept for a song at the beginning of summer 1963—a song that would be one of "the most explosive pop records ever made," according to Ian MacDonald in *Revolution in the Head*.[35] "She Loves You" remains the Beatles' best-selling single in the U.K. and went to Number One in the U.S. It was recorded in July of 1963.

According to Ian MacDonald in *Revolution in the Head*, although John and Paul had written many songs by early 1963, "their confidence in all but a few of them was low."[36] They had a local following, had garnered publicity and had made a respectable showing with their first album, but according to biographer Philip Norman, the Beatles' popularity was slumping by fall of 1963.[37] A single by the Dave Clark Five had displaced them on the charts, and they were met with indifference on a tour in France. Then, they came back after the release of "She Loves You." "Beatlemania" would officially begin in October 1963, with their televised performance at the London Palladium. Ian MacDonald writes that "the Beatles brought their set to a climax with 'She Loves You,' and overnight, Britain took the Beatles to its heart."

I suggest that what Paul encountered at the Asher residence forms the hidden subtext of "She Loves You." In tandem with "I Want To Hold Your Hand," "She Loves You" was also their breakthrough to U.S. audiences. Both songs were a co-write with John. John said later "She Loves You" was "mostly Paul," and that the concept was Paul's. John told the interviewer that "She Loves You" was when "Paul began to put a third thing in there."[38] Let's look at the lyrics of this groundbreaking song.

"She Loves You" has a conceit of the singer(s) (Paul and John singing in harmony) breaking the ecstatic news of the song's title. It is not common that someone jumps for joy telling someone that another person loves him. It was an unusual premise. Ian MacDonald described the lyrics as "prodigally original, yet instantly communicative."[39] I suggest that Paul had done something very simple, but what no songwriter had done before: to sing a song from the point of view of a third person who interceded between two parties. I propose this song, which was a hit and really captured people's attention as something unusual, was Paul posing the Beatles-as-therapists.

Instead of writing a song from the typical point of view of the lover, Paul's concept put the Beatles in the space between, bringing news ecstatic to relate. The precise relationship is undefined; however the concept is akin to a therapist who has consulted with both parties. "She said you hurt her so/She almost lost her mind/But now she says she knows/You're not the hurting kind." And: "You know it's up to you/I think it's only fair/Pride can hurt you too/Apologize to her." The Beatles were mediating between a couple, while singing directly to audiences.

If Paul had written the song from first person, and not from the point of view of the "third thing," the song title would have been "I Love Her," and it would have been unremarkable. "She said I hurt her so/She almost lost her mind/But now she says she knows/I'm not the hurting kind…. She loves me, yeah, yeah, yeah!" The relief of the singer over reconciliation would hardly have endeared him to audiences. He would have seemed to have benefited from his girlfriend's confusion more than anything else.

But instead, "She Loves You" brought something new to the relationship mix, an intermediary, and also a hint of a different dialectic. It put the Beatles in the space between people, similar to but not necessarily exactly as a therapist. It introduced a hint of absurdity as well, the singers or person in the song bringing news about something they actually know nothing about except what the two parties told them. And it was done to a setting of music and vocal power that was so high-energy as to be unprecedented. This was *news*. The song, or blast, was I suggest taken subconsciously almost as if here was being presented an heretofore-unknown *dimension*. It was the use of psychological subtexts, which John called "when Paul started to put the third thing in there." Although it was often playful, often joking, it was in effect creating in people's minds a new horizon of (possible) interactions, depth, relatedness, and feeling. This new dimension was the "interval" Paul created, that I will explain more of later.

Much attention was focused on the refrain of "yeah, yeah, yeah," which John said they had copied from Elvis Presley. MacDonald wrote, "Beyond doubt, the record's hottest attraction was its notorious refrain 'yeah, yeah, yeah,' from which the group became known throughout Europe as The Yeah-Yeahs. (Almost as celebrated were their falsetto 'ooo's, stolen from The Isley Brothers.)"[40] However, MacDonald, writing in the 1990s, missed that a new Beatles' "way," the "third thing," had been created. The Beatles' music was taken from many musical ideas and mannerisms of other artists, but it had that something different. I submit that the song's impact wasn't due to its Americanism of "yeah," with its sexual innuendo. I suggest that the high-energy song sounded so novel, even alien, because Paul had found a world to resonate with in the psychological texts and the world of mental therapy and acting at the Asher's. In "She Loves You," he transposed the dialectics of therapy (that is, a therapist being a third party to a relationship, inserting themselves as arbitrator, and essentially attempting to explain two people to each other) into pop music. This was a new approach to writing songs. The Beatles also tell the second party (and the listeners) how to *feel*: "She loves you, and you know you should be glad."

Not only did he do all this, but he also essentially wrote a satire of dialectics into the song, an implausible situation mending a rift between two people and presented as resolved beyond a doubt.

The force of the Beatles' delivery in "She Loves You" was disproportionate to the situation, but this was attributed to *joie de vivre*. This same abundance of energy, with a "live" sound was in "I Want to Hold Your Hand." One suspects more than a hand will be held, but the song lyrics were acceptable to radio programmers. Released in November 1963, the latter song finally reassured U.S. radio programmers and Capitol Records.[41] Both singles paved the way to the Beatles' high-visibility U.S. promotional tour a few months later. (Before that, according to MacDonald, Capitol had declined to widely promote Beatles singles. "Please Please Me" was thought to refer to fellatio.)

And I Love Her

The Asher's worlds of psychology and acting continued to influence Paul. He was beginning to develop a "way" of writing songs. Paul's third song written after meeting the Ashers examines the difference between acting and being sincere. It raises the question of doubt, and then settles the issue – makes, in effect, a diagnosis. He does love "her," even though, as the song acknowledges, there is a huge grey area in human relations.

"And I Love Her" was the next song Paul wrote after giving Peter Asher "A World Without Love." It was, I suggest, fruit of his new fertilization by the Asher household and the realization that he could put lyrics through the vise (devise, sieve or filter) of psychology and the world of acting. The song alludes subtly to the intersection of acting and truth. The lyrics are conventionally poetic, but they give a nod to the possibility that all words, no matter how loving, could be an act. "The kiss my lover brings, she brings to me," the singer (I will sometimes employ this designation instead of the Beatle name) sings, then adds, "and I love her." The line subtly implies that it is possible for her to bring a kiss, (that is, to kiss him) but to be kissing another lover mentally while she kisses him (or even that he is not always "himself"). "And I Love Her" is extra confirmation for the words we have just heard—"Bright are the stars that shine/Dark is the sky/I know this love of mine/Will never die"—but it also hints that a lover's words or actions might be acting. The song is a strange little wraparound, meeting its own potential for meaninglessness in the middle. The instrumental middle eight, although romantic, veers dangerously close to parody, its legato guitar solo asking for "whispered words in French." For all its sweetness and tenderness, that the listener *feels*, the listener has also been told in so many words that words and actions can be false. Paul had to add, "and I love her." ("You were all right up until then," Sir Paul commented later about the lyric.) But then, could the confirmation "and I love her" possibly be an act, too?

I believe this song, recorded in February of 1964, was the fruit of Paul learning and thinking about acting and also his own capacity for feeling and emotions. (I am not a psychological expert. Maybe there is a difference technically between feelings and emotions, but I leave it to someone else to explain.)

Jane and Paul attended the theatre in London several nights a week,[42] so the craft of acting was on his mind. But there was something else growing in this early song, which I suggest could have been fruit of being immersed in an acting family. The absence or dislocation of "All My Loving" was fusing with acting in "And I Love Her." Beatles' songs were moving in a different *direction* from other songs.

It would be in these songs written post Paul's move-in that Beatles lyrics would begin to captivate listeners. By late 1963, "Beatlemania" set in. Not every song Paul wrote would have the hidden subtext of therapy, mental patient, acting, or the asylum; from 1963 to 1965, I count about half of his songs to be so (now that it is possible to verify with certainty which songs Paul wrote, by consulting numerous lists on the internet). There was seeming insight to their songs, which made the appealing, well-publicized, mop-topped Beatles stand out even more. This was the "emotional complexity" that would launch the Beatles into unprecedented fame.

Things We Said Today

The "different" quality of Beatles songs continued with Paul's next song, "Things We Said Today," released in June 1963, two months after he met Jane and the Ashers. The situation of the song again has distancing, where the singer is thinking of the future even though he is supposedly singing about the present. "Someday when we're dreaming/Deep in love, not a lot to say/Then we will remember/Things we said today." Paul is not letting the listener know what was "said today." He does share some thoughts –"These days such a kind girl/Seems so hard to find…. Love me all the time, girl/We'll go on and on." Like "All My Loving," the song has dislocation in that the point of the song is something that hasn't happened yet. Paul later commented that the song did "quite a good trick" in that he alluded to nostalgia for the present, in a moment in the future.[43] (A mood of dreamy nostalgia is also reflected in the music.) The lyrics, in alluding to "things we said today," might have been Paul's thinking of therapy sessions where people go to "say things," and the therapeutic conversation is to be remembered for later, but one cannot be sure.

Every Little Thing

Paul followed up "Things We Said Today" with "Every Little Thing." Ian MacDonald called this song "passionate" and "one of the most emotional tracks on the album." He saw it as confirmation of Paul's feelings for Jane. Yet, he noted that it was "a puzzle" that it ended up as "filler on Side 2 of 'Beatles For Sale,' only lowly regarded by its composer."[44] I think it is understandable why, not only that it might not have been the strongest song musically. It could be that Paul was finding his lyric territory, and in "Every Little Thing," he found that even though he could express a lot of feeling in a song, it would have to have something more going on in it. The song expressed strong emotion, but it did not have "odd logic," or novel phrases. Other songs Paul wrote at this time, including "What You're Doing," and "And I Love Her," did. "Every Little Thing" didn't have that different angle, that unusual phrasing. Therefore, for all its emotion Paul saw, maybe ruefully, that "Every Little Thing" would not be a song important to fans. There had to be something else to attract them, in Beatles songs: the third thing.

The third thing had worked with "She Loves You," and John and Paul's harmonies atop high-energy ringing guitars and Ringo's high-hat cymbal told audiences that the Beatles were onto something. They were co-writing using conventional song structures during those early days, but the third thing (or as I call it "the interval") would expand in songs, led by Paul's interest in psychology and acting while at the Asher's.

What You're Doing

Paul next put the "different" element into "What You're Doing," also recorded in fall of 1964. What I am going to suggest may shock some readers, but, when I read these lyrics in context of what was happening in psychology of the time, it does seem that the song's lyrics could have been found in a mental patient interview transcript.

Dr. Asher would have read patient interviews every day, in his post as supervising physician of Central Middlesex mental hospital. He would use them to reach a diagnosis. These "work-ups" or interviews, excerpts of which were quoted in psychiatric literature of the mid-Fifties to early 1960s, show patients using a mixture of polite, almost formal language, and a particular type of emotion. The patients use somewhat formal language, that is, "proper" language, both because they are British, and because they are being interviewed by a doctor or therapist. But there is also a particular undercurrent of desperation; the patient is *in extremis*. They want to be understood; their future depends on it, at this point. They are almost powerless, being interviewed by a doctor who might decide whether they need treatment. Hence there is in these transcripts a politeness mixed with strong feelings and emotion. I argue that this point of view, this voice, is found in Paul's song, "What You're Doing." The lyrics describe the feelings of a young man who is feeling "done to" by his lover/girlfriend – but it is very like a patient's situation who has been admitted to a mental hospital and does not know what doctors are "doing" to him. The song's protagonist has no control over his situation. He asks, "Why should it be so much to ask of you/What you're doing to me?"—a mixture of desperation and conscious formal request in one phrase. (This type of question anticipates Gregory Bateson's complaint that a child can't make meta-statements to his parents, in Chapter Two). I think it likely that Paul could have been looking for material in Dr. Asher's library, and found a good phrase—spoken by an asylum patient. The protagonist explains he is "feeling blue and lonely," and has "been waiting here for you/Wondering what you're gonna do." Yes, this could be his waiting by the phone for a girlfriend to call—but it is really suitably describing a committed mental patient's reality. They are powerless, not knowing what is being done to them or why, feeling manipulated, and in the uniquely vulnerable spot of not knowing if it is "too much to ask" that the doctor clarify what the treatment will be. The song implies that he wishes he could ask the girlfriend/ doctor, but feels he can't. There is a sense of desperation while the protagonist tries to maintain self-control.

After, I suggest, Paul transposed or was inspired by mental patient interviews to write these lyrics, he then used his method of writing a middle-eight which contextualized the song as being about a conventional situation: romantic love. He sings, "And should you need a love that's true, it's me." This brings the listener an odd string of communications following one upon the other, not very logically: a desperation-tinged wish, followed by reassurance of the other person. It is this mix that makes the song memorable, and in what would come to be a Beatles trademark, not completely understandable. The lyrics match effortlessly to the clever melody and chord changes, and the lyrics, fitting perfectly to meter and yet, not fully understood, are duly filed away. Many Beatles songs would be filed away, as something "important that we listen" to. They would be listened to with "half an ear."[45] This is similar to what children do when they hear phrases they do not understand: they remember them, filing them away for later.

The treatment of the mentally ill was much different in the early Sixties than it is today. I ask the reader to imagine the schism then, between the general population and those in mental hospitals or asylums. The world was different than today. Every medium-sized to large city in the U.S. and the U.K. had an asylum to house the mentally ill, often located on the outskirts of the city.[46] Their lives, their forms of expression were as unknown as their feelings. (And yet, somewhat relatable, psychiatrist R.D. Laing would insist.) There was an institutionalized divide between sane and insane and another marker of that divide was popular culture and songs. In rock music, the most rebellious form of popular music at that time, there were in the Fifties still quite straightforward lyrics and images. For example, Elvis Presley sang," Don't be cruel/To a heart that's true ... I don't want no other lover/Baby it's just you I'm thinking of." If there were metaphors, they were used obviously: "Oh, let me be your Teddy bear." Charming the audience and undisturbing context were also important factors in mainstream acceptance. Frank Sinatra could sing that his lover's powers over him might be "witchcraft," but he didn't smear his face with coal, clasp a snake and grimace. He smiled, snapped his fingers, and wore a tailored suit. Elvis did jut out his pelvis, but his lower body was cropped from view for television audiences.

I do not want to give the reader the impression that I am ignoring the emotional pull of the Beatles songs, their appeal, freshness, and all the great things about them. I wanted to look at Paul's artistic process, how he wrote his songs. This is a process I have never seen done before, and as I followed the line of my thinking, which was simply that Paul could have been influenced by Dr. Asher, I was able to find more and more in Beatles songs which supported my theory. I will cite all the psychological sources I believed influenced Paul, in this book. I suggest the reader have on hand a copy of the complete Beatles songs lyrics, published by Hal Leonard, to refer to. If my book seems like dry analysis, please understand that emotionally, musically, I have respect for what the Beatles did. But this book will also tell a deeper story that some might find disturbing, or even be upset at me for thinking it. I went chronologically through Paul's entire Beatles *oeuvre* to track his process, before sitting down to write this book.

The patient transcripts in the Asher library would have contained strong, but somewhat controlled, expressions of feelings. In 1963, Paul might have been interested in reading about feelings; he had been accused of having none. A few years previously, his love affair with young Dorothy (Dot) Rhone had ended when she miscarried his child. He was seventeen, she was sixteen. Her miscarriage ended any plans of marriage. Dot's mother then told her "don't see that boy anymore. He has no feelings."[47] The mother of his subsequent flame, Iris Caldwell, had told him, "You've got no heart, Paul."[48] These comments were bound to have sunk in. They implied that Paul was a beautiful façade; an actor's mask if you will, who didn't have the feelings that one should have in a romantic relationship. But at the Asher's, Jane and her father Dr. Asher made it their professions to know where the dividing line was between acting and reality was. And there were on the shelves, I suggest, a trove of patient transcripts with people exposing inner feelings. It may have been subconscious or conscious on Paul's part to choose this family to move in with, but it is my contention that it was what Paul sensed he needed.

Paul, before meeting the Ashers in spring of 1963, had written on his own "I Saw Her Standing There," "P.S. I Love You," and "Love Me Do"—simple songs with limited poetic content. He knew he could be an accomplished songwriter, but he needed, as all writers do, material.

Dr. Asher, although a responsible professional working with the mentally ill all day, was not above a bit of nonsense. He loved practical jokes, and one of his favorite writers was Rupert Crawshay-Williams, author of *The Comforts of Unreason* published in 1947.[49] Dr. Asher would have had this book in his library, and it is possible Paul read it. The book is a philosophical treatise on madness, irrationality and psychology, which examines "motives for irrationality," fantasy, and how society (a group determination, that is) might determine objective reality. Crawshay-Williams held that irrationality was a welcome anodyne to the constrictions and limitations imposed upon people when they held as universal the ideas of "truth" and "goodness." He argued these were subjective constructs. Crawshay-William's examination of motives for irrationality would have resonance with Asher in his study of Munchausen Syndrome. Crawshay-Williams also wrote about circular logic in his book. *The Comforts of Unreason* is the sort of playful yet underneath, serious questioning of authority and ideals which both Paul and Dr. Asher would have appreciated. The Beatles' irreverence was to be influential during the Sixties. Paul was beginning a process which would become his preferred way of writing songs, and which would influence millions.

Paul wanted to be recognized as a songwriter, not an anonymous one who cranked out the hits in New York's Brill Building, but a new breed. The Beatles had been inspired by the example of Gene Vincent, who wrote his own material. The Asher family environment of psychology and acting would be of great help to Paul. And the mental patient interviews, which I am suggesting Paul read in Dr. Asher's library, could have been a source for memorable expressions of emotion. In a sense, to be "locked away" at the Asher's was the perfect environment for an aspiring songwriter who might desire to make personal statements. As icing on the cake, Margaret Asher, who suffered from migraines which gave her insomnia, was often up late to fix a meal for Paul after his evenings out.[50] At the Asher's, there were not only "comforts of unreason," but also comforts of home.

* * *

In Chapter Three we will look at a psychiatrist who would present the poetry in the words of the mentally ill: a psychiatrist at whose "altar" the Beatles reportedly "worshipped." But for now, imagine Paul, secreted away in Dr. Asher's library, browsing this book here and that book there. The library might have contained many interview transcripts of the mentally ill, read by very few other people in the entire world. Paul reads a few pages of interviews, and then picks up a book by R.D. Laing. He reads about a woman who calls herself "the ghost of the weed garden." He picks up a book of patient interview transcripts – and reads an interview with a depressed man who tells the interviewer, "There's a shadow hanging over me." Why that is interesting, thinks Paul. Usually shadows are under people. What an interesting phrase.

He reads more. Some of the mentally ill, whom Dr. Asher listened to, diagnosed and treated every day, describe themselves in compelling language: "I feel transparent, like glass," says one woman in an interview with her therapist. "As if everyone can see through me."

Then, imagine Paul putting the book back on the shelf in the library, and pondering as he ascends the stairs to his attic room. How is that woman insane and I'm not, he thinks. She's rather perceptive. How real are the self and its boundaries, he thinks abstractedly. Where does acting leave off and reality begin, in a person?

These stairs are a bit dusty, Paul might think, as he continues up the staircase.

"Hello?" Paul hears Jane's voice inside her room, below the attic. He puts his hand on the doorknob and walks in.

"How was rehearsal?" he asks.

"It was all right. I will be leaving in another two weeks' time," says Jane.

He knows that Jane, his young love, can act with the pose of her elbow; on film, the angle of her eyelashes can communicate a character's thoughts. Jane has learned about the various schools of acting: how to act a scene of great emotion with every muscle in her body relaxed, or how to act the same scene with her body tense as a coiled spring—trying to feel inside herself the same emotion of the character.

* * *

In February 1964, the Beatles were introduced to millions of viewers on U.S. television, with cutaways to girls screaming even more ecstatically they had to pop acts on Fifties television shows. Previously to the Beatles, pop acts were greeted by mostly young female fans applauding, often while they were chewing Beechnut gum, provided by the show sponsors. Sometimes the fans would appear to "melt" with emotion, for instance over Paul Anka. The Beatles seemed to provoke a more intense response than other pop acts, however, one verging on hysteria. The reactions could have been staged; only recently it has been revealed that fans were paid to be bussed to the airport to greet the Beatles on their arrival in the U.S. Likewise the news story about Beatlemania at the band's October performance at the London Palladium was said by Dezo Hoffman in Shout! to be a gross exaggeration. Hoffman said that only a handful of girls were screaming, and the photo was cropped and captioned that there was a crowd of manic fans. Norman, author of Shout! concluded that the riots had been "faked."[51]

After playing on Ed Sullivan for two nights, broadcast to an estimated 73 million people,[52] the Beatles were booked to perform at Carnegie Hall. This was no struggling band; through Epstein's connections they were "opened wide" in film distribution terms. The public was meant to take them to their hearts immediately. Their debut in the U.S. was bolstered by a wave of spin-off merchandising, from synthetic Beatle wigs to Beatle-imprinted dresses. Epstein almost "gave away" these concessions;[53] but it was effective nonetheless because all the merchandise in stores, publicity and radio play would contribute to the idea of "Beatlemania." It would aid in keeping them talked about in the media, and in the forefront of people's minds. Beatlemania was reported to be sweeping the U.S. when they returned later that year to tour.

In July of 1964, the Beatles released the film "A Hard Day's Night" which emphasized fans chasing them about. On the soundtrack were "And I Love Her" and "Things We Said Today" by Paul.

In October 1964 Paul recorded "She's a Woman," (some say, written on the spot in the studio) a "wire-taut" song praising a lover's fidelity and understanding.[54] This he followed with an old song of his, written in 1960, "I'll Follow the Sun." By this time he had been at the Asher's almost a year; in November of 1963, he had moved into a top-floor attic room in their home. He had been visiting there and eating dinner with the family for months, so it was a natural progression.

* * *

By November 1964, Paul had come some way since he first started hanging out with Jane and her family. He had co-written and come up with the idea for "She Loves You," and written the much-admired "And I Love Her": he was writing songs with depth, praised by critics. His songwriting was now regarded as on par with John's. He had been validated as a songwriter, and was no longer just "the cute one."

Initially, The Beatles hadn't picked any one musical style to be known for. The group's versatility was forged in clubs in Hamburg, where they were regarded as a musical jukebox, and attracted audiences with their energy and eclecticism. Their 1962 audition for Decca Records showed them capable of performing in many genres and in a sense, having many "identities." However, this didn't really help define them. In a 1962 televised performance in Sweden, the Beatles performed before a small studio audience of neatly dressed teens. John belted out "Twist and Shout." But Paul following this with "Have Some Fun Tonight" seemed (and not only because of his microphone not being loud enough) rather redundant. The audience was appreciative, but their applause gave the impression that one tough screamer was enough in the band.

Paul could scream-sing, and had a side that was as much a "Teddy Boy rock 'n' roller" as John's; but now he had found a trove of inspiration which could help him form his own songwriting identity. He had a wellspring, discovered at the Asher's. Paul began his journey, his "praxis," of what would become his identity fracture project, or IFP. I am not saying he labeled it thus; it could be he would never assign his artistic process any label. It is the name I assign to his artistic process, which I will argue had in all its facets, that general result. Paul's "IFP" would mean that he could retain many facets of himself, while being the "cute, sensitive Beatle."

Once Paul's identity was nailed down in 1964, the rest of the group could be arranged around it. The other Beatles could be presented to the public with complementary images that ensured if you didn't find the quality you wanted in one Beatle, you could find it in the other. Biographer Albert Goldman in *The Lives of John Lennon* described it as a "dialectical completion": If you thought John wasn't spiritual enough, then George was. If you thought Ringo was slightly dim, John was witty; if you thought John was cynical, then Paul was sensitive – "round and round in circles ... and it all made for a comforting sense of completeness."[55] Instead of being an interchangeable-looking boy band (although they were this too), they were now able to claim separate "identities." Each Beatle took a piece or two of the personality puzzle: cute, sensitive Beatle, rough, witty Beatle, quiet, spiritual Beatle, and salt-of-the-earth, clown Beatle, or what their producer Walter Shenson called "the adorable runt of the litter."[56]

Paul's IFP and having these different "selves" in the band would greatly help The Beatles because it could allow them to present songs in as many compositional styles as they wanted. The IFP, as I will show, produced a lyrical subtext that would give cohesion to and a reason for (although not overtly stated) the band's eclecticism. From henceforth The Beatles could distinguish themselves as separate Beatles and be more accessible than before to fans ("Who's your favorite Beatle?"). This gave them a comforting conformity on the surface and "branded" them for Stateside audiences. But at the same time, this and the IFP would allow them to bring a veritable potpourri of musical styles to audiences.

Underneath their music was the broken bedrock of Paul's Identity Fracture Project. It came out of Paul's personal drive to fracture himself, which I shall explain possible personal reasons for in Chapter Six. This drive, I suggest, is what made the reading of mental patient interviews so fruitful for his songwriting. The world of psychology and the asylum became so reliable a metaphor for songwriting, that Paul's IFP eventually ate the band. All the Beatles could write using that subtext of therapy, psychology, the mental patient and the asylum, and did. They could present ontological concepts, Vedic Transcendentalism, ideas from therapy, whole and hole, patient meltdowns. The subtext Paul discovered would be the continuity, whether the songs were nursery rhymes, group sing-a-longs, rave-ups, noise concrete, near-psychotic "rants," or tender love ballads. Each Beatle wrote songs that used it. The IFP subtext allowed them to be extremely eclectic in their song styles and instrumentation, and their music still perceived as "Beatles music." It meant that after a certain point it seemed that there was nothing they couldn't get away with musically and lyrically. It could *all* be The Beatles.

To be freewheeling and experimental was to be the tenor of the times. But paradoxically, the Beatles were to use the words and metaphors from the world of those "locked away," or at least under analysis. The way the group formed their songwriting identity and that of the band, after mid-1963, was around psychological and acting subtexts. Initially, it was not in every song: but after 1964 an increasing percentage of their material was drawn from it. In 1963 they were not confident of their abilities, but after Paul had been frequenting the Asher residence for several months, they effected their breakthrough, "She Loves You," based on the concept of psychiatric therapy.

The lyric approach of "She Loves You" wasn't found in other songs of the day. The world of psychology was "something new" to mainstream audiences, so new as to go unrecognized. You might get the humor and some insight from a song like "The Wanderer" sung by

Dion, but the Beatles lyrics, taken from this other world, seemed on a different order of magnitude.

George Martin commented later, "They just blossomed like an orchid in a hothouse. Once they had their first success, they realized they had a way of writing songs that would appeal to the public."[57] Paul, I am suggesting, was the instigator of this "way" of writing songs, that had "the third thing," such as in "She Loves You." A hothouse plant flourishes in an enclosed environment: "locked away." The asylum was to be an important motif in the Beatles' artistic trajectory.

When Paul met Jane Asher in April of 1963 the Beatles were experienced on the club scene, had some talent, and had been picked up and packaged by Brian Epstein. They had released one album, almost half of it cover songs. Entering the world of the Asher family, Paul was a young man trying to find out what would sell – and what resonated with his own muse. What would enable the group to reach a wider audience was the "something new" in their lyrics. There was logic of non-logic in Beatles songs, but also a new approach to songwriting, hard to pin down. I assert this was due to Paul's moving into a household that immersed him in the worlds of psychology and acting. Soon, through Peter Asher, Paul would read books published by the "avant-garde." Through Jane, he learned about acting and theatre. Paul later said about this period of his living at the Asher's, "I often felt the other guys were sort of partying, whereas I was learning a lot. Learning an awful lot."[58]

CHAPTER II

Backdrop: The 1959 LSD and Psychotherapy Macy Conference

A few years before the Beatles' debut, a series of conferences were held on a drug which would be an integral part of the Sixties: LSD-25. In 1959, the *Conference on The Uses of LSD-25 in Psychotherapy* was held in Princeton, New Jersey. The Conference, held and co-sponsored by the Josiah Macy, Jr. Foundation, was the fourth and final of a series on LSD. It is interesting to read the transcript of the proceedings, held at a time before LSD was promoted either directly or indirectly to the public, and in this chapter I will attempt to link some of the topics discussed at the Conference to the Beatles.

The Conference was supported in part by Sandoz Pharmaceuticals, "in line with studies of LSD-25 and Psilocybin in the realm of experimental psychiatry." [1] Four papers were presented: *Psychoanalytic Psychotherapy with LSD* by Harold Abramson, *The Nature of the Psychological Response to* LSD by Ronald A. Sandison, *Symbolysis: Psychotherapy by Symbolic Presentation* by C.H. Van Rhijn, and *The Study of Communication Processes under LSD* by Henry L. Lennard and Mollie P. Hewitt. After each paper was presented, there was an open discussion among the twenty-five participants. The proceedings were taped with the attendees' permission and a 300-page transcript of the proceedings published by the Macy Foundation.

Even though the combined data presented at the Conference covered approximately 2,000 subjects tested and over 12,000 LSD sessions,[2] the Conference attendees could not reach consensus on how LSD did what it did, nor could they agree on what LSD was intrinsically good for: what it did that other drugs couldn't do.

Attendees, (a full list is in the Appendix) many of whom were working on government grants, represented a variety of research projects and included Paul Hoch, Chairman of the Department of Psychiatry at Columbia University; Sidney Cohen of the Neuropsychiatric Hospital, Veterans Administration Center in Los Angeles, California; Psychologist Gregory Bateson of the Veterans Administration Hospital in Palo Alto, California, Ethnology Section; Charles Savage of the Center for Advanced Study in Behavioral Sciences at Stanford, California, and Louis Jollyon West of the departments of Psychiatry, Neurology, and Behavioral Sciences at the University of Oklahoma School of Medicine.

What had these researchers been doing with LSD that they could go on the record talking about in the late 50's? Dr. Harold Abramson had given LSD to over four hundred people, a hundred of those in tandem with what he called "quasi-Freudian" psychoanalysis.[3] He had also administered the drug to Siamese fighting fish as well as snails, and filmed its effects.[4] (Abramson and the Conference moderator, Frank Fremont-Smith, were friends from college[5] and Abramson had given Fremont-Smith his first dose of LSD.) Dr. Peck reported he had given LSD therapeutically to over a hundred people, frequently with hypnosis. Dr. Sidney Cohen of the Los Angeles Veteran's Administration had given it to seventy people for psychotherapy and to several volunteers in a creativity study. Dr. C.H. Van Rhijn from the Netherlands had given it to about twenty people at the two large mental wards he supervised. These researchers, who were administering the drug in psychoanalysis or for treatment of neuroses, were generally positive about its effects, stating it enabled a person to interact better with their families and workplace afterward, although acknowledging the results were highly subjective.

Whether using it for therapy or mind research, most of the researchers at the Conference had been first introduced to LSD through the military. One researcher, trained as a biochemist, commented that he "came through the front door." "At least one of us did," Fremont-Smith replied. There was also crossover between mind research and therapy, as evidenced by Dr. Charles Savage, who first used LSD to treat shell shock. In the Sixties, Savage would continue to be based at Stanford University. I quote Savage's background given at the Conference because it is pertinent.

Savage: "In 1949, under Navy auspices, I was looking for improved methods of inducing psycho-catharsis and facilitating psychotherapy, as I had found sodium amytal and Pentothal disappointing. I ran through the gamut of alkaloids, from mescaline and cannabis, through harmine, harmaline, scopolamine, and cocaine. I was primarily interested in mescaline, but was dismayed by the intense nausea it produced both in me and in my patients. When I learned from Dr. Beringer that LSD produced *ein susser rausch* (a better dream) than mescaline, I began to use it and have been working with it on and off ever since.

"Concurrently, I was attempting to integrate psycho-pharmacological and psychoanalytic data and particularly, to understand the meaning of the LSD experience. The similarity of processes in the LSD-induced state and in schizophrenia impressed me more and more. In the Public Health Service, to which I was subsequently transferred, I attempted to develop objective measurements of the LSD phenomenon, in order to assess various LSD antagonists that might be useful in the treatment of schizophrenia. Dr. Evarts and I worked with monkeys for a while, in order to find out how LSD affected their visual learning behavior. In small doses it did not affect them; in large doses it tranquilized them; I might say, it stupefied them.

"Then I went back to work with humans, though Dr. Evarts continued to work with monkeys and discovered, as you probably all know, a specific blocking effect of LSD at the lateral geniculate body. By this time, chlorpromazine and reserpine had already come on the market and had proved to be effective LSD antagonists.

"We have used LSD in psychotherapy for a number of years. Our results have been inconstant, and we have blown hot and cold about its value, sometimes feeling that it was revolutionary and at other times feeling it was actually detrimental.

"At the present time, I am consultant to the Palo Alto Mental Research Institute, where Dr. Adams and Dr. Jackson are working on the influences of LSD on personality structure and defenses: how LSD heightens, mobilizes, outlines, and liquidates defenses and how these defenses are subsequently dealt with in psychotherapy. The primary focus has not been therapy *per se*, but research in therapy and personality structure, although from time to time we see some surprising therapeutic reactions from LSD. I am also using it strictly for therapy at the Livermore Sanitarium."[6]

Savage's work in Palo Alto was "not therapy *per se*." He was researching how a person is who they think they are—how a person forms their own sense of self. Savage observed that LSD "heightens, mobilizes, outlines and liquidates defenses" of a person's self-image. I interpret this statement to mean that a dose of LSD would enable the person to bring out material which would indicate what their weak spots were; what were their core anxieties and their core "texts." This is the material that is usually hidden.

To the psychoanalyst, the hidden "material" that has been "repressed" supposedly comes out under LSD. Savage's statement that LSD "liquidates" the defense of the personality is the military researcher's way of describing it. He wanted a truth serum – one which would break down the defenses of personality. LSD allowed for vivisection of the personality, in that the material brought out would indicate what the person's "walls" or boundaries were, while at the same time the drug would break personality defenses apart.

Louis Jollyon West stated that he "was surprised at the developments in the use of LSD as a therapeutic agent, and so perhaps I am here under false pretenses. I have never used LSD in psychotherapy."[7] West had tested for LSD's specific effects and antagonists on military recruits.[8] He also had conducted animal trials, including injecting a dose of 16,000 i.u. into an elephant named Tusko. The elephant fell into a comatose state, and then when West injected an antagonist to the drug, Tusko convulsed and died.[9] (West would later monitor with his staff a fake "hippie pad" in the Haight Ashbury District, which we shall discuss in Chapter Four.)[10] West had been using LSD to isolate its chemical effects and then develop antagonists (antidotes or blockers); other military researchers at the Conference were using LSD to "regress" patients mentally (of one subject, horrifyingly, they noted that "we took her back to a two-year-old"). LSD could be used in combination with other drugs, in order to erase memory and then "replace" traumatic memories, in effect re-programming the subject. West's other area of research at the time of the Conference was to administer LSD and then re-enact traumatic situations with film and sound effects, supposedly in order to erase Post-Traumatic Stress Disorder, or PTSD in military personnel. (It was not called PTSD at that time.) At the Conference there were references to this type of experimentation using the term "Reconstructive therapy."[11]

* * *

Behind several of the attendees' statements about their research is the ominous fact that many of them were trying to find out the workings of the mind—to find the key to and power of emptying a mind and how to program it. Less ominous, but still ethically dubious was research by psychotherapists who contended that LSD in smaller doses had positive effects on the personality.

Dr. Sidney Cohen was especially interested in LSD's effect on creativity. He also felt that LSD opened "doors" to deeper perception. Cohen, who had given LSD to Clare and Henry Luce of Time-Life publishing in the 1950s,[12] was at the time of the Conference administering the drug to veterans and testing volunteers in creativity experiments at the Neuropsychiatric Hospital, Veterans Administration, in Los Angeles. He later became an authority on drugs and addiction for the National Institute of Mental Health.

Cohen stated that he was "interested in physical diseases and drugs which have psychic reverberations. About six or seven years ago, I wrote a paper on the delirial states. It was an easy jump from the examination of toxic psychoses to my own provocation of these states with LSD. My first subject was myself, and I was taken by surprise. This was no confused, disoriented delirium, but something quite different."[13]

Cohen's area of interest was rather similar to Dr. Asher's. Both were interested in physical diseases which caused abnormal mental states. Cohen also researched those drugs which caused "psychoses." Even though he studied LSD as a toxin which caused mental abnormality and hallucination (psychosis), when he took it himself, he decided it had benefits.

Then, Cohen went on to administer the drug to test its effect on creativity.[14] Creativity is a rather amorphous thing—but he was trying to find whether LSD either inhibited or spurred creativity.

Even though some data presented argued for abandoning research with LSD and also raised serious ethical questions—five suicides were reported, one directly attributable and four some months later when the patients worsened[15]—researchers positive about the uses of the drug outnumbered the skeptics. Many reported positive results using the drug to treat neuroses and alcohol addiction. Those who were negative or skeptical of its usefulness included pure scientists and those who were using it in military applications along with other disorganizing and psychosis-inducing drugs currently available. One scientist reported nine or ten "prolonged psychotic reactions" among LSD test subjects.[16] Cohen kept track of statistics on negative outcomes.

In just a few years the drug would be promoted to an extent these researchers would never have imagined. In the same year of the Conference, psychiatrist R.D. Laing at the Tavistock Institute of Human Relations in London finished his second book, challenging the basic assumptions of psychiatry (the doctor-patient role), as deeply flawed. Harvard psychologist Timothy Leary would take up Laing's anti-psychiatry banner in 1963, sharing a friendship with Laing. Both would promote and distribute LSD to the general public as a kind of stealing of Promethean fire from the psychiatry-gods.

But that was still in the future. In 1959, the Macy Conference attendees thought of LSD not as a "psychedelic," but a psycho-mimetic or model psychosis drug, because it produced some of the mental states found in psychotics and schizophrenics. None of these top-level mind researchers on the cusp of the Sixties gave the slightest impression that this was a drug for widespread use, and that the Western World needed to "turn on."

Attendees agreed that LSD did increase "symbolization," (talking)[17] and could produce hallucinations (particularly in higher doses).[18] LSD caused de-personalization (loss of ego, a feeling of looking at oneself from outside oneself, a feeling that one was not like one's usual self);[19] de-realization (reality looked different and objects took on different meanings than formerly), and it was noted to cause an "exquisite suggestibility"[20] and "massive increase in association."[21] Other effects were hallucinations, lack of homeostasis (loss of orientation, or means of stabilizing oneself in relation to the environment) and altering boundaries between the patient and therapist, or even between the patient and other objects.[22] "Dialectics are altered," observed Bateson. "The person becomes that which they are looking at."[23]

The researchers knew, then, that the LSD state broke down the personality; "You can't tell the difference between yourself and the other person," noted one researcher;[24] "ego-dissolving" and "the ego gets another notion of itself," said another.[25] The closest mental state to these effects was schizophrenia, although a few researchers said the LSD state was not exactly like schizophrenia in that speech was not as garbled. One researcher, Sandison, stated that LSD caused permanent personality change even with one dose, described as "long-term and permanent neuronal rearrangement."[26]

LSD's effects were not unique, however. Data presented at the Conference showed other drugs could achieve the same effects. Nor were its effects unequivocally attributable to it; in one test, subjects hallucinated on the control, tap water, after they were told they had been given LSD.[27] Several other "related compounds" (there were about nine others, which researchers knew about but the public is ignorant of, except for MDMA) were noted to produce hallucinations or temporary psychosis.[28] There were many compounds being used in research which could produce similar effects.

Still, there was insistence from several researchers that LSD was something different. Mostly, it seemed to work differently for each person who took it, and in each setting it was given. The drug had been used in experiments as a truth serum for interrogation. If given with no expectation of its helping, the experience was negative and the subject never wanted to take it again. If given in therapy with expectations of improving the patient's condition, then some patients "willingly took it dozens of times."

Some researchers saw LSD's effect as a "psycho-catharsis" or another means of shocking the system. Researchers were familiar with the use of shock or catharsis in treating mental illness. Insulin comas, electroshock treatment, chemically induced seizure, or wrapping patients in ice-cold sheets had been used in asylums since the Thirties, after which the patient might be calmer, reorganize their scattered thoughts and behavior, and show improvement.[29] Seeking this result, some researchers had given LSD in high doses to chronic schizophrenics. The patients reportedly showed remarkable improvement while on the drug, speaking normally and with insight about their personal problems; but then, they were noted to "remit rapidly" (go back into schizophrenia) only a day or two after having taken the drug.[30] A few had worsened markedly afterward and researchers indicated at the Conference that hope for LSD as a treatment for schizophrenia was waning.

Other patients who were less afflicted—neurotics and compulsives—were given the drug: many showed remarkable improvement in symptoms "for about two weeks, and then they go back to their old patterns," said one researcher. However, LSD in low or threshold doses (100 i.u. and lower) was thought to be a possible promising area for further research, as was using the drug in psychotherapy with "normals."

So on the one hand, some military-linked researchers used LSD to break the mind; their application did not argue for anyone wanting to take it at all. On the other hand, among the therapists, positive results were reported (at much lower doses than Savage et al. were using). "Could this be a nail soup?" one researcher asked. He related the tale of the beggar who made a bargain with a peasant that if he could make a delicious soup using nails, he could have the soup. He asked the peasant for water, vegetables, beef and spices, and then added nails to produce a "nail soup." "It just might be that LSD is the nail in the nail soup," the researcher observed.[31] The results seemed to him entirely based on the circumstances of the test.

Other attendees were having none of this. Some waxed eloquent about the potential of the drug. Many of the psychotherapists (including Cohen and Abramson) had taken it themselves. "The enthusiasm of the therapist seems to be a side effect of the LSD," noted another researcher dryly.[32]

The data on LSD, like the attendees, were a mixed bag. Although military researcher West was skeptical of LSD having any therapeutic value at all and thought it might be even detrimental, Dr. Van Rhijn envisioned giving it to dozens of patients at a time: "I had a vision, and I still have this vision, of mass therapy," he remarked.[33] With over two hundred patients, he could not devote time to each one. He could just administer it to a group of patients and leave them to figure things out for themselves; that would save him time. He had treated outpatients with it and had done no follow-up, but he assumed they were much better, since they hadn't returned for more treatment.

This all-over-the-place meeting of the minds did not succeed in forming one mind about what LSD was intrinsically good for. The moderator, Frank Fremont-Smith, stated that he had hoped for more than just data. He had hoped the "model psychosis" research would add dimension to an understanding of personality. He stated that he had hoped the researchers could "create" a psychosis- or LSD-influenced model of the personality from the data—"form a model of personality that includes psychotic reaction."[34] I take his statement to mean that instead of there being an incomprehensible gap between sane and insane, a bridge between would be forged.

Possibly with implications for the mass administration of LSD that was to happen at rock concerts in the Sixties, one researcher made the comment that "to give LSD or other psychomimetics to a stable population was a way of examining socio-dynamics." If psychomimetics were given only to the mentally troubled, he explained, then researchers would not necessarily learn anything germane to society or the normal personality, because an insane person is already damaged in some way mentally. Hence to understand social function and as he termed it, "group procedures toward deviants" in a normal population, then administering psychomimetics (LSD) to "normals" might be "helpful."[35]

It is remarkable that the researchers were so unconflicted about administering mind and personality-breaking drugs. LSD was still legal and many of the researchers had administered it for years, working on grants in connection with research facilities. Several operated in close proximity to college campuses such as Stanford, New York University and the University of California campuses. A few researchers complained about colleagues objecting to their giving mind-drugs to student volunteers. In any event, it was observed by one researcher that "among more sophisticated groups of test subjects (that is, college-educated young men and women) the personality structures are not as deeply affected (and) that the experience can be dealt with on a more superficial level with less long-term 'rearrangement.'"[36] These researchers were MK-Ultra, that is, mind-"kontrol" researchers doing work for the CIA, under former OSS operative Richard Helms.

The Conference attendees discussed briefly the ethics of what they were doing. "Some of (the legal liability) can be obviated with blanket waivers," one observed.[37] Moderator Fremont-Smith stepped in to note that they needed to always consider the ethics of what they were doing with any research, "because that is the most important thing." That being said, another researcher went on to note that there was legal risk, especially in the State of New York. "In New York State," he observed, "even if you get a blanket waiver from the patient, you can still be sued because it is illegal there to ask a person to sign their life and soul away."[38]

Above all, the subject and therapist's expectation about the drug experience was important, more so for LSD than for other drugs. Abramson related that during his administration of LSD to snails that he subsequently filmed, he had inadvertently absorbed some of the drug through his skin (it was distributed in liquid form in ampules at that time, by Sandoz labs). "I went home and I didn't know what was happening: I felt terrible. But then I told myself it was LSD; I must have gotten some of it on my skin. I was going to be all right, it was just LSD. I was not dying. I calmed down and went to sleep."[39]

However for all their strict attention to collecting detail, if not strict attention to ethics or lab procedure, researchers were hampered in codifying the drug's effects. They could describe LSD in terms of crossing the blood-brain barrier, increasing metabolic rate, and so forth; but to describe patients as "improved" was subjective language. Hence, there were many signs at the Conference, Fremont-Smith remarked, of the "murkiness" of the psychiatric profession at that time.[40] The attempt to exchange information between researchers pointed out the subjectivity of the terms they used. Discussions about terminology began with the very first presenter, and continued until the Conference end. The researchers argued the meaning of every term except medical or scientific ones to stalemate: "regression," "improvement," "adaptation," "conception" versus "perception." Researchers reach a state of détente on one term only to encounter another. It was thus difficult to reach firm conclusions about uses of the drug when being used therapeutically.

One researcher objected to Abramson mixing Freudian terms (ego, super-ego, repression) with biological data in his presentation. Fremont-Smith stepped in: "at this stage, we are in new terrain as far as mapping what words to use ... to combine soft terms with hard science is allowed and even desirable." However the effects of LSD did seem to defy classification more so than other drugs. Another researcher, in an attempt to chart the responses in his patients, had them use a 300-card system with one-line descriptors of what they were experiencing.[41] When further reduced to ten major groups and represented as icons, the dots he plotted on a chart clustered in the middle like a black hole eluding definition. LSD seemed to do everything – maybe. Taking the patient's word for what it did for them was dubious in itself.

Researchers acknowledged that, similar to any therapy session, a person could be just making up their "astonishing visions" or saying they felt better.[42] Whether they had truly improved after taking the drug was found to be difficult to quantify.

Abramson, who had given the drug to over 400 patients, used the word "magic" in connection with it, although in kind of a tongue-in-cheek fashion. He had been giving it in tandem with analysis to his psychotherapy patients. His administration of it, however, was on the brink of getting out of control; he noted that he was "besieged" with people wanting to try the drug and have the experience of it.[43]

Word was getting out; people at other people's homes, no longer in supervised clinical settings, were taking LSD.

Sidney Cohen did not comment on being "besieged," but he would have been aware, having given it to people himself outside a clinical setting, that LSD use was spreading outside medical and research circles. In the mid-Sixties Cohen would go on campus at University of California at Los Angeles and lecture about LSD to a packed auditorium.[44]

The Words Got in the Way

Not only were researchers frustrated in their efforts at communication: so were the insane. Attendee Gregory Bateson, who would continue to be at Stanford in the Sixties, discussed the problems that schizophrenics face in getting their "point across."

"The schizophrenic knows the (language) conventions, really, and is using them all the time," Bateson asserted. "The patient's problem as a schizophrenic is to find out, within the limits of certain rules he has learned by bitter experience, whether or not it is safe to try to communicate about material for which language is very unsuited."[45]

Bateson: It is very tender, it is very – I don't want to say "vague" material, because it is not vague at all, but very –

Hartman: Incommunicable.

Fremont-Smith: Or difficult to describe.

Bateson: No, it is not incommunicable, because obviously, we are able to communicate with each other a great deal. There would be no psychotherapy if it were incommunicable.

Fremont-Smith: It is difficult to circumscribe with words. It is very fragile, friable material. And when it is incorrectly circumscribed with words, the whole dance is essentially destroyed.

Bateson: Yes.

Fremont-Smith: And this hurts the patient.[i]

Bateson: This hurts the patient every time the destruction occurs… The problem is: What function does the very dramatic LSD experience have in establishing between two persons the

---

i This recalls the poet T.S. Eliot's lines from his poem *The Love Song of J.S. Prufrock*: "And when I am formulated, sprawling on a pin/When I am pinned and wriggling on the wall/Then how should I begin/To spit out all the butt-ends of my days and ways?/And how should I presume?…. If one, settling a pillow or throwing off a shawl/And turning toward the window, should say: /"That is not it at all/That is not what I meant, at all."

notion that they are going to share material of this kind? I think the stage is set by the very fact that the LSD material (researchers call "material" the thoughts that a patient communicates under LSD) is organized in terms of these rather more basic epistemologies, characteristic of the unconscious or of dreams. In this setting it is possible to communicate ostensively. It doesn't have to be expressed flatly in words, in order to communicate about it. You can point to the LSD experience, or to a picture of the LSD experience, or something like that. Ostensive rather than verbal communication can be used, and this can be done within a frame, which is itself defined by the LSD. This is a frame which says, "This is the sort of discussion we are having."[46]

Van Rhijn commented enthusiastically, "Yes ... that is the perfect situation, in which words are no longer needed to express one's self."[47]

Bateson then goes on state that the therapist too needs to have the ostensive frame of reference, that is, therapists too should take LSD, so as "to be aware of a world organized in terms of these premises." When the reception to this seemed frosty, Bateson then said, "whether or not we have actually had the LSD experience, we are all psychotic enough, really, to understand psychoses."[48] Again, this is going too far; but it seems Bateson was more interested in bridging gaps of communication than in diagnoses which would effectively separate one population from another.

* * *

Bateson's exchange with Fremont-Smith about communications and the ostensive culture pertain, to my mind, to what Fremont-Smith hoped to have happen at the Conference.

I think the comments Bateson made above, about an ostensive frame, went some ways toward summing up what became the Sixties' concerns – changing and creating new "frames of reference." Bateson's idea of a frame to-point-to can be read as a template of what the counterculture would be. Paul's process and The Beatles' evolution into psychedelic music would create an "ostensive" culture. Paul's process, I suggest, is similar to what Bateson described above.

At first, the patient who was "locked away" presented "fragile, friable material." This was what Paul was putting into his early IFP songs – vulnerable tales of "emotional complexity," as critics put it.

Then, so that the "dance would not be destroyed" (by which Fremont-Smith meant the "dance" between therapist and patient, but this "dance" was also between one and another, or even the Beatles and their public) – categorized and dismissed with limiting, unmagical terms – there had to be a frame of reference put around this material so that it would not be "killed" by the wrong sorts of words. This could be a simple shrug, yawn, as well as being panned by critics, lambasted, or even disinterest in whatever the "fragile" person is trying to get out. With an ostensive frame, however, the Beatles' news of new "feelings" would remain untouchable by critics – and the Beatles could continue to be cultural leaders of youth.

As Laing and Bateson argued, a patient does not want to be dismissed. R.D. Laing and Bateson[ii] regarded madness as a social construct rather than a fact that some people were deranged. Laing wrote that "words are the most effective tools to shrivel up the reality of another person." As Bateson explained above, the patients want their "fragile" perceptions and expressions to be understood and not even necessarily classifiable. I argue the Beatles, with Paul's praxis, positioned themselves in this "magical" way. They, and their fans by association, were unclassifiable. John commented later that if you want to subvert, you have to be "subtle" about it.[49] His comment implies the Beatles were trying to subvert, and I suggest they were doing it in a "magical" way with unclassifiable "material."

[ii]   Author, cyberneticist, anthropologist and social scientist Gregory Bateson was one of the founders of the Josiah Macy Foundation. Bateson was in the core group of the Macy Conferences on Cybernetics (1941–1960) and Group Processes (1954–1960). His wife, anthropologist Margaret Mead, served as president of the World Federation for Mental Health, as did Frank Fremont-Smith, John Rawlings Rees, and G.M. Carstairs.

The fear of being identified, classified, judged and pinned to a wall like a bug (a Beatle, perhaps?) had been expressed in T.S. Eliot's poem *The Love Song of J. Alfred Prufrock*; his depiction of both being a nonentity *and* being drowned by human voices (which implies having a self to drown), maintains a "homeostasis" of poetic vision that is conceivable on paper, but not in real life. However, The Beatles' young listeners, like Bateson's and Laing's mental patients, could be "non"-entities, but also unique, *unclassifiable* and not able to be dismissed.

Bateson's "dream," as I call it, of an ostensive culture of implicit understanding between people (Abramson, at the Conference, dismissed this idea as falling under the banner of "total psychoanalysis. And anyone who wants total analysis is dreaming")[50] I think describes the Beatles' process with their audience fairly well.

In the next presentation, "The Nature of Psychological Response to LSD," Dr. Sandison discusses the release of subconscious material on LSD. First, LSD overcomes "resistance." Then the patient's liberated unconscious material must undergo symbolization, that is, be put into words or drawings. Van Rhijn shows several paintings which patients made on LSD. (These are similar to paintings made by Christiana Morgan in the Twenties, when she was under deep analysis with Carl Jung. We will discuss Morgan later.) Then Van Rijhn presents an illustration, which depicts the symbolizing function as a layer of the psyche with various symbols floating around it.

> Murphy: Are those floating things in (the illustration) symbols?
> Van Rhijn: I don't think they are floating, but possibly they are well oiled.
> Fremont-Smith: Are they a lock-and-key situation? (He is referring to them emerging or being "unlocked" due to key or "trigger words," such are used in hypnosis.) It is a lock-and-key mechanism which appears there. Those are narrow channels of different shapes.

Van Rhijn: Some notions go through the channels easily; they don't have any resistance at all. Some can't come through, just because the person is not ready for them.[51]

Some researchers were using LSD with hypnosis, to test suggestibility. Louis Jollyon West commented that LSD "widens the holes and greases the skids." It enabled more suggestibility and liberation of subconscious material.[52]

I will suggest in Chapter Ten that a similar door-or-hole template for the subconscious is depicted in animated form in "Yellow Submarine," released in 1968. There is a scene with a corridor of doors and bizarre unexpected "material" pops out of them. Another scene shows "holes" through which the Beatles travel to other "lands."

Younger listeners especially were being asked to identify with the Beatles: publicity for them was everywhere, in international media. Their songs worked on both a conscious and subconscious level, and it was felt that they did not need to be "explained;" in fact critics trying to categorize the Beatles' music were scoffed at. It was the new "feeling" in the music that was thought to be the important thing.

For Bateson's ostensive culture to be achieved, a frame had to be constructed that would be what Bateson describes as "undefined," but still able to be pointed-to. (It would not be achievable in the real world, just as Eliot's artistic homeostasis wasn't.) Although not confined, defined and adjudged, it would be something to be pointed to by those who were aware of it. The counterculture "frame" which was to be pointed to and interpreted freely by the largest possible group was the creativity of the Beatles themselves. Their "magic" was the indefinable X-factor that audiences worldwide could point to, and would be used to frame a "new awareness." LSD, too, was "ostensive" and the drug that no one could define at the Conference.

Thus after 1966, depending on how aware listeners were of the drug scene, Beatles music would constitute a major ostensible frame of reference for the cultural changes that we understand were to comprise the Sixties. Their lyrics could plausibly refer to anything: yet, to those who were aware of the frame of reference, Beatles songs after 1966 were communicating based upon their referring to the drug-state or an "evolved" state. They could be listened to on many other levels, too, as children's songs, parodies, experimental, old-time ditties and so on, by those who were not aware of the frame of reference. Thus, those who were initially affected and identified with the "fragile, friable" emotional material of the Beatles' earlier songs were receptive to accepting the "frame" as being almost indivisible from LSD or an LSD-like awareness (ego-loss). And new listeners, too, could become aware of the Beatles' Aesopian (hidden) language of drugs and "evolution." However, the glue that held it all together was the Beatles lyrics, as I shall show. The lyrics had a subtext that was unknown to listeners, but told a story, subconsciously. The lyrics increasingly were written by referring to a psychology subtext after 1966, to where almost every Beatles song, unless it was an old song or a satire, was written using this approach.

Continuing to look at Bateson's "dream," however, it is interesting that Bateson used the word "ostensive." "Ostensibly" is defined as that which is shown outwardly, professed, ("her ostensible motive") or to all outward appearance ("he was ostensibly frank, but deceitful in actuality"). It is combined from the Latin infinitives of to show and to stretch. "Osten*sive*" is defined as "to-point to." It is interesting that Bateson used ostensive indicating the external, to "show" but to avoid the potentiality or connotations of deceit attached to ostensible. Perhaps aware of Bateson's liberal attitude toward the insane, the Conference attendees did go on to question his assumptions about schizophrenics and how they symbolize (create mental forms as in drawings or language). Bateson, like Laing, believed that schizophrenia was not "real"; he thought it a sane reaction to an untenable situation. If the schizophrenic were understood, this would dissolve the schizophrenia. Bateson told them that "the peculiarity (in symbolization, or communications), if there be one, is below the horizontal line in Figure 24 (he was referring to an illustration depicting layers in the subconscious where symbolization occurs). My view is that the symbolizing function has been very heavily penalized, particularly the one dealing with all the premises of relationship to another human being."

Bateson goes on explain that for a person classified as schizophrenic, it is taboo for them to accuse the therapists or doctors of intentionally misunderstanding them. "These are (also) the rules of the game in (their) families, and if you look at the families you will see these rules working out very melodramatically. He can't say to his mother, especially, and usually not to his father, 'You, Father,' or, 'You, Mother, are doing such-and-such to the relation between us.' That is the abstract statement which cannot be made."[53] This is Bateson pointing a finger at the "normal," implying that the hierarchical structure of the family breeds schizoid or schizophrenia, rather than saying that families have some rules, *and* the child is mentally troubled. He also ignores the fact that the child is unable to make such meta-statements because of their stage of development.

More of these ideas will be discussed in the next Chapter on R.D. Laing and David Cooper. Here I only want to point out that ideas expressed at the Conference have some bearing on the methods of the Beatles.

The Words Get in the Way, Part Two

During the Conference, the "unknown gap" between people, which is both the reason for and the inevitable condition of the therapist's profession, comes up again and again as researchers struggle with words. It began with the first presentation: Abramson, in using the word "transference," a concept basic to therapy, is challenged as to what was the "transference" he was talking about with that patient, and how "transference" is generally defined. After discussion fails to reach consensus, Fremont-Smith intervenes: "Let the man get his statement out."

"We use symbolic language and terms all the time, without defining them, but then when we try to, we find we don't know what we're talking about," says Dr. Hoch.[54] "Despite all our charts, our graphs, our tests, our data, the core of the LSD experience remains in the dark, quite untouched by our activities," Dr. Cohen observed.[55]

Most researchers agreed that the LSD state did get people to talk (to symbolize), and would cause in some but not all subjects hallucinations. Subject behavior could mimic that of psychosis, under large doses of the drug. One thousand micrograms was enough to put a person "over," in their terminology,[56] and under lower doses subjects became "exquisitely suggestible," as one researcher described it.[57] Data presented showed in both schizophrenia and under LSD there was observed to be hallucinations, abnormal emotional states, de-realization (seeing other meanings in common objects) and de-personalization (feeling outside of oneself, or feeling a complete change in body image).

This much the conference researchers codified in tables and charts, using commonly agreed-upon adjectives and terms. However, saying what the drug actually did for people was a much larger stumbling block, or wide-open terrain, depending on how you look at it. Some researchers, such as Sidney Cohen, asserted that the drug opened the channels on repressed "material" that would be visualized and then discussed with a therapist present at the session. Other researchers such as Van Rhijn reported good results doing no therapy whatsoever—simply handing them the vial of LSD (at this time it was typically given in liquid form) and leaving the patients by themselves to sort it out.[58]

West proposed further study in animal and human testing in combination with other drugs to isolate LSD's particular properties. He cautioned that people were too quick to assign it attributes and that its particular properties should be defined exactly. Others contended that LSD did not do anything different than what was already available. "There are many other drugs we have that produce similar effects," one researcher noted.

In talking of LSD, a new *terra incognita* had been discovered, which gave some of them hope. In the mutability of results tabulated, in which seemingly any result could happen, it was as if a huge blast of fresh air had entered the stale confines of mind research. Abramson said LSD brought out repressed material which years of talk therapy could not do. He commented, "In my experience, the use of LSD seemed to introduce a new era, a new search for magic. It (has) a glamorous appeal. Magazine articles distorted the situation very much. I, and I am sure many of you, have been besieged by people who wanted to take the drug, who wanted to experience the LSD reaction."[59]

> Savage noted, "LSD heightens perceptivity and empathy tremendously."
>
> Malitz challenged him. "I wouldn't completely agree that it heightens perceptivity and empathy as we ordinarily regard it. Perceptions may be heightened, but they may be distorted in being heightened.
>
> Savage: Yes, that's true. You can't tell the difference between yourself and the other person. But perceptions are increased, while reality testing becomes diminished.
>
> Malitz: That's the point. The patient's empathy with the therapist is also quite distorted in many instances. I would think, then, that when both therapist and patient take the drug, they would compound these distortions.
>
> Fremont-Smith: A third physician is needed, one who has not had the drug, to watch the physician who has had the drug watching the patient who has had the drug.[60]

Reconstructive Therapy

The sense among many of the Conference participants was that here was a drug with promising, if hard to codify, benefits. However, one man's therapeutic rehabilitation was another man's re-programming: at one point in the discussions, the psychotherapist and the military brainwasher met themselves in the middle.

> Abramson (speaking of psychotherapy): The patient was taken back, on LSD, to earlier states, and then could frame her thoughts in a new manner.
>
> Savage (speaking as a military researcher): It sounds analogous to growing a new brain.
>
> Abramson: No.[61]

At the close of the Conference, moderator Fremont-Smith stated, "We have not communicated."[62] The researchers had, as far as he was concerned, fallen short of bridging gaps or integrating their data; some evolved form of communication remained just out of reach that could only be glimpsed by Fremont-Smith. He concluded, "The main lesson of Conference was the difficulty of communication."

But to this reader, a lot had been communicated. Each researcher had their own uses and purposes for LSD, and that they each had a niche of study was not necessarily a bad thing. After all, their field of research was the human mind and the human individual. In such a broad field, LSD didn't intrinsically bring their research together to have more than a few results in common. But Fremont seems to have hoped that LSD could enable a new language to mesh of interdisciplinary scope, forming a model of the personality "that incorporates psychosis." Or perhaps he hoped for a language that would signal a change in the very personalities of the researchers themselves—not defending their areas of research or challenging others, but reaching toward unity.

* * *

Let's go a little further, if the reader bear with me, into what I call Bateson's "dream." His "ostensive" frame is like the frame of an in-group; for example the military or the world of hospital staff, with its own in-jokes and references. The in-group does not change reality, but has a frame of language whereby they interact with it and with each other. It is their social reality, but it does not constitute ultimate reality. However, if "reactions to psychosis" are incorporated as a model of personality research, as Fremont-Smith wanted them to be, this could have the effect of shaking up every construct or frame of reference of *any* group. This would be the major "consciousness shift" that the Sixties was said to represent.

This is what is most germane to the situation Paul found himself in at the Asher's. It is my suggestion that the Beatles put both Bateson's "dream" and the aims of Fremont-Smith into an artistic medium. The unavoidable reality that each person has a separate mind from another was the problem that therapy addressed, but also the very basis that gave therapy its *raison d'être*. Thus, the dialectical "problem," which seemed to be expanding minute-by-minute at the Conference, was put into songs and then transformed by the Beatles into a colorful spectrum of possibilities. If only we could accept less sanity in our world – more "fun," more undefined "freedom." The fuzzy grey areas where communication came up against subjective roadblocks would go from lonely non-connection to a free mind of mutual communication, based on the ostensive frame.

Bateson's vision of Prufrockian rejection (if I may call it that) was the core of what he saw as the problem of relations between people. The Beatles, especially in "Sgt. Pepper's Lonely Hearts Club Band," would parlay the lonely, grey "gap" into a veritable feast of changeable, often non-identifiable feelings, chords and color. There would no longer be loneliness (rejection) because there would be no distinctions. No high or low. If you just "tuned in," then you would join (so their sub-narrative went) the new in-group, with the ostensive frame of reference.

And this would form a group for everyone – with its word, Love. Love would be the only word (because after all, as soon as you added any more words, you risked battles over meanings of terms, as happened at the Macy Conference). With love, boundaries would drop – and "no" turn to yes.

A way to bridge that "gap" is what the Beatles songs ostensibly held out to youth – to erase boundaries (Abramson's words) in "a new search for magic." This seems rather obvious in retrospect, but the purpose of this book is to both map out exactly where it occurred (by focusing on lyrics primarily) and how, through looking at psychiatric literature of the time.

Help! and the Stablemate

In 1965, John wrote "Help!" It is possible that this song was inspired by a term used at the Conference, which pertained to the procedure for LSD psychotherapy. The final paper presented at the Conference was "Symbolysis: Psychotherapy by Symbolic Presentation," by C. H.

Van Rhijn.[63] He explained an alternate therapy procedure he followed (when he was not simply giving unattended patients LSD).

> Van Rhijn: In the auto-analytic procedure which I call "symbolysis," we give the patient LSD in a totally dark room, where he is not left alone, to the point where he hallucinates. Everything he says is recorded, and the next day it is read back to him. We then let him work out in writing his ideas and interpretations of the material. The therapist-physician follows this process closely from the copy he gets of everything the patient writes. Only on the patient's request will he be there for assurance, advice, or interpretations of the symbolic material.
>
> Fremont-Smith: It is not the therapist who is with the patient in the dark room, but merely someone who records everything he says?
>
> Van Rhijn: The material is recorded on tape. The man who is with the patient is passive and silent. He often does not say anything.
>
> Fremont-Smith: He is a reassuring figure?
>
> Van Rhijn: Yes, indeed; a quiet, reassuring man.[64]

The idea of this man, I suggest, influenced John to write "Help!" in the manner that he did: a situation that calls for a "reassuring man," or as this person is described elsewhere in Van Rhijn's presentation, the "stablemate."

> Van Rhijn: He (the mental patient who has been given LSD) knows he can call me, because there is a person in the room, a very quiet person, who doesn't say anything but with whom he can discuss the things he sees.
>
> Fremont-Smith: You mean that he can discuss it with the quiet person?
>
> Malitz: Who is this person?
>
> Van Rhijn: He is a male nurse. He is 55 years old, married, and has seen many types of therapeutic situations of this nature.

He has not taken LSD himself yet, but he should... He is a rather passive person, there to give the patient one contact with reality.[65]

I suggest that John wrote "Help!" with this scenario in mind, after reading the psychiatric literature about it: Help! describes the LSD therapeutic session, and the "help" given by the "comforting man." John began taking LSD in early 1965 and by the time he wrote the song had taken it many times. "Now I find I've changed my mind, and opened up the doors," he writes. The "doors" refer to Aldous Huxley's underground bestseller, *The Doors of Perception*, which no doubt the Beatles were exposed to through their association with Barry Miles, and the Indica Gallery and Bookstore (more on Indica in Chapter Four). *The Doors of Perception* (from which the band The Doors took their name) was Huxley's account of taking mescaline. "Help! I need somebody/Help! Not just anybody!" cries John, to the "stablemate." "Help me if you can, I'm feeling down/And I do appreciate you being 'round/ Help me get my feet back on the ground!" John sings that now he's opened up the doors, "my independence seems to vanish in the haze!... I know that I just need you ("the reassuring man") like/I never done before."

Given that John had taken LSD and was reading books he would pick up in the Asher's basement on their way to being shelved and sold at the Indica bookstore and Gallery, it is reasonable to suggest that John could have browsed other psychiatric texts available and was inspired by LSD psychotherapy to write "Help!" We could say that it was simply from out of the blue that he wrote the song, or he just randomly put those words together – but, my suggestion is that the Beatles (mainly Paul, but also John) were reading psychiatric materials and literature for new ideas, phrases, inspiration and material that would resonate.

I suggest that John found this psychological scenario and wrote "Help!" inspired by it. Whether he found it in the Macy Conference transcript is unknown, but the "stablemate" who gives the LSD-tripper their one grounding in reality was a story too good for John to pass up, I suggest. He even gave the music a Country-Western feel in the rhythm, to go along with the "stable." The term, as explained at the Conference, is taken from horse trainers who put a calmer horse in the stable alongside a nervous horse which is being trained.[66] I suggest this psychological term would also to some extent define the later role of the Beatles – that of "experienced" guides, reassuring listeners to go on inner exploration. Thus the "stablemate" is an important motif for the Beatles. We see that role also sometimes taken by Ringo in the style that he delivers his songs – as the "stalwart man."

John often told a story about the genesis of "Help!", that he wrote it fast, because the name of their forthcoming film had been changed from the working title of *Eight Arms to Hold You*, to *Help!* He had to come up with a title song. Yes, he wrote it "to-order"; but John would display again and again that his spur-of-the-moment songs would sum up the latest development in what I call Paul's Identity Fracture Project, or IFP. I am not suggesting anybody sat the Beatles down and told them, "This is what you have to write about, and here is how to do it." I am only asserting that many of John and Paul's songwriting ideas and their path as Beatles came from their reading psychiatric literature.

The B-side to "Help!" was "**I'm Down**." This Paul wrote as one of his "joke" songs, but it too is written using allusions to a therapy situation. The singer, markedly upset, sings that he is "really down," and then accuses the other person in the room, "how can you laugh, when you know I'm down?" It is a literal flip side of "Help!" It addresses the same person, the therapy stablemate. On the single, the Beatles present an A-side, John appreciating a comforting "mate" in the midst of his existential crisis, and a B-side, Paul as a patient who thinks his "mate" is laughing when he admits depression. The single therefore, though full of energy on both sides, and delivered with engaging, emotive singing by both Beatles, shows at bottom no resolution on an ontological level (that of basis, or formation of self).

If you are a young man with a sketchy art-school education, who has made a minimal living singing songs like "Twist and Shout" and emulating singer Little Richard's screams, as John was from 1956 to 1963, what do you do to find complexity? Where do you find something to say? I am suggesting that both Paul and John read psychiatric literature, and/or Paul told John about his discoveries. John's eyesight was very poor, which is an important thing to realize about him. We shall discuss it later in context of his songwriting.

I find that some core ideas (the ostensive culture) of the Sixties as well as details (the stablemate) were in evidence at the Macy Conference. As I analyze the songs, I could see that psychological motifs formed their lyric scaffolding. This meant the Beatles exhibited an understanding of relationships well beyond their years, that captivated critics and listeners and put the Beatles at "the toppermost of the poppermost."

CHAPTER III

Contemporaries: Laing, Cooper

D r. Asher's consultation room on Wimpole Street was on the first floor, above the basement. The basement had many uses: it was where John and Paul met to write songs, and also where Margaret Asher would give music lessons.[1] Book shipments bound for the Indica Gallery and Bookstore were initially stored in the basement, and John and Paul could easily pick out a book from a stack or box and read the latest missives from Basic Books and Penguin, among others.

Peter Asher, who had (with Gordon) gone to Number One in both the U.K. and the U.S. with Paul's song "A World Without Love," was a co-investor in the new Indica Gallery and Bookstore. The other investors were John Dunbar (friend of the Rolling Stones and husband of singer Marianne Faithfull), and their mutual friend Barry Miles. Miles, who became a good friend of Paul's, had owned a few bookstores before opening the Indica and had managed the paperback section of "Better Books,"[2] an arty London bookstore which both published and stocked "Beat" writers such as poet Allen Ginsberg. Miles left Better Books in 1965 to start the Indica. Tony Godwin, owner of Better Books, was also manager of Penguin Books, a major paperback publishing house.[3] Thus, the mainstream press and the

Beat avant-garde had a confluence of influence, notably meeting in the Asher basement where Paul and John wrote songs. Tony Godwin is an example of connections between the supposed avant-garde and established imprints. In a similar situation, the ideas of Tavistock-based psychiatrists R.D. Laing and David Cooper would first be published by Tavistock Publications, and then by Penguin, a mass market publisher. It is thus hard to call the Indica Bookstore and Gallery entirely avant-garde. It was *known* as such, but its "radical" or "consciousness-raising" books were in some instances coming out of research institutions like Tavistock. The Tavistock Institute is a social research center with strong ties to British military intelligence. And, then, consider that the "new," irreverent, youth-oriented Beatles were recording at EMI, an electronics research and recording facility of the British military.

This chapter will examine the influence of psychologist R.D. Laing and to a limited extent his associate David Cooper, on Paul's writing. Laing had essentially the same job at Tavistock clinic as Dr. Asher did at Central Middlesex. Asher left his post as Ward Chief at around the same time Paul entered the Asher household. Reportedly this change was precipitated when it was decided that Asher's position should be filled by a psychiatrist instead of a doctor of medicine. Asher would have been aware of Laing's research and publications, as they were working in the same field.

Laing wrote popular, influential books, introducing a different attitude toward mental illness and a new way of assessing its causes. According to the *UK Guardian*, "The Beatles, Jim Morrison of The Doors and the poets Sylvia Plath and Ted Hughes all worshipped at the celebrity court of this charismatic high priest of Sixties counterculture, the so-called "acid Marxist" considered by some to be a less wacky British version of America's anti-Establishment, acid-head psychologist, Dr. Timothy Leary."[4]

* * *

Laing had for some years studied the mentally ill when he gathered together patient case studies for his first best-seller; he completed the clinical work for it by 1957. *The Divided Self: An Existential Study in Madness* by R.D. Laing was published in 1960 by Tavistock Publications. It met with such interest that a sequel, *Self and Others*, was published in 1961. *The Divided Self*, although a best seller in the U.K. in 1960, was not published in the U.S. until 1962 on Pantheon. Then, Penguin (on its imprint Pelican) published a mass market U.S. edition in 1965. Penguin published several of Laing's books including *The Politics of the Family*, *Knots*, and another bestseller, *The Politics of Experience*.

Since the Beatles reportedly "worshipped" at Laing's altar, one assumes they would have read his books. The *Independent* article describes Laing as an "acid Marxist," but at the time of his initial success Laing was not perceived as such. One has to read his books to understand his appeal at that time, and the particular flavor of his observations. Laing would have it that he was the sole introducer of sensitivity to psychiatry; he was not; however, he was one of its most publicized critics and a founder of the "anti-psychiatry" movement. Amidst the perceived cultural sea changes of the era, Laing became a rock star of sorts, standing for empathy, liberation of self, finding one's own creativity, while at the same time advocating to abolish barriers between "mentally ill" and "sane" and criticizing society's "insanity."[5]

The foundation of Laing's work began in the mid-Fifties with his research into communication patterns of families of schizophrenics. He co-authored with Aaron Esteron *Sanity, Madness and the Family*, published by Tavistock Publications. Laing and Esterson interviewed the immediate family of schizophrenic patients, (usually at least five persons) and attempted to show, by the convoluted ways the family communicated, how their child had been driven insane.[6] The interviews were presented with little commentary. To those who read attentively the book might have made its point, but the format was not accessible to mainstream audiences.

For *The Divided Self* Laing changed his presentation and used an anecdotal approach. He interspersed literary observations about existential alienation with descriptions of patients, then let them describe their feelings in their own words. In the poetry of their language and the commonality of their struggles, many readers found something to relate to. Readers felt probably for the first time a feeling of empathy for the schizoids and schizophrenics described within its pages. Laing related how "Mrs. R." felt nervous, self-conscious in public: "In the street, nobody knows who you are. No-one cares about you … no-one gives a damn."[7] Mrs. R. wanted to be at home where everything was "familiar"—common enough feelings that many people could relate to. One schizoid young man, "David," wore a cloak and always felt he was acting a role in front of others, but kept his real self hidden.

Let's look some more at the schizoid and schizophrenic patients Laing brought to readers with a shock of recognition in *The Divided Self.* Although they were suffering from mental illness, there was a certain poetic force in their (and Laing's) use of language.

The self-conscious Peter was "split," and "felt guilty for being in the world in the first place."[8] His parents had ignored him, growing up; "they had simply carried on as if he were not there." "David" was "not simply eccentric; I could not escape the impression that this young man was playing at being eccentric," wrote Laing.[9] David always had to keep in mind that he was playing "a part."[10] His real self, he kept hidden. Laing describes the schizophrenic feeling that he is "made of glass, of such transparency and fragility that a look directed at him splinters him to bits and penetrates straight through him."[11]

One patient whom Laing said could be "anyone, anywhere, anytime" described herself as, "I'm thousands. I'm an in-divide-you-all. I'm a no-un."[12] Another schizophrenic called herself a "tolled bell," or told-*belle*, a play on words. Her mother would give her advice, and dress her up to be pretty, (*belle*) "until she resembled nothing so much as a life-size, painted doll." Laing remarked that "even as a psychotic statement, this seems a very cogent point of view and it gives in a nutshell the gist of her reproaches against her mother."[13] A schizoid young man described his feeling that he had no core of self, or basis, using a vivid metaphor: "I am only a cork floating on the ocean."[14] There was poetry in these phrases, and the patient's difficulties seemed to resonate with Laing's readers. Laing's characters seemed to be saying things about common feelings, and even to be talking about the larger frustrations of human relations.

I call these patients characters in a novelistic or stage sense, because Laing admitted much later on that he made some of them up. He used feelings and perceptions from his own experience to make the patients more relateable. Thus, he mixed the perceptions of a sane person (himself) with the perceptions of those who had been diagnosed as schizophrenic or schizoid. In retrospect, it is also obvious that Laing was careful to present those patients who were relatable to readers—not the schizophrenics who were smashing their dishes at mealtime and writing on walls.

Laing's point in writing his books was essentially that the insane were closer to sane than not, and that the system that treats insanity is itself insane. He advocated for more convergence of the two worlds, sane and insane, for better treatment of the existential condition of the individual, and more tolerance.

If he needed such assurance, Laing's books would have given Paul a philosophical reason to mix the words of the broken-minded with those of the normal. Paul had apparently read Laing's works and, according to the *UK Independent*, liked his approach.

In Laing's work, more than *I Never Promised You a Rose Garden* by Hannah Green which related a girl's fantastical world of schizophrenia, readers were introduced to mental patients who seem as least as perceptive as ill. Readers and critics could relate to the vulnerable, confiding Peter, and the poor girl who felt "transparent." Laing's work made it seem that the insane were possibly not so insane after all and might only need to get away from their families, and be around people who understood them.[15]

In Laing's work, we encounter the confiding-yet-relatable mad person. Readers and critics could relate to the misunderstood, poetic existentialism of Laing's patients. Laing's books "make the process of going mad comprehensible," according to the back blurb of *The Divided Self.* Laing's work was *on its way to a peak in popularity* when Paul met the Ashers in 1963. I suggest that Laing's success could have further inspired Paul to put mental patient language or "illogical" observations—that nonetheless summed up the song character's entire condition—in his songs. And these words, in song, would form "a subjective work, a work, however, which moves in all its forces toward objectivity." This phrase was on the frontispiece of Laing's *The Divided Self,* and it is also a fairly concise description of a song. A song is a subjective work of art, but it is pushed into objective reality on the radio, and taken for objective reality by the millions of young people listening to Beatles songs by mid-1964.

Many ideas Laing took credit for were not his own. D. W. Winnicot, who wrote its forward and read *The Divided Self* in manuscript, had already come up with the theory of a split in the personality of a growing child caused by trying to meet familial expectations for conduct.[16] The idea of family members causing a child to become schizophrenic had been discussed extensively by Gregory Bateson in his "double-bind" theory. In this situation theorized by Bateson, the parent (usually the mother) gives conflicting messages to the child, contradictory body language, and so on, to such an extent that the child's formulation of self is hopelessly frustrated. Bateson at the 1959 Macy Conference discussed this situation in terms of the child's inability to challenge authority: something that Laing would pick up and take much further. Bateson commented at the Conference that "both a child, and a schizophrenic," could never make a meta-statement questioning the "authoritarian's" motives for behavioral rules. Blockage of a child's meta-processing from early on, as Bateson saw it, was the germ that formed a schizoid detachment from self, which could later lead to schizophrenia.

The idea that the inner life of and communications a person receives are to be considered is an excellent point and one that needed making at that time; Laing was to be an ardent supporter of it. Letting a child dictate to his or her parents was not something most parents would consider. The "anti-authoritarian" idea could be experimented with at mental institutions, however. Copying another colleague's idea, that of David Cooper who had set up Villa 21, Laing founded in 1965 the Philadelphia Association, which would house mental patients without locks or involuntary drugs. Inmates would decide on their own rules for the asylum. The idea was that conversation was to be the main modality of therapy, and also, voluntary use of LSD. Villa 21 lasted for five years, until two patients on LSD jumped from the roof to their death. Then it was shut down.

Cooper's experimental Villa 21 was adjacent to the main mental hospital at Tavistock; Laing's two inmate-run asylums were located in residential districts in London.[17] Celebrities such as Sean Connery were frequent guests to Laing's inmate-run asylums, and they had a party atmosphere. LSD was kept in the refrigerator, as a kind of "spiritual laxative," as one ex-inmate put it.[18] "Normals" mixed with the "insane" and boundaries were intentionally blurred. (According to a visiting journalist, "It seemed to me the psychiatrists outnumbered the patients, who were all female and uniformly good-looking. Ronnie would be pompousing about dressed in white robes looking like Jesus, and I'd be asking him, 'Why has that bloke got his hands all over that girl?'")[19]

However amidst the party atmosphere, I suggest that the same unethical and invasive research was going on as the military had done under clinical settings a few years previously. One example is that of a patient named Mary Barnes. Barnes was given regression therapy followed by "reconstructive" therapy. It is not stated what drug was used – but given that there was LSD in the refrigerator, and Laing was a well-known supporter of LSD, it is likely they used LSD just as military researchers used it. Regressed, she was a full-blown psychotic, smearing her excrement on the walls. She was then "brought back." In other words, she was re-programmed and they grew her a new brain, as Charles Savage would have put it. She was given paint to use, and discovered a talent for art. She was brought back to adulthood and gained a new identity as an artist: her pieces sold in galleries. Although the outcome was positive, there was the same horrifying removal of a mind that had been performed by military researchers. So, Laing's inmate-led asylum was not so benign, although they might have thought than in giving LSD to Mary, she had nothing to lose.[20]

Laing was also looking closely at how identity is constituted. If the perceptions of the insane were relatable, on some level, and families had the power to "brainwash their children," as the back blurb of *Sanity, Madness and the Family* put it, then, is our very identity and sense of self compromised from the get-go? Where are we? Our true selves could have been already taken away by society. Consider this rather wordy passage from Laing's *The Facts of Life* lecture excerpt: "Winnicott proposes that when a baby looks at its mother's face, the face is the baby's first mirror. It's in that face that one sees oneself reflected. The image one develops of one's own face is built up in very complex ways. Once it is established, I suppose many people feel they are somewhere-or-other behind a face which they can't see because they are on this side of it, but if they could see, if they could look into a mirror, or if they could get around in their imagination from behind and look at themselves from outside, then they would see their 'face.'

"But what is one's original face before one is born? The face that we take to be our face is far from our original face, and if we identify ourselves with that face, then we're already in a sense deracinated, uprooted and captured by this magic spell of reflected images reflecting each other, wherein we can become lost by identifying ourselves with any part of it. There's no way to describe one's original face. One can only allude…. If I felt shaky, scattered, unaccountably frightened, or in any state of bewilderment or consternation or disarray or perplexity or confusion … the best way to drive myself crazy would be to go to a psychiatric institution. In such places there is complete local power to chop and cut people up, physically as well as theoretically, in the name of the exact opposite of what is said is being done."[21]

It is interesting the Laing chooses the metaphor of a kaleidoscope: "reflected images reflecting each other," to describe losing oneself.

That same image for a loss of self would be used to describe the girl in "Lucy in the Sky with Diamonds" who has "kaleidoscope eyes" and is "gone."

As the Sixties wore on, Laing, like Leary and Ginsberg, distributed LSD to the general populace, especially artists and influencers. Laing took to using Dr. Van Rhijn's preferred method of "giving them their LSD, and then leaving them alone to figure it out for themselves." Novelist Edna O'Brien, who had been welcomed into the publishing scene in "swinging London" with her imagistic stories set in Ireland, decided in 1970 that she needed a refresher and invited Laing to administer the "shamanistic drug." By this time Laing was held in awe, somewhat like the Beatles had been, as a voice of the Beyond – a keeper of mysteries that could be unlocked by LSD. She thought the drug would help her creativity, and she also admitted she wanted to become closer to Laing somehow. Laing gave O'Brien the drug, left shortly afterward, and then for the next twelve hours she underwent an experience of hallucinatory hell. O'Brien felt unstable for many months afterward, having to leave a performance in a theater because "my head was being lifted by swords to the ceiling." She had hallucinations in a hotel room, and also made some dubious choices later on, buying a home on the remote coast of Ireland when she couldn't even drive.[22]

She had probably wanted to remain somewhat Edna O'Brien, and just be a better version of herself; instead she felt for some time afterward that she "became somewhat unhinged."[23] I mention O'Brien in tandem with Mary's experience to show that the military research idea of growing a new brain was more or less the same idea as the acid-guru's goal of "transcending larval identities of class, race, and society" (Timothy Leary's statement) which was supposedly brought about by taking LSD and other hallucinogens. It was the same breaking and re-constituting of one's personality. The other aim of the Sixties "gurus" Laing, Ginsberg, and Leary was to turn society inside out. (Or rather, to turn the *perception* of society inside out.) The sane were to be seen as insane, the Establishment was to be seen as insane authoritarianism. *The Divided Self* was a key publication to introduce this process to the mainstream reader. It would make the "process of going mad, comprehensible," and so would introduce the figure-ground idea (is it mad, or is it understandable, and thus perhaps not mad after all). Willis Harman, director of Stanford Research Institute that had strong ties to Harvard, also stated that one of their goals was to make people live more "inner."[24] That is, to literally put your "inside out."

This *ungrounded* model, of neither-vase-nor-face-but-both going on simultaneously was akin to Sidney Cohen's idea of "unsanity." He stated that creativity and the outstanding achievements of human-kind were attributable to a region of activity not quite sane, and not insane either. He depicted the region schematically as a small slice in a circle. At the top was sanity, almost to the other side of the circle was insanity; but in a small slice, between the two, was "unsanity." This, he claimed, was where creativity lay.[25]

Thus, the psychiatric world which Paul was living in proximity to, which he had a front row seat to, was the sort that may have encouraged him to enact his very own identity fracture project. He had perhaps personal reasons to do this, which I will explain in Chapter Six. Plus, the evident relatability of Laing's "characters" could have encouraged him to put the words of the broken-minded into song lyrics. He would be writing songs as if what Laing said was right – that the world of the insane is the sane world, and the outer world is the insane one. This is the core idea, as we have seen already, of "A World Without Love." Paul would go on to create in the Beatles *oeuvre* the notion of the asylum, where everyone is "all together now." This would be the "Yellow Submarine" (literally Villa 21, adjacent to the main clinic) where "our friends are all aboard/Many more of them, live next door," as the music tootles and sways somewhat vertiginously.

The Beatles would be in a sense the vertiginous in-house band of Villa 21 and Laing's Philadelphia House. Their songs would cause, in Ian MacDonald's phrase which he used to title his valuable and well-written reference on the Beatles recordings, "a revolution in the head." Their songs would allow for an over-turning of conventions and "usher in a less deferential society" (as quoting author Salman Rushdie), along with increased drug-taking to find, in Sidney Cohen's phrase, "the beyond within." A person could experience, vicariously, LSD's "lack of homeostasis," "increase in symbolization," and "increase in association," in just the space of listening to music. Timothy Leary commented that "listening to a Beatles album is thirty minutes of de-programming." As I shall explain in Chapter Twelve, this was, at least in retrospect and in Paul's opinion, in order to pave the way toward a more tolerant society, a more liberal society, and a therapeutic society. This was Laing's vision too. The Beatles would do it on a mainstream level, reaching all the way into bedrooms of youth and children across the planet, leading millions to try LSD; and Paul was on the selection committee of the first large outdoor rock festival, Monterey Pop, for which almost none of its performers were paid, but at which LSD was in abundance.

Laing was the first mass-published psychiatrist to relate his sympathy for the "test subjects" of psychiatrists, both animal and human. He describes in *The Facts of Life* how the nervous system of frogs is examined: "I would hope if someone wanted to get to know me, he would not bash me on the head, cut my brain out of my head, take my head from my neck, cut my body in half, turn me upside down, burn me with acid, and torture the whole and all the bits with electricity and God knows what." He relates as inhumane how nurses and doctors describe their patients: "we've got a hemorrhoid in bed three, we've got a couple of veins, and we've got a good gallbladder coming in tomorrow."[26] Laing observed there was "a lot of genuine humanity among the doctors and teachers and clinicians in Glasgow, but at its very best, medical training was be-deviled, and still is, by its own *insane* theory and *insane* practice."

I am merely pointing out that for his time, in the early Sixties, this kind of "break from the establishment" was something new in mainstream publishing. Laing was criticizing the medical establishment, and also, the establishment of the family. Laing's books did all kinds of things: they made "going insane comprehensible," they attacked the medical and psychiatric establishments; they argued that going insane was part of a healing "praxis." And at his time, in the Sixties, all these ideas were considered.

In 1963, then, Paul began living in the home of a doctor who diagnosed the insane, during a time when there were changes in the air in attitudes toward the insane. There had for some time been interest in studying madness and the boundaries of it: the Rockefeller family put millions toward studying schizophrenia in the Sixties, and had long funded psychological research connected with Harvard University.

Laing later went on to re-enact the experience of birth with his patients, and wrote *Knots*, which examined dialectics to the brink of absurdity. But it is Laing's early work, where he posed as the compassionate, literate therapist and the confiding, existentially lonely patient that I suggest is echoed in the Beatles: "if you're lonely you can talk to me."

However, Laing can be accused of simply pathologizing normal states and refusing to admit the possibility of insanity. Laing does certainly ignore, in his books, the possibility that a person could be somewhat relatable, sensitive, *and* insane. (Just like Bateson ignored that a child could need some rules.) Just because the family of a schizophrenic's communication style is familiar to readers, doesn't mean that ergo families in general drive their children insane. But Laing's eloquent descriptions of families and lonely schizoids and schizophrenics (one patient calls herself "the ghost of the weed garden") give us only lonely, misunderstood individuals with cold, blinkered families. Because of his insistence that families and society were to blame, Laing was later lumped with theorists of the so-called New Left such as Herbert Marcuse.

Laing did make some contributions to psychiatry, in that his books argued for better treatment of the insane; for our purposes we will discuss his ideas in tandem with David Cooper, another influential psychiatrist in the U.K. during the Sixties.

* * *

David Cooper

David Cooper was a colleague of Laing's at the Tavistock Institute. Cooper had worked in military psychiatric research, and also in "counter-ops" in South Africa. Cooper's books, published by Tavistock, were aligned with Laing and Gregory Bateson's ideas, but much more convoluted in style. However, Cooper did write one book for which he became famous in the early Seventies: *The Death of the Family*. In this work Cooper stated that he wanted to

"cover the social functioning of the family as an ideological conditioning device (the non-human phrasing is deliberate and necessary) in any exploitative society – slave society, feudal society, Capitalist society from its most primitive phase in the last century to the neo-colonizing societies in the first world today. It also applies to the first-world working-class second-world societies and third-world countries in so far as these have been indoctrinated into a spurious consciousness that, as we shall see, is definitive of the secret suicide pact conducted by the bourgeois family unit, the unit that labels itself the 'happy family'; the family that prays together and stays together through sickness and health till death us do part or releases us into the terse joylessness of the epitaphs on our Christian tombstones erected, for want of any other sort of erection, by those who mourn for us in the curious mode of remembering very hard to forget us very hard. This false mourning is just and poetic in so far as no authentic mourning is possible if the people who mourn each other have never met each other. The bourgeois nuclear family unit has become, in this century, the ultimately perfected form of non-meeting and therefore the ultimate denial of mourning, death, birth and the experiential realm that precedes birth and conception."[27]

Cooper's fundamental basis in Marxism was much more obvious in his prose than in Laing's. He hated that dialectics, or the relationship between two separate people, even had to take place. To Cooper, any difference between people was something impinged on them by society and above all by the egregious construct of the family. He saw the family as a construct, rather than a core unit of human behavior. Cooper, in the same book quoted above, wrote, "the ideal end of therapy is the final dissolution of the duality of therapist and 'therapeutized' – an illusory state of non-relation in which therapy, of necessity, has to start and which derives from the family binary role system of bringer-up and brought-up. When will parents allow themselves to be brought up by their children?"[28]

That these ideas were mooted about at Tavistock would be influential upon the rise of communal living, and alternative family structures. Cooper saw communal living as a realization of human potential and of self-knowing that had been denied by what he called "the fur-lined bear trap" of the "bourgeoisie" family.[29] Of course that he called it a "bourgeoisie" family was a tip-off. He hated the Capitalist system and would describe in *The Language of Madness* "the class and national struggle against Capitalism, against bureaucratic degenerations of Socialism, and against imperialism all over the world."

In 1962 Cooper set up Villa 21, as "a deliberate attempt to abolish the traditional hierarchy between doctor and patient."[30] Cooper went farther than Laing in his vision for changing society and human interactions: he hated dialectics, or what he called "the control that lies in the spaces between us."[31] To Cooper, the space between therapist and patient, parent and child, teacher and pupil, was a space for control and distortion. He wanted that space removed, somehow; even though attendees at the Macy Conference (Abramson and others) had noted that "total analysis was impossible" and that "to record all the data about every session, every feeling I had and the patient had, and analyze each sensation and thought over the course of a half hour, would be impossible." "We are unable even to produce an accurate description of the fluctuations between two people just exchanging 'Good Mornings' at the breakfast table," Fremont-Smith agreed.[32]

But the attitudes of 1959 were given less shrift in the Sixties—they were taken for "resigned" attitudes. Cooper could argue in effect that "total analysis" *was* possible; and that the "language of madness" should be used "to destroy an actual, objective persecutory situation that one is caught up in from even before one's beginnings.... I have shown the polar opposition, in terms of the truth of a life, between normality (which is the sorry fate of most of us) and sanity and madness which meet each other at the opposite pole."

Cooper alluded to what I am calling Paul's creation of "the interval" in *The Language of Madness,* writing that "as the medical attitude always seems the concrete, the substantial, the locatable, the idea of finding supposedly pathological processes going on as it were in the empty spaces between entities is disturbing to the medical consciousness; everything in the field of investigation becomes flux, contradiction, the negation of the negation and the vertiginous spiraling of endless 'meta-levels' of discourse. The objective perspective is lost in a field of intersubjectivity; it is as if *the method of studying the field of madness must itself be involved in that madness.* Not a method in a madness, but a method of madness." (Emphasis his.)[33]

Cooper stated in 1971 that "non-psychiatry means that profoundly disturbing, incomprehensible, 'mad' behavior is to be contained, incorporated in and diffused through the whole society as a subversive source of creativity and spontaneity, not 'disease.'"[34] In a more boiled-down version of this idea, Cooper also stated that "society should be seeded with its own madness," which relates, in my mind, to the feedback experiments which writer William Burroughs was carrying out.

Burroughs's idea was to go about taping news broadcasts, traffic noise, lectures, any sounds in the manmade universe and then play them back as a kind of magic reversal charm;[35] a form of parroting as parody. To put the language of the insane into familiar discourse, in the form of song lyrics everyone would come to know, would be a form of this "seeding." Another one of Burroughs's ideas was tape loops. Loops of media broadcasts, records, film, music, could be used to the same effect – as a commentary or mocking critique, or even a magic charm, to nullify the effect of what he called "Capitalistic (and heterosexual) transmissions."[36] Burroughs was quite literate behind his crusty façade, and it is almost certain he would have read Laing and Cooper, interested as he was in U.K. publishing. Burroughs had famously challenged U.S. obscenity laws and eventually won with his anarchic novel *Naked Lunch* in 1966. In 1964 Burroughs was living in London and sharing a small recording studio with Paul McCartney.[37] Paul was inspired by Burroughs's tape loop experiments to make his own loops, and he played a demo of "Yesterday" for Burroughs's critique. Paul was introduced to Burroughs and other Beat writers through Barry Miles, a friend of Peter Asher's.

In that Paul was hanging out with William Burroughs (who also pioneered the idea of "cut-ups" or cutting into and then randomizing text to allow divination of its "real message") he was very close to the ideological basis of Laing, Cooper, and Burroughs, which was fundamentally subversive. Denis O'Dell, Apple Corporation's film producer, described the Beatles as "gentle subversives" in his memoir;[38] but a gentle subversive is still a subversive. However if this is so, Paul did it, at least in most songs, rather gently and with tender vulnerability. His voice would be akin to Laing's sympathetic, maligned and misunderstood "cases" who poetically confide in the listener.

This was not a new idea. There have long been "mad" poets, or writers who benefit from an association with the mentally unstable: the famous author F. Scott Fitzgerald used his wife Zelda's letters to him from the mental hospital in his novel *Tender is the Night*.[39] But the Beatles' unusual lyrics weren't just to sell the songs, although they did; by putting in relatable-but-not-quite-logical apperceptions, the Beatles also conveyed the idea that the average person had been emotionally starved without knowing it. The Beatles seemed "deep" beyond their tender years, emotionally insightful in songs like "Tell Me What You See," "Yesterday," and "I'm Looking Through You." They seemed to be familiar with emotional climates and perceptions that the average person had had no clue of until then. In "She Loves You," the whole approach to that song (which I am suggesting was that of a therapist speaking to a couple) really *was* something new. The Beatles' lyric communications were of great interest; the emotion in the songs was something to buy for oneself to listen to many times – something to get up to speed on. The Beatles weren't just singing about romance as usual and maybe alluding to sex. This was like a new land had been discovered.

I am suggesting that the Beatles were perhaps positioning themselves from early on as "guides" in a process (stablemates) and that they put themselves, like Laing, in a mediating space between "sane" society and the insane. They were the kaleidoscope-eyed artists seeing both the shattered Infinite, and at the core, the only true reality.

When they arrived in the U.S. in February 1964, according to *The New York Times* the very first question the press asked of them was, "Do you believe in lunacy?"

"Yeah," replied one of the Beatles. "It's healthy."[40]

CHAPTER IV

"Yesterday" and "Rubber Soul": Paul's IFP Gels

P aul's songs were perceptive, complex, and the poetry in his lyrics sometimes had this slight oddness, which came off as wry sophistication with, one assumed, heartfelt affirmation underneath. Paul's new songs charmed millions; they were what people hoped to hear from such a sweet-faced young man, and they had a confidence and sophistication that hinted at deep emotion. "All My Loving," "And I Love Her" and "She Loves You" were the beginnings of Paul's artistic process, what I call (as Laing used the term[1]) his "praxis." Paul's early song which he gave to Peter Asher, "A World Without Love" functioned as "proof of concept," in a way. I think that Paul found, if not exactly a formula, an approach or process for writing songs. Acting, dislocation, even a split – these were the ideas that spoke to him. And, the emotions in patient interviews (I suggest) gave him a way to put something truly "new" in his songs. If we give credence to the *UK Independent* assertion that the Beatles liked Laing's ideas, then these were reasons also for putting words of the broken-minded into songs. In any event, by 1965, the Beatles no longer had to fill a good portion of their albums with cover songs. They were writing with insights and an approach not previously encountered in pop music.

Prior to the Beatles, and during their era, there were plenty of songs about the ecstasies, breakups and makeups of romance; but there hadn't been lyrics describing relationships in the sense of a person being seen as transparent, needing ontological assurance, or implying that words might be false. These were born out of Paul's IFP, I suggest, which would shape Beatles songs from mid-1963 onward. His IFP (psychological subtext), along with other motifs (including surrealism and dislocation) gave the listener a real sense of encountering "something new." However all of these things were hidden; the primary thing was the *feelings* the songs gave the listener. John would write during this period some non-IFP songs that also were revealing of feelings: "This Boy," "When I Get Home," "In My Life," "I'll Get You," and the accomplished "No Reply." Both Beatles had talent, to be sure; however I will show how Paul's process or "praxis" ultimately defined the Beatles (if you could say they are anything definable) and how it later dictated the songs they would release. In 1965, Paul would continue along his praxis and write a very successful song that would gel the process he had begun at the Asher's.

* * *

Sometime in January or February of 1965, a dentist friend dosed John and George unsuspectingly with LSD.[2] Although the experience was nightmarish, John took to the drug (as he would take to many pills and powders over his lifetime) and began using LSD regularly. John was no stranger to drugs, but Paul was only using alcohol and pot at this point, although he was spending time at various (intellectual) drug hangouts, and was a friend of heroin users The Rolling Stones, William Burroughs and Allen Ginsberg.

Around the same time that John was dosed with LSD, Paul recorded "**Tell Me What You See**."[3] This song is in the same vulnerable, confiding mode as his earlier "What You're Doing." "Tell Me What You See," which John said was mostly written by Paul, is a song about a love relationship, but the boundaries of give-and-take are not defined, and neither is the singer's sense of self. "If you let me take your heart, I will prove to you/We will never be apart/If I'm part of you." If the "other's" heart is taken, then it is not given. "Open up your eyes now, tell me what you see/It is no surprise now/What you see is me." He then changes the chorus to "Look into these eyes now, tell me what you see/Don't you realize now/What you see is me?" The last verse repeats insistently: "Listen to me one more time/How can I get through?/Can't you try to see that I'm/Trying to get to you?" Even though Paul adds lyrics like "if you put your trust in me, I'll make bright your day," to make it sound like a romance song, I suggest this song was inspired by reading of patients in therapy sessions; that is a situation where the person, like the singer in the song, wants to be "seen," "known" and understood by the therapist. (Laing wrote of psychotherapy: "In a word, the patient wants to be understood.") The singer in "Tell Me What You See" asks for verification of his self from the other. "What you see is me," he sings, but then pleads, "*Tell* me what you see." Interestingly, she is not being asked to open her heart, but her eyes, in order to *see* (comprehend) him. Eyes only see the surface; so the song is contradictory.

I suggest that these lyrics are very much like a therapy situation where a patient wants the therapist to hand himself over to himself on a plate. In that era's pre-Cognitive Therapy psychiatric world, it was more often up to the therapist to analyze the patient's material and tell him what she or he "saw." Dr. Asher, too, had written an article for Lancet, "On Seeing," which described how observation of the patient, taking in their appearance and manner, could aid in reaching a diagnosis. I submit that Paul got the idea for this song from reading about diagnosis and analysis. He transposed such a situation, after reading about it, to a love song, and again its lyrical insight seems deeper than that of a typical love ditty. Nobody would (and hasn't until now) make the connection that he might have taken ideas, or even the words of a patient demanding self-definition, from the world of psychology.

It's odd to think of Paul intent on a book for his inspiration, but, it is not so far-fetched. He used to read his mother's medical books, and thereby knew about human reproduction far ahead of his classmates. Browsing through medical texts was something he'd done profitably since he was a boy.[4]

I think it reasonable to assume that John, too, was sampling the library at the Asher's or at least browsing piles of books that were arriving in the Asher basement, on their way to the Indica Bookstore. The Asher basement, as we have noted, was the initial delivery location for books bound for the Indica Gallery and Bookstore. It is a fact that John's song written in 1966, "Tomorrow Never Knows" was inspired by his finding some lines in Timothy Leary's *The Psychedelic Experience* – based upon the *Tibetan Bardo for the Dead* – while shopping at the Indica.[5] Although this anecdote shows John was very interested in picking up new books to read, it also underscores that it was Paul who was the leading intellectual light of the group. Paul's intellectual curiosity and discoveries were the basis for much of John's inspiration. If Paul had not been as gregarious toward intellectual, psychological and literary ideas, or living with the Ashers, there is little chance John would have been exposed to these things all by himself. Paul sought out stimulation and John then picked up on it. John at this time was married; he and his wife Cynthia had a son, and were living in quiet Weybridge, "the stockbroker's belt." Paul meanwhile was hanging out with old Beats, baby-Beats, going to theatre with the Ashers, discovering tape loops, avant-garde film and music. For song structure (so to speak), lyrics, and for his own personal reasons, Paul delved into books in Asher library for inspiration and material. He would often go out alone to clubs, and be prince of the social scene. By contrast, John "was quite happy to stay down in Weybridge, doing fuck-all," as Epstein's assistant Tony Bramwell noted.[6]

But John could always come back with a song; he would be exposed through Paul to ideas, and then with his customary facility, "sum things up." Almost spur-of-the-moment, John wrote "Help!" which took country-styled strumming one existential twist further. Instantly the Beatles were back at the top of the pops. It was a pivotal moment for the group, because it meant that John could put his powerful songwriting skills behind the psychological content that Paul had been drawn to for some time. John's upbeat-downbeat "Help!" was a song of identity loss – sung with such naked emotion as only John Lennon could muster. This was no *hiding* ontological insecurity or *subtle* dislocation, as in Paul's songs. The singer in "Help!" needed to be grounded now, and fast.

Ian MacDonald wrote in *Revolution in the Head* that even by early 1965 and with their worldwide fame, The Beatles were considering doing comedy songs.[7] They recorded a few clinkers in this period: "That Means a Lot," and "If You've Got Trouble." There were signs that their brand might be fading.[8] Critics were taking bets as to how long their popularity would last. But then in late March or early April of 1965, John wrote "Help!" which would be another huge hit. This was a brash confessional, but it also introduced ontological insecurity in rock-pop songs to the public. I have suggested John's newfound interest in LSD, and his possibly reading about LSD sessions and the "stablemate" inspired this song. In any artist's synthesis of material there are various skeins which come together and overlap; but the basic "story" of "Help!" parallels almost exactly the Macy Conference attendee's descriptions of the help given by the LSD-session assistant.

* * *

Yesterday

In June 1965, two months before their second film *Help!* and its soundtrack were to be released, Paul finished his signature song, which would gel his IFP – "**Yesterday**."

Ian MacDonald wrote that according to George Martin, Paul wrote "Yesterday" while staying at a hotel in Paris in January 1964. Other writers state that Paul wrote the melody for "Yesterday" very soon after he came to live at the Asher home; some date it to the same month he moved in, November 1963. In any event, it is agreed that Paul had no lyrics for it for months. He spent some time after writing the melody asking around for people's opinions if it was indeed original, not really believing it was. According to MacDonald, Paul assigned the words, "Scrambled eggs/Oh my baby how I love your legs" to the melody, as place-markers.[9] Paul played the melody for friends until John, for one, was tired of hearing it. Paul's biographer Miles said Paul "took his time" and finally finished the lyrics.

"Yesterday" was instantly recognized as a signature song. It encapsulated so much that was latent about the Beatles, and in Paul's way, not John's. Where John's "character" in a song would scream "Help!," Paul's would mournfully and poetically confide his muddled sense of time, self and place. "Yesterday" was its composer's most successful gelling of the hidden subtext of mental patient fracture, self-alienation, lack of basis, and failure to communicate, with normality. In this song, I think Paul was able to fuse both his readings in mental patient texts, and his own sense of loss, deep down, from the death of his mother. Patient-like phrases are there – in "I'm not half the man I used to be/There's a shadow hanging over me." "Yesterday came suddenly" is the first sad observation in the "patient interview," accompanied by mournful strings. Paul, as the "character" of the song, is summing up what he knows and it falls short. To listeners, the character's words don't make logical sense, but/and we the listener can only empathize with those words and Paul's beautiful way of singing them.

The song's middle section is where a deeply personal admission came, I think. In the middle eight, Paul for the first time acknowledged to himself (except perhaps once previously in the unreleased "I Lost My Little Girl") his sadness and bewilderment over losing his mother suddenly to cancer. "Why she had to go/I don't know, she wouldn't say." His mother wouldn't say that she was ill because she didn't want to worry her children. He continues relating his memory of this time, placing mounting emphasis on each word: "I – said – some – thing – wrong/Now I long for yesterday." Here, Paul possibly was (I intuit) remembering when he blurted out, "but what will we do for money now?" after his father told him and his brother that their mother had died. He always castigated himself for saying that.[10]

The last part of the song resumes the Victorian-cramped string arrangement and reprises the muddled resignation of the depressed, yet unthreatening schizophrenic or the institutionalized, passive neurotic. "Oh, I believe in yesterday," the singer concludes. Though he exists in the present, he is never to be brought into any present.

I will point out that the type of "inmate" Paul would derive inspiration, and I suggest, lines from, was not just any mental patient. He was not taking material from psychotics or dilapidated hebephrenics. He was, I suggest, taking lines from schizophrenics under treatment, who were interviewed at some length in mental hospitals at that time. (These were the categories of mental patient that Laing presented to the public in *The Divided Self* as "understandable." They were, to Laing, relatable and some were undergoing a rejuvenating "process" in their schizophrenia to become a new self. They had no self at the present, because their self as they wanted to define it was invalidated—it had been lost along the way. This was allied with Bateson's theories of invalidation.)

"Yesterday" was a brilliant synthesis of the words of the broken-minded with heartache; as we have seen him do before, the middle eight clarified the "unusual" phrasings of the verse to be in the context of a love relationship. "She" who "had to go" we assume to be a wife or girlfriend. The net result was that again the Beatles were delivering to listeners "new language" about love relationships. And, it was in a clearly superior melody line and arrangement: a real piece of *music*.

One could say a line like "yesterday came suddenly" was just Paul's using poetic license. True, but I ask that people look at the overall consistency of pattern in Paul's and the other Beatles' songs. I took the songs chronologically and went carefully through them, all along doing research into psychology of the time to verify if my theory could be true. Perhaps my theory's consistency is that it was always myself looking at the songs. All I ask is that the reader consider my assertions.

It is also important that the reader understand the synthesis achieved in "Yesterday" was one of making fracture into a whole.

The character of the broken-minded confessor (which was seen most recently prior to the Beatles in the verse of Fifties Confessional poets) had been fused and made indivisible from the normal. The Beatles were not labeled "confessional poets." They were simply "talented young lads." Their songs were accepted as poetry of normal feelings about romance. "Yesterday" was speaking for all. This was, in effect, working backwards from Laing, but achieving a similar effect, that is, the Laingian fusion of insane with sane. To synthesize is to compose and to combine – to make whole. The opposite of synthesis is to decompose, divide and separate. So, Paul had successfully done *both* of these things, in one work that spoke to *all*. He put the words of the broken-minded (that is, the identity-fractured) into a composition and through his synthesis, made a "w/hole."

Just a year or so before meeting the Ashers, Paul was wearing a "quiff" hairstyle in emulation of Elvis and screaming like Little Richard. In the month Paul met the Ashers the Beatles were covering a Larry Williams song "Anna (Go With Him)." By the end of 1964, Paul was writing songs like "What You're Doing," from a very different level of awareness.

His art was in effect, I suggest, making a new "type." It is the same way an artist hopes to create a "body" of work. It was making a new statement about personal reality and thus making a new *person* possible to emulate.

Paul must have intuited that he had opened up some of his own psyche, or at least his inner feelings, to write this song. "Yesterday" wasn't only a Beatles song. It was Paul's song. To him, the song was proof that he had feelings. Paul called up Iris Caldwell's mother and told her to watch him sing "Yesterday" on television that weekend, "and then tell me that I've got no feelings."[11] The hidden subtext he had used in some songs had fused with his own emotions, borne fruit and eclipsed anything The Beatles had released to date.

Henceforth, boundaries could continue to be profitably blurred by The Beatles between the illogical and the logical, through their art. Nobody could challenge *oddities* in songs after "Yesterday" in the face of such a resoundingly successful artistic synthesis. It was as if a cultural home truth had been spoken. "I believe in yesterday" – in that resigned yet muddled confession was a summation of loss, one that resonated with the state of the British Empire.

No matter what its associations for listeners, "Yesterday" was to be a gateway song. It is The Beatles' most recognized and covered song of all time (a fact which John chaffed at).

Its triumph was confirmed when the Beatles were awarded Members of the British Empire or MBEs, in October 1965. The Beatles were henceforth officially not just a "Beat group" (they never had been). They had had unprecedented publicity and promotion for almost two years, and were opened wide in the U.S. in early 1964 before they even toured the U.S. Now, they had delivered the goods. They weren't just a flash in the pan or a fad.

After this, listeners all over the world would go on to enjoy the new sensitivity and feelings plumbed in "Rubber Soul," recorded in October and November, and released in December of 1965. Paul could go on confidently and expand the "interval" he had opened, using the "comforts of unreason" he had found at the Asher's.

Rubber Soul

The Beatles' music, for all its brash energy, was not easily classifiable. "Our music is just, well, our music," replied John to an interviewer asking him to categorize it. The "odd" words gave them a mystique over other bands. The Beatles' joking and evasive interviews with the press did not clarify matters. The Beatles knew that as soon as they became classifiable, they would lose some of their mystique. Very little was known about them personally in the United States – where they had gone to school, for example. Theirs were irreverent, new voices taking youth culture by storm, according to all their publicity. They consciously sought novelty in their use of instrumentation after 1966 and their many studio manipulations of sound.

The 1965 album "Rubber Soul" would be "when something really got going," John commented later, "with our music. Whatever it was, we just let it happen and tried to control it a little bit."[12] I suggest that with "Rubber Soul," which came out the same year as "Yesterday" and "Help!" John, Paul and George started gathering together their forces to write songs informed by the issues that Paul had been working so assiduously on, and thinking about, at the Asher's – loss of identity, ontological insecurity, and the viewpoints of the mentally ill.

"Rubber Soul," especially the U.S. version of it, has an emotional, earthy feel and depth of insight in the lyrics. It was with this album that the Beatles began to be looked up to as artistic leaders, even savants. It had more of Paul's IFP on it than any previous album. There were five IFP songs on "Rubber Soul," and nine on "Revolver." Before, Paul had scattered his IFP songs here and there, and on singles. Now they were being presented in a more concentrated manner. "Rubber Soul" would present the Beatles finding their own voice (so to speak).

"I'm Looking Through You" I suggest had its idea taken from Paul's reading of psychiatric literature or mental patient transcripts. A schizophrenic described himself in Laing's "The Divided Self" as feeling transparent. This feeling was common among schizophrenics, because they experienced lack of boundaries. Laing also used the phrase "looking through" to mean diagnosing someone, or getting to know them. In Paul's song, "I'm looking through you" is used both ways; he is both getting to know how "you" are, and discovering that, surprise, "you" are not there. "Where did you go?" he asks. "I thought I knew you, what did I know?" This is also alluding to acting, that "you" were false.

Paul in "I'm Looking Through You" writes, "Your lips are moving, I cannot hear/Your voice is soothing, but the words aren't clear." She (we assume) is talking in a soothing manner, like a therapist; but her communications no longer reach him. He has "seen through" her. But instead of merely using that common expression, Paul has broached the subject in an entirely new way. She is transparent, gone: "Where did you go?" And, roles have been reversed. She was above him, but now she is "down there." "I'm looking through you/And you're nowhere." This is a Laingian idea, of exchanging the seat of authority.

This was more intriguing "news" about relationships and even, reality: with "I'm Looking Through You," the idea of being "nowhere" or being transparent, entered popular culture. Before this, similar existentialist ideas about the self were found in the plays of Edward Albee, Samuel Beckett, Jean-Paul Sartre, and pre-dating all those, possibly the Transcendentalists, but who knew about them? Only highbrow adults or literature majors. The Beatles were bringing existential, ontological concepts to the average person sitting in Peoria. The lyrics were novel *and* memorable because the song had harmonies, rhythm and a guitar break.

Music makes words more relatable on an emotional level. Chords define emotion. Words in books – dry, compared to lyrics in music. Lyrics are chosen by some songwriters very carefully because they know that the music amplifies the words so that they carry much more weight than if there was no music behind them. If words "work" in a song they have a good shot at passing for "truth." (At least, among teenagers and young people.) If the song "works," it goes right into people's minds (even if bad—this is known as an "earworm" in German). I could go on, but the reader probably is aware of these properties of pop music (as Zelda Fitzgerald reminisced of her youth, "when we still believed … in the philosophies of popular songs").[13]

Beatles songs were telling new kinds of stories. The unusual phrases asked that people see relationships and themselves differently. The youngest and most impressionable listeners surely entertained, in fantasy, that the Beatles were singing directly to them. They gobbled up the thoughts and the re-framing of relationships more eagerly than any lesson taught in school.

Now That I Know What I Feel Must Be Right

The Beatles "news" about relationships and the feelings discovered or uncovered (seemingly) in their songs gave young people confidence that they had "news" of their own to bring to society. They were not just immature young people who had not yet had life experience and who should follow in the footsteps of their elders and betters. Many young people thought that the new bands, and especially The Beatles, were showing that youth had its own way of looking at things, its own sensitivity that could build a new society. "It was like a new world had opened up," said a photographer interviewed in a documentary on Twiggy. Youth suddenly had a voice.[14] There were skeptics, though, one young man (in the BBC documentary *Why I Hate the Sixties*) interviewed at the time saying, "The younger teenagers in this country have been made up by the people that run fashion and pop business and the newspaper men, so they themselves have come to believe it." Current-day columnist Peter Oborne in the same documentary noted that the Sixties invented the "idea that young people were interesting; which they're basically not, actually."[15]

A song John and Paul co-wrote, "**The Word**" accordingly gave youth the news that "the only word is love." A sunny, simple rock song easy to dance to, "The Word" had broad, layered harmonies while the lyrics stated, "It's so fine, it's sunshine/It's the word, love." At almost three minutes, this song was not a vignette of fraught communication as many other Beatles songs. It was a tonic, a dance number and a celebratory song.

The lyrics I suggest were setting up the "ostensive" "dream" of Bateson that was explained in Chapter Two. The youth had been made to feel more, through the music of the phenomenal Beatles; they were empowered because the Beatles were recognized, praised, validated, given MBEs and world fame. Therefore, to those youth (and other older fans, and children), "what I feel must be right." Now that the feelings evoked by the Beatles had been validated, by Royal recognition, feelings were right. Consequently, in "The Word," the Beatles tell their rapt public that feelings are like a beam of sunshine that is "right," this "light" is the way (echoing Christ's words to his disciples, of I am the light and the way). The word for what is "so fine, it's sunshine" that is, these sunshine-like *feelings,* is "love." John sings the verses like he is delivering a testimonial; he is relating his story about how he came to understand the word. "In the beginning, I misunderstood/But now I've got it, the word is good!" And, "Now that I know what I feel must be right/I'm here to show everybody the light!"

The song could be taken as a quasi-Christian reduction, a simple advertisement for "love." But let's look a little closer at the lyrics. They begin, "Say the word and you'll be free/Say the word and be like me/ Say the word I'm thinking of/Have you heard the word is love/It's so fine, it's sunshine, it's the word, love."

Then in the next verse, listeners are enjoined to "spread the word and you'll be free/Spread the word, and be like me/Spread the word I'm thinking of." Followed by "give the word a chance to say/That the word is just the way/It's the word I'm thinking of/And the only word is love."

So, in this song, the Beatles were saying that behind the "way" the band had (which was not really obvious as to how they had become so popular) and the feelings they had brought to people, (which were various and subjective) was this word: love. So, one must say it, spread it, and accept it as the only word. In doing all these things, the listener would then "be like me." And, in being "like" The Beatles, they would also be "with" other people, just as they were "with" The Beatles. And, everyone in this group would be free.

"The Word" was giving people something to "point to," as Bateson theorized. A framing of the "way" as being love and light. "It's sunshine." It's every color in the spectrum. That it is a one-word "dream" club or in-group is necessary because to add more words would have introduced debate and therefore, doubt. So, one word, love, will be the banner. Those who have been made to "feel" by the Beatles are told, "What I feel must be right." They are enjoined to "show everybody the light." To enlighten others, too, and spread love. However, love also sounds a lot like LSD in this context: It is "spread," you have to "give it a chance to say" to you, you "get it," and with it, "You'll be free" and "be like me." You will lose yourself, that is, on love, and also on LSD. No ego boundaries or troublesome dialectics. LSD, or love, will spread like a virus.

"Say the word, love," the Beatles intone. "Love" is also a form of address in England, akin to "you, dear," but the song does seem to mean "love" in the universal sense. However, John almost snarks the sunshine-love-rock cult before it even gets off the ground. He sings his interjections in almost a campy way: "In the beginning, I misunderstood/But now I've got it, the word is good!" and especially when he sings, "I'm here to show every*body* the light!" His delivery is *almost* a parody of a convert. However, the positive message of "say the word, love," comes across. This song would set up the "ostensive" frame of reference that would give people something to point to that was no longer internal, but had been externalized. The new "depth of feeling" which Beatles songs had alluded to had stirred energy in people that needed to be externalized in some way, and now, they could join the cult of "love" which would be the ostensive frame.

Several songs were left off the U.S. release of "Rubber Soul": **"Drive My Car,"** John's **"Nowhere Man,"** **"If I Needed Someone,"** and **"What Goes On."** I think these were left off the album for U.S. audiences because the West Coast hippie/love movement needed to be launched and couldn't be confused or, worse, brought down by a John-summation song like "Nowhere Man." Better to release "Nowhere Man" as a separate single, and not confuse people at the outset by including it on the album.

"What Goes On" is a direct allusion to psychiatry: "what goes on, in your heart?/What goes on in your mind?" sings Ringo. The rest alludes to "your lies," betrayal, but these lines fit right in with the psychiatric subtext. The hidden psychiatric sources were the group's power base, providing compelling lyrics to put into songs. The critics marveled at the Beatles' sophistication. But critics focused on the musical originality (where they could), and did not address the content of the lyrics other than to say that for such young men, they seemed to have an advanced understanding of relationships.

Hence, the tuneful Beatles came to be trusted sources of information and as familiar, even more so in some cases, than the listener's family members. The therapeutic letting-go of boundaries, even of self, is what came to define The Beatles, and I think, possibly their audiences. They promised that it was possible to "get to" someone else, see their and one's (shared) core(s), if one could only give up a bit of oneself in the process: this is like therapy, but with the addition that the therapist meets the patient somewhere in the middle (it could be likened to LSD psychotherapy where both therapist and patient take the drug). In the songs, the therapist and patient are transposed onto self and other or boy and girl in a relationship. I am just showing how the therapy template was used in Beatles songs; and the fact it appeared there at all, I attribute to a process Paul was undergoing in himself, and a songwriting method he stumbled across at the Asher's.

At this point, each little jangle of the guitar, small breath taken between phrases and careful middle eight played by George Harrison, Paul or George Martin, was relished as another treasured message and communiqué of intimacy, and the songs were about, after all, "just what one was thinking." One's inner psyche was being explicated in song. The Beatles had gone beyond being a pop phenomenon, with half of their songs a British take on blues songs.

A beloved song on "Rubber Soul" was Paul's "**Michelle**." It pre-dated the Asher's.[16] Paul had written the song and some of the lyrics when he was a teenager. Typically he had presented it as a "joke" song, and told people it was "a way to draw birds (attract girls)." He would make up words on the spot when performing it. But I suggest that by 1965, after he found some way to put his emotions into song with "Yesterday," Paul could now sing this song and sound sincere. He had earned his sensitivity, so to speak.

"**You Won't See Me**" is more vulnerability from Paul, and the lyrics are also subtly allusive to being "not there" or "gone." It is reasonable to assume Jane's leaving town so often on her theater tours inspired this song. The singer of the song feels awful about it: "Though the days are few, they're filled with tears/And since I lost you, it feels like years/Yes, it seems so long, girl since you've been gone/And I just can't go on, if you won't see me." The "twist" is in the refrain, which implies that if she isn't here, he won't be here either any longer. He both needs her here, and needs her to exist (to be seen). This threat-to-self recalls the condition that Laing wrote in *The Divided Self* that one of his patients suffered from: a need to be seen in order to feel that one exists. "To her, *esse is percipi*," Laing commented. (To be is to be seen.)[17] Paul could use his unhappiness about Jane, synthesize it with the perceptions of the mentally ill and psychiatric concepts he was reading, and come up with another poetical yet interesting song.

The Beatles had become as familiar to fans as their own family, and fans felt a deep connection to the group. That this happened with the fans knowing almost nothing about them was due to the first phase of the IFP: poetry about "feelings."

Holding Hands Under the Table in the Mad Poet's Club

Of course, words of the less-normal in books and poetry were not something new. There had been a long history of "mad poets" by the time Paul was writing songs. "Mad" poets had been gaining accolades in the Fifties in the United States, and would continue to do so into the Sixties. Robert Lowell's poetry class at Boston University could be regarded as a Petri dish for such poets. Lowell's distinguished relative James Russell Lowell, a poet, had co-founded *The Atlantic Monthly* and was professor of Linguistics at Harvard.[18] Lowell was eventually appointed Ambassador to the Court of St. James, which is the court of the British Monarchy. Lowell believed in the poet as a prophet and critic of society. Poet Robert Lowell taught poetry seminars and occasionally checked himself in to the nearby McLean mental asylum.[19] Lowell would receive acclaim for his book of poems *Life Studies* and was awarded a Pulitzer Prize. Two of his students, Anne Sexton and Sylvia Plath, also were treated in mental hospitals, Plath at McLean for several months following her first suicide attempt in 1953.

Lowell, Plath, Sexton, and John Berryman were labeled the "Confessional Poets." Regarded as self-revealing poets, they wrote about relationships and their own feelings of inadequacy. To many, their poetry was taken to be illuminative of the human condition and expressed feelings usually hidden under the façade demanded by society. Although (according to her biographer Anne Middleton) most of the critical debate around Sexton centered on whether she was mentally ill or not,[20] her verses gained more and more acclaim and in 1967 Sexton's collection *Live or Die* was awarded the Pulitzer Prize.

Plath, an aspiring novelist as well as poet, took Lowell's class in 1958, and had the Lowells to dinner. She wrote in her diary in 1959, "There is a terrific demand for this kind of stuff (stories from the insane asylum). I am a fool not to take advantage of it."[21] Plath hoped she could write something marketable about her experiences at McLean, which had included ECT.

Plath was noting in her diary even in 1959, "I will write mad stories,"[22] and "a series of madhouse poems."[23] She worked at Massachusetts General Hospital, adjacent to McLean, for two months in 1958 typing up mental patient interviews (just such interviews as I am suggesting Dr. Asher had in his library). The job apparently gave her much-needed inspiration and material. Plath wrote in her diary, "I feel my whole sense and understanding of people being deepened by this: as if I had my wish and opened up the souls of the people in Boston and read them deep."[24] She wrote a short story, "Johnny Panic and the Bible of Dreams," based on her experience typing up the transcripts. She noted with this story that "I have gotten some of myself into my writing, at last.... It is queer and quite slangy, so I think it may be publishable."[25] By "slangy," I think she meant it had terms specific to the mental health field. Another story, "The Mummy," she called a "psychiatric fantasia" but later dismissed as a "morbid psychological sketch." Neither story found a publisher in her lifetime. She then worked as a secretary for a professor of Sanskrit and Indian studies at Harvard,[26] and continued seeing her psychiatrist from McLean, Dr. Ruth Beuscher.

By the early Sixties, Plath and her husband, poet Ted Hughes, were familiar figures in the London arts and publishing scene, occasionally featured on BBC poetry broadcasts, and acquainted with literary lights such as Stephen Spender (who gave her comp tickets to the obscenity trial for D.H. Lawrence's novel *Lady Chatterley's Lover*).[27] Plath and Hughes were invited to T.S. Eliot's home for dinner and Eliot offered to read, and discuss, in manuscript any plays in verse Hughes wrote.[28] The London theatre scene was a "fantastic market" for young talent, Plath wrote in her diary.[29] Plath must have felt perfectly placed to bring out her own news, as she rubbed elbows at dinner tables with well-known publishing figures and invited eminent poetry critic Albert Alvarez to visit her home in Devon.

Plath also might have been encouraged by Laing's success to push forward with writing a fictionalized account of her own breakdown and mental asylum experiences. Plath published her novel *The Bell Jar* in late 1962, a year and a half after Laing's *The Divided Self* and only one year after Laing's sequel, *Self and Others*.

Plath's protagonist Esther Greenwood in *The Bell Jar* was not like Laing's somewhat relatable, poetic patients, however. Esther is cynical, killing in her observations, and darkly comical, as we ascertain from her diaries that Plath was herself. An editor who rejected Plath's novel commented that Esther's observations were merely those of a clever young person, her transition to madness was not adequately explained, and thus, Plath did not handle her material well.[30] The editor, knowing Plath's real-life "material," her experience in a mental ward and with ECT, had expected insight which the book did not deliver. Between the dark humor and Esther losing her mind, there was a gap. The book did sell, initially, but Plath was disappointed to be "patted on the head for good writing, criticized for weak structure, and dismissed," according to biographer Anne Stevenson.[31]

Laing's *The Divided Self* was the first to erase, or at least blur, that gap. Laing's presentation of his patients, as the book's back blurb said, "makes the process of going mad comprehensible." This type of claim attracted readers, as did Laing's dark Scots good looks and large, sensitive eyes. It helped that Laing quoted poetry and literature, which in psychology books was unheard-of. However in Laing's world, the "gap" between sane and mad was explainable, in nonfiction. The frontispiece to *The Divided Self* had a quote from E. Minkowski, "Je donne une oeuvre subjective ici, oeuvre cependant qui tend de toutes ses forces vers l'objectivité." (I am giving a subjective work here, a work, however, which leans with all its force towards objectivity.)[32] This covered both bases and implied that Laing was aware he was presenting art as much as fact, and that he wanted the "subjective" to be taken for real.

Plath's protagonist had perceptions quite different from the subtly shaded melancholy of the vulnerable and misunderstood individuals of Laing's partial invention. Esther lambasted everyone from a magazine editor wearing thick spectacles and a hat of imitation lilacs ("She looked terrible, and very wise")[33] to her mother, whom she in one scene fantasized strangling to death.[34] This was pitiless black humor, which then jumped off the deep end into psychosis: entertaining, perhaps, but not to be taken seriously (until, one might argue, after Plath's suicide).

The well-connected Harvard poet George Starbuck (whom Sexton had an affair with) most likely helped Sexton's progress to a Pulitzer.[35] Starbuck in turn was put in his position at Houghton Mifflin Books through the efforts of Archibald MacLeish, a poet who had been briefly head of the Library of Congress and Secretary of Cultural Affairs under Franklin D. Roosevelt.[36] The MacLeish connection to Starbuck and by extension Sexton, Lowell and Plath is not insignificant because MacLeish was also a close friend of the F. Scott Fitzgeralds and Ernest Hemingway during their expatriate period and for some time afterwards. MacLeish also believed in the poet as social leader. In addition to being awarded three Pulitzer Prizes, MacLeish, a lawyer, worked for British military intelligence in the Office of Strategic Services (OSS), and was an editor for Henry Luce's *Fortune* magazine. MacLeish read an early copy of *Tender is the Night*, drawn from Zelda's time in a mental asylum. Possibly MacLeish had some interest in promoting the "insights" or language of those who suffered from mental illness into literature. He was a Boylston Professor of Rhetoric and oratory at Harvard from 1949 to 1962, so was there at the time Plath and Sexton were attending Lowell's poetry seminar at nearby Boston College.

Another friend and colleague of MacLeish's was Henry (Harry) Murray, who was to mentor Timothy Leary. Murray was analyzed by the psychiatrist Carl Jung in the Twenties in Zurich (along with Edith Rockefeller) and was captivated by Jung's mapping of the subconscious depths. For many years Murray led (funded by members of the Rockefeller family) the Harvard Psychological Clinic, and incorporated Jungian ideas into research there. Murray was a leader in the area of personality "typing" and research.[37] Beginning in the Twenties, he and his staff at Harvard formulated detailed personality assessment tests, interviewing and testing fifty college men for the first major study *Explorations in Personality* published in 1938.[38] In WWII Murray worked for the OSS testing and selecting candidates for intelligence service. Murray had a tower built near Harvard in emulation of Jung's tower at Bollinger, where Murray and his mistress, clinician Christiana Morgan, explored extreme states of anima and animus based on Jung's theories of internal archetypes.

Jung's influence on research into the "psyche" and personality was thus to some extent entrenched at Harvard. Jung wrote an extensive study of associative language and also of archetypes in the subconscious, both subjects of strong interest to academically guided poets.[iii] While attending Lowell's poetry seminar, Plath was reading several books on psychology, including Jung's work.[39] T.S. Eliot, who had attended Harvard, was also fascinated with insanity and the unmoored perspective, according to an article by Ronald Bush in the *Oxford Dictionary of National Biography*.[40] Eliot was also seemingly familiar with Jung, writing a poem in the Twenties entitled "Animula," and was friends with Herbert Read,[41] who was both a Modernist and co-edited Jung's *Collected Works*.

The Wallace Stegner Writing Program at Stanford was a similar incubator of talent to Lowell's poetry classes in that it also was closely connected to a research institution, Stanford Research Institute (SRI),

---

[iii]   The Swiss psychiatrist and psychoanalyst Carl Jung wrote a short Gnostic treatise in 1916 called the *Seven Sermons to the Dead*, which theorized a God higher than the Christian God and Devil, "Abraxas," that combines all opposites into one being.

which we will discuss in Chapter Five. Participants in this program included author Ken Kesey, screenwriter and novelist Robert Stone and Robert Hunter, who would become a lyricist for the Grateful Dead.

When Plath killed herself, Sexton felt cheated somehow; her biographer commented, "it was as if Plath, the savvy rival, had leap-frogged right over Sexton's project of becoming famous, in which a well-publicized suicide was to be the goal."[42]

However, at least one writer in the Sixties questioned whether Plath's last poems should be taken for poetry. Critic David Holbrook wrote in 1968 and again in 1976[43] that Plath's poems were the work of a "schizophrenic," that her troubling imagery did not have any cohesion, and therefore should not be taken to have artistic merit.[44] In rebuttal, critic Judith Kroll in 1978 pointed out Plath's senior thesis at Cambridge was on "The Double" in Dostoevsky, in which Plath observed "a certain understanding of the mechanics of schizophrenia is desirable" to understand what she saw as a necessity of the artist – to create a double of herself in her art. Kroll contended that Plath was mixing myth, queasy imagery, acerbic observations, and creating Jungian-style archetypes intentionally: as a poet, not a mentally ill or distraught person writing words onto a page.[45]

After Plath's demise, rather than dismissing her poems as they had her novel (or seeing that she had been cannily reaching for the audience Laing had tapped two years previously) the critical assessment was that Plath committed suicide because she had *seen too much*. She had gone down in a blaze of visionary angst; she had comprehended too much, more than she should have, about women's roles, and the knowledge drove her to suicide. According to this subsequently well-promoted reading of her poetry, her verses were poetic genius, and she was a feminist. Her husband Ted Hughes, who collected her poems that were published posthumously through T.S. Eliot's firm Faber and Faber, suppressed for years the information that he had left Plath for another woman shortly before her death.

Anne Sexton taught poetry classes at McLean to inmates, before her own suicide. McLean might not be only a mental hospital sympathetic to troubled artists, or to potential artists who are currently troubled. Like Lowell's seminar and the Stegner program, it seems that McLean might be interested in *making* artists. A quote from an article by Alex Beam on James Taylor's website alludes to this, saying that "For James Taylor and many other affluent young people, it was a combination of progressive music school and country club, with barred windows." Critic Charles Gullans, reviewing Sexton's poetry at the time, remarked "the Romantic stereotype says that the poet is sensitive and suffers; the neo-Romantic stereotype says that anyone who is sensitive and suffers is a poet. These are documents of modern psychiatry and are a result of a confusion of standards in the public mind."[46] Singer James Taylor, role model for the new "sensitive man" of the Seventies, was an inmate at McLean before his rise to pop fame.[47] He was one of the first songwriters signed to Apple records, and has for many years been managed by Peter Asher.

Author F. Scott Fitzgerald, at least as familiar to English litera-ture majors as Ernest Hemingway, set his novel *Tender is The Night* at a Swiss sanatorium. Fitzgerald's protagonist, Nicole, writes letters to her doctor; for these sections Fitzgerald quoted his wife's Zelda's actual letters to him from mental hospitals. At one point, to the ther-apists it seemed kind of a mash-up: was Scott perhaps the unstable one, and Zelda the "genius," or was it vice versa? Psychiatrists were drugging Zelda (at the same time, encouraging her to write). Zelda, whom therapists discouraged from being a ballet dancer, wrote a novel and many short stories while in asylums. She once wrote to a friend, "Don't *ever* fall into the hands of the brain and nerve special-ists unless you are feeling very Faustian."[48] Some of Zelda's therapists at the many asylums she stayed wanted to "treat" Scott also. Treating two writers, one commercially successful and the other thought-to-be-insane, would have given researchers an ideal A-B to find what makes an "artist." Scott did not undergo "therapy," but noted that he would probably "be carried off by four strong guards, shrieking … while Zelda is followed home by an adoring crowd … and offered a vaudeville contract."[49]

Paul, through living with Margaret Asher, had a connection to Harvard and T.S. Eliot: Margaret and T.S Eliot share a distant ancestor who was a long-term president of Harvard.[50] Charles William Eliot was president of Harvard from 1869 to 1909, and is credited with "secularizing" the university to be a premier research institution. Eliot was himself a bit of a mental Argonaut into the creative propensities of abnormal states of mind; as noted above, he was interested in the topic, and he was treated for a mental breakdown in Switzerland before he wrote *The Waste Land*.[51] Eliot's wife Vivienne, according to her biographer in *The Painted Shadow*, was inspiration for (and contributed to) Eliot's famous poetry of the early Modern period. She had the unfortunate fate to be committed to and later die in an asylum[52] (or, "a glorified rest home, with some measure of restraints needed," as a friend of hers put it). Thus, there are similarities between what I suggest Paul's wellspring was, and that of Eliot and other Modernist poets and writers.

* * *

The Queen of England awarded the Beatles MBEs in October 1965, two months after the album "Help!" including "Yesterday" was released, and about two months before the release of "Rubber Soul." The *Beatles Book Monthly*, the Beatles' official fan magazine, explained that bestowing the award was the idea of U.S. teenagers "across the pond":

"Earlier in the year, 75 teenagers from Pennsylvania had petitioned the Queen to have the Beatles knighted. While the timing was not yet right for that high of a Royal honor, Prime Minister Harold Wilson saw his way clear to submitting each of the Beatles' names for receiving the MBE, or Members of the Most Honorable Order of the British Empire, a prestigious annual award.

"The Beatles arrived at Buckingham Palace on October 26th, 1965 at 11a.m. for the Royal ceremony in which they would receive medals from Queen Elizabeth II. After the ceremony, a press conference was held at the Saville Theatre in London. The Beatles' manager Brian Epstein was also in attendance. At the time of the press conference the Beatles were well into the recording sessions for their next album, "Rubber Soul."[53]

According to the press release, fans in the United States initiated the Queen of England's award to the leaders of the "British Invasion." Youth in the U.S. had been inundated with Beatle publicity for months, since February of 1964. The Beatles paved the way for what was publicized as a welcome invasion by British bands.

The reader could take this book as my theory based on my own neuroses. All I ask is that the reader consider it. There are always the lyrics as the Ur-text to refer to, and they are what I base my theory upon. Critics state that to extrapolate from an artist's work into their private life is a mistake, and then go on and do exactly that. I don't think I am reading too far into the lyrics; there is that "third thing in there," which I am asserting is psychiatric literature of the era.

In writing this book, I analyzed each of Paul's songs chronologically. Most Beatles songs I had initially thought of catchy, poetic, compelling, and sometimes impossible to figure out. But then as I launched my research into psychology of the era, with each song, to my sometimes amazement, I could see the pattern. Reading about Sixties psychiatry and Laing, I first made the intuitive connection; after that, even though it was odd to see the subtext I had to admit its existence.

*   *   *

Sometime in mid to late 1965, Paul and Jane did a photo-shoot of Paul in and around the Asher home. Jane took the pictures, and Paul did a few poses – sideways on a bench with one leg propped up, gazing out a window, standing beside an automobile, looking at the camera through leaves.[54] His white collar is high to his chin, and his eyes are deep and yet fathomless. However, his expressions all seem of a piece. He had arrived as an artist in his own right, and his eyes somehow showed this. He and Jane might have taken the photos to help him "own" his artistic identity, which the public now perceived as the cute and *sensitive* Beatle. I intuit the photo shoot was a benchmark in that Paul felt confident he had achieved a songwriting identity.

He had solidified it by writing "Yesterday." Although the song and his artistic process were based on motifs of acting, dislocation and schizophrenese, it was like a new man had been launched. Now, Paul could go forward and be as many voices as he wanted, with his IFP "praxis." And it could all be synthesized successfully, as he had done with "Yesterday." Could what we see in those photos perhaps be the real Paul looking sadly at the world through the identity he created for himself? I think the real Paul *can* be glimpsed in Jane's photos. He still retained some of his innocent qualities, which he would later seemingly dispense with, adopting a somewhat impatient, brusque manner in interviews.

That relationships and sense of self could be complex was one of the big revelations of Beatles songs. That a lover could ask his beloved to see him completely—how different that was from "Bee-bop a lu-lah, she's my baby."

Rockers like Chuck Berry, Elvis and Dion were hip in a kind of wink-wink way; it's not that they were unaware of their allusions to sex or misbehavior. But the Beatles were saying new things about what supposedly went on in relationships. It was like a page had been turned. The new(er) "rock and roll" sexuality, not ending in marriage, was supposedly going to have an awareness to go along with it. It would (supposedly) be a new terrain—a new examination of dialectics—even of phenomenology. This is-it-you-or-is-it-me territory "existential psychiatrists" such as Cooper and Laing were familiar with. And because of Paul's discoveries at the Asher's, ideas from existential psychiatry and Transcendentalism would be introduced to the world. After 1966 most of their songs would have these ideas overtly or in subtext, as I will show.

The "Summer of Love" was just beginning to dawn in 1965, barely visible on the horizon. Soon, the Beatles' communications to their fans would be fused with and almost indivisible from the drug LSD. But in mid-1963 to the end of 1965, the Beatles had their own hour in the sun, when they distilled most purely the artistic process Paul found at the Asher home.

CHAPTER V

Here, There, and Everywhere: Paul's IFP Expands

P erson X: "It will let you see inside yourself."
Paul looked down at the sugar cube in his hand and
frowned.
Paul: "Just for the sake of argument, how would *I* know that
I am looking at myself? Maybe I will be *imagining* that I'm
looking at myself – or, making even *that* up! Or, *if* the whole
enlightenment thing about this drug is bosh, how would I
know whether or not what I'm seeing is just visions of brain
damage, *if* I've been brain damaged?"
Person X: "Well, I donno. …But, don't you want to 'look
through'… yourself? To find out who you really are?"
(Paul thought: *Hell, he's using a line from my own song to persuade
me … as if I don't do this drug, I deny my songs … my Beatle Paul
identity.*)
Paul: "I don't do hard drugs."
Person X: "But LSD isn't like heroin. It isn't addictive."
(Paul thought: *John has been taking LSD for almost a year, and has
gotten closer to George. Ringo took it, with apparently no ill effects.*)
Paul: "Hm. John does like it."

Person X: "Jane is out of town, on tour. She doesn't have to know."
Paul, unsure, looked at the sugar cube again.[iv]

* * *

Paul had his praxis – and it was so effective. And yet in late 1965, after the release of "Rubber Soul," Paul took LSD.[1] He had had a critical success with "Yesterday." But his songwriting was still not as prolific as John's at this point. John had written the stronger songs on "Rubber Soul" – "Norwegian Wood," "It's Only Love," "Girl," and "In My Life." These wonderful songs John had written after he had taken LSD. Paul had written the music for "In My Life," but John was moved to write the deeply felt lyrics. Perhaps Paul thought that taking LSD might help his own songwriting.

Paul held out from taking LSD for at least half a year after the other three Beatles had taken it. "The demon drug," he thought of it.[2] But by 1965, controlled and uncontrolled substances were all around him. LSD, pot, heroin and other drugs were in use among other musicians in the scene, at various "crash pads" Paul visited, at parties and in nightclubs. William Burroughs, a heroin addict, shared a recording space with Paul, where they both experimented with editing recordings on audiotape. Other Beat writers, including Paul's friend Allen Ginsberg, promoted or distributed hallucinogens. But Paul, although he played his new song "Eleanor Rigby" for Burroughs's critique, helped build the bookshelves at the Indica Gallery bookstore,[3] designed its wrapping paper and read its "avant-garde" books, had not tried LSD.

After all, why should he take a drug that psychiatrists said caused "de-personalization"? LSD enthusiasts, of which there was a growing number, said that "de-personalization" was only an uptight Western term for seeing the Infinite and losing your ego—shedding your veneer of society's programming, like an outmoded chrysalis. LSD

[iv]   In this fictitious scenario, I am merely showing Paul's ambiguity toward LSD, which he has stated he felt in several interviews and in Barry Miles' biography.

was touted not as a "permanent neuronal rearrangement with permanent effects upon the personality," as the Macy researchers had described it,[4] but a "transformative" drug. It was praised as a quick route to what psychiatrist Sidney Cohen called "The Beyond Within." Cohen had published first-hand accounts of people who had taken the drug in 1964.[5]

Cohen did not acknowledge that his LSD subjects might have simply been making things up about their experiences, or that their brains could have been adversely affected by it. That would be a concern in the world of psychiatric research, and to some extent publishers are also responsible for assertions they make; but published interviews or testimonials such as "Constance Newland's" account of her LSD psychotherapy, *Myself and I: LSD 25* published in 1963,[6] or Cohen's book of interviews need not be factual. And to Paul, as an artist, the "murkiness" of the psychiatric profession was not a hindrance. It was actually something in its favor that it faced a gigantic blind spot in its knowledge, which was the inability to ever know exactly what was in another person's mind. This was the terrain where "dialectics" came into play, which so frustrated Cooper and Laing. It was to be the precise grey area the Beatles would make their own.

Paul had earned his identity as a songwriter with hard work: He was by late 1965 the cute, rich, famous, *and* sensitive Beatle. Only he, and maybe John, knew how he wrote such interesting lyrics and had such insight into relationships. The next step for the Beatles would be to expand and embellish his IFP and the interval he had created.

Young and old liked the Beatles' music. Their songs were sufficiently insightful that youth were gaining by association a new status in society. No longer were the young perceived, in the press at least, as ignorant – they were being interviewed, published, their opinions aired and their tastes marketed to.[7] At the pinnacle of this new interest in youth, this hopefulness and sense of fun, towered the Beatles. The Beatles' songs were so different. No one could say why exactly their sound was so compelling. They were beacons – seemingly shining, as the Sixties wore on, from a higher plane of understanding. This was due, I assert in this book, to Paul's IFP. It opened up possibilities where none had existed before. If one thinks of relationships between two people as a gap between the numbers one and two, now it seemed as if an infinitude of numbers in between one and two could exist. In the songs they created (which seemed sincere, therefore real and originating from them) it was as if new vistas of communication were possible – that a new kind of *person* was possible.

Then abruptly, in 1966, the Beatles' image implied that they might be "taking drugs." The change was obvious in the photo on the back of "Revolver." They were in a dark studio, wearing shades or tinted glasses, and had shaggier hair. This was a daring change in their image, but I will argue that both their image change and the change in their sound were accepted because of the process of the IFP that was already in place.

What the Beatles had been doing, that is, placing concepts of ontological insecurity, motifs of dislocation, and using psychological texts as "news" about relationships (which was the art of Paul's "praxis" or IFP) could by 1966 be rolled forward into promoting LSD's "de-personalization" and concurrent "new awareness." The same subtext worked for each. To the public, it would then seem that the counterculture (that is, the "ostensive" culture dreamt of by Bateson) came into being spontaneously. It would not be a case of obvious parties marketing ideas to youth or to the general population. Rather, the counterculture was perceived to have formed spontaneously. This perception was due to the IFP subtext filling (mysteriously) the gap of dialectics, and inserting the Beatles themselves into the figure-ground relationship. New ideas about relationships had been expressed in Beatles songs. And the more porous boundaries of self underlying songs such as "What You're Doing," "I'm Looking Through You" and Help!" would dovetail into songs giving listeners a musical simulation of a drug experience that could also take one "somewhere else" (such as on "Tomorrow Never Knows"). The Beatles could now use the language of patient transcripts and scenarios of psychology and therapy just as effectively to

CHAPTER V | 109

allude to drug awareness, spiritual enlightenment, or counterculture "awareness." This they did.

Strangely, though, it was kind of a loop, or an ouroboros: The "model psychosis" drug, LSD, was initially administered to study schizophrenia. Then, the words of schizophrenics, put into Beatles songs, gathered people together in a new kind of "counterculture," which then led people to consider taking LSD.

Life was going to follow art, and art follow life, in the "mad" Sixties.

*   *   *

In December 1965, Paul himself went in somewhat of a circle. By taking LSD, he made the artistic mistake of "buying yourself." This is my term; I will explain it, if the reader bears with me. In buying yourself, I mean that an artist should never buy or adopt the outer world's interpretation of what he or she has created as being representative of their own identity. This is because other people's interpretation is just that – an interpretation. People encounter the artist's art in their own way. They never see the process that was uniquely the artist's own. The artist needs feedback, but it should never be taken as the definitive statement of what they are doing, because it has been filtered through observers, it is not straight from the source. If a piece of art evokes something really new, then people will seize upon it, interpret it and compete to classify, to put a net around it and thereby make it vicariously their own.

The Beatles resisted categorization. This was partly because they were always trying new sounds. (For discussion about their sonic innovations, see Chapter Seven.) But more importantly it was because the synthesis or process (which included Paul's IFP) was in effect hidden from view. Their phenomenal success and creativity were the "unknown" X-factor that the Macy researchers had encountered around LSD – in what Abramson had called "the search for new magic."[8] The Beatles were perceived as the new magic. They always had something new to give; and a new culture could supposedly grow off of this and come into being.

The Beatles did have some creative magic, in that songs would sometimes come to them, as happens to certain songwriters. However, for Paul to take LSD, that offered (ostensibly) the magic awareness he already had achieved was a symbolic gesture that carried not a little risk. LSD was held out to millions in the Sixties as the key to be, in a sense, "like the Beatles" or "with" the Beatles; to have their insight, their ability, their magic; but no one could be *them*. Paul was in a unique situation in that he could draw upon materials that spoke to him, and synthesize songs which were an unusual palliation of modern stresses. John also picked up on his method of writing songs based on psychological texts. Theirs was such an engaging and creative synthesis that it seemed to point to a new awareness.

The "Interval"

Their music had such a new approach, that it was as if it created what I call "the interval." This is my term, and it stands for the subliminal effect of their songs on people. The Beatles brought news of "feelings" and seemed to describe new emotional possibilities of relations between people. This begat, or rather a "counterculture" was built up around, this initial perception of something having been "opened up."

Sheila Whiteley, a lecturer on popular culture in the UK, describes the formation of the counterculture in similar terms in her book *The Space Between the Notes: Rock and the Counterculture.* Examining the image of a prism splitting light on the album cover of Pink Floyd's "Dark Side of the Moon," she writes:

"Aesthetically, the image can be seen as a literal signifier of the psychedelic effect that Floyd hoped to achieve through the fusion of sound with light. At a deeper level, it can be interpreted as inspiration (clear white light) converted through musical and technological transformation (the prism) into the psychedelic range of sound and meaning (the whole spectrum). So the image encapsulates not only the philosophy of the group but also the philosophy of the counterculture itself with its emphasis on alternative structures of meaning."[9]

This is similar to the same way I conceptualize the "interval." As Paul's "praxis" expanded, so did the behavioral and communicative processes allowed in the new alternative culture.

Whiteley also noted connections between Pink Floyd's music, surrealism and madness on "Dark Side of the Moon." "The montage of bizarre sound images and taped emotions ... create an often disembodied, hallucinatory impression of the threat of madness. Just as surrealistic art speaks directly to individualized secret fears and emotions through universal signifiers, so the juxtaposition of images ... creates an experience of madness."[10]

Front man Syd Barrett was given LSD prior to joining the band. This might have been another creative "experiment." As many know, Barrett quit Pink Floyd in 1972, and lived with his mother from 1978 onward.

Related to my analysis, Whiteley finds that the familiar, when mixed with bizarre and emotional content at one remove, evokes a feeling of madness or instability. I suggest that this is very like what the Beatles were doing: they were mixing the familiar (primarily music genres, but also rhythms of nursery rhymes, images of gardens and tea, and so on) with the IFP subtext.

I conceptualize the "interval" as something Paul made possible, an opening being made into which a sense of new possibilities and new personality were theoretically possible. I compare it to the infinite amount of numbers that theoretically can occur between two numbers, but you could also think of it a "rainbow" spectrum suddenly being created from white light, or Sidney Cohen's "unsane" wedge of creativity.

Thus, this wedge, or interval, made by Paul's artistic process, seemed to point toward new perceptions and possibilities. LSD was offered as the open sesame to what the Beatles were seemingly onto.

* * *

Paul, I am asserting, led the band. John might come up with brilliant summations of what Paul was interested in, but Paul had to initiate research and introduce John to various artistic and philosophical, as well as psychiatric, texts and ideas. Did Paul feel his synthesis of texts, ideas and situations into art was not enough, and that he had to organically "break" himself? This would mean that he wanted to risk taking himself, the artist, out of the equation. It could be an erasure of soul. Taking this kind of risk would imply that he had an inner drive to fracture his own identity.

Paul has mentioned that he took LSD due to "peer pressure": that in fact, Peers of the English aristocracy were pressuring him to take it.[11] The London scene was awash in drugs; he was a lysergic holdout. Biographer Barry Miles stated that Paul was "still insecure," after receiving his MBE. He was afraid that "his career would be over at age thirty" and felt he needed to write some long-lasting standards.[12] Perhaps, although taking a boundary-dissolving drug and writing "standards" would seem to be incompatible activities. According to biographer Steve Turner in *Beatles '66: The Revolutionary Year*, Paul first took LSD in December 1965 at Tara Browne's home. Browne, the heir to the Guinness brewery fortune, would die in a car crash in late 1966. As I will discuss below, other parties could have persuaded Paul that LSD would improve his songwriting, or make it more prolific. LSD was found to have "massively increased associative language and symbolization" among subjects, according to a researcher at the Macy Conference. Associative language and symbolization are songwriter's tools, if they are lyricists.

By late 1965, through the efforts of Janiger, Cohen, Abramson, Ginsberg, Leary, Al Hubbard and others, LSD had permeated into various strata of society. Poets, actors and peers had tried it. Students, businessmen and housewives had taken it. Psychiatrists offered weekend sessions, which they called an "executive's special."[14] By 1965, by conservative estimates, 40,000 people in the U.S. had taken LSD; small numbers in relation to the overall population, but Timothy Leary's 1963 expulsion from Harvard had brought LSD to the attention of millions through mass media publicity.

The LSD phase of Paul's IFP coincided with his moving away from the Asher home. In early 1966, Paul made the important step of buying his own house in St. John's Wood. Prudently, he chose a large, but well-fortified residence that was near Abbey Road studios.[15] Jane was at this point frequently on tour, and in April 1966 turned twenty. Turner states in his book that after Paul first took LSD on December 14, 1965 he took it several times again in 1966. Jane has commented that returning from touring in a production of *Romeo and Juliet*, she found that "Paul had changed so much. He was on LSD, which I knew nothing about.[16] There were fifteen people dropping in all day long. The house had changed, and was full of stuff I didn't know about."[17] She did not want to take the drug.

Paul was going to look less clean-cut and boyish from then onward. Even his face looked different; his jaw seemed thinner, the top of his head less round. He was becoming a man with a house of his own and a songwriting identity. How could he top himself, though, after writing "Yesterday?" An interviewer in *The Beatles Book* monthly, November 1966 issue, asked him if he ever worried about not being able to come up with new material. "No," Paul replied. "I used to think that, and was frightened that I was going to dry up, but now I realize that it won't happen if you're interested.

"Our songs are changing because we're changing, but you still get the type of person who sticks to something even if they don't like it—everyone can do something else, even a bank clerk or a laborer. I get annoyed with people who are too nervous to change their way of life.

"People say that 'Yesterday' was my greatest piece of work, but I hope I will write a better one."[18]

It is interesting that Paul thought it important to criticize those who didn't change. A pluralistic approach to identity was to be one of the hallmarks of Leary's "philosophies" as well. A primary roadblock to change, of course, is lacking motivation. And lacking motivation is also perceived as a roadblock to creativity. Arthur Koestler would publish a 700-page-plus tome in 1964, *The Act of Creation*, that stated creativity is suppressed by "the automatic routines of thought and behavior that dominate (people's) lives."[19] Koestler, who observed experiments in creativity at Harvard and was given psilocybin by

Timothy Leary there, went on establish a Foundation with editor David Astor of the *Observer* to bring arts programs to prisons.[20] Although positive, this does seem to be more of the "creative experimentation under observation" that seems to have been such a holy grail to researchers in the mid-Fifties through the Sixties.

A related problem is that what often spurs a song or poem to be written is emotion. And thus it can be hard to write a song, if one is feeling "uninterested." Paul didn't have to feel strong emotion, however, to write songs with his IFP: he could write some good music he liked, and then use a psychological subtext as the lyric framework. This meant he could potentially write a song based on almost anything that he encountered. His IFP allowed him to write in all kinds of styles. Eclecticism was the Beatles. Irreverence, rock and roll was the Beatles—but so was heartfelt confession.

I suggest the changeover to psychedelic rock would be accepted by their audience due to Paul's IFP, which he had been putting since 1963's "She Loves You" into Beatles songs. The IFP psychological subtexts were the lyric umbrella under which the four Beatles could venture into all kinds of styles. Now, at the beginning of the "psychedelic era," they could use the same approach and also add, via the studio, the emotional musical language to go along with the psychological lyric subtext. They could paint feeling-pictures in sound, that they wouldn't have to reproduce live. The Beatles had already been "leading" people: they had introduced new phrases, ideas, and new *feelings* about dialectics. Paul was the instigator of all of this. He would now take the reins as co-producer with George Martin as the Beatles moved into their "psychedelic" phase—which was the same old IFP.

"Although John was thought originally to be the leader of the band," writes biographer Philip Norman, "by the Mid-Sixties the elastic-sided boot was firmly on the other foot"—of Paul.[21] Emerick noted that Paul began to take over production of every song, selecting each instrument and tone color, and supervising the mixing, starting with "Revolver."[22]

The use of schizophrenic non-logic which he incorporated in songs pre-1966 would henceforth segue into "drug logic" as the ostensive culture metamorphosed. It would be conflated into the "kaleidoscope eye" of the "new type," that John (or rather, his "Pepper" personae) sang of in "Lucy in the Sky With Diamonds." A creative, flexible new type would be the person born of the expansion of the interval.

This new type of person, which Paul was gesturing toward in his art, lived, so to speak in a space that was neither "sane," nor "insane," according to psychologist Sidney Cohen, a creativity researcher working with LSD and volunteers at the Veteran's Hospital in Los Angeles and who tested student volunteers at UCLA.

Cohen was one of the leading researchers in LSD and creativity, along with Oscar Janiger, Allen Ginsberg's cousin, who was also based in Los Angeles. Cohen had a theory about creativity derived from his research with artists and LSD. He depicted it as being in a circle, with the point at the top of the circle representing complete rationality, then going all the way around to insanity. Near the top was a wedge where creativity was located. Cohen labeled the wedge "unsanity." The creative wedge was neither rational nor irrational. In this wedge or interval, according to Cohen, dwelt the creative mavericks—those who could invent and break new ground in all fields of endeavor.[23]

Paul, I suggest, whether wittingly or unwittingly, had given people a feeling of this creative, "unsane" interval when he started to put the IFP subtext in songs. Cohen's idea was also related to Rupert Crawshay-William's writing in *The Comforts of Unreason*, that humor could be a creative force. Arthur Koestler (who was personal friends with Crawshay-Williams) wrote in *The Act of Creation*, published by Hutchinson and Company in 1964, that jokes and humor were a creative state of mind, along with dreams and trance-states. I will discuss more about Cohen's schematic circle as it regards "Lucy in the Sky With Diamonds" in Chapter Eight.

* * *

Revolver

For "Revolver," Paul wrote six songs: "Eleanor Rigby," "Good Day Sunshine," "For No One," most of "Yellow Submarine," "Got to Get

You Into My Life," and "Here, There and Everywhere": over half of the U.S. album release. (For the U.S. release, George wrote three songs and John wrote only two.) Also in that same year, Paul's "Paperback Writer" A-side (B-side, John's "Rain") zoomed to Number One in the U.S. This was the beginning of what I call Paul's "Expando-Paul" phase, when he would expand on all fronts of the IFP subtext, and take expression of it to a state of mastery.

It might lend perspective to consider first some other songs that were charting during 1966. Songs that charted at Number One in the U.S. included "When a Man Loves a Woman" by Percy Sledge; "My World is Empty Without You" and "You Can't Hurry Love" by the Supremes; "Last Train to Clarksville" by The Monkees; "Strangers in the Night" by Frank Sinatra; "The Ballad of The Green Berets," which held at Number One for several weeks; "Sunshine Superman" by Donovan; "Paperback Writer" by The Beatles; "Good Vibrations" by The Beach Boys; "My Love" by Petula Clark; and for one week, "Paint it Black" by the Rolling Stones.[24]

Thus there was an abundance of creativity in popular music of the time, giving the Beatles plenty of competition. The Beatles by no means dominated the Top Ten; they would have their week or two at the top of the charts and then drop down, just as their competitors did. The Supremes were a great pop group; Percy Sledge sang probably the most human song of the lot. But these artists, although making lasting contributions, were not perceived as leaders. The Beatles (and, with the symphonic tripiness of "Good Vibrations," The Beach Boys) were thought to be, by the end of 1966. Why were the Beatles perceived as such? It was, I am arguing, due to the IFP subtext.

1966 brought change: not only did they change their image, it was their year of transition from touring group to studio group. "Revolver" and specifically the track "Tomorrow Never Knows," which depended on tape manipulations and studio techniques for its effect, would signal their change in style and delivery if not in basic approach. Now, the Beatles would give "news" or guidance into the experi-ence of ego-loss and what *that* felt like. Where in 1965 John had penned "Help!" about needing a stablemate, with "Tomorrow Never Knows" the Beatles became the stablemates. "Turn off your mind, relax and float downstream," John instructed listeners. The Beatles took on the mantle of experienced, trusted figures who would guide youth through the "experience" of taking LSD or smoking pot. They assumed the role of LSD psychotherapy stablemate, the same role Timothy Leary had taken on occasionally at Harvard and would assume after he left Harvard.

John wholly grasped Paul's identity fracture. He would "sum it up" in bold, yet rather loose, compositions. "Tomorrow Never Knows" began as "a muddy wash," according to Abbey Road audio engineer Geoff Emerick.[25] MacDonald stated that Paul's production of the song was integral to its impact.[26] It is an out-of-body-experience of a song, still vivid today. By comparison, Paul's songs of the IFP are classical miniatures, written with a balance of form to content. However, no one suspected Paul's "content" was just as fractured, underneath, as John's. John, Paul, and George could all fit their songwriting styles under Paul's IFP. "Revolver" would be the first Beatles album to be almost entirely IFP songs (nine out of eleven songs, on the U.S. release). Each song talks in a different way about identity fracture, therapy, psychiatric concepts, dislocation, or void.

Let's look at songs on "Revolver," released in August of 1966, as they reflected or embodied his IFP.

"Revolver" opens with a harder rock sound. A snarling, sinuous guitar riff (played by Paul, actually)[27] opens George's "**Taxman**" after someone counts in one, two, three, four to the backdrop of a cough, "as if they were stoned in Tibet" (MacDonald). The immediate impression is that these Beatles are not going to play "nice" anymore. After the song fades out on Paul's guitar solo, then follows "**Eleanor Rigby**" with a rush of strings, indicating that we are about to receive what everyone has really come to hear: another televisual scene of emotional depth. Because this is the real breakthrough of the Beatles: emotional complexity combined with immediacy—a sense of you-are-there.

"Eleanor Rigby," although televisual and memorable, would be less intimate and bleaker than "Yesterday." It was, like "Yesterday," scored with a string arrangement. However, although "Yesterday" was sung in the first person, the character of Eleanor Rigby is sung about in third person, which creates a bit of distance. Also, "Rigby" does not have a vulnerable, muddled (mental patient's) voice. Instead, the song depicts deep emptiness in people. Father McKenzie darns his own socks, not believing in companionship; he is alone. Eleanor keeps empty watch for company. She "waits at the window/Wearing a face that she keeps in a jar by the door/Who is it for." No one visits, and her face has faded to nothing, is the implication; she must put on a face to be seen at all. (This recalls T.S. Eliot's line of the face one puts on to greet other faces.) "All the lonely people, where do they all come from? /All the lonely people, where do they all belong?" asks the refrain. An existential perception of emptiness pervades everything; one can't turn to the Church or to other people for comfort. Father McKenzie writes the "words of a sermon that no-one will hear." Even if lonely people might show up to a service, they are "no-ones" who won't hear or understand the words. When Eleanor dies, "and was buried along with her name/Nobody came." Father McKenzie wiped the dirt from his hands as he walked away, reflecting that no one came to the funeral. "No-one was saved," implies both that no one can expect to be "saved" by the Church, and that the Father only attended Eleanor's funeral to do his job.

"Eleanor Rigby" sat on Paul's musical shelf without words for some time before he enlisted people to help him finish it.[28] He wrote the music in 1964 while living at the Asher's. He wanted the song to tell a story, but didn't know quite what. As with Brian Wilson's "feels,"[29] Paul had an evocative piece of music, and needed help with lyrics. (Wilson referred to his unfinished pieces of music, without lyrics, as "feels.")

In its finished state, the song makes the listener subtly aware that Eleanor Rigby is an empty person. And that like the "Nowhere Man," she is "a lot like you and me." In fact, she is one with "all the lonely people," all of humanity. She waits at a window, wears makeup, and she helps at the church. But her externality is all she is. These activities are presented along with images that bespeak their emptiness—her face is "in a jar by the door/Who is it for," she "lives in a dream," that is, in a fantasy of her own mind, and if Father McKenzie darns his socks alone at night, "what does he care." On the chorus, Eleanor is multiplied to thousands—millions—like her, "all the lonely people," who don't know where they belong or "where they all come from."

It is true that our human origins remain mysterious, and how we got here, another mystery; but this present-day part of the human condition is in "Eleanor Rigby" wedded to emptiness or void in the (written-by-committee) lyrics.

Here is a "type" presented, again. Like John's "Nowhere Man," it's that of the "empty" person, detached from their inner feelings. I don't think it extreme of me to read this song in this manner. MacDonald writes, "Eleanor died without ever expressing her true feelings." Father McKenzie didn't "care," either. And because (the song implies) there is no God, feelings are all we have. Paul could have rhymed, "thought of her face, as he walked from the grave/At least she was saved." That would have provided some relief (at least, to Christians). But instead we get, "wiping the *dirt* from his *hands* as he *walks* from the *grave*," emphasized in meter, like hammer blows. "No one was saved," ends the verse. MacDonald called the final verse "brutal."[30]

However, that the song was taken as being sympathetic to old people and to "loneliness" says a lot about how Paul was perceived at that point. It was taken to be that Paul, sensitive and bringing "news," had just sung another truth about how people live. With "Eleanor Rigby," the news was that people in general are all lonely. And this was somehow (in art) accepted: I am not so sure this would have been a generalized assumption cropping up in a song of the 1950s. The lyrics, although coming down hard on the Church, were perceived, because of prior songs Paul had sung, as more of the same from him—feeling, sensitive, even compassionate. However, somewhat sneakily (and in a split sense), the song asks the listener to both feel for, and be one of "all the lonely people." The lonely people and the listener come from nowhere, have nowhere to go, and are empty. They need to express their *feelings*, or suffer the meaninglessness of Eleanor's fate. (I will also note that the psychiatric Behaviorist approach does not allow for God or a concept of a soul.)

Another song Paul wrote for "Revolver" is "**Good Day Sunshine**." This song, its chorus sounding close to an advertisement jingle for orange juice, is aural sunshine. "Sunshine" could be referencing Liquid Sunshine, which was a name of LSD in vials being distributed at the time. There was also LSD in bright orange pills, lab grade, being distributed in California, and orange blotter LSD that was called Orange Sunshine. The Brotherhood of Eternal Love was set up at this point in Los Angeles to manufacture tens of thousands of hits of LSD.[31] The *Saturday Evening Post* published "Drugs on Campus: A Coast-to-Coast Survey" (a rather offhand title) in May 1966, and its author stated that drug distribution had spread from its initial center in Greenwich Village, New York, to campuses nationwide. Pot and LSD were the two favored drugs, and "every campus had its Jewish drug dealer with a suitcase full of pot."[32] Many of the students interviewed had posters on the wall of the Beatles, and were listening to the new music.

Paul was in proximity to the Beats; he was friends with drug connoisseur and distributor Allen Ginsberg, who had gone around for a year or two with Timothy Leary turning on tastemakers, the intelligentsia, and whoever else crossed their path.[33] Since Paul had taken LSD himself and was friends with the Beats, it is reasonable to assume that "Good Day Sunshine" could be a nod to a "trade" name for LSD, a drug that does according to the Macy researchers change the subject's sense of their own identity and makes colors as bright and shiny as the fade-out harmonies of the song.

John and Paul during this period colored their lyric sheets to make sure they rendered in sound the "colors" of the lyrics.[34] "Good Day Sunshine" was beneficed with sun-spectrum harmonies – implying all the colors in the rainbow can be seen if you "lie beneath a shady tree."

All through 1965, Paul had been, in his off hours, smoking pot and experimenting with tape loops.[35] William Burroughs, who shared a recording studio that Paul sometimes used, had introduced him to this idea. Paul also had two Brennel tape recorders set up in his room at the Asher's. He would tape bits of sound, then splice, reverse, and create looping Mobius strips of no end and no beginning. Paul mentioned in an interview that he wanted to "break apart sound and find something new in it." This is a Burroughsian idea.

Burroughs had his own philosophy about tape loops: like just about everything Burroughs did, it could be taken as subversive. Burroughs wanted to bypass the mind, which he saw as "programmed"—society had brainwashed people to accept sex roles, competition, jobs, University degrees, and a house in the suburbs. Society was to Burroughs and his friends, including Allen Ginsberg, not a reflection of basic human needs, but an inhuman, artificial, and pleasure-destroying construct. Reality could only be found by scratching deep below its controlled surface, or scrambling it: So, Burroughs and his various creative collaborators, among them Brion Gysin, cut up texts from newspapers, from books, and collaged bits of audio, seeking to find "the real message underneath." Paul echoed this idea when he told an interviewer that he wanted to "take a note and wreck it and see what else is in it."[36] Gysin also said language itself was to blame, that "we must rub out the word."[37] Tape loops, which made nonsense out of sense, were an ideal aural assault on language. Gibberish loops both illustrated and achieved their aim of control-destabilization. In all this Burroughs's set were similar to the Dadaists. Burroughs and Ginsberg were also avid drug users. If one couldn't scratch down deep below the surface, then one needed to rise above it.

Oddly, where counterculture came from, in 1965, was rather close to where some of the Macy researchers left off. And where the Beats had been all along. The fascination with drugs and altered states of Burroughs and the poetic Beats was pretty close to the "study of the creative possibilities of deliriants and of transcendent visions" of psychiatrist Sidney Cohen. The dinner parties that Harold Abramson held to give LSD to a select few friends were only smaller and with no door charge than the Trips Festivals of 1965 and 1966.

the TRIP -- or electronic performance--is a new
medium of communication & entertainment.

FRIDAY, JANUARY 21
america needs indians, sensorium 9 - slides, movies,
sound tracks, flowers, food, rock'n'roll, eagle lone
whistle, indians (senecas, chippewas, hopi, sioux,
blackfeet, etc.) & anthropologists. open theatre -
"revelations" - nudeprojections. "the god box" by
ben jacopetti. the endless explosion, the congress
of wonders, liquid projections, the jazz mice, the
loading zone rock'n'roll, steve fowler, amanda foulger,
rain jacopetti, & the unexpectable.

SATURDAY, JANUARY 22
ken kesey, members of the s.f. tape music center,
big brother & the holding company rock'n'roll, the
don buchla sound-light console, overhead projection,
anthony martin, ramon sender, bill maginnis, bruce
baillie. "the acid test", the merry pranksters & their
psychedelic symphony, neal cassady vs. ann murphy
vaudeville, the grateful dead rock'n'roll, allen ginsberg,
roy's audioptics, movies, ron boise & his electric thunder
sculpture, the bus, hell's angels, many noted outlaws, &
the unexpectable.

SUNDAY, JANUARY 23
high energy experiments conducted in the cyclotron of
dome-shaped longshoreman's hall by america needs
indians, open theatre, s.f. tape music center, the
merry pranksters, gordon ashby (light matrix), henry
jacobs (air dome projections), kqed, don buchla, the
grateful dead, the loading zone, big brother & the holding
company, & many others still being assembled. since the
common element of all shows is ELECTRICITY, this evening will be programmed live from stimuli provided by a
PINBALL MACHINE. a nickel in the slot starts the evening.

the general tone of things has moved on from the self-
conscious happening to a more JUBILANT occasion where
the audience PARTICIPATES because it's more fun to do so
than not. maybe this is the ROCK REVOLUTION. audience
dancing is an assumed part of all the shows, & the audience
is invited to wear ECSTATIC DRESS & bring their own GADGETS
(a.c. outlets will be provided).

design:
Wes Wilson

printing:
Contact Printing Co.

TICKETS = $2 PER EVENING
= $5 FOR SERIES
AT CITY LIGHTS, S.F., ASUC

There were researchers in the psychiatric community who would have favored making even Paul McCartney a guinea pig and spokesman for LSD. At Stanford, research labs such as Myron Stolaroff's were studying the effect of LSD on creativity. At Harvard, Leary had given the drug to poet Robert Lowell, and to many other creative influencers. Dr. Oscar Janiger, Allen Ginsberg's cousin, administered LSD in Los Angeles to over a hundred volunteers to study creativity.[38] Sidney Cohen was also doing work in this area.[39] In the late Fifties and early Sixties the Rockefellers[v] funded a Harvard Psychological Clinic study on creativity,[40] headed by Henry Murray, who mentored Timothy Leary. Murray took LSD under Leary's guidance in the early Sixties, but Murray was never was able to complete the book he wanted to write on Herman Melville. Nor did Murray's investigation into extreme states of consciousness in the "tower" he had built to emulate Jung's tower at Bollingen stimulate his writing about a "new" consciousness. Of course, the general public was (and is) as ignorant of this research as it was about Fifties-era research into LSD's hard-to-define applications.

However, the general public *was* being thrilled by Paul's songs and encouraged toward a sense of new creative possibilities. The Beatles, however, would introduce the concepts of emptiness and void into their songs after 1965. This might go along with the subtext of a mental asylum, therapy and so on because the ultimate invalidation of an individual is to be locked away in a mental hospital, as actress Gene Tierney observed of her experiences in asylums.[41]

"For No One" describes an estranged couple who are physically and emotionally separating from each other. "You stay home/She goes out." And: "She wakes up, she makes up." "She takes her time and doesn't feel she has to hurry/She no longer needs you." She applies a mask—like an actor's mask. "She says that long ago she knew someone/But now he's gone/She doesn't need him." The "he" (not identified as the singer

---

[v]   The Rockefellers also funded the Harvard Poet's Theatre and poetry fellowships, according to Stevenson, Anne, *Bitter Fame: a Biography of Sylvia Plath* (Houghton Mifflin Company/A Peter Davison Book, 1989) p. 139

but who we assume is) she knew is "gone." Then, in the penultimate scene of this televisual drama, she is crying in a way that hints at her own emptiness as well as her lover's emptiness. "In her eyes, you see nothing/No sign of love behind the tears/Cried for no one/A love that should have lasted years." Her tears, which function as a barrier or a glass, are like the mirror before which she composes her face. Both sides of her eyes reflect that there is nobody home. Her eyes are a double-sided mirror, which reflects vacancy. We will find this idea in George's song about the Beatles, "Only a Northern Song." "No one home" is also found in many other Beatles songs: "Nowhere Man," "Eleanor Rigby, " "A Day In The Life," "Strawberry Fields Forever," and "Within You Without You." Each "whole" or person contains "a hole" in the Beatleverse.

Is "For No One" an IFP song? It does not contain "illogical logic," it is more employing formal imagery such as the metaphysical poets would use: that of the eyes, and the empty glass/mirror. It's also a bit surrealist, a motif we find in other songs by Paul. But I think it is an IFP song. Somewhat like "Eleanor Rigby," it questions the individual's capacity for having a self. It is broaching the idea of emptiness, a motif in Beatles songs. Love between two people sometimes does not sustain, nor did the Church help Eleanor Rigby.

"Here, There and Everywhere" is perhaps the sweetest piece of music Paul ever wrote, but its lyrics suggest, like the "lipless kisser" in "All My Loving," a sense of dislocation. Each "place" shifts in soft-focus dissolve to the next, until he hopes he will always be in her eyes, "here, there, and everywhere." The song is not about any one moment, but about several which fade into each other. The effect is of blissfully dissolving into love, and thus into "everywhere." So, the singer does not gain anything, in a sense, for themselves in love, but rather a blissful sense of formlessness. They hope to blissfully be here, there, and everywhere, and thus, nowhere, excepting in her eyes.

The effect is like a kaleidoscope. Actually, her eyes could be interpreted as kaleidoscopic, because if he is everywhere when he is in her eyes, he has been fractured into many different images. "Here, There and Everywhere" is basically a picture of loss of identity when in love, as it is traditionally understood in literature. But, although he is in her eyes, he is also everywhere: which was something new to say about this "love." I suggest that in this song, Paul has again put an IFP idea: he is describing a scattered person with no basis, and one must point out that having no basis is the definition of schizophrenia. Then he frames it as a song about love. This was Paul's basic method of writing: to find an unusual idea from psychiatric literature, whether it be mental asylum texts, therapy, or split identities, and then make these odd phrases apply to a romance situation. This was saying "something new"; but it was also implying that one could be "someone new." (John also sang, "When I think of love/As something new.") This is the idea of Sidney Cohen's "pie-slice" of creativity: which interestingly is also a schematic of a kaleidoscope, two mirrors leaning onto each other inside a circle.

An important IFP song on Revolver is "**Yellow Submarine**." This song with its nautical theme was an unexpected novelty from the band, but it somehow fit right into the emerging spirit of the Sixties. It was often sung in solidarity at student and protest gatherings. Even though light-hearted in tone, complete with sound effects, I suggest that it too has the IFP subtext of the mental asylum. Paul wrote most of the song; I submit that the idea of it is based on Villa 21 and Kingsley Hall, Laing and Cooper's inmate-run mental asylums. The *UK Independent* article cited in Chapter Three stated that celebrities, authors and other influencers visited these asylums during the Sixties. In any event, Paul (a "worshipper" of Laing's, according to the same article) would have been aware of these well-publicized experimental "homes," where rules were decided communally among the inmates, and they could choose their activities with less supervision than formerly. Villa 21, adjacent to a conventional mental hospital in Hertfordshire, opened in 1962. Dr. Asher, having been a mental ward supervisor, would also have been interested in the experimental asylums. Many celebrities and hipsters visited Laing's asylums in London to commune with the inmates or "hang out."[42] I suggest that the song "Yellow Submarine" describes this happy nut-house-party situation.

"And our friends are all aboard/Many more of them live next door." On a real working submarine, no one would "live next door" and they wouldn't be chortling and making funny noises. But the inmates are all aboard at the experimental asylum, and many more of them do indeed live next door at the adjacent conventional mental hospital. "As we live a life of ease/Every one of us, has all we need." Working submariners definitely do not live "a life of ease." But, in an asylum, all basic needs are met. The inmates in the song identify not as each one, but "we." So, it is a song of solidarity. Also note that sub-mariners are "the silent service," in that they can't talk about what they do, and where they go. The metaphor perfectly fits both the asylum subtext of the Beatles, the Beatles themselves who had to maintain a "clean" image, and their fans themselves, who are invited to join in this sing-along about the ostensive, new "alternative" counterculture which was just beginning—the covert "silent service." The song was written I am asserting out of, once again, Paul's subtext of mental asylum, mental patient, and loss of self.

"Yellow Submarine" was given to Ringo to sing, in his role as stalwart Everyman. He would later pen his own version of this "sub-marine" community in "Octopus's Garden."

For the Beatles, gathering everyone under the asylum or nut-house banner came with a sense of celebration—everyone's life could be, "with" the Beatles, happy and joyful—in contrast to the depressive, cramped lives of the Eleanor Rigby's, the Nowhere Men, or "people who think they know better." Living "with" the Beatles on the "Yellow Submarine" promised to be a liberation from *mores*, and from, in a sense, one's own burden of separate identity. People would be "no-ones" all together. All pressure was released, as when pressurized air blasted in "Yellow Submarine."

"Got to Get You Into My Life" is an ambiguous "love song." The words are rather generalized. Paul has said on occasion that it was about his liking for pot. If nothing else this gives proof that his songwriting process could include his having other things in mind. I suggest this song is possibly about Paul finding his own artistic inspiration. He arrived at the Asher's: He was alone, taking another road, where maybe he could see "another kind of mind." Then, "And I suddenly see you." I suggest that the "you" he found, was among other books, patient transcripts. He could pick a book up and hold it; it didn't run; it "didn't lie." (Perhaps a bit of a joke there: the book didn't "lie" around but was always put back to sit on the shelf.) He would always beat a path to find "You," the information, again: "if I'm true, I'll never leave/And if I do I know the way, there." My analysis might be a bit of a stretch, but given the pattern of the other songs, it is possible that he wrote this with his creative discovery in mind, the moment when he found "another kind of mind, there" to "get into" his life. He is thrilled about it: "Did I tell you I need you?" "Say we'll be together every day."

If so, this wouldn't be the only time Paul would pen a song about his songwriting process. It does seem unlikely that he could write such an excited song about discovering pot when he had had it in his life for quite some time at that point.

Whether or not the song is about finding inspiration in the Asher library, the effect of the song, like many other Beatles songs, is to imply that there is more to relationships than one realizes. The immediate intensity of the song that manages to increase on the chorus, the blasting trumpets, George's burbling-over guitar solo, and the screaming-high trumpet fadeout as Paul declares over and over again the "find" of "You" affirms this find is something new and out of the realm of normal life. The *feeling* of emotion stirred is the important thing.

The song also shows how Paul combines several ideas in one song: it is a love song, (one critic called it a love song "of sorts") and an implied "new" awareness (a new emotional plane to dwell on) with a hidden subtext—I suggest inspired by the "story" of his IFP. The main takeaway is the extreme emotion and that something out of the ordinary has happened. And as in his other "relationship songs" such as "And I Love Her," "She Loves You," "What You're Doing" and "I'm Looking Through You," relationships are being sung about and represented in an entirely new way.

Looking at the Beatles songs on "Revolver," the psychiatric influence is obvious. From the so-transparent-that-one-overlooks-it allusion to talk therapy in "I Want To Tell You," by George to the not-obvious-at-all "Yellow Submarine," the other Beatles were using the same psychological subtext as Paul. I think it is this subtext that made their songs form cohesive albums. Let's look at more songs on "Revolver" with IFP subtexts.

"I Want To Tell You" is sung from the point of view of a therapy patient: "I want to tell you/ my head is filled with things to say," sings George. "Sometimes I wish I knew you well/Then I could speak my mind and tell you/Maybe you'd understand." This is transferring the therapy session to the dialectics of the "romantic" relationship. No songs had phrased the lover's need to communicate using quite this language before, and so the lyrics sounded quite new. It is the situation of a patient with his or her analyst. Even the idea of a limited time to speak "my mind," due to the therapist's clock is in the song: "I'll make you maybe next time around." And: "I don't mind, I can wait forever, I've got time." Here, the singer is comparing his session with a prospective lover to a patient who has to abide by the therapist's clock. The patient runs out of time to tell what they are thinking, but the singer won't: he's "got time." There is also a psychological split in there: "But if I seem to act unkind/It's only me, it's not my mind/ That is confusing things." He also says, "I want to tell you/I feel hung up and I don't know why." This is transparently a "romantic" meeting-as-therapy session.

John's old song, "What Goes On," ("What goes on, inside your head?") could fit in with the IFP, and it was included on the U.K. release of "Rubber Soul."

John's "She Said She Said" was supposedly inspired by an LSD trip he took, during which actor Peter Fonda was reputed to have annoyed him by saying, "I know what it's like to be dead." This is a plausible beginning for John to write a song. However, the song is really, I assert, about the emotional breakthroughs that are possible on LSD, and the form of the song is that of a therapy session in a psychiatrist office. As he did with "Help!" John has put the LSD therapy setting into song. "She," the psychotherapist, knows what it's like to be dead, and she also knows what it is to be sad. The therapist, having taken LSD, knows what it's like to be ego-dead, and also about being sad (depressed)—she is a therapist who has taken LSD, as Leary and some of the Macy researchers recommended.[43] John replies, "You're making me feel/Like I've never been born." This is both an expression (you're making me feel as if I'm as naïve as a baby), and is another emphasis on, or even a rebirth into, new, intense *feelings*. The singer is being made to feel so intensely, it is as if he'd never been *alive* before. It also could be a reference to the experience of being "born again" which some clients reported during LSD psychotherapy.

Again, I am assuming that John had access to the same psychiatric literature Paul did. He and Paul hung out and wrote songs in the Asher basement, where many books headed to the Indica Gallery were temporarily stored, and would have been able to browse Dr. Asher's library. John also would visit the Indica bookstore in person. Dr. Asher's library could have contained information on LSD psychotherapy going back to the early Fifties. The therapist then accuses John, "You don't understand what I said." John counters, "No, no, no, you're wrong/ When I was a boy, everything was right." The soaring vocal line on "when I was a boy," is like a look backward in time, and also, at an older style of therapy – Freudian, recalling one's childhood. Then the insistent guitar line returns. "Who put all those things in your head?" John asks, "things that make me feel that I'm mad?" He ends the session by telling the therapist, "even though you know what you know/I know that I'm ready to leave." (He would make a similar comment later to the Maharishi.) However the music is ecstatic, not dismissive. He repeats, "You're making me feel/Like I've never been born."

This was extraordinary for a pop song of the time, and maybe since. It compressed the (supposed) breakthrough of LSD therapy, a door opening into feelings, and Cooper's vision of erasing dialectics into one song. The LSD therapist is trying to reach him with empathy. John (the singer) is saying no, you're wrong. But there is a sense, in the music, that she is somehow right. The music itself, and his *feeling*, seems to bridge the gap between minds. Accordingly, new vistas of consciousness are suggested to the listener. At the end, as John repeats "she said, she said," the words spiral "cosmically."

I am suggesting that John had LSD therapy at least in mind, "having read the book" when he wrote this song. If he didn't experience a therapy session himself, he could read about it—he would refer later to his living vicariously through books in "A Day In The Life." Perhaps, the song really is about falling in love, when "Love" is the only "word" to say; and everywhere he goes he hears it said, "in the good and the bad books that I have read." In any event good and bad, you and me, up and down, are supposed to fuse in the "new awareness," and I suggest that John was picking up books for inspiration at the Asher's and at the Indica bookstore, as was Paul. "She Said She Said" is a psychedelic song, based on LSD psychotherapy – an intentionally "mind-blowing" lack-of-dialectics song. It is about therapeutic psychedelic awareness – in John's inimitable way of summing it up. It was but a hint of things to come, but a powerful one indeed.

Listeners were walked through a letting-go of self on John's **"Tomorrow Never Knows,"** originally titled "The Void." The song is literally a visualization exercise such as a psychologist would do with a patient. It is a "session" and also mimics hypnosis in its effects. The song started out as "a muddy wash … of loops," one chord, and John chanting, according to MacDonald.[44] John wanted to sound as if he was chanting from the top of a mountain in Tibet. But how to illustrate in "music," "the void" or loss of "ego"? At this point in the recording sessions, "McCartney's role in clarifying harmony and texture was crucial." Paul had tape loops from either Burroughs or that he had made himself, "a collection of bizarre sounds," according to audio engineer Geoff Emerick, which included backward tape of him playing guitar.[45] As they layered sounds and effects, the song became massive. George Martin related that assistants manned tape players and hit play on the tape loops as they recorded to track, making the recording one-of-a-kind.[46] The concept of identity fracture or loss was in the song, for which Paul had been laying the groundwork; when it came time to produce a dissolution of self into a void, he was at the ready. "Tomorrow Never Knows" is still hypnotic and convincing today, due to the powerhouse combination of John's writing skills and Paul's creative production.

The buzzing, disturbing insect-like sounds in the song call to mind the poem "Jewelled Indifference" in Leary's "Psychedelic Prayers," published in 1966[47] and which Paul and John might have read. In the poem, a "puny ego" is begging for mercy not to be sucked into the void. There is no answer to his or her pleas, but "jeweled indifference of the relentless diamond eye," floating somewhere up above him. The shining, multi-faceted "indifference" of a diamond eye would be re-visited by John in the "kaleidoscope eyes" of "Lucy" on the Sgt. Pepper album.

John, posing in "Tomorrow Never Knows" as a guide, is in the void with the listener. The listener is invited to be in the void with The Beatles. Fans would always be "with" The Beatles—the Nowhere Man was "a bit like you and me," one was understood to be grouped with "all the lonely people," and the lonely-hearted would pick The Beatles as their "lonely hearts club band."

Paul's "**Paperback Writer**" is another song connected to his IFP, I suggest. The paperback writer feels he has no identity yet. Even though he has written a paperback book, he will only be a paperback writer if "sir or madam" read his book and publish it. Moreover, he is willing to give away all the rights to his book: "If you really like it, you can have the rights/It can make a million for you overnight... I need a break, and I want to be a paperback writer." Paul has stated the song is about people in the London scene who wanted instant fame, but it is interesting that he wrote a song about a writer, a creative, who is writing a letter asking in effect for an identity. Again, there is dislocation. The writer, although having written a story "based on a novel by a man named Lear," (perhaps a reference to the nonsense writer Edward Lear, a favorite writer of John and Paul's) does not think of himself as a writer. If he is conferred this identity, however, a burst of power and glory will open up. Could Paul have been thinking of himself, a songwriter in hopes of having a songwriting identity, who is conferred that identity by giving away his "rights" to his own sense of self? At any rate the song is about a person who has no sense of his value or identity. The music does confer a sense of power and exultation (feeling), in this false situation, although the Beatles' vocals at the end slightly snark it.

Beatles songs thus in 1966 had what I call IFP in them, but also had more than a little "void": they often depict emptiness of self. Besides "Paperback Writer," there was "Nowhere Man," released as a single in the U.S. and on an Extended Play disc in the U.K. that year; the crying girl of "For No One"; Eleanor with her face in a jar; "the void" one was told to surrender to ("it is not dying"), in "Tomorrow Never Knows." The Beatles would continue using the emptiness and ego-loss motif, along with psychological metaphors of the IFP.

At any rate, I am just pointing out that the IFP was in "Revolver" added to with the, by 1966, LSD-associated idea of de-personaliza-tion and de-realization (seeing reality differently than formerly). The same language was now segued into meaning the identity fracture of the LSD experience and the loss of ego experienced on that drug. If listeners had been captivated and mystified by the Beatles' emotional complexity and seeming insight into feelings and relationships between people (courtesy of psychological texts), they now could see the Beatles pointing the way to the same state they enjoyed was via turning off the rational mind, and taking supposedly consciousness-expanding drugs. People browsing indie bookstores were coming across Aldous Huxley's *The Doors of Perception*, translations of Vedic philosophy, books on interpersonal relationships, tantric sex, and Yoga—a smorgasbord which was lumped into the category of New Age. In a circular sort of way, both large and small publishing houses (if one wants to even make that distinction) were at the ready to supply information both to the

Beatles and to their audiences about what one could be with the new "awareness." Publishing could be called the Fifth Beatle.

With "Tomorrow Never Knows" as the finale, "Revolver" did point the way: toward one's head. The message was to take LSD and other "consciousness-expanding" drugs. This would be to further the new frontiers that had been breached as early as mid-1963. John said in 1968 that the early albums were "embarrassing": "it was embarrassing then, because we wanted to be like *this*."[48] He also later commented, "Changing the lifestyle and appearance of youth throughout the world didn't just happen – we set out to do it. We knew what we were doing."[49] Of course, this could be John boasting after the fact, but it implies that the "third thing" and the words for their songs were carefully chosen, and not the off-the-cuff, spontaneous randomness they would have listeners believe. Paul's IFP began as his own process, but then the opportunity for identity-fracture and loss of self would become real with the distribution of LSD in the U.S. in 1966 and for many years afterward. The IFP would not just be something to be entertained by, and thus absorb, unconsciously; you could try it chemically. Everything from John's insistent voice to the broken-meter drumming of Ringo on "Tomorrow Never Knows" heralded the "new awareness."

And so the "interval" of "a new type" who had deeper feelings – Paul's original invention – became an LSD-aided expansion into (supposedly) more creativity and fascinating new change into different attitudes, lifestyle and morals. The passkey to get to be this "new type" was to take drugs, especially LSD. "Are you experienced?" Jimi Hendrix would ask onstage at Monterey Pop. Not even a child would be able to miss that to answer "yes" was to have taken LSD. To take it would be supposedly to become someone new.

Gears Are Turning

> "Monterey was the nexus – it sprang from what
> the Beatles began, and from it sprang what followed."

– *ROLLING STONE* PUBLISHER JANN WENNER

It might seem inauspicious to begin a section with a quote from Jann Wenner. However I found Wenner's observation to be quite *apropos*. In the course of my research, I found that no matter how unaware of each other they appeared to be, beginning in late 1965 many people embarked on promotions and actions leading up to the Monterey International Pop Music Festival. It was as if gears were turning in London, New York, Los Angeles and San Francisco. Monterey Pop, held June 16 to June 18, 1967 at the Monterey County Fairgrounds, would be a focus point defining the perceived cultural momentum; afterward, it would be pointed back to as an event "defining a generation" (as would its sister event Woodstock, held in 1969). For those who had something to gain from these perceptions, it was essential that Monterey Pop happen. Not only that it happen for itself—an outdoor music festival at which LSD was distributed. It was important that it happen as something to lead up to, and then as something to document and refer *back* to.

First, there had to be young people who wanted to attend it, for it to exist. Small events would have to happen before such a large event could be promoted successfully. The pilot programs would be the first underground LSD parties, begun in 1965 in the San Francisco Bay Area.[50] The first Trips festival was officially held in San Francisco, at the Longshoreman's Hall, January 21st-23rd, 1966. Although it is not known who planned the 1965 LSD events, it is documented that Stewart Brand, Ken Kesey, Lawrence Ferlinghetti and Chet Helms were largely responsible for organizing the first official Trips festival. Brand and Kesey were both connected to research at Stanford.

Willis Harman, director of Stanford Research Institute (SRI) and a promoter of the New Age, stated later "one of our goals at SRI was to make people live more 'inner.'"[51] Harman noted in an interview in 1975 that LSD was being used to bring out more material from the subconscious. In an interview with the Australian Broadcasting Commission, Harman made the provocative claim that Albert Hoffman did not synthesize LSD. He said that that was a cover story, and that the drug had actually been synthesized in Germany in the Thirties by chemists who were members of the cult of Rudolph Steiner. Harman stated the synthesis of LSD was not publicized at that time because of the political climate in Germany in the Thirties.

While on the faculty at Stanford, Harman became "impressed with the educational implications" of techniques in psychotherapy and group therapy which were developing at the time, and how they could affect "the human personality." He stated that in 1956 "we started (at Stanford) to do some very serious work with (psychedelics)... We were exploring creative problem-solving, educational aspects of drug experiences as well as religious and psycho-therapeutic aspects. You can't really separate them."

There is no doubt that SRI in Palo Alto, California, about one hour's drive south of San Francisco, was a West Coast counterculture incubator. Harman and SRI were connected to Stewart Brand,[52] who was supervising the South Bay communes under the auspices of the Portola Institute. Several researchers at Stanford had military connections: Brand had served in Navy, and Charles Savage, researching LSD's effect on the personality at the Center for Advanced Study in Behavioral Sciences (CASBS) and at the Palo Alto Mental Research Institute and VA hospital,[53] had previously worked for Navy Intelligence.[54] Anthropologist-cybernetician Gregory Bateson was at Stanford during this time as well.[55] Also at Stanford as a Visiting Fellow was a co-founder of London's Tavistock Institute of Human Relations, Eric Lansdown Trist, accompanied by his son, Alan.[56]

Alan Trist was nineteen when he arrived with his father at Stanford in 1960. He would become an early manager of the band The Grateful Dead, and later run their publishing company, Ice Nine. Lead singer and guitarist Jerry Garcia and lyricist Robert Hunter were both guinea-pigged on LSD and other psychotropic drugs at the VA hospital through auspices of the Palo Alto Mental Research Institute, along with Ken Kesey.[57] This was during the same time period Gregory Bateson and Charles Savage (whom we met in Chapter Two at the Macy Conference) were there doing LSD research.

Alan Trist was reportedly influential in forming the Grateful Dead. In *Sweet Chaos: The Grateful Dead's American Adventure*, Alan Trist told biographer Carol Brightman, "What we were interested in was art. It was the business of being an artist that totally captured Jerry (Garcia) and (Robert) Hunter." Trist added, "art in the sense in which art is free of the political frame of reference."[58] "Alan," said Grateful Dead lyricist Hunter, "was a heavy prime mover in getting us together to recognize ourselves as a *group*."[59]

SRI's part in seeding and guiding the emerging "countercul-ture" is confirmed by looking at the invitation for the first Trips Festival, which was held over three nights in January 1966 at the Longshoreman's Hall in San Francisco. The list of performers and exhibitors show that most had a connection to SRI.

Stewart Brand (of Portola, and SRI) did a photography exhibit; The Grateful Dead (managed by Alan Trist, thus connected through Trist's father to SRI) played their inaugural gig using their new name; Chet Helm's two bands, Big Brother and the Holding Company and Quicksilver Messenger Service, played; the Music Tape Center, par-tially funded by the Rockefellers[61] and whose co-founder was friends with Stewart Brand of SRI and Portola, exhibited; Ken Kesey and his "Pranksters," guinea-pigged at Stanford, offered LSD-spiked punch. A young Steve Jobs, future leader of Apple Computers, worked alongside Stanford computer innovators on "The Congress of Wonders" and "The God Box." [62] It was as if a Petri dish of coun-terculture had been set up, to be observed by people acting as if they were looking the other way. They set up the medium, and then they added people.

The first Trips Festival had connections to the Beats as well. Allen Ginsberg appeared onstage, and Lawrence Ferlinghetti's bookstore City Lights sold tickets to the Trips festivals and Fillmore Auditorium events.[63] City Lights Publishing was connected to Better Books (since Better Books distributed City Lights' Beat authors, as did Indica Bookstore in London. Both bookstores as we have mentioned were connected to Paul's friend, Barry Miles). Neil Cassady, one of the

Beats, had driven the Kesey "Furthur" bus, and Ginsberg had been distributing LSD with Timothy Leary to influencers.

As word got around in San Francisco and the Bay Area, and the Trips events continued with music and free drugs, a "scene" started to snowball. A larger venue was needed, so the Fillmore Auditorium in San Francisco was used for Trips events and weekly concerts. Its proprietor, the successful black entrepreneur Charles Sullivan, who booked jazz acts, was found murdered in mid-1966. After his death, Chet Helms and Bill Graham took over the Fillmore Auditorium live performance permit.[64]

Some people would pop up and further the "movement" along, then sink out of sight. Oddly, Sylvia Plath's former lover, Richard Sassoon, made it out to San Francisco to edit the pilot issue of *The Oracle*, entitled *P.O. Frisco*, (Psychedelic Oracle Frisco) in the fall of 1966. Sassoon is a member of the powerful Sassoon opium trafficking family, connected to the Rothschilds. Sassoon left after editing the pilot issue.[65] *The Oracle* was famed for its colorful graphics and third-eye illustrations and ran for little over a year, ceasing publication at the end of 1967. It was the paper of record for the hippies in the Haight. *The Oracle*'s run spanned Monterey Pop and the Summer of Love; Allen Cohen and a poster artist named Michael Bowen produced and edited the paper. Bowen's mother had reportedly been the mistress of a powerful figure in the Jewish Mafia, "Bugsby" Siegel.[66] Prior to being an art director, Bowen had illustrated the cover of Timothy Leary's *Psychedelic Prayers*, published in 1966 by New York University Press. The cover, a multi-headed horse with a large penis and breasts, was a representative example of what came to be known as "drug art."

In October 1966 LSD was declared illegal, but a "Love Pageant," openly flaunting the law, was held in the Golden Gate Park "panhandle" and featured the Pranksters, Big Brother and The Grateful Dead.[67] Richard Alpert, of Harvard, visited. In January 1967, Harvard psychologist Timothy Leary, on stage with Allen Ginsberg, introduced a slogan to thousands of the curious gathered on the grass in the park: "Turn On, Tune In, and Drop Out." (Leary's friend, advertising pundit Marshall McLuhan, had suggested the phrase). The Human Be-in at Golden Gate Park in San Francisco featured (not surprisingly) Leary, Ginsberg, music by the Grateful Dead and free LSD, and was proclaimed to be historic.

A month or so after the "Be-in," the Beatles met at Terry Melcher's house in Los Angeles to discuss the upcoming "Summer of Love" and the Monterey Pop festival, and songwriter John Phillips, Beatles/Beach Boys publicist Derek Taylor and Paul McCartney would work together to pick the bands for the festival. Phillips, Lou Adler, the Beach Boys and the Beatles were on the festival's organizing board.

John Phillips, whose group The Mamas and The Papas had a hit debut album in 1966, would write not one, but three songs enticing youth to California: "California Dreaming," released in December 1965 and on their debut album in 1966, "San Francisco (Be Sure to Wear Flowers in Your Hair)" released in early 1967, and "Young Girls are Coming to the Canyon," (referring to Laurel Canyon, in Los Angeles) in August of 1967.

"San Francisco" was timed to lure tens of thousands of youths to San Francisco, and painted a picture of youth "all across the nation," set "in motion," presumably taking Greyhound busses, cars, or planes, to converge on the Haight Ashbury district, where "gentle people, with flowers in their hair" will be having during the summer "a love-in, there." About forty thousand runaways flooded into the city, and an organization called "the Diggers" provided free food for them.[68] All was in readiness for Monterey Pop.

But what was the very first shot fired over the transom from the new "counterculture"? Again, it had something to do with psychiatry and mental illness, and the Laingian idea of abolishing barriers between sane and insane. I believe two initiating counterculture events could have been in 1962: a folk ditty called "Walk Right In," asking "do you want to lose your mind?" had radio airplay, and the novel *One Flew Over the Cuckoo's Nest* by Ken Kesey became a bestseller. Kesey's novel was a fictionalized exposé of mental hospitals. In the novel, a large-breasted Nurse Ratched whom the inmates call "Big Nurse" terrorizes the inmates. The most anti-authoritarian and spirited of the patients, Murphy, posing as insane to avoid serving time in a work camp, is given a lobotomy. He is then smothered with a pillow by his (supposedly) sympathetic fellow inmate, Chief, who subsequently escapes.[69]

The book and movie promoted ideas similar to Laing's, that mental hospitals are inhumane and that the insane could be saner than the "normals." In Kesey's novel the idea is given a few twists: a statutory rapist is the "anti-hero" and posed as the sane person in the bunch, who is treated as insane. The book and movie encouraged empathy for, even identification with the insane (along with of course, saying that they weren't really insane.) Both Tavistock psychiatrists and SRI-supported writers were saying the same thing.

We will now discuss a little more about the goings-on in and around Stanford. As we mentioned earlier, writers including Ken Kesey and Robert Hunter were attracted to Stanford though the Wallace Stegner Writing Program. Kesey, Jerry Garcia, Robert Stone and Robert Hunter were given LSD through the Palo Alto Mental Research Institute at the time Kesey was working at the nearby Veteran's Administration hospital,[70] where Charles Savage was doing LSD-and-personality experiments. Stewart Brand received his first LSD trip at Myron Stolaroff's International Foundation for Advanced Study (IFAS) laboratory in nearby Menlo Park. Electrical engineer Stolaroff was formerly of Ampex (reel-to-reel tape recorders) and had been at Harvard, where he in turn had been given his first LSD experience by Richard Alpert.[71] Stolaroff's lab would administer LSD and mescaline to over 300 volunteers to study creativity and "the reformation of values and personality" possible through taking the drug, as he wrote in a paper co-authored with Willis Harman, director of SRI. Kesey, writer Robert Stone, and a group of other guinea-pigged intellectuals formed a commune near Stanford campus, on an oak-lined street named Perry Lane. There they indulged in wife-swapping and drugs, and attempted to interest the sons and daughters of upper-class Palo Altoans in LSD.

"They went after the daughters, in particular," remembers Alison Kennedy, who was a teenager in Palo Alto at the time. Kennedy, a petite, blond, articulate teenager, had been kicked out of parochial school with her girlfriend and both were enrolled at Palo Alto High School when they met Kesey. "He and his friends used to hang out at the East-West Bookstore," she recalled, in tiny downtown Palo Alto. Kennedy and her girlfriend attended a party where Kesey gave a reading of his new novel, in manuscript. Kennedy's girlfriend, who was also underage, befriended Kesey's girlfriend, and "was spirited into the Perry Lane commune, where she was given LSD and also the drug IT-290."[72] (IT-290 is listed as an "empathogen" which increases empathy and induces vomiting.) When the girl's father located her, he had the police raid and bust the Perry Lane commune. This event forced some of Kesey's group into the hills near Santa Cruz.

A few years later, communes had sprouted on the hills of Berkeley and Los Angeles. The communes, according to Kennedy, were overseen by The Portola Institute, which was publishing Brand's magazine, the Whole Earth Catalogue. "The grand-pooh-bah of the East Bay communes was Stewart Brand."[73] The Portola Institute was connected to SRI and reportedly the umbrella organization for the East Bay communes. There were six "divisions" in the Palo Alto hills and one was a preschool named The Big Rock Candy Mountain Preschool. "Those kids were *really* free," Kennedy said.[74] The communes were "of every stripe." Hers had "gestalt, meditation and yoga. The same as Esalen. But we had better food. Food was important."[75] The communes were reportedly supported by state funding.

Meanwhile in 1964 Kesey and his coterie, including Beats Allen Ginsberg and Neil Cassady, left their Santa Cruz mountains commune and traveled across the U.S. in their "Furthur" bus, distributing LSD along the way. They called themselves the "Merry Pranksters," but their activities were more than pranks, in that they would dose unwitting people with LSD. Even people who took the drug knowingly were risking permanent damage to their minds.

Aldous Huxley, prolific British novelist of *Brave New World* who had written about his experiences in *The Doors of Perception*, visited

SRI and also lectured at UC Berkeley. He befriended Kennedy and corresponded with her until his death in 1963.[76]

It is very telling that the son of Tavistock Institute co-founder Eric Trist, namely Alan Trist, was present at the very beginnings of The Grateful Dead, from the time that they called themselves The Warlocks.[77] Trist was there when Garcia's bandmates chose the name the Grateful Dead in late 1965, which Garcia reportedly picked at random, from a dictionary.[78] The name itself seems to be an invitation to destroy the ego (so-called ego death) and become a "dead-head," which the band's followers called themselves. The name is reportedly from a folk tale about a deceased spirit who was thankful to be given a good burial. Wherever the name came from, its distasteful implication is to "kill" the mind. The band's logo, a skull with a lightning bolt inside it, can be interpreted as an ECT shock to the brain. The sound and drug experience of Dead shows are, not surprisingly since they sprang from the same place where Dr. Savage was researching "psycho-catharsis," an immersive experience in electronic amplified sound, with peer-pressured use of LSD. The Grateful Dead's soundman, Stanley Owsley, was also an LSD manufacturer.[79] Owsley provided them with audio equipment and created the first sound systems that made large outdoor concerts such as Monterey Pop possible. "Dead" shows would provide for decades the set and setting for a communal drug-taking party, primarily LSD.

The San Francisco concert venues and the Haight Ashbury district were near either clinics or hospitals where drug overdose victims could be examined and LSD antagonists tested. According to Tom O'Neill in *CHAOS: Charles Manson, the CIA, and the Secret History of the Sixties*, Macy researcher Louis Jollyon West set up a fake "crash pad" on Frederick Street, just up the hill from Haight Street, to lure kids to form their own counterculture under the noses and clipboards of students hired to examine them.[80] Charles Manson was one of the many criminal types and predators floating around the scene in the Haight-Ashbury.

Monterey, the town selected for the first outdoor rock festival, is maybe not coincidentally the site of the Defense Language

Research Institute, the largest military intelligence languages training school in the U.S. It employs several thousand people in a town of today only 25 thousand (I could not find its population number for 1967). The Institute could have provided hundreds of young intelligence personnel to mingle with and observe the festival audience.

Thus there was no small amount of MK-Ultra type researchers and artist-intellectual guinea pigs running around the nascent hippie scene. The Mamas and The Papas were regarded as role models among youth living in communes, relates Kennedy.[81] But the hippie scene was not what one could call a grass-roots phenomenon.

The Mamas and The Papas also had a short trajectory. Producer Lou Adler formed the band in late 1965, and it started to fizzle out by the end of 1967, after a mediocre performance at Monterey and an August show at the Hollywood Bowl in Los Angeles with Jimi Hendrix as opener.

Plenty of bands had sprung up in Los Angeles (many of them produced by Terry Melcher). There was the Haight-Ashbury scene and the communes. So why would Jann Wenner say it was specifically the Beatles who put in motion what would lead to Monterey Pop Festival? The reason is that (besides Paul helping choose acts for the Festival) the Beatles were the spark, the hope of hundreds of thousands of youth drawn into this new scene. I suggest that young people were convinced by their response to the Beatles' creativity and lyrics that a new way of being might be possible. They were the "young generation, and we've got something to say," (as the replacements for the early Beatles, The Monkees, put it on their asinine TV show). It might seem a little unbelievable to people born after the Beatles' era, but the Beatles were perceived to have moved to a plane of higher awareness, and were regarded as consciousness leaders.

"Two albums above all completed the Beatles' transition from a singles band to a studio band: 'Rubber Soul' and 'Revolver,'" noted biographer Barry Miles, adding, "there was a complex maturity in the work."[82] "Revolver," released in August 1966, would contain a counterculture anthem, "Yellow Submarine," *and* a guided tour into the LSD trip or ego-loss, "Tomorrow Never Knows." In early June 1967, just before Monterey Pop, the Beatles would release "Sgt. Pepper's Lonely Hearts Club Band." On each of these albums there were songs with the subtext of the asylum, mental patient and therapy, or what I call Paul's IFP.

As it happened, after all the Beatles had taken LSD, they would increase the IFP subtext in their songs, because the IFP metaphors of the asylum, mental patient, therapy, and loss of self would segue neatly into the LSD experience. Lack of ontological security and lack of homeostasis was segued into the "love generation," because oddly, the Beatles chose to use the same hidden subtext to gather followers into the asylum of the new counterculture. LSD provided, in effect, yet another allusive layer over what they were already doing. It would allow for additional tone colors and sounds being added to their IFP. From mid-1963 roughly half of Paul's output (songs he wrote on his own, not co-written with John) was what I call his IFP. From "Revolver" onward, *85 percent* of the entire band's output would be the IFP. Whether it was IFP or LSD was now in some sense lyrically interchangeable.

* * *

Paul was drawn to beginning his own IFP; whether it was innate in him or something imposed on him at the Asher's, I do not know. However, Paul's paintings even today show depictions of emptiness and dislocation. His "praxis," developed at the Asher's and which led to his taking LSD, might have changed his sense of self permanently. Or, he is attracted to those ideas.

Meanwhile youth, gathered together in events and scenes through a combination of idealism, good intentions, self-interest, curiosity, intellectualism, and boredom, wanted to follow the Beatles' example. LSD's very failure to be codified by the Macy researchers became paradoxically its major selling point in the Sixties. It would (supposedly) open a door that was specific to each person taking it. However what was not publicized was its documented schizogenic effect on the brain and personality. It caused a temporary schizophrenia-like state, and even those researchers enthusiastic about the drug said it caused "permanent neuronal rearrangement."[83]

Whatever the "experience" really was for participants—whether they took the drug or just pretended they did—the fact that Monterey Pop did happen would give those around at the time something to point to—that they were present at "the birth of the counterculture." This was the ostensive culture Bateson had wanted. The counterculture event, repeated at Woodstock and Altamont, would be a shared experience not circumscribed by words. This is still in effect today when people refer to the Sixties: "if you remember it, you weren't there." The Sixties and the birth of the counterculture were framed as something open and hopeful, not to be circumscribed. The Beatles, too, seemed to be open to all and everything, like global romantic partners upon whom anyone could project.

It's the Same Guy

There are a small percentage of Beatles fans who believe that Paul died and was replaced sometime in late 1966.[84] Paul's change in appearance could be attributable to his face maturing, taking LSD, or any number of reasons. His face could have thinned out possibly because he had moved out of the Asher's and was no longer enjoying Margaret Asher's cooking; he also had become a vegetarian. If the reader will put a picture of 1965 Paul next to a picture of 1970 Paul, taken from about the same angle, and then switch both of these photos to be upside-down next to each other, one's mind will stop the recognition of subtle changes such as wrinkles or expression, and just see the basic features. And using this test, it is clear to me that Paul was not "replaced." Looking back and forth quickly from one photo to the other, especially comparing the eyes, one sees that early Paul and post-1966 Paul are the same person. Of course, this test might not convince because people might contend that plastic surgeons who worked on creating "fake Paul" used the same method to verify their work was done correctly. The debate will probably continue, but the picture test convinced me that it is the same Paul.

Was This a Test Too?

It is remarkable that roughly at the same time, in late 1965, the pre-eminent songwriters of the Western World, Paul McCartney and Brian Wilson, both were given LSD in close proximity to a member of the Asher family and to psychological influences.

First, let's backtrack a bit. In late 1964, Brian Wilson met Loren Schwartz at Terry Melcher's home in the Hollywood Hills.[85] Apparently Schwartz's father, in what might not be such a coincidence, was a psychiatrist.[86]

Schwartz introduced Wilson to pot-smoking,[87] and then in spring of 1965, he offered Wilson some LSD. Schwartz told him it was from Stanley Owsley (who was soundman for the Grateful Dead) and said to Wilson, "Brian, you're unique. An artist … I know of something that can really expand your vision. Really open you up to music."[88] Wilson took the drug and then wrote "California Girls."

By fall of 1965-1966, Wilson had a number of song fragments lying about, emotional chords which he called "feels." These "feels" needed lyrics, however. Through Schwartz, Brian connected at Melcher's house parties with Tony Asher. Asher, who also worked for a Los Angeles advertising agency, had written advertising copy for the Beatles' first promotional launch in the U.S.[89] Wilson called up Asher to offer him the job of lyricist, replacing his usual writing partner, band mate Mike Love. Asher agreed to work with Wilson on what would become the *Pet Sounds* album. Then, in fall of 1965, Wilson took LSD again, which he says was provided by "a friend."[90]

Tony Asher is the son of Irving Asher,[91] a film producer who initially made his career in Los Angeles working for Warner Brothers Pictures, then moved to London to head up Warner Pictures U.K. I realized it is likely the Asher family whom Paul was living with and Tony Asher were all related. All three Asher children were acting in film or radio, and Peter Asher had acted in a movie produced by the

Irving Asher studio as a young boy. Family connections to Irving Asher would be a likely reason for all three Asher children finding gainful employment in film.

According to Steve Turner in *Beatles '66*, Paul McCartney was given LSD for the first time in December 1965 at Tara Browne's home.[92] At that time, Paul was still living at the Asher's. So, it appears that in 1965 Paul McCartney and Brian Wilson had similar influences: they were in the presence of psychological ideas, the drug LSD, and in close proximity to at least one member of the Asher family. They were also connected through EMI, of course. The Beatles were on EMI, and EMI owned Capitol Records.

Wilson and Asher collaborated on *Pet Sounds*, which was hailed as a breakthrough in pop music.

Van Dyke Parks was Wilson's next songwriting partner. Parks's father was also, as it happens, a military psychologist.[93] During 1966, Parks and Wilson took LSD and other drugs supposedly for creative fuel while they worked on songs for *Smile*. However, they came close to losing their creative discernment and as Wilson related in his autobiography, every composition sounded as good as the next.

In April of 1967, Paul McCartney dropped by for a visit and he and Wilson played each other material they were working on. Wilson had a table laden with vegetables, to get in the mood for recording his new song, "Vegetables."[94]

A month later, Wilson wrote, "I began to lose it."[95] He felt his mind going. "The buzz is that you are creating something that is intensely personal," Parks told Wilson accusingly. "Yet you refuse to act remotely so."[96] Parks was writing obscure wordplay lyrics, evocative of the history of America; Wilson wanted to write "a teenage symphony to God."[97] But he was not able to do this.

Both McCartney and Wilson had tremendous pressure to come up with material, of course. But putting this picture together, it is reasonable to ask whether McCartney and Wilson were given LSD as a creative experiment, such as had been enacted at Harvard, SRI and elsewhere. It is also possible that providing the top composers LSD was done intentionally so that they would write songs for an ostensive culture such as Bateson described, and that Alan Trist described as one being free of a political frame of reference.

It could have been either, both or neither. McCartney and Wilson were at a peak of fame and creativity, Paul having just written "Yesterday," and Brian having written many hits. They were contracted to the same parent company, and used the same publicist. Beatles publicist Derek Taylor arrived in Los Angeles in 1966, after Wilson had taken LSD. Taylor was integral to promoting *Pet Sounds* in the U.K. He would make-over the Beach Boy's clean-cut image, and promote Wilson as a "genius." The Beach Boys and the Beatles were both on the Board of Governors for Monterey Pop. The organizing committee included Lou Adler, Terry Melcher and Derek Taylor. You couldn't call The Beatles and The Beach Boys "rivals."

After Paul took LSD in December 1965, he went on to produce "Revolver," released in August of 1966. Brian Wilson released the single "Good Vibrations" in October of 1966, which went to Number One. The Beach Boys had "found a new sound," "to compete with The Beatles," as the British press put it, disingenuously.[98]

By late 1966 in California, The Doors, The Byrds, and Chet Helm's bands were playing the Avalon Ballroom and the Fillmore venues, the Trips Festivals were distributing LSD, various liturgical-folk harmonies filled the airwaves, subsidized communes dotted the hills and hinterlands in Laurel Canyon and the Bay Area, "California Dreaming" was still on the charts,[99] and the top composers for pop music had taken LSD. The Sixties were in full swing and the Summer of Love was still to come.

CHAPTER VI

Identity Fracture as
Self-Protection: Henry James

U p until now my progression through Paul's "praxis" has been chronological; in this chapter I will step aside from the timeline for a moment to discuss possible reasons for what I suggest was Paul's drive toward fracturing his identity. They vary from implied social critique, forging a "new" voice, to Paul's own need for self-protection. I will also compare Beatles song motifs with those used by novelist Henry James, who used similar imagery in his writing.

Social Critique

The record-buying public, from older children to the middle-aged, had delighted in the light-hearted, fresh and irreverent Beatles, and were impressed by the new sounds on "Revolver" and "Pepper." "Pepper" had been for many an imagistic, colorful vaudeville in sound. In September 1968 *Life* magazine tempered the upbeat feelings with a somber photo-editorial that connected Beatles lyrics to social critique. For the September 20, 1968 issue (just prior to the release of the White Album) photographer Art Kane was given the assignment to travel to England and take pictures to illustrate the lyrics to Beatles songs. First, Kane listened to his stack of Beatles records. He reported "when you hear them with half an ear, as I'd been doing, some are gay and bouncy, like the one called 'When I'm Sixty Four.' But almost all, when you really listen to them, with their nostalgic echoes of fairy tales and Mother Goose, ring with loneliness and abandonment."[1]

Kane took pictures around central London and created photo collages which were presented alongside Beatles song lyrics and a brief editorial blurb. Kane's photo-illustrations intuitively illustrated the IFP. The first is of an older woman; her face tinted blue-green, she looks out a window framed in peeling paint and plaster. She wears red lipstick ("a face she keeps in a jar by the door"). Opposite her is a close-up of an angel statue in a graveyard, with a caved-in head and "empty" (masked, or dead) eyes. Lyrics to "Eleanor Rigby" were printed alongside the illustration. The editorial copy stated: "A living face peering out of a window and a masklike memorial in a church-yard reflect the poignancy, expressed in the song, of being unloved and anonymous both alive and dead." Combined in this image are ideas of fracture, double, emptiness, implied atheism, and a literal image of a "broken" head.

For the next illustration, lyrics to "A Day In The Life" are printed alongside collaged faces of Londoners, mostly women, their faces expressionless against a backdrop of grimy London row home exteriors. Juxtaposed is a man in a bowler hat inside a shiny black limousine. Collaged across his face is a "forbidden" diagonal sign. "The line 'I'd love to turn you on' seemed to many people to refer to taking drugs," the copy reads. "But Paul McCartney says it means 'turning people on to the truth about themselves' – to make them see how materialistic they are." The snippet-collages are arranged in kaleidoscope-fashion, the faces resembling each other. The copy and illustration implied that everyday people were depressed, fragmented, and materialistic.

A sad, young headband-wearing "mum" with a crying baby was juxtaposed with an image of a vacant, sad baby face superimposed on an empty institutional bed, to illustrate "Lady Madonna." The caption read: "The baby in the East London hippie pad has a mother, but another child, whose image emerges from an institutional cot, may not. The photographer felt the song implied a threat of abandonment, jarring against the innocent nursery-rhyme quality of the lyrics."

The last illustration is a tinted photograph of two naked children, a boy and girl, running with backs turned to the camera. The copy stated, "A Salvation Army hostel bears the lovely name of Strawberry Fields. To the photographer, the lyrics are a call for the lost innocence of childhood."[2]

The photo-feature gave *Life* readers some social critique to munch on, alongside a visual representation of the IFP and the lyrics. Even if by now they weren't familiar with the Beatles' music, they could look at the fracture and malaise of the eight-page feature. That the Beatles gave *Life* permission to reproduce the lyrics in full shows that at this point in 1968 the group or those managing them wanted them to be perceived as bards of social criticism, albeit by proxy through a magazine editorial.

However, the particular appeal of Beatles songs was that each person could interpret them as they wished. *Life* magazine added an editorial slant for its readers. But millions more listeners, in encountering the basic indefinability of the Beatles music, experienced it as freedom to experiment and a beacon to a new awareness.

It is worth pointing out that the Beatles had as strong ties to publishing as they did to the music industry. John had penned two best-selling books by 1968. Paul had a direct connection to Better Books and by extension Penguin Books, the linchpin of the paperback press, through his close friend Barry Miles. The Beatles were at the peak of a "new awareness" but they were also writing for, and being inspired by, the publishing world. Books on behavior, psychology, spiritualism, ecology, and so on were echoing and relaying the "feelings" the Beatles engendered, often on small imprints connected to a larger publishing company. An "indie" press in name only could test-market books to be later published in larger print runs for the mainstream market. As we have mentioned, the same man, Tony

Godwin, managed an avant-garde bookstore and Penguin Books. The trendy youth of London and other urban centers were "expanding their knowledge" in bookstores. (In his autobiography *Wouldn't It Be Nice* there is a photograph of Brian Wilson browsing a Los Angeles bookstore in 1966 with a Penguin edition of *Psycho-Cybernetics* in his hand.)[3]

Psychologist R.D. Laing benefited too from publishing interconnections. Laing's books were first published by Tavistock Publications and then by Penguin, then mainstreamed at a certain point into the U.S. market on Atheneum Press. Paul had created an "interval." It seemed to mean, I argue, that new feelings, new ways of seeing were possible. Publishing on both sides of the Atlantic rushed to fill in the gap. Because the Beatles said their lyrics were arbitrary or "random," and yet the songs cohered, this gave people permission in effect to go far afield, searching outward from the normal (in "a new search for magic" that the Beatles seemed to confirm was there) and the search meant, naturally, one would want to read about all sorts of "new" topics. Sensing change was afoot, and being told constantly by the media that "the times they are a-changing,'" youth and portions of the mainstream public wanted to read as much as they could about topics previously the purview of specialists, researchers, academics, meditators and bibliophiles.

* * *

A New Voice of Pluralism

Many a writer, if aiming to break into publishing, hopes to attain a distinctive voice and widespread appeal that the Beatles had achieved. The group wrote in all kinds of music genres, yet each song sounded like a "Beatles song." The Beatles had several advantages over a literary writer; to name just a few, they could communicate feelings, associations, even images in sound, without having to write full sentences or even a word if the music "told" the story. As time wore on, the band's output was categorized as being about "love," and that they were "inclusive" as well as "irreverent." It is worth wondering

CHAPTER VI | 153

if their pluralistic "voice" in some sense replaced the need for more individualistic voices in literature, or at least made achieving such a voice in some sense harder than before.

Just a few years previous to the Beatles' breakthrough, Sylvia Plath, who wanted to be a novelist as much as a poet, was casting about for possible "voices" to learn from and then to make her own in order to break into the mainstream literary market. In 1957 she wrote in her diary: "I could write a terrific novel. The tone is the problem. I'd like it to be serious, tragic, yet gay & rich & creative. I need a master, several masters. Lawrence, except in *Women in Love*, is too bare, too journalistic in his style. Henry James too elaborate, too calm, and well mannered. Joyce Cary I like ... or J.D. Salinger. I have time. I must tell myself I have time."[4]

Plath mentioned these particular novelists because they were social critics. Her politics were generally Left, although she was not a feminist. Like many aspiring writers, Plath did not mind using another writer's style until such time as she developed her own. "I will imitate until I can feel I'm using what he can teach," she noted about another writer in her diary.[5] However it is worth noting that she was thinking of *several* "masters" and of producing a potpourri of effects (serious, tragic, gay, rich and creative). Plath intuited that a lot had to be served up to a mass audience. The obverse of a "deep" psychological novel would be "a limited, folksy, vivid style that limits the girl, defines her."[6]

However, her goal, which she states over and over in her diaries, is to find her *own* voice. Plath was determined to find a voice that encapsulated *her*. She had watched the literary market closely, and had shifted from wanting to write "women's stories"[7] to "mad stories."[8] To find herself through writing, however, was her true desire; this is the desire of many writers. One wonders what Plath would have made of the Beatles who were just entering public consciousness at the time of her death. She died in February 1963 when the Beatles had released two singles. Although one does not usually mention Plath and the Beatles together in the same sentence, after doing some research, I saw some connections between what Paul was doing and what Plath wanted to do. The Beatles, although initially less original in their music than in their approach to it, were letting out "feelings" and then were able to move toward a broad pluralism in "voices" that were yet perceived as their own. They were able to employ a wide range of styles, feelings and effects—similar to what Plath wanted to do.

Plath also, as I suggest Paul did, read mental patient interviews. She worked at Massachusetts General Hospital for a few months as a secretary, and typed up patient files. This gave her insight into people, which she desperately wanted—to open "up the souls of the people in Boston and read them deep."[9] The job gave her material for short stories, as we have mentioned, including "This Earth Our Hospital" (a phrase she lifted from a poem by T.S. Eliot).[10] Plath wanted to get "her own voice" into her writing; she felt she had achieved this initially in these stories and in her novel *The Bell Jar*, but then later dismissed these works as "psychological fantasia,"[11] and a "potboiler."[12] Besides reading patient interviews, she had written her senior thesis at Cambridge on "the double," discussed schizophrenia and the necessity for a writer to understand it, read Jung, considered pursuing a degree in Psychology, and had personal experience with ECT and mental institutions.

In the early 1960s, Plath and her husband Ted Hughes were immersed in the same milieu as Paul: Ted was writing plays for the theatre, Plath befriended dramatist Alan Sillitoe and his wife,[13] and went to a party for the Guinness Prize, given by relations of Tara Browne's. (During this time, as we recall, Paul said "the really big thing" each night was attending the theatre, and Paul was a friend of Tara's.) In addition, she was meeting people in media including the BBC, and had met T.S. Eliot, a relative of Margaret Asher's.

The Beatles used the subtext of the mental patient world to great advantage and so consistently in their image and their communications as to saturate their audiences with it. One wonders, would Plath have recognized the subtext in their songs?

Leaving Plath for now, we will examine motifs used by the English novelist Henry James. A consummate literary stylist, yet too "well-mannered" for Plath to emulate, James as it happened used in his *Fin de Siècle* era similar motifs that the Beatles used. The Beatles wanted to use conventional literary motifs when they could. However, they would use motifs in ways more penetrative than James did, in part because of the nature of their chosen medium. I will next discuss the Beatles' and Henry James's use of the motifs of the eye and acting.

The Eye

Henry James's novels revel in description of the surface of things, and of people. He implies with the motif of the eye and the impressions received by it that a fixation on appearances is a trap both for those providing the show, and those attracted to it. The character Peter Sherringham looks "like a Titian"; Miriam Rooth looks "like the finished statue lifted from the ground to its pedestal"; Lady Agnes has a "face of a fine austere mould," and her skin has "a singular polish."[14] His characters that are creatures of mere appearances are described in terms of being paintings or dolls. But the seekers of "truth" also are caught, trying to penetrate surfaces with their eyes. The narrator of *The Aspern Papers* probes in vain: "I turned my eye on every article of furniture," he relates, trying to locate the papers. The eye motif is used a little differently in James than in Beatles songs. James seemingly describes the surface to make the reader aware of the show; he does not intentionally scramble what meaning the sense organ has. The person seeing the glittering facades is understood to exist. The readers can, through the narrative point of view, decide for themselves if looking like a statue or a painting is a clue to the character and if so in what way. The sense of identity being fixed *somewhere*, allowing a reader's sense of discernment, is maintained.

The Beatles also employ imagery of the eye in their song lyrics. But the eye is not just an organ of perception in Beatles songs: it becomes a transformative organ. It undergoes an evolution just as the person(s) in the songs using it do.

The motif of the eye and seeing occurs many times in Beatles songs. Early on, Paul wrote "I Saw Her Standing There." In this song, written prior to 1963, eyes are used simply to see. They do not get in the way of the action. The singer uses his eyes, and so does she; "well she looked at me/And I, I could see/That before too long/I'd fall in love with her." The eye enables identification and attraction ensues—or even love. But in later songs, Paul develops the eye imagery as he introduces complexity in relationships. The singer is "looking through you" and a person can be transparent. In another song the singer asks (as I suggest, a therapy patient would ask) his love to "tell me what you see," as if looking implies much more than seeing externals. The eye motif is used to mean inner comprehension, but it also can be an empty mirror; "no sign of love behind the tears/Cried for no one." As the Beatles apparently brought more "news" of complexity possible in relationships, or of self-image, so did the burden increase on the motif of the eye. In "Here, There and Everywhere," the singer hopes he will always be in her eyes, and thus be everywhere within her eyes. By the time of "Revolver," the eye motif is used to "see the meaning of within/It is believing." The eye is not seeing out-wardly: it is asked to look within, and to see the un-seeable—see the meaning of emptiness. Tough to do, but the guided visualization in "Tomorrow Never Knows" is accompanied by a swirling, swarming, shimmering instrumental break depicting a void, while tape loops and backwards-guitar squawks. That helped listeners to see the void, because one was hearing the ostensible sounds of it. The eye had a lot of homework to do, in Beatles songs.

John had his own personal reasons for using the motif of the eye. He often wrote of the eye as unseeing. In "Nowhere Man" he wrote, "He's as blind as he can be/Just sees what he wants to see/Nowhere man, can you see me at all?" That the nowhere man is pathetically limited, in his awareness of others and of his own potential, is taken to be the meaning of the song. I am not saying that that is *the* mean-ing of the song, any more than I am saying Paul's songs have specific meanings; I am only pointing out a subtext, and how I suggest Beatles songs were written. "Nowhere Man," I suggest, stemmed from John's day-to-day reality of having poor vision. His eyesight was so weak that he could not recognize someone from a few feet away if he took his glasses off.[15] According to Emerick, with his glasses on John could not read lyrics on a music stand; so, looking at himself in a mirror from a few feet away, he would have not been able to see clearly his own face. Imagine being so blind that you can't make out your own face in a mirror, and then imagine growing up this way. It would make a child feel isolated; and then imagine not having your parents living with you either! Both of these conditions could have been a major factor in John's character and in his art.

John's poor eyesight had to have had an effect on how he learned about the world. It would have affected him while growing up. John gave off the appearance of being a man of wide experience. But, his experience of the world had been limited because of his vision. Growing up, he would not have been able to compete in athletics and similar group activities. As an adult, he would not usually travel far alone. If he had lost his eyeglasses, he would have been virtually marooned and vulnerable. He *needed* a band of friends around him, and companions like Mal Evans to "lookout" for him when he wasn't at home at Weybridge. Accordingly, John was not a good driver. He would travel in his psychedelic-painted Rolls Royce, as a rich man with a chauffeur. Later when he and Yoko ventured with their children on a vacation to meet his relatives, John drove; but when needing to let a car pass, he pulled the car into a ditch on a narrow road, and they sustained multiple injuries.[16]

Because of his weak eyes, most of John's knowledge about the world had been gained not by moving about unaccompanied in it, but through books. Wearing strong prescription glasses, John could read books, the paper, and watch the "telly." His poor vision was a limitation. But this might have been a limitation that led him to become an artist, and such an inventive one. Because of his limitation, he was more alone with his own perceptions about things. He learned guitar, drew, wrote songs, and developed to a fine degree the skill of gleaning information from the sources he could access. John became a quick study; astute in his perceptions, if rather quick to dismiss. His assessments of the media and the printed word were insightful and humorous, if often bitter. Although John was described as "confrontational"[17] and he was sometimes downright aggressive with people, John was also a master at "summing things up." He had developed this insight, or caustic way, depending on how you view it, due to a combination of poor eyesight, an isolated childhood, and his bright mind.

But John could also be quite naive about people if they convinced him that they had special knowledge. Magic Alex was one example – a charlatan who had John convinced he could do phenomenal things with audio equipment.

John wrote some of the Beatles' most powerful lines using the eye motif. Besides the image of the "kaleidoscope eye," he penned the famous line in "Strawberry Fields," "living is easy with eyes closed/ Misunderstanding all you see," the meaning of which we shall discuss in Chapter Nine.

But by the time of "Sgt. Pepper," the eye was used as an "inner eye" to visualize the journeys the Beatles would take the listener on. The eye was also transformed to embody the new LSD consciousness. "Lucy" was a visualization song, engaging the listener like a therapy patient, describing "tangerine trees, and marmalade skies." The girl the singer is seeking has "kaleidoscope eyes." Lucy's eyes are a kaleidoscope of everything: seeing everything, expanded in vision, but also of no one color, seeing in fragments, and uncommitted to any one vision. Nor does she speak (this is analogous to the "silence which is everything" in Seymour's analysis of James). I suggested John might have taken the idea of "kaleidoscope eyes" from a poem in Timothy Leary's "Psychedelic Prayers," published in 1966. John would likely have read this poetry book. In the poem "Jewelled Indifference," a "puny ego" is begging the Void that his sense of self be preserved.[18] The Void has no answer, but "jewelled indifference." It is immune to his pleas to preserve his sense of self. The Void is described as a "relentless diamond eye." This is a description of a kaleidoscope. "Lucy" in "Lucy in the Sky with Diamonds" is also "gone." She is John's depiction of such a void. She is found only in the sky, and hovers above the singer much as "Jewelled Indifference" does above the "puny ego." In the poem, the ego is sucked upward into the jeweled, diamond Void. "Here – we – go – good – bye," Leary wrote, of the ego's dissolution in the Void. In the poem's final line comes another image that will be important for the song "Strawberry Fields Forever" (which the Beatles recorded at the very beginning of their sessions for "Pepper" but kept for the subsequent album): "And you shall be as immune to the passing of men as to the passing of straw dogs."

Thus in Beatles lyrics, the eye motif evolved from an everyday romantic notion of its use, in finding a girl and falling in love at first sight, to a signifier of transcendence of the Ego. The "diamond" or "kaleidoscope" eye became a symbol of the ego-annihilated non-self. The eye was no longer used to identify anything, but to be a reflection of the void, or of fragments. I also must note that a kaleidoscope is drawn schematically as a triangle inside a circle, much like Sidney Cohen's slice in the circle of "creativity." As a "kaleidoscope eye" could be depicted as an eye atop a kaleidoscope's two mirrors leaning together and forming a triangle, this is also a Masonic symbol of the all-seeing eye.

After Lucy and her kaleidoscope eyes, the eye continues to signify a "progression" in Beatles songs. In "I Am the Walrus" the eye is dead, dripping custard from the (baked?) egg-mind in back of it. Then, eyes appear in "Blackbird" as "sunken eyes" from which the Blackbird is instructed to see. By the time of the White Album, then, the eye as signifier of the self is "dead" (as in the ego being annihilated). The "deadness" of the eye is passed on to the Blackbird, so it can "arise." We will examine this song more closely in Chapter Eleven.

Thus while James used motifs of acting and of the eye in ways that assumed a point of view, The Beatles used these same motifs in a way that reached a state where everything could be refracted and fragmented into everything: a relativist state of non-identity. This "ego-death" is found in Jung, who discussed the "annihilation of the ego" way back in the Thirties.

James was a writer of The Gilded Age: The Beatles came along after Wittgenstein, Freud, Jung, Adler, Einstein's theory of relativity, and the Atomic Bomb. They did use the same motifs as James, although writing almost a century later. But the Beatles used the motifs of the eye and acting in a much more pervasive sense. They pointed the way toward a supposed "new race of laughing freedmen" as Leary put it, and did much to create a new "ostensive" culture. In a way, the Beatles' art seemed to prove relativity. They successfully piled "everything" into their music, made it seem all of a relative, and subjective nature (that is, no high or low) and yet paradoxically were also given validation of their *own* identity (which they shared with fans) as the "*best* band that ever was." However I am asserting in this book that the means by which they achieved the supposed breakthrough was by "letting the crazies out." For several decades some in the psychological establishment had taken note of the crossover-factor of the world of the insane with the sane, the possible arbitrary nature of what was sane and insane. Laing was the first to break ranks, but only on the surface; he voiced the "concerns" of many in the psychological and liberal establishment. By the Sixties, such theories would be presented to a receptive audience as feeling-fact by artists who could present them in the right context. That Paul did this in the method I am describing does not argue necessarily for his IFP and the Beatles being a planned "op."

The Acting Motif

In his novel *The Princess Casamassima* James describes several characters using the imagery of acting. There is something "theatrical" about Hyacinth Robinson: "he was to go through life in a mask, in a borrowed mantle; he was to be every day and every hour an actor." Robinson "masquerades" both in "high life" and in low. Lady Aurora suggests "a personage in comedy"; Vetch suggests "the odour of stage paint." And it is in a box at the theatre that Hyacinth meets the Princess—a box that "framed the bright picture of the stage and made one's own situation seem a play within a play."[19]

Surrounded by opulent interiors, James's characters move in stage sets of their own making. But they are seen to be only acting roles in society, and their settings confine them.

The nature of their ambiguity, in particular the governess of *The Turn of the Screw*, is part of their (possibly) acting a role. James's stylistic technique is to conflate ambiguity upon ambiguity until the reader is left only with questions, and no answers. James wrote to a friend that it was his intent to keep the governess "impersonal" and it was left to other critics, notably Edmund Wilson, to assert that she was a classic example of the sexually repressed character as posited by Freud.[20]

James's father was an influential psychologist, as was his brother William, and his family reportedly had "a fascination with the supernatural," according to Dr. Claire Seymour in her forward to an edition of his novellas.[21]

This much James gives his readers: the message that society itself may be an "act." Society, James implies, makes actors out of people who do not need to or care to explore their own inner lives or address inequalities in society. (It is only the elite in James who are "acting.")

James gives readers a "portrait" of a Lady, who may or may not be acting. But the Beatles extended the acting metaphor to include, I suggest, everyone and everything. Paul questioned the idea of words being meaningless "lines" in "And I Love Her." The idea of people emptily acting their roles permeated such songs as "Nowhere Man" by John and Paul's "Eleanor Rigby." The cover of "Revolver" had the Beatles peering through masks, symbols of the stage, and "Sgt. Pepper" structured the entire work around the conceit of it being The Beatles acting as "another" band. James used acting as a motif to criticize roles people took in society. But the Beatles saw almost everything as an act. They saw themselves, of course, as an act and John was to tell Hunter Davies, "We're a con as well … Beethoven is a con."[22] Part of their appeal was their irreverence. They "saw through" people, as Laing would have put it, and as it was echoed in "I'm Looking Through You," to see the emptiness of a personae.

This recalls Shakespeare's (uttered in separate plays) edicts of "all the world's a stage, and all the men and women merely players" and "It is a tale … full of sound and fury, signifying nothing." However, the Beatles were not actors-as-tragedians; they wanted their act, if act it be, to be perceived as fun, irreverent and playful.

I have suggested that in moving in with the Ashers Paul was sub-consciously seeking boundaries between the genuine and the actor. Acting permeated his art, as a songwriter: he performed for audiences and took on the guise of a character each time he sang a song. John and Paul seemed to think about acting in ways similar to James. James gives the reader a basis to work from, as a reader, and then gradually erodes the moral and narrative signposts until in the words of Dr. Claire Seymour, "there is a silence at the centre of *The Turn of the Screw*, which stubbornly refuses to be filled…. The promised revelation is never supplied and the text retains its secrets. James's silence may be the silence of 'everything,' an infinite panorama of all possibilities."[23]

According to writer Daniel Schneider in his analysis of James titled *The Crystal Cage*, James used the imagery of acting and people as being "onstage" to hint at moral ambiguity, or what James called "the terrible mixture in things."[24] However an acting motif also allowed James to maintain his own distance from judgment, and to allow for a wider audience being drawn to his work.

Paul's motif of acting also allowed for the Beatles to maintain ambiguity, and thus widen their appeal. Millions could relate to what Paul projected, and if he implied words were an act, that was just adding a flavor of sophistication. The Beatles were acting as Beatles, but never telling people what their script really was, until they allowed that it was "the word, Love" which if you say, you will "be like me." The energetic music along with Paul's IFP would allow for a mixing of every sort of musical statement, a "voice" that could seemingly incorporate an infinitude. "The equation between the love they took and the love they made was intact into infinity," gushed their publi-cist Derek Taylor in later years.[25] This only means that their "use" of materials was not ascertainable, and thus was not able to be dismissed or eventually become passé. Thus, Paul out-ambiguoused (my coinage if the reader will indulge) James in using the acting motif. Acting and the IFP were not just a literary/songwriting device, but also an umbrella under which the Beatles were possible. Where James used the motifs of acting to (possibly) imply the empty façade of the well-to-do, Paul would use acting motifs to (possibly) question all society, and ontological reality itself. James may have "doubted in man's undiluted goodness," but the Beatles, I suggest, went about diluting *any* self-concept and then deeming a self-concept unnecessary. This was the outgrowth of Paul's own personal IFP and his use of texts that initially he found at the Asher's.

The Beatles would expand on the acting conceit with their 1967 album "Sgt. Pepper's Lonely Hearts Club Band." Paul proposed the album's concept as a way to "not be ourselves ... it would be nice to lose our identities."[26] We will discuss this album in Chapter Eight.

Acting permeated everything, in the Beatleverse. In "Penny Lane," the nurse, "although she feels as if she's in a play, she is anyway." Even if she attempts to feel real, she won't be able to be real, because everything is an act "anyway." This is a Munchausen patient who has lost the dividing line between acting ill and actually being ill, or the schizophrenic who feels full of other people, not himself. An actor could also be a person who is compelled to act like someone else. If an unstable person is adept at acting and "fools everyone that he is an 'actor,'" then he is validated in that role by society. (Peter Sellers seems to have veered into this territory.)[27] The Munchausen patient, the schizophrenic, however, are not given any place and role in society. Laing argued that a schizophrenic is just a person who got caught up in the wrong circumstances, or simply has the wrong audience. I suggest that Paul transposed this basically relativist idea into his lyrics, that there should be no dividing lines.

However, as a Beatle he could equivocate. While out walking his sheepdog sometime in 1968, Paul encountered an actor acquaintance. The man told Paul in an affected way of his upcoming acting job, refused to tell him what part he would play, and then strode away. Paul commented to Hunter Davies walking beside him that the man was typical of actors: "He can never relax. Can never be himself."[28] It is ironic that an actor refused to tell Paul what his role would be. Paul could have easily alluded to some bit of that role in a song (Zelda Fitzgerald referred to this as putting "in your books the perfume I used last year" to a writer friend, who was taking close note of her).[29] But the actor, while acting like an actor, also protected his own interests.

The Beatles were at the top of the artistic world, and saw things at the very moment they were introduced to the public; they saw the latest of everything and this enabled them to be fresh and new themselves.[30]

Schneider in his book *The Crystal Cage* observed, "The artist lives the largest possible life because, in his daring, he enjoys the greatest possible extension of experience and consciousness. The freest life is the largest life, the largest the freest: life unconfined to a single perspective. Freedom is expansion, flexibility; it is the recognition of "variety, variety," a happy pluralism, being as complete and wide-ranging as possible."[31] But, Schneider observes, pluralism has its drawbacks. "The artist setting out to pack as much life as possible into his work is inevitably confronted by tremendous problems. Art has a way of resisting the diversity and variety of life."[32] An artist needs some filter, some way of both presenting details and making it seem like a guiding artistic intelligence is behind the selection of them. Paul and the Beatles used the subtext of the IFP and this enabled them to cram all sorts of experimentation into music and by extension, to enlarge people's sense of freedom.

Pastiching the Normal

Although they seemed to have supra-normal abilities, the Beatles' use of traditional music genres reassured their fans that they were not aliens. Paul could write in familiar, even old-time genres. He would also include on each Beatles album at least one song which was seemingly unburdened with introversion, which provided reassurance that the Four Lads from Liverpool were coming from a place familiar to everyone. There was thus the perception, bolstered by Paul's compositions, that their music was an evolution of the habits, behaviors and institutions that everyone had grown up with (and had fought to protect). One example is "Michelle"; but that was after all an old song, that Paul had written on Forthlin Road. Paul's traditional (non-IFP lyrics) songs that appear on Beatle albums include "Michelle," "When I'm Sixty-Four," "Your Mother Should Know," and "Honey Pie." Three of these songs Paul wrote before he moved in with the Ashers.

Paul had a very firm grasp of the ordinary—an almost oppressive grasp of the ordinary. He would never lose his awareness of what constituted high and low cultural tradition. He had an ear for composing with song forms he had learned from his father, that the family had enjoyed whilst gathering around the piano. Even as a rock star, Paul would wear a jacket or a shirt with a collar, sometimes ate "Liverpool slag" beans on toast,[33] and his dog was an English sheepdog. Denis O'Dell, producer at Apple Films in the Sixties, wrote of Paul's "love of the ordinary and a desire to exist in the same world as the rest of us."[34] Paul's awareness of ordinary British life, which John had no use for, would go a long way toward endearing the Beatles to fans and keeping them in millions of people's affections.

However, on the White Album, the group would write in familiar styles to make a satirical point, or to deliver up what MacDonald calls "genre-parodies." "Bungalow Bill" uses a pre-recorded sample of classical guitar to introduce a tale of a "mighty hunter" whom children mock. The ornate keyboard harpsichord on "Piggies," George's song, flourishes around the greedy piggies in mock tribute. The Beatles parodied the Beach Boys' "California Girls" with "Back in the U.S.S.R." ("Well, the Ukraine girls really knock me out/They leave the West behind.") Every form can be used, and nothing is sacred. "Paul became a master of the pastiche, (combining selections from different works) which was a popular form at the time," noted MacDonald. Parody, nonsense verse and satire were pervasive in

Sixties media, on television, in books and on film. (To name a few, the Goon Show, Firesign Theatre, Monty Python's Flying Circus, comic Peter Sellers, new editions of Lewis Carroll and Edward Lear. In the U.S., the Smothers Brothers Comedy Hour, as well as The Monkees and numerous television sitcoms.)

Paul's "familiar" sounding compositions, written from a solid awareness of genre, were effective juxtaposed with John's less-structured songs. John's songs, as many critics have noted, were slightly "crablike" or "horizontal": they seldom had jumps in vocal line, and some of them amounted to not much more than one chord. However, when put side-by-side with Paul's on albums, this had the effect of making Paul's tidier compositions sound "trippy" or detached. John and Paul's songs would create a synergy of detachment from "the normal," or normality tinged with psychedelia.

Identity Fracture as Self-Protection

Because an anxiety about loss of ego, vulnerability, and loss of self underlies Paul's choosing a mental patient and asylum subtext, one can hardly avoid the conclusion that this was not merely an aesthetic necessity, but was the expression of anxieties that Paul had lived through in his childhood. The loss of his mother Mary could have been experienced as such a blow that refuge in art, song, music, unreal worlds and fantasy was seen as crucial to his carrying on. In creating masks and guises in song, Paul could try to protect himself from further exposure and vulnerability to loss. He could speak through the guise of Beatle Paul, who was in turn speaking the words of others (the patient transcripts). The mask or split self idea extended to the other Beatles, as evidenced by the cover of "Revolver," where their real eyes peek out from behind line drawings which are masks of their own faces. This is the subliminal message of the cover—Laing's idea of the "divided self," or the false self that one adopts to fit into society. The Beatles "came out" as counterculture leaders in 1966, when "Revolver" was released. The "other kinds of mind(s), there," were their scripts. But they were only partial scripts, sometimes probably only a phrase of a few words. The Beatles had to synthesize, add more lines, and make the sad song better: this they did. In all this synthesis of psychology texts, Paul was the leader.

In *The Crystal Cage: Adventures of the Imagination in the Fiction of Henry James,* author Daniel Schneider discusses R.D. Laing's idea of the "divided self" in relation to James's interest in acting and psychology and how these interests also informed James's fiction.

Henry James was the son of a philosopher and psychologist. His novellas and novels, written from 1871 to 1910, frequently point out the highly decorative surfaces and the ornate décor of Edwardian lives, while hinting at deeper conflicts within the characters. Schneider's premise is that James's fixation on acting and "the divided self" was due to James having to choose the identity of the "good son" for his mother, a role at odds with his true self. James chose this role because his older brother gathered all the academic accolades. "If (Henry) could not be superior, he could be good."[35]

I don't want to wander too far into amateur psychoanalysis, but perhaps this sort of situation could have applied to Paul as well. Paul's brother Mike was the "good" brother. Their mother was a nurse and an authoritarian, in contrast to Paul's sensitive, easygoing musician father. Mike was his mother's obedient angel, and Paul early on learned how to be dutiful, too, on the surface, to compete. But there was some hidden rebellion: Paul felt cramped by the rules, and he used to go in and secretly pull apart the lace on his parent's bedroom curtains, thinking, "That's got them."[36]

After their mother died, Paul at age twelve no longer had a mother to compete for. If he had formed an identity, somewhat, by complying with what Mary had wanted, that identity was now lost. The same year his mother died, Paul took up guitar, and then met sometime-art-student and "Teddy Boy" John Lennon. It is interesting that Lennon in effect replaced Paul's brother in his life after his mother died. Lennon, a bit older than Paul, already had a reputation of being a bully, intractable and cheeky. Paul would defend him to other people: "He's all right, really."[37]

Whether Paul really felt at sea in himself in the sense I am describing is not clear; one can more readily conjecture that John typically felt himself a bit unmoored. John told biographer Hunter Davies in 1968 that he sometimes felt depersonalized: "On my own, for three days, I almost leave myself completely. I'm just not here … I have to see the others to see myself. I realize then there is someone else like me… It's frightening, really, when it gets too bad. I have to see them to establish contact with myself again and come down."[38] "They seem to need you less than you need them," John's wife Cynthia remarked.[39] It is worth noting that even though Paul's brother Mike was also a musician, it was John with his rebelliousness and unstable sense of self with whom Paul could work creatively. John was inspiration to Paul, and John would in turn be inspired by and brilliantly "sum up" intellectual ideas Paul came across.

Schneider notes that Henry James's rivalry with his brother and adoption of the only role left to him might have given him long-lasting anxieties that informed his character studies in his novels.[40] A person with a "false front" would both be fearful of exposure, and yearning for other people to interact with and know "the real him." A feeling of "not acting as one's real self" toward others would then by projection extend to a projection that others are doing the same. (This recalls the line, "Although she feels as if she's in a play, she is anyway," Paul wrote for "Penny Lane.")

In 1964 Paul released "And I Love Her," which was, I suggest, his way of addressing the question of how real is the affection we have for someone and how do we know if they are acting. All of "Sgt. Pepper's Lonely Hearts Club Band" is, in a sense, about acting because it is performed by the Beatles, acting as another band (Sgt. Pepper's). There is no indication who Sgt. Pepper is, other than an illustration on a paper cut-out inside the album. The album is a series of filters, whereby we listen-in on a performance by The Beatles acting as another band, performing songs for another audience. This is "dislocation" in the extreme. If the schizoid individual is in fact only an "individe-you-all," as one of Laing's patients described herself, she can only divide herself into "everyone" to be "herself." By pitting actors-acting-as-actors opposite the listeners' mirror of a manufactured audience, Paul was setting up funhouse mirrors where the "real" image can never be detected and possibly no real-reality does exist— that is, no core of anything exists.

The same idea but applied to language we saw earlier in "And I Love Her," where the lyrics themselves acknowledge their potential hollowness: "And I love her," Paul assures us, at the end of a series of tender words praising "her." Implying that the words he just said, might be mere empty convention or even meaningless.

Paul uses acting motifs as part of his own Identity Fracture Project, as we saw in "And I Love Her," and will discuss regarding Sgt. Pepper. He was drawn to the questions acting itself raised: how does one decide what is "good" acting? Based on reality? But then, how does anyone know if some person "in reality" is real or an act? Paul had good reason to be interested in acting and the theatre, being in show business; and he had good reason to be drawn to reading about psychology, to find material for songs. However in being drawn to the theatre, and to the patient transcripts of the mentally ill, I suggest that Paul also had a personal need to know where his own dividing lines were, where his feelings resided. He also I suggest had an inner drive to step back, to distance, to divide into several minds, to be in a sense more of a perceived person, but also less vulnerable. Also, there can be a sense of freedom involved in being "someone else," similar to traveling to a city where one is unknown. This shuttling-between could be a spur to creativity. Paul, in being "locked away" in the asylum of the Asher's, was finding his way to both his feelings, and then back to the protected personae of Beatle Paul.

The IFP blurred boundaries and music genres. In this way Paul could compose, in effect, using all sides of himself. But we could also level the same criticism toward Henry James's lack of fully fleshed-out characters, as we could toward the Beatles' inability to consistently come up with "real songs." The Beatles wrote many songs, but only a handful can be placed alongside and compete on the same level as classic songs. Think of a song like "Octopus's Garden," or "She's So Heavy," and then place it beside a song like "Traces Of Love." Of course, they are three different genres, but my point is the Beatles sometimes got by on their innovation more than in fitting into any preconceived standard of aesthetic merit. Coinciding with this, Beatles songs mean a lot to people, but they can't tell you exactly what. Some Beatles songs do stand as classic and tell a story: "In My Life," "Yesterday," and some of Paul's later songs for the Beatles come to mind, including perhaps "The Long and Winding Road." But in being "Beatles," from whom anything could be expected, they created for themselves a certain pass. James, it could be argued, also created a character (of ambiguity) whereby he could avoid fulfilling certain requirements of his art. He could write stories about people being empty at the core. By being preoccupied with acting, appearances, and "multiple selves," James had a way of telling a story with a big hole in it—that of basis of character. This would allow him to avoid figuring out certain things for himself. "There is a silence" in the middle of James's novella *The Turn of The Screw*, notes Seymour, (essentially a guessing-game of who is moral and who is not, and whether anyone should care) and I suggest that it is James's fiction device itself that puts it there. His works were for all their encompassing detail and ornate surface, almost shaggy dog stories. Similarly we could see Paul's songwriting with its hidden subtext of non-self, ego-loss, mental patient language and the asylum, as, if not shaggy dog stories, although they might come close, then a means of having "something to sing about," and of giving the Beatles' erratic mix of songwriting styles continuity and a unique voice.

By 1965, after tutelage from Burroughs in tape loops, tape splicing and other sonic experiments, Paul knew what this "voice" or sound of identity fracture was. But, since he had his "ordinary" side, he would write traditional-sounding ditties, but put them through a filter as it were. His sonic innovations, done in close collaboration with engineer Geoff Emerick and producer, composer and arranger George Martin, would be henceforth linked in people's minds with the new culture and also to LSD and drug use. Notably the odder sounds on Beatles records would *not* be linked to schizophrenia, or mental patient's reality, in people's minds—even though those very words and allusions are there in the lyrics. Through his immersion at the Asher's and with some cues taken from his fellow creative colleague Brian Wilson, Paul could confidently "stage" the sound of psychedelia. In Paul's hands, it would be a mixture of all the influences he had come to love—a smidgen of Stockhausen, a bit of Burroughs. "Pepper" would bring the flavors of the avant-garde to the turntables of America, in one listening session. All one had to do to get the de-stabilizing effects of avant-garde music, which hardly anyone knew about save academics and a very small section of the record-buying public, was to listen to an album produced by George Martin and Paul. Better than George Martin could know, Paul had a sonic feel for internal fracture, dissolution, insecurity, that would and should accompany the lyrics of the Beatles' songs. Even if a song's structure was traditional, he made sure that by the end of producing it, the overall effect sounded like the Beatles. Using his production skills and the IFP subtext in the lyrics, Beatles songs sounded as if they came from some "other" state of mind. So, music hall songs could sit right next to the "transcendental" of George Harrison's Vedic-philosophy-lesson and sitar.

Dividing one into different personae was integral to the Beatles' image. The Beatles, resembling each other, were intuitively both one person, and four different persons. One of the early scripts their film producer commissioned for them was about a multiple personality; the idea was that John would have three other multiple personalities in Paul, George and Ringo. Producer Walter Shenson commissioned the script for them sometime in 1964; it was entitled "Beatle 3," and later renamed "Shades of a Personality."[41] The project was still in development in late 1967, but was finally shelved.

In leaving the world of the false (society, appearances) and constructing "roles" to enter the world where "nothing is real" (everything is art), one can be in Timothy Leary's words, "anyone this time around." Psychiatrist David Cooper at the Dialectics of Liberation

Conference in London in 1968 stated that the schizophrenia was "simply the project … to rediscover a pristine wholeness."[42] According to Cooper, the schizophrenic has the most exquisite and true take on reality. Herbert Marcuse then envisioned in his lecture a society that will be "a work of art."[43]

Writer Henry James examined the character of the artistic "free-spirit" in his 1875 novel *Roderick Hudson*. In this novel James examined the plight of those who can't be pinned down by society or anyone. James's protagonist is "nature's child—impulsive, wild, amoral, like some beautiful, restless, bright-eyed animal, whose motions should have no deeper warrant than the tremulous delicacy of its structure."[44] Hudson is incapable of making decisions and sticking to them. He drifts from experiment to experiment, impulse to impulse, and from woman to woman. In the end, he simply dries up. This description brings to mind both the image and the artistic side of Paul: the free spirit, the person who never wants to become set in his opinions. Paul's curiosity and flexibility to adapt to different situations sat alongside his skills as a consummate mixer. But would Paul always be able to sit down and write songs about what he was experiencing? He felt he had to "stay interested,"[45] and his girlfriend Francie Schwartz noted what she called his "desperate curiosity."[46]

James was examining ideas of a split self, contrasting the search of some individuals toward a "truer" existence versus (what he saw as) hollow conformity. Sixty years later Laing would argue that a split self was a pre-condition of growing up in a family, and that typical "repressed," "authoritarian" families effectively either brainwashed their children, or drove certain of their more sensitive children insane. For Laing, as for James, the problem was all about conformity and inequalities in a society which damns even generosity toward the less fortunate as a self-serving act. In the words of James's father, "it was really impossible to help anyone without an acknowledgement of the gross social inequality which permitted that situation."

In the Beatles' creation of the ostensive culture the idea of "high" or "low" would be replaced with the egalitarian-communalistic concept of "help from my friends," or "all together, now." Riding the Beatles' flying wedge of new "feelings," young people would gather enthusiastically in communal living arrangements, at rock concerts, pay for group therapy sessions, and enroll their children in non-hierarchical schools, trying to live differently than in the old competitive/ Capitalistic order. The Sixties ostensibly gave people more choices in how to live their lives.

However, as Henry James said in 1907, "the imagination incurably leads a life of its own."[47] It is easier to imagine a society of equality in every way than to create one. Life was trying to imitate art, or Utopianism, and the efforts were being closely observed by those who wanted to know about human nature and behavior. Meanwhile Paul, although leading the culture, was concerned primarily with his own art. His IFP created a new way of thinking about things: it wasn't real, it never would be, but millions bought it and tried to act as if it was. The Sixties were what author Ken Goffman called a "mimetic culture" (in his book, *Counterculture Through the Ages*).[48] That is, much of it was based on imitating or even "acting" as-if. Author and journalist Simon Heffer (on the BBC documentary *Why I Hate the Sixties*) described it this way: "it was a decade of the replacement of reality by illusion."[49]

The problem with thinking that everything is connected, is that one sooner or later meets oneself in the middle (a loop). This was what James called the "awful mixture in things," or what (academic mentor to Sylvia Plath at Cambridge) Dorothea Krook termed as the state where "the selfless motive is inseparable in experience from the selfish, the beneficent action from the acquisitive."[50]

Sidney Cohen in his book *The Beyond Within* made an interesting comment about this perception vis-a-vis psychosis. He stated that LSD could give a person a transcendent vision of connectedness, along with the feeling that this was all okay—but that this same awareness of connectedness or mixing under normal circumstances would be a psychotic experience accompanied by terror and dread.[51]

According to Schneider, James developed a vocabulary that would "permit him to render in virtually every sentence and with maximum expressiveness, the ambiguities of experience in an enslaving world. Every image and epithet would flow from the center, the imaginative source; not a word would arise accidentally. And it was because he now had so complete a grasp of what he could do in his art—of what he wanted every word to do—that he had created virtually a new style.... Since the enslaving world is one of base, deceiving appearances, James is driven to develop an immense vocabulary relating to acting and 'showing'... as contrasted with the invisible and inner worlds."[52] Paul also used the motif of acting as we have seen in "And I Love Her," and "For No One," and his use of acting motifs usually betrays a person's inner emptiness, as in Eleanor Rigby's TV-movie-of-the-week staging, or what MacDonald called its "televisual vividness."[53] A motif of acting is in some ways unavoidable in music because once a song is produced it takes on an outer shell and in a way becomes an actor on a stage. The purest form is the melody line, unaccompanied. Even a single chord added to a melody line "types" it into a certain statement, music genre, emotion or mood. Paul had taken on the task of producing the Beatles—a gargantuan task on the face of it. But it was not really such a huge task since Paul already knew intuitively just what the Beatles wanted the songs to "say" underneath the chords, melody lines, and harmonies. The songs would thus all fit together on albums, even though their genres would vary widely. As long as they had production that hinted at that instability, that "other world" of the mental patient, the lyrics that alluded to therapy, acting, lack of ontological basis, or even the asylums themselves, the consistency of their subliminal message and of the albums would be maintained. Hinting at instability was easy—and the fun part.

John took LSD repeatedly in an attempt to "erase himself" (according to MacDonald, and also Barry Miles).[54] Although John had a pattern of abusing drugs from his teenage years onward, John's LSD-taking might suggest an "experiment" being undertaken which was to create artists who lack any sense of conventional self—who are, in fact, insane—but are nonetheless accepted in culture as visionary. If a young person (such as John) so hates conventional culture, they might be convinced to donate their minds to such an experiment in an effort to bring something entirely new into the world (such is the hope). This is related to the kind of experimentation and research that was going on at Harvard at the time Leary was there, under Henry Murray, who it should be noted tried to "de-program" students in feedback experiments.[55] Murray attempted to "de-program" the brilliant math prodigy Ted Kaczynski out of his values (they called him the "lawful" student), by giving him repeated interviews along with discussion with an older participant skilled in rhetoric, who challenged his views. (Archibald MacLeish was lecturing at Harvard in Rhetoric at this time, and he was also a lawyer. He could have provided the person skilled in rhetoric, if he did not do the job himself!) Electrodes were attached and monitored Kaczynski's physiological reactions. The interviews and debates were videotaped and then played back for Kaczynski to see his expressions and how he was being out-debated. Taping in order to play back and undermine is a Burroughsian technique. Interestingly, after this unethical, boundary-blasting experiment, which went on weekly for three years, Kaczynski went on to write a thesis on boundary functions in mathematics. He later became a recluse and was convicted for murder as the so-called Unabomber. The prefix Una replaced the prefix "uni" which was for "university," since he targeted university professors.

Journalist Arthur Koestler was also at Harvard during this time, collecting information on experiments with personality and creativity research for *The Act of Creation*. Leary gave Koestler psilocybin pills. Some hours into the trip, Koestler commented, "This is marvelous, no doubt. But it is fake, ersatz. Instant mysticism." He told Leary about people in Austria who would climb a seven-thousand-foot peak and then had schnapps at the top, and that he would rather do something like that, with sweat and effort involved.[56] As we mentioned, after writing *Act of Creation*, Koestler co-founded with David Astor of *The Observer* a foundation that sponsors art-making in prisons.[57]

In the encapsulation of society-as-mental-hospital, which we will see in Paul's later song "Penny Lane," and already were introduced to in "Yellow Submarine," there is the idea that a person can now have the freedom to form their own identity, but they will be also, comfortingly, part of the new ostensive culture. The mental hospital metaphor, although hidden, was used to convey the new loosening of roles or of what one is "supposed" to be; more open expression and possibilities along all the expected trajectory of one's existence. These ideas of increased freedom, including sexual freedom, had of course been mooted for over a hundred years before the Beatles, if not for thousands of years previous. Since the early 20th century psychiatrists had theorized of "repressions," and "neuroses" stemming from repressions. But it took, perhaps, more than psychiatrists writing about these ideas to effect change across society and the mainstream population. It took an artist who was immersed in psychological ideas and synthesizing them into song, as if groping in the dark and then fashioning something entirely new out of these concepts. The Asher's Edwardian home, with its staircase, libraries and many floors, was a dimly lit incubator.

"Nightmare Alley" and Acting

An examination of the particular combination of acting and psychology having an influence on others can be found in the 1946 film "Nightmare Alley" which starred Tyrone Power.[58] Power fought to be in this film, because of its pertinence to the particular adulation and awe reserved for some actors, as if they possess godlike attributes.

Tyrone Power felt himself to be, in a sense, multiple people. He wrote in a biographical sketch for a novel that he was a conglomeration of mannerisms he had picked up from other people. "Little things have rubbed off … this gesture I use … this manner of speech, this way of walking … where did I get them?"[59] He might have only known a person for a few minutes, but in that time he picked up something from them that would stay with him for the rest of his life. This relates to the statement made by Fremont-Smith at the Macy Conference: "How much does a person influence another person? That is the real problem." To Fremont-Smith, this was the core puzzle researchers intended to solve: how is identity and sense of self constituted?

There is another aspect to being, like Power's protagonist, nothing if not informed by other people. If you have no identity, you could possibly be all things to all people. This idea was explored in many films, but "Nightmare Alley" is worth describing for its parallels to the Beatles' "non-self" dynamic. Its protagonist, Stan Carlisle (played by Tyrone Power) is what was called in carnival acts a "mentalist." He purports to read people's minds or see the future. He has powers of intuition, but Stan cons his way to success by stealing information, and also by conning his customers. He and his partner use a hidden code, and then he also gains inside information about his clients through a psychotherapist who has been clandestinely recording her patients' therapy sessions (actress Helen Walker combines concern with creepiness in her role as the psychotherapist). An elderly indus-trialist promises to give Stan tens of thousands of dollars if Stan can summon from the spirit world the man's deceased girlfriend, so he can apologize to her for past sins. Molly, Stan's wife, agrees to act as the girlfriend, but then has a change of heart. Stan's un-masking as a fraud, by his wife Molly, is the key moment in the film. Past and present collide, artifice and reality collide, and the con is exposed.

It is interesting that the emotions of both the movie audience and the gullible industrialist are most acute when the artifice of the con is at its height. Are emotions at their height in unreal situations or situations "framed" for public consumption? It is something to ponder and argues for the power of art to "be the axe for the frozen sea within us," as Franz Kafka put it. Not that the emotion felt is necessarily the *appropriate* one, but that art *can* liberate emotion.

The rise of Stan to The Great Stanton has similarities to the Beatles: the use of hidden knowledge, words that mean something else, the rise to fame, the attribution of special powers, and even perhaps that people *want* to be deceived. Stan, like the Beatles, was able to use words such that he convinced the public that he had special insights into the human mind. As he gained fame, the public became convinced that he had special powers, was not an ordinary person, and was possibly in contact with the Divine. The Beatles were similarly rising higher and higher with each album. People with disabilities would show up at Beatles concerts, wanting to be healed by their touch. "Cripples!" John would yell, if he wanted Mal Evans to clear unwanted visitors out of the green room.[60]

Neil Aspinall, the Beatles' road manager and personal assistant, commented to Hunter Davies that the Beatles "have always come across as being so good and kind and nice, when they're not particularly, not more than other people. I think people wanted them to be like that…. It's strange, isn't it, how people take to an image?"[61]

Molly's moral conscience did not allow her to continue the fraud. But no such pangs trouble an artist. The Beatles said all along that they were only entertainment. They promised no truths. Their magic trick was to get the public to *accept* anything they did—and this they succeeded in doing, because of Paul's IFP.

I would suggest that the Beatles were coming close to Stan Carlisle's compromised position, however, by the time of "Pepper," which is why John launched a pre-emptive strike to bring down their image in "Walrus." The Beatles were at that point far above their fans. But that wasn't supposed to be the new egalitarian reality. A way to get around this dialectical problem was to invent the device of Sgt. Pepper's, where they were not really being "themselves," but another band led by Sgt. Pepper. In that false subsidiary position, they could go ahead and give Aesopian cues to their followers and paint aural pictures of expanded awareness. And, similar to the Great Stanton, they rose even further as their artifice increased. "Pepper" was perceived as the Beatles' creative peak, the high summer of the Sixties.

* * *

There was a class-consciousness and conflict in Henry James, and a finger leveled at society's "falseness" in R.D. Laing; but no one had acted in mainstream song as if Laing was "right." So, Paul took Laing's critique of society farther in that he created in his IFP a fun-loving mask behind which to "act" as if *"everything* is all right." Behind which he was subverting society just as Laing and even as

David Cooper wanted. The Beatles never came out as rebels; that was supposedly the Rolling Stones' job. No one could accuse the Beatles of being subversive if it was "all a bit of fun," and they always had plausible deniability (i.e., John's son drew a picture he named Lucy in the Sky with Diamonds, so the song is not about LSD). For "Pepper," no one could even accuse the Beatles of putting out substandard songs, if it was in concept, "another band" playing the music. It is of course obvious to all it is the Beatles playing the entire thing. But, it was a type of acting-through-acting-through-acting idea of Paul's, similar to his writing-songs-through-using other minds, which made Sgt. Pepper's work, at that particular time and maybe for ever after. The Beatles were becoming change agents through filters, masks, dislocation, diverting, fracture and over-determining to the point of possible infinitude. There was no way to challenge them. Paul became such a master of the Beatles' language of IFP, that he placed his critics and public in positions from which any opposition became impossible—he held them or "fixed" them. Toward this end on "Pepper" Paul created the idea of a fictional band, singing to a fictional audience, obviously fake, who applaud it; the songs tell stories, and the singers with all the novel sounds and effects are obviously singing through some other filter of reality. The "Pepper" album was called "fraudulent"[62] and "drug-soaked" by critics at the time. Which, it was—but who cared? The characters of the album and the Beatles as those characters exist in a world where nothing is real and a lot of freedom is permitted.

In fact when one writes like this about The Beatles, more and more a big circular void opens up. Or rather, empties out. Nobody had to be anything. Least of all The Beatles. All pressure was lifted.

That Paul took the information at the Asher's and "made it better," indeed huge, is similar to Timothy Leary making his own name worldwide with the data gathered about LSD and its ambiguous, different-for-everyone effects. Most in the (contentious) psychiatric community wanted to still keep the drug under wraps, study and control its applications, but Leary wanted to give it to everyone, particularly teenagers, to "change the world." Paul said similar things in 1967, when he gave his first "official" post-LSD interview: "It would mean a whole new world ... there wouldn't be any more war or poverty or famine."[63] However, Paul didn't need to wax eloquent about LSD; he already had LSD's "model psychosis" embedded in the subtext of his songwriting. The Beatles were also the bringers of news about the emptiness of self and creative leaders of communal relativity. Paul, in "opening wide" to reach the broadest segment of the public with his art, took an approach similar to Leary's in that both would use information that was heretofore controlled within the psychiatric community as a springboard for fame. John later called Paul "a good PR man ... about the best in the world."[64]

CHAPTER VII

The Beatles' Look and Sound: "All a Bit of Fun"

That the early Beatles wrote songs by following on musical ideas by other musicians, there is no doubt. John commented later, "We stopped being a band when we stopped going into record stores and stopped trying to improve on our favorite singles."[1] But John is revealing (as is usual with his statements to the press) half of the truth. When the Beatles quit the "please" department in 1966 is when the psychedelic "revolution" in rock had begun. Paul's "third thing," as I have attempted to explain, began in mid-1963. John's remark seems to imply that they "stopped being a band" exactly when they found their own voice; this was taken for one of John's jokes because the remark doesn't make sense. I suggest John said this because once Paul found his own process of writing songs, they were no longer "improving on" musical ideas from other artists, and singing about "diamond rings" and "hold me tight." Paul had found a way for the Beatles to write seemingly deeper songs about feelings, and from henceforth John was less the leader, and Paul and his IFP was (were).

In this book I am focusing on Paul's lyrics. But there were other elements that contributed to both the hidden subtext, and to the

Beatles' mass appeal. Most of the things that can be said on the topic of their look and sound are well-known to any Beatle fan. So I will omit description of their charm, talent, charisma, and compositional skills, which have been covered by others already. In this chapter I will discuss some of their musical innovations and how they pertain to Paul's IFP. To discuss every aspect of the IFP as it affected their music (rather than solely the lyrics) is unnecessary as I ask the reader to judge for themselves, using their ears, if they hear it after considering my theory. The primary evidence of the IFP, the Ur-text, are the lyrics, and the synthesis of their sound and word in the IFP was what brought them such acclaim.

However, there were elements of the Beatles that contributed to their gaining attention even before the IFP began.

Their Look

The early Beatles (at the time of their U.S. television debut in February 1964) were original to Stateside audiences in that they sang with British accents, had longish hair and played loud electric guitars. What initially drew attention was their energy, their looks and their unusual style. They were lively and boyish, shaking their hair not like sexualized rockers with greased Teddy boy "quiffs" (which look they had sported, including the leather jacket, just the year previous),[2] but in seemingly simple high spirits. With a professional window-dresser's eye for what would be appealing to the consumer, Brian Epstein had styled them as neatly and identically as he would have a NEMS window display. They were boyish—they were charming—there were four to pick from—they all looked and acted similar, and their look was a bit strange.

I believe that their hair, a type of cut called the urchin haircut, was an important factor in the Beatles' acceptance. It is almost a bowl-cut, such as children wear. The urchin covered their foreheads, made their faces more alike, and also obscured their physiognomy: no one could by observing their forehead height make a judgment about the intelligence of each Beatle. This was important because at the time, teen and adult beauty magazines were somewhat obsessed with facial shape, giving advice on how to hide some features and emphasize others. There was much emphasis on appearance, proper etiquette in social gatherings, and so on. The Beatles seemed to exist outside of this. The urchin cuts subconsciously made them appear innocent, cute and charming as they sang songs about everyday things, like holding hands and dancing. A columnist in *Teen*, May 1964 issue (Ted Persons) observed that the strong emotions the Beatles expressed about holding somebody's hand only made sense if you imagined them as a little boy who had lost his mother in a department store. Their emotion, in other words, was that of children, not of adults, and was out of proportion to the scenes their songs described. Persons also wrote that the Beatles, with their childish haircuts, appealed not to the rebellious instinct in girls, but to the maternal instinct. This, he said, was "commendable. So, long may they weave ... their non-art of the non-song."[3] Ian MacDonald writing decades later similarly noted that the early Beatles songs were about releasing emotion, and that the lyrics were secondary.

Unlike popular singers of the day, the Beatles were a team. The identical haircuts, pointy black boots and collarless suits constituted a team uniform. Yet they were also introduced as personalities, so a fan could cheer them on as a team and also "pick a favorite Beatle." They seemed safe for parents, children and teens. You couldn't go wrong picking one or the other as a favorite, and they weren't sexy, at least outwardly.

As early as 1964 it was prognosticated that they were only a passing fad, and that once the novelty of the haircuts had worn off, their vogue would fade. Then Paul and John came in with "deeper" music and they showed they had something "new," after all, artistically, to say. Their lyrics seemed not entirely logical, but as noted earlier, they were extraordinarily confident in their delivery, and "it seemed important to listen."

A key component of their early recordings and performances was that they were almost shouting the songs, and sometimes scream-singing in the manner of Little Richard or Chuck Berry. John especially could scream-sing with emotion, and this was definitely meant to evoke excitement.

However, the younger set didn't always know what to make of the groups' higher than usual energy – how to react. For instance at an early concert when Paul sang "Some Fun Tonight," the audience of neatly dressed Swedish girls did not bring their hands up to their face and scream, but clapped politely to the song's simple back-and-forth beat.[4]

By late 1963, I suggest, advertisements, articles and photos depicting "Beatlemania" had shown the proper public reaction to have to the group. The message was that the Beatles were a band that it was finally (this adverb is important) "okay" to let go and scream to. As we have mentioned, a news story in October 1963, covering their London Palladium show, carefully cropped around eight girls[5] and captioned it as a mob of teenagers. The screaming and jumping up and down at shows affected how the young people felt. Letting go was understood to be a group activity. Nobody screamed and writhed in the privacy of their room while listening to the Beatles on a phonograph. The Beatles started to sing about "inner" feelings by 1964, and as I have noted, brought into their songs concepts of ontological insecurity. (Screaming for mother, Persons described it.) It was the group's physical proximity (and of course, music) that was supposedly the instigator of audience hysteria, when they played live. But one can question whether the mass screaming of audiences was an existential acknowledgement of collective futility. Were the belly-deep screams an acknowledgement of an heretofore-repressed fact that idols can never be reached, and that a fan is one speck in millions? To Persons, the Beatles were depicting themselves as children that their audiences wanted to mother, and yet their songs also invoked, and created, a collective screaming for attention, I suggest, also for ontological security. The Beatles and their fans were an ontological mirror. In any event each fan felt the Beatles somehow knew them (due to the manner of the IFP as I have described). Further, many a young female fan felt that the Beatles should meet her, sooner or later—that such knowledge of her inner state could only mean that they already knew her and that it was fate she would meet her Beatle. This was a collective feeling that as one writer put it decades later, "if every girl of my generation had had her wish, she would have ended up marrying a Beatle."

The Beatles, using Paul's IFP, worked in the terrain of dialectics, and of erasing divisions between people. They did it by appearing initially almost as children. Children are loved simply for being children. Early on, the combination of their haircuts, trim suits, lack of muscularity, glib pronouncements, upbeat stage presence, and songwriting approach made a synergy. Fans were instructed to scream even louder to the brink of hysteria, more so than they did to singers such as Paul Anka (although the film clips of some of his fan reactions are similar). The energy fed back into the recordings. One can almost hear the high-pitched screaming at the beginning of "She Loves You" and "Tell Me Why."

There is no disputing that the upbeat, irreverent Beatles, after they were signed to Parlophone, had at their disposal the best recording stages and equipment the world had to offer. Parlophone was at EMI Studios, or Electric and Musical Industries, a research arm of the British Military. Anything developed in audio was "heard here first." To be a truly novel recording group, the Beatles had to record at EMI Studios. There was no comparable studio in the U.S.—no "United States Military Electronics Musical Industries." (At least, that was known as such.) Also at their disposal at EMI Studios was the entire British Broadcasting Corporation archive of sound clips and sound effects (the BBC is another arm of the British government).

Their producer, George Martin, had been previously headed another division at EMI recording experimental electronic soundtracks. He had subsequently worked with several comedy artists, "illustrating" their routines with appropriate sound effects. Martin was a classically trained pianist and multi-instrumentalist; he said that he originally wanted to be "Rachmaninoff the 2nd."[6] This is notable because the

Beatles were to bring new sensations and feelings to people, and Rachmaninoff was a composer of drama and force. Martin did not become a classical composer, but his production of the Beatles' music would convey the maximum amount of feeling in the material. His contribution was inestimable to their success: he would score parts, play keyboard middle eights, hire and conduct the session musicians. Martin and his inventive audio engineer Geoff Emerick, an audio effects innovator, would toil for hours after the Beatles had recorded their parts and gone home. They could fulfill almost any arty request from the group—John asked Emerick to make him sound like a monk on a mountaintop, to evoke the smell of sawdust at a carnival, and one time asked Martin to produce the sound of an orange.[7]

The imaginative but also somewhat authoritative Martin was the perfect choice to produce a band that wanted to be new and brash, convey a lot of feeling, and have artistic credibility. Epstein provided them with their reputation for professionalism, the suits and tours. Martin and Emerick's instrumental scoring and innovations fulfilled all their goals of production.

Of course, what sold the Beatles most was John and Paul's vocal blend. The blend was unusual. John's voice was an amazing instrument that could express sadness, pride, anguish, sarcasm, you name it. Paul, unusually cute, had a sweet voice with a delivery and accent which could charm millions.

Their Sound

Of course, this is the entire point. I will not go into details about this except as it pertains to the IFP and what I call the interval.

The Beatles felt they had to be new and different in everything they did. Their guitars, Emerick noted, could not sound like guitars; nor could a piano sound like a piano: "I was constantly wracking my brains trying to come up with ways to make things sound different."[8] They were continually trying out new, exotic instruments and electronic sound effects. There had to be a sense that the Beatles were always going to be breaking new terrain. "It seemed to us to be crucial to never do the same thing twice," Paul noted. "In fact, as they say now, 'they never did the same thing once!'"[9]

This sense of nothing-as-usual supported the feeling that the Beatles had broken ground into new awareness. The untraceability of their approach, and uncategorizeable music, created in listener's minds possibilities—literally giving people "somewhere to go" as a type.

Early on, one of their innovations was that their vocals were often close-miced.[10] Putting the microphone close to the singer creates an intimacy and immediacy; it sets up the singer as "confiding" or singing to the listener directly, more so than if they were standing some distance away from the microphone.

A key instrument of the psychedelic period, but not necessarily of the Beatles, was the Hammond organ. Although the Beatles were not known for that sound, they did make ample use of its oscillating Leslie in their recordings and a discussion of the Leslie is relevant here.

The Leslie cabinet contains baffles rotating in front of the speaker cone, and it is the sound of signal fracture—it breaks a chorus tone into "bits" with gaps in between. The Leslie was very appropriate for Beatle's songs because it illustrates fracture. It became the keyboard and vocal sound of the Sixties and was used on into the Seventies (a recording of Allen Toussaint singing his composition "Southern Nights" sounds very much like John Lennon singing, so closely is the Leslie effect associated with John).[11] I suggest that the flicker of the Leslie, when used on vocals, broke up the traditional idea of a voice having presence, and of the singer having a solid identity in telling a story. John would repeatedly ask Geoff Emerick to use the Leslie on his voice. The reason was not because John didn't like the sound of his own voice (that is absurd—John loved singing), but because a voice put through effects fit with the Aesopian language of drugs, and also of ego-loss which is part of the IFP. The broken-up voice came to mean a "trippy" Sixties consciousness, such as on the song "Crimson and Clover." New intervals were being heard and explored—sonically, as well as emotionally and mentally. Like "the flicks" (the old term for movies), which hypnotized as their frame-intervals rapidly scrolled, the broken-Leslie voice could entrain the listener into a fantasy world. Emerick toggled the switch to do a Leslie wobble: "No one there to tell us what to do."

A flange effect also doubles and warps the sound. John used the flange on "Tomorrow Never Knows." It doubles the voice (a fracture in sound) and puts the double at a slight varispeed off from the original. A flange effect is not the same as simply double tracking. A flange always sounds "bent" and can be over-used. It was appropriate to use in Beatles songs at certain points.

The novel treatments of vocal effects and instruments created "our little hideaway, beneath the waves." Under the sound waves, one would gather. The asylum which was brought into the world by the Beatles had more in common with particulate disintegration than arousing the maternal instinct, such as Persons had described them doing.

The Beatles were in a sense reaching back to the intense feelings of childhood and putting them into songs supposedly about adulthood. The release of feelings and the insight into relationships were what sold their songs to the public after 1964—not simply their songs and their hair. Brian Wilson was also working with going back to childhood feelings, at the time of his collaboration with Van Dyke Parks. Wilson, after taking LSD, set his piano into a sandbox,[12] to evoke both the beach and the feelings he had felt as a child in a sandbox (although it is possible Wilson seldom went to the beach, except for his *Saturday Night Live* skit). In any event, the Beatles were working in intervals, particles and waves, so it was natural that Brian Wilson would place his piano in a sandbox as a representation of this as well.

The use of new sound effects and news about feelings evoked the sensation of when everything was new, in childhood. To a child, everything is a discovery. Both Wilson and the Beatles wanted to evoke and express this sense of wonderment and they did it primarily using psychedelics and psychology concepts or texts. I am asserting this primarily in the case of the Beatles, but Wilson was exposed to similar influences—psychology and LSD. By contrast, Elvis was not bringing childlike feelings to listeners, nor was a singer like Petula Clark. However, when the Beatles segued from "new feelings" into an Aesopian language of drugs was when The Monkees had to step in to fill the void for the children and pre-teen market, in 1966. Then, it was appropriate for corporations like Yardley of London to sponsor The Monkee's television sitcom.[13]

The Beatles' use of adult humor mixed with the evocation of childhood feelings, and compounded with "illogical logic" created a situation much like the incomprehension experienced by a child toward remarks made by his or her parents. Beatles lyrics might be stored away in a person's mind much as a child will remember unintelligible actions of his parents for years afterward. The puzzle is stored away and remembered. It is possible it could be subconsciously pondered for years, mulled over in the mind as an experience or words that made them feel emotions, and yet was not sensical.

I think these reasons, in addition to the IFP, are in large part why the Beatles' music was so compelling.

Here is a partial list of aural inventions the Beatles brought to conventional music:

- Tape loops
- Reverse recordings
- The Leslie on vocals and instruments
- The sitar
- Fuzz distortion effect
- Flange effect
- Varispeeding (speeding up or slowing down tape to raise or lower pitch, either while recording, or while mixing down or mastering the recording)
- The Mellotron and many other new keyboards
- Unconventional use of conventional instruments (such as hitting piano strings with a mallet for "Getting Better")

- Close-micing
- Inventive use of dynamics—experimenting with peaking sound levels intentionally
- Feedback (as on the beginning of "I Feel Fine")
- Echoe (such as doubling an accent beat with an effect placed on drums)
- Nursery-rhyme cadences
- Sound effects
- "Modal" songwriting (this term means writing songs in distinct sections, such as "A Day In The Life")

The Beatles were one of the first bands to use fuzz distortion, before the Fuzz box (a step-on effects pedal) was marketed to the public.[14] The "Tone Bender" fuzz-box and WEM-Rush Pep Box (advertised as "Fractured Sound"[15]) were two fuzz distortion pedals tried out by the Beatles, then marketed to the burgeoning electric guitar market among young men.

The spectral keyboard sound at the beginning of "Lucy in the Sky With Diamonds" and the Mellotron at the beginning of "Strawberry Fields Forever" are but two of the unusual and new keyboards they used. They were the first to use tape loops and sampled sounds in a commercial recording on "Tomorrow Never Knows."

Their new sounds, of course, went hand-in-hand with their bringing "news" about feelings in relationships, and then "news" or felt-landscapes for the "new awareness." But they also did inspire a lot of inventors to tinker on designs for keyboards, guitars, or effects, and then the Beatles might be first to try them out. Geoff Emerick in *Here, There and Everywhere: My Life Recording the Music of The Beatles* goes into details about the Beatles' recording process. I also refer the reader to *Beatles Gear* by Andy Babiuk, a chronological encyclopedia of Beatles instruments, which will tell you everything you want to know about the instruments they used on recordings.

* * *

You can think of Paul's IFP as opening a big open pit, or sand-box, for him and others to fall into. And play in. The Beatles did increase public interest in music, in their quest for inventive sounds and unconventional use of conventional instruments.

Because the Beatles had this subtext hidden in their songs, and were master "early adopters," they were kings of what became the Sixties' musical-mental sandbox. Paul had created a world where one could be "locked away" from the harsh adult world, hearing the latest installment of the "other world" which the Beatles seemed to bring "news" from. That this "news" was sometimes culled from testimonies from broken minds, people never suspected. People have intervals between A and B, in normal conventional reasoning, and one of them had been breached without anyone suspecting it. Therefore, an interval, somewhat like a mathematical interval, which theoretically can telescope into an infinite series of numbers, had been opened—a sandbox of infinite tone colors. It wasn't really: and this is the import-ant point I am making—Paul knew the limits of his method and where he got his texts and subtext. But to the listener, who had no idea of this, it did appear like an "infinite interval" or paint box of a million colors, a sandbox of billions of sand particles, had some-how been "opened" or "created." The "selling" or fabrication of this perception is what really made the latter part of the Sixties an era of colorful explosions of one sort or another (as if "shot from guns!"). The particles were now liberated, the colors flowing out, however tunefully or gently—because of the subtext Paul began to incorporate at the time he released "She Loves You."

CHAPTER VIII

Sgt. Pepper: Brian Epstein Cried, and Lucy Would Be in the Sky With Her Eyes, Scattered Diamonds

"In their music, (the Beatles) have an instinctive awareness of what to do. They are always ahead of everyone else. But in much of their other thinking, they tend to be juvenile psychologists."

– GEORGE MARTIN[1]

The "murkiness" of the psychiatric profession that created division among the Macy Conference researchers was by 1967 in direct proportion to the Beatles' mystique. The Beatles *were* that gap, and the gap was also LSD. Their songs re-fashioned the terrain of dialectics—of relationships between self and other(s). In that terrain the Beatles were putting across the message that there need be no opposites, no disagreement, just "love" which was taken to mean infinite shades of understanding, feeling and communication. In "Hello Goodbye," Paul iterated, "You say high, I say low/You say why, and I say I don't know/You say goodbye, and I say hello." It was happening piecemeal, but in small, chewable doses, the Beatles were pushing a concept of no dialectics and the universal Yes, when they weren't telling people that the "normals" were empty. Psychiatrists such as the Macy researchers did know about "emptying" people out, with mind-breaking drugs. Leary's idea that LSD could allow the user to reach a Vedic transcendent state was a typically Western approach to self-improvement: Take a pill (or a tab, or a drop of ampule liquid), and see God. The uncharted terrain of therapeutic encounters would be in direct proportion to the mystique of the "interval" which Paul had created. The wasteland of the gap between one person and another would be (supposedly) filled with colors, myriad options and infinite changes.

Paul said later that having had not such a bad time on LSD that he took it on a few more occasions. However as we shall see, the Beatles would use the same subtexts of therapy, the asylum and so on in their songs after they had all taken LSD. The same lyric motifs could and were taken for expanded awareness due to drugs. This was the evolution of the synthesis of broken-with-whole that Paul had achieved in "Yesterday" and which I discussed in Chapter Four.

The Beatles' manager Brian Epstein cried when he saw the "Revolver" album cover.[2] Epstein had believed in the eventual success of John, Paul, George and Ringo since he had begun managing them in December 1961. He explained his tears by saying the artwork captured the idea of the Beatles' music perfectly. It did: they were looking through masks of their own faces. Epstein cried because this was proof that the era of the teenybopper Beatles, "carefully sweetened for public consumption," as Ian MacDonald put it, was coming to an end. The Beatle's old selves would next be presented on the cover of Sgt. Pepper as waxworks dummies. Epstein had planned their image carefully and had an instinct for what would appeal. But in August 1966, this old image was a cartoon, a dummy, and a mask that was about to be shed. The group was moving into a different phase, although in a way they would be doing the same things.

Soon after they released "Revolver," the Beatles told Epstein that they were stopping all touring. Epstein knew he no longer had any integral function in the Beatles enterprise. "What do I do now?" he asked a friend.[3] He had been their guide into the industry, their negotiator, coached them how to behave for the public and the media, and emotionally had been like a family member. Epstein had been close to John, especially, who had sent him flowers and a note saying he loved him one time when Epstein was in a clinic taking a drug cure.[4] Now Epstein's tears were because it looked like his "boys" would need him much less.

Although Paul might not have known it, his IFP had laid the groundwork for John's unstable personality to really shine. John would achieve a level of genius in his songwriting. He would write several songs about Paul and his IFP, which by 1968 would begin to annoy him. Paul in 1966 in effect became the band's leader. He would produce "Sgt. Pepper's Lonely Hearts Club Band" in 1967 again with his IFP in mind, confidently working closely with George Martin and Geoff Emerick. "And there I am, producing the album," Paul commented[5] (in a BBC documentary on George Martin) looking at a photograph of himself at the mixing board, moving the sliders, taken just after he had grown his moustache. Paul could expand his lyric process of dislocation, absence-in-presence and emptiness under the auspices of the new drug culture, using the psychological subtext of mental asylum, void and therapy. The IFP musical language could expand to vividly illustrate or evoke altered states, now that the Beatles were freed from having to reproduce the sound on tour. Paul would have the surest ear for the language of what the songs were communicating: he believed in his ability to produce as he believed in himself.

As Hunter Davies observed at the recording sessions for "Pepper," The Beatles were intent on working on songs over and over. "It's often hard to see what they're still looking for, it sounds so complete ... their dedication is impressive, gnawing away at the same song for stretches of up to ten hours each. Paul often appears to be the leader in all this ... mainly because someone has to say it's not good enough ... he's still the keeny."[6] The other Beatles were contributing songs that were "Beatles material," because their lyrics could allude to the same Beatles IFP universe (or Un-verse). The Four No Ones would be right there with their listeners. They would act as "stablemates." "Pepper" was to be the penultimate statement of the communal spirit of the Sixties and a soundtrack for the drug culture.

* * *

> "The Beatles were a little model... It was like saying, you can be young, you can be far-out, and you can still make it."
>
> –JERRY GARCIA[7]

To the record-buying public it was obvious that something new was afoot: The Beatles were singing in code about the new counterculture. Musical and lyrical references to drugs and drug awareness in "Revolver" were caught by listeners; the Beatles were writing what is called an Aesopian language. Aesopian language is a coded language which is only recognized by those in the know. The ambiguous Aesopian language of their songs (is it or is it not about LSD?) gave the Beatles and their followers a filter and smokescreen they could always dodge behind. The counterculture had a new language that would not "pin it down."

This was Bateson's dream. It was the birth of a new ostensive culture, one where specificity was not the coin. The members of the asylum were mental Argonauts, going in different directions, but they were all loosely bound in the new counterculture, while remaining unclassifiable. Although many youth groups were political and had specific aims, the Beatles' music, being unclassifiable, formed an umbrella organization. The counterculture "umbrella" was the Beatles' IFP, I am asserting. "Forget the inmates taking over the asylum," commented Paul later, on seeing a photograph of himself with George Martin at the mixing desk at Abbey Road. "There we are—working it."[8]

On "Sgt. Pepper" the Beatles would use much of the same approach to songwriting, namely the IFP subtext. Even so, Paul still needed inspiration, something to come to him, in order to write songs. He might have become "Expando-Paul," but now by doing so he was still being The Beatles (and vice versa, to the other Beatles' increasing annoyance). He wasn't really himself anymore, at some point on the road to writing, recording and producing a "Beatles" song. That is, his art had been expanded, codified, and split-off, in a sense. It must have been hard to wonder where he himself would go next, but he didn't have to do that just yet. The Beatles as "The Beatles" had a formula. But Paul still needed a seed to write a song—someone's story that interested him, new information, and new material. But how much storage space did he have? Did he need either to a.) be interested in everything, in order to find new material or b.) lose more of himself (by meditation, or by taking drugs) to let the inspiration in—or if it was a combination of both, what was the right proportion? How could it be *foolproof* to write "Beatles" songs, with the IFP subtext of not being "anybody," or as George would sing about it in "Only A Northern Song," "nobody's there"? Or would there be a line beyond which Paul wouldn't sound like Beatle Paul anymore or his music lost the plot?

This was what seemingly had happened to Brian Wilson, after taking LSD. His music touched on an almost alien, otherworldly beauty on his composition with Van Dyke Parks, "Surf's Up." Watching Wilson play this song on Leonard Bernstein's show, one can almost sense Wilson leaving *everyone* by the last notes. It is truly heartbreaking. Wilson, overwhelmed by stimuli and demands, took to his bed.

By classical definition, a poet has a point of view. In the 20th century Modernist poet T.S. Eliot had famously insisted that great poetry was *im*personal.[9] The Beatles were continuing this idea of Eliot's to an extreme. They were de-personalizing *themselves*. John had been taking LSD frequently since early 1965 in an effort to "destroy his own ego": he would be brilliant at summing up "the culture" of the Sixties spun-off of his and Paul's identity fracture process. (John did later on occasion come out with personal statements, such as "Julia.")

Did Paul find this "way" of writing songs because he was influenced by Eliot's ideas (he was living within the Eliot family, after all, by way of the mother Margaret Asher) or did he not have faith that inspiration could come to him? Did he not believe in the identity of the artist, or did he think such a notion of identity was passé? Pluralism is certainly borne out in his music. His time at the Asher's gave him ample opportunity to put words to the many different music styles he knew already, and to be exposed to avant-garde music, literature and theatre.

The Beatles had scored a critical and popular success with "Revolver," and so with his production of "Sgt. Pepper" Paul moved into what I call his "Expando-Paul" phase. He identified with his own syntheses of broken-with-whole, as did his audience, and so the interval of expansion he created had been proven to be viable. He could produce the album with a confident sense of what it should communicate to listeners.

Why do I call it Paul's IFP? Why not just say he was writing songs with a psychological subtext? I call it the IFP because I sense he was drawn to psychological materials for personal reasons. He was also writing songs with motifs of dislocation. He was enamored of R.D. Laing's theories of the "divided self," or false identity. In addition, he eventually took the "identity-fracturing" drug, LSD. I think Paul had an inner drive to fracture, or split, his identity.

Meanwhile, messages the Beatles had encoded in news of "feelings" were being enacted in media. Messages were in novels, film, and advertising: for girls and younger women, pick yourself off the sofa, dress colorfully, go downtown, and try something new. You don't have to be stuck in one role—you can have a different identity for every day of the week. As explained a girl in the Yardley Slicker lipstick ad in 1967: "I have this thing about my identity. I never look or act the same way two times in a row. Yesterday I was the darling of the Discotheque. Today I'm Carnaby Street. Tomorrow? Tomorrow I think I'll be demure little Girl-Girl. How do I do it? How do all London girls do it? With Yardley Slicker... (There follows a description of the similarly hued frosted lipsticks.)… It's all up to me, and my mad mod mood of the moment."[10] Change, or even to be someone else each day, was marketed to women perhaps more than men. The "Georgy girl" had "another Georgy deep inside/Bring out all the love you hide/And oh what a change there'd be/The world would see/A new Georgy girl." She was also told in the song, "Don't be so scared of changing/And rearranging yourself." Songs were celebrating the girl who can "change with every new day" ("Ruby Tuesday") or in Jimi Hendrix's words, "covers me with smiles and then leaves." The "flower girl" of the Cowsills hit "The Rain, the Park and Other Things" was there for a few minutes, spread euphoria and then took off for some unspecified destination. Young men were a little less all over the place: to be "hip" they had to have longish hair, be style conscious, intellectual, and ideally either had a connection to a drug dealer or played an instrument or both. They were in other words like the Beatles.

The new person was open to new experiences—a type that was un-typable. One good way of being unclassifiable, of course, was to be high half the time. The drugs mixed with the deafening atmosphere at rock clubs made detailed self-revelation in conversation impossible; but the clothing indicated the pluralistic outlook. Instead of being a slave to one fashion, youth was encouraged to dress like a walking collage of fashion, which in turn became its own fashion.

Paul's "praxis" discovered and developed while at the Asher's was being reflected in the motley of youth (in contrast to fashions of the early Sixties where the straitjacket white tunics, staring eyes and pale lips made the models resemble shock treatment patients). Beatles music had made it seem like there was "more" lurking unexpressed in people; it expanded ostensible possibilities. However behind all this display there needed to be some core to the matter. Accordingly music was saying that now was the time to change society. In many songs flooding the airwaves, the message was given that the answer was blowing in the wind, consciousness was changing, and the old ways were that of "Mr. Jones" who didn't understand and couldn't see. Enlightenment was to come with drugs, rejecting dialectics, and unification in "love."

The creativity and expressiveness of the Beatles seemed to be proof that the youth would know what this society could be, and the Beatles could lead.

Before "Revolver" was released there had been signs that the popularity of the Beatles was waning. The single "Paperback Writer" did not reach Number One, people in the Bible belt burned Beatles merchandise, and seats went unsold at some of their tours. However "Revolver" released in August of 1966 put them back on top, and had shown that they were "the evolving Beatles," as George Martin put it. By late 1966 they had the attention of a good portion of youth and adults worldwide almost desperate to know what they would do next.

That their popularity did wane just before "Revolver," however, shows that even though "Yesterday" achieved a synthesis, it was quickly understood and then consumed by the public.

In June 1966, there appeared another sign that the Beatles could not be pigeonholed. A compilation of their hits, titled punningly "Yesterday and Today," showed the group dressed in butcher smocks festooned with animal blood and pieces of baby dolls. The "butcher" cover, part of a triptych, was quickly pulled after protest, but whether or not this brief glimpse of the "edgy" Beatles was planned to be just that, and retracted on purpose, or that they seriously thought the public would buy it, the "gaffe" leaked the message that the Beatles had quit being "please"-men. I suggest that the photo triptych which included the Beatles connected by an umbilicus to a naked woman, her back to the camera, and George play-acting about to hammer nails into John's head,[11] illustrated transparently what I call their "concerns." The Beatles ostensibly wanted to (by meditation, at that point) "open the channel to enlightenment" which in some esoteric schools is thought to come in as white light through a channel through the top of the head. The umbilicus could also be viscera—that is, "evisceration of identity." Of course they showed these ideas in typical joking Beatles fashion, with plausible deniability.

The "Butcher" cover was quickly replaced. The photo and triptych hardly saw the light of day in the United States where the Beatles had maintained a cleaner image from the beginning. The "gaffe" did build anticipation for "Revolver"—where would the Beatles take listeners next?

For the cover of "Sgt. Pepper's Lonely Hearts Club Band," released in the U.S. on June 1st, 1967, the Beatles, dressed in colorful band uniforms, stood beside Beatles wax figures. There was a large group of figures out of history propped up in back of them, with a floral arrangement in the foreground. It resembled nothing so much as a funeral, although the Beatles made no statements about its meaning. (Paul later said it was inspired by "floral clocks" in parks in England.)[12]

The Cover, Hypnosis and Suggestion

Dr. Asher was a hypnotist, practicing at the time Paul lived with him. Dr. Asher wrote an article for *Lancet*, "Respectable Hypnosis," about hypnotherapy for ailments such as hair loss. He seems to have been successful in treating people with this method. Hypnosis was featured content at the Macy Foundation-hosted *Cerebral Inhibition Meeting* in 1942. (Again, this is the topic of what are you *inhibited from* seeing.) At that meeting, Milton Erickson introduced the topic of hypnotism. Erickson, born in 1901, was a hypnotist, psychologist and psychiatrist, and the founder of the American Society for Clinical Hypnosis. While working in military psychology during WWII, he formed a lifelong association with Gregory Bateson and Margaret Mead. Books about Erickson's methods include *Uncommon Therapy* and *My Voice Will Go With You*. Descriptions of his methods of hypnotic suggestion are found online, but there is not space to discuss them here.

Gardner Murphy, head of the Menninger Clinic Foundation, was also interested in hypnosis along with the paranormal, as was Harvard-linked psychologist William James, as we have mentioned. Murphy wrote the forward to Sidney Cohen's *The Beyond Within*, and worked with Thelma Moss, who published her account of LSD psychotherapy, *Myself And I*, under a penname. Later while in Los Angeles Moss also supposedly scientifically verified that the famous "spoon-bending" charlatan, Uri Geller, was able to affect measuring instruments with his thoughts.

At the 1959 Macy Conference on LSD-25 there were several discussions of using LSD with hypnosis, and how LSD increased suggestibility in patients. Doctors related that they were administering LSD frequently with hypnosis. Some researchers observed that the subjects were unable to be hypnotized using the usual methods during the LSD session, but that during it they were "exquisitely" suggestible; which is in essence the same thing. That is, messages could be given that would go readily into the subconscious mind. This area of psychological investigation, suggestion and hypnosis, also could be somewhat analogous to the Beatles putting an asylum subtext into their songs, and psychological motifs into their lyrics in order to bring about changes in societal *mores*. This could have been what John meant by "sticking bits in." In any event the Beatles, or at least Paul, were likely aware of hypnosis and suggestion being researched in psychology, since he lived with a hypnotist. To what extent the Beatles *planned* on changing the lifestyles and habits of Western youth, I leave the reader to decide. John implied that they did ("We knew what we were doing"), but my task in this book is to track their *artistic* process, and Paul's "way" of successfully writing songs, which was their primary activity. To a certain extent, all art contains suggestion.

However, one thing I noticed, subliminally, about the "Pepper" cover proves to me that the Beatles were probably aware of subliminal suggestion. I glanced one night at the Beatles' bright uniforms on the front of the "Pepper" album and a word popped out at me: Love. I was surprised, having never "seen" this before. I invite the reader to see it (or rather the suggestion of it) for themselves. George's trim has the E, Paul the V, Ringo's trim suggests an O, and John, holding the horn, hints at the L. There is also another word on the back cover, which features Paul's back turned to the viewer. This word was even more of a surprise. I chalk this rather shocking word up to the Beatles' sense of humor and their having fun with the idea of subliminal suggestion. Subliminal imagery became the subject of books on advertising, a little later on. George's uniform showing an "E" on both the front and back covers, and the "V" of Paul's back-of-uniform trim on the back cover are the easiest letters to "see."[13]

* * *

The core of the matter, as always, was the feelings which the Beatles and their music produced. On the cover, Paul wore a neutral expression while the other three looked solemnly, even stonily, at the camera. Inside, the four were all smiles and affectionate gazes toward the viewer. Here was the prize, for looking inside: love. Their bright satin uniforms did indicate, if taken only on a consumer-message level, a new and improved Beatles. However they also bore insignia of the "counterculture": a badge that looked like a colorful hand-painted block of wood, and a daisy on one epaulet. Could the "funeral" that the dead-looking cardboard figures seemed to be attending be of the old self, and the record buyer invited to the death of the old (Beatle)-self for the birth of the new (Beatle)-self?

Without allusions to history on its cover, "Pepper" might have been accused of being an opportunistic soundtrack for the upcoming Summer of Love. Which, it was; but the cover lent the music an historic dimension and also a sense of hidden significance. It might have been the first album cover to hint at occult meanings.

Paul's idea was to frame the entire album as a performance by another band. "I got this idea," he told the other Beatles. "Let's not be ourselves. We could say, 'how would somebody else sing this?'"[14] The concept reflected his earlier concern with acting, and also, splits: the Beatles would act as the band of Sgt. Pepper, who "taught the band to play." Such an artistic device also provided insurance for any artistic gaffes, and gave them more freedom to play with sounds. But it also fit with his ongoing IFP.

Paul was expanding into "the interval" his IFP had created with confidence—a sure hand and ear. He reportedly made decisions on every aspect of production, and played the album's most startling guitar solos. He also demonstrated or told Ringo on occasion how he wanted the drums played. Making an album at this point became "Paul's project," John commented later; "He would go off and write ten songs, and then come to me and say we need a few more. He would get a concept ... then I would write songs ... it was like a job."[15] But John was more than able to write-to-order for the IFP. The 1967 permutation was the "trip" of "Pepper." The album has a persistent sunny attitude that was the sunshine-synthesis of the fractured kaleidoscope. Certainly if anybody other than Paul had produced it, it would have sounded much different. The fanciful, vaudevillian whimsy of the overall effort was Paul's. The album *was* Paul.

* * *

The first track set up the acting conceit of the album. "**Sgt. Pepper's Lonely Hearts Club Band**" comes in with a burst of rock, chorused harmonies, and a laughing, canned audience. Clearly, fun is in store with a dose of humor, and the Beatles sound exactly like they always have. Nobody will be left out in the cold: "You're such a lovely audience/We'd like to take you home with us/We'd love to take you home." The Master of Ceremonies (Paul) breaks in to announce: "The singer's going to sing a song/And he wants you all to sing along." The Beatles are using no "different" voices to be "Sgt. Pepper's band." Sheila Whiteley in *The Space Between the Notes: Rock and the Counterculture* called the opening song effective because even though the group is saying they aren't the Beatles, the listener is reassured that he or she is in the hands of the same Beatles.[16]

Then Ringo delivers his vision of the helping, even therapeutic community, in track two. The confiding character in a typical Beatles' song is back again; but he is in a better place on "**With a Little Help From My Friends.**" Ringo, as "Billy Shears," self-questions while the prompting voices of Paul and John fill in the descriptive gaps. It is as if we are listening in on "Billy's" mind. We hear his inner feelings. But, "Billy" is not sad to be on his own. "No, I get by with a little help from my friends," he declares. The other Beatles join him on the refrain—"a little help, from my friends." This sing-along ditty impresses the listener that now, a sole soul—a person who has lots of feelings, and is vulnerable (this was the template for the Beatle fan which their songs had assumed or set up) can be given "help." Support can come not from just one person, as was implied by John in "Help!", but from many people. Billy can try, get by, and get high with a little help from his friends. It was a reassuring opener to a "show" that started off as patently fake, with a canned audience. Billy's friends (the Beatles) are right there reassuring everyone. They are (all four of them) the "comforting man" of the LSD psychotherapy session.

David Pichaske (in his book, *A Generation in Motion*) wrote that "Friends" was "a very important song in the story of Sgt. Pepper and his band." "Friends" was more meaningful than "Yellow Submarine" in that it could not be taken for a children's or novelty song: it is sung "straight out" (except for the artifice of Ringo being "Billy Shears"). Pichaske wrote that the song introduced the notion of community support as part of the new awareness. Paul wrote it, I suggest, using an IFP subtext. The song, with its question-and-answer, resembles a therapy session. "Billy" questions his own feelings. John and Paul, like therapists, are prompting him to reply. They are probing, expanding on his feelings: "Does it worry you to be alone?" "Are you sad because you're on your own?"

Feelings, and lessons about loneliness, were of course found in many a popular song: "Laugh, Laugh" by the Beau Brummels, for example. But loneliness had never been explored this way before in this format. "Billy" is split, questioning himself. After the session, the chorus comes in affirming that friends help "Billy," and by extension the listener, with loneliness and feelings. Existential problem solved.

Communes were in the news by 1967, and Paul could have simply written the song with communes in mind; but there are also many precedents for community awareness in the psychiatric literature. It seems that Paul was never far away from a good shelf of psychiatric literature to inspire him to structure a song. Psychologist and

M.D. Morris Carstairs gave several lectures for the BBC in 1962 which were published two years later by Penguin Books (after first being published by Hogarth Press) as part of the Reith Lectures series.[17] Carstairs posited that a person's personality could be figured out through group activities. In this assertion Carstairs was aligned with other psychiatrists such as Gardner Murphy, co-head of the Menninger clinic. Murphy, putting his ideas in practice in various structured activities for mental patients at the clinic, favored less individuality because he believed individuality fostered a competitive attitude. The psychologist Maxwell Jones, so-called father of group therapy, took these ideas in a different direction, publishing a book which would inform Paul's lyrics on a later song on "Let It Be."

The idea of community support comes very early on in "Pepper." The "lonely hearted" are reassured with the first song after the opener. The song states that problems of self-definition and feeling alone are solved by being in a group of friends. Coming after the introduction's "fake" (canned) group of people applauding and laughing, along with the fact that "Billy Shears" sounds exactly like Ringo—*is* Ringo—the disarming effect of "Friends" is to convince the skeptical that there may be something to "Billy's" statement.

The psychological subtext to the song made it distinctive. If Ringo had sung, "When I'm alone/Want to pick up the phone," that would have been banal in the extreme. Instead, Billy is asking himself internal questions, and they are being expanded upon—as if by helpful therapists. The therapy subtext in "Friends" framed the idea of a community where people would explore newfound feelings and identities, would be heard, included in a group and looked after ("helped"). This is the therapy subtext, extended to a group therapy setting. People with "friends," it was implied, would no longer feel empty or lonely-hearted. A therapeutic community would form. This was an ideal of communes which was being tried out across the U.S., but especially on the West Coast, as overseen by Portola Institute. In theory, at the very least a respite from normal reality would be found in the commune. Drugs would (usually) be available. Sex may also be had with no strings attached. Work will be shared; creativity will flower, and "different" behavior will be accepted, even encouraged. All this was prognosticated to come into being and grow. And it was growing day by day under the artistic auspices and guidance of trusted stablemates, the Beatles.

The therapy subtext was artfully hidden, but this "help" from "friends" was sounding better than your parent's therapy. This was not a stay in a loony bin, then a return to the harsh world of society, where "rainclouds hide the moon" and "birds sing out of tune" (as in "A World Without Love"). That had been the only available option for the listener's parents, careworn individuals with burdens on their shoulders. Now, "therapy" (as presented in subtext) could be found in the new society, not sought "outside" it. An isolated, frustrated life was in theory a thing of the past, according to pundits of the Sixties, Leary among them, and stemmed from a limited and confining sense of ego. Ego had put prior generations in a rut. Now was a new time, a new era, to lose your "ego" and see how many options were available. Then everyone could help each other and expand (like the Beatles seemed to be doing) into new consciousness possibilities.

"We were all on this ship in the Sixties, our generation—a ship going to discover the new world. And the Beatles were in the crow's nest of that ship," recalled John, in 1974. This whole scenario was thought feasible due to Paul's praxis and creation of "the interval."

In 1966, Timothy Leary was putting on multimedia shows with lights, music and his own voice to simulate the LSD experience for audiences along the East Coast.[18] He was assisted by his partner at the time, Rosemary Woodruff. The intent was to pile on enough stimuli to produce an altered consciousness, and then guide audiences through it. The multimedia shows were also a bit of a social experiment, which Leary was interested in doing. He and Woodruff were in effect offering a guided visualization for people who found it hard to visualize, and also were less likely to take the drug. Also this was a legal way to publicize LSD—by simulating its effects. Leary and other writers were touting loss of the ego or "ego-death" as a path to individual freedom of thought, a new dawn of shared community, or both.

LSD was made illegal in October of 1966. Accordingly by early 1967 many clubs were incorporating light shows, projections and other audio-visual stimuli to get their audiences "out there." Clubs featured flashing strobe lights, multiple audio-visual stimulations and de-stabilizing drugs available from the house drug dealer. What had been in the hands of military researchers a means to de-stabilize, demoralize and de-program people was now being charged admission to. The hoped-for transcendence was not usually found in such venues, but one could go home and read about what one had just experienced.

* * *

To return to "Pepper": After "Friends" comes "**Lucy in the Sky with Diamonds**." Spectral keyboard announces the beginning of a guided visualization, sung by John. The listener, having "sit back" to "let the evening go," or perhaps lit up a joint, can be led into envisioning another reality, with John as guide. The shimmering keyboard sound is to depict the "enhanced" reality the listener is supposedly being transported to. Like a therapist doing a guided visualization on a patient lying on the couch, John intones, "Picture yourself in a boat on a river, with tangerine trees and marmalade skies."

He doesn't sing, "Let's all go out on a boat on a river." He uses the phrase "*picture* yourself." Just that choice of words makes a difference. It asks you to picture the scene – go somewhere. It works because ideas and phrases used in therapy work.

It was also important that some of the scene visualized be edible. It makes it more enticing, and some might be reminded of the children's board game of Candy Land (a perennial favorite, released in 1949, Candy Land is a "simple board racing game ... with no strategy involved; players are never required to make choices, just follow directions" according to Wikipedia). The song depicts a colorful landscape that promises no terrors (or decision-making). "Cellophane flowers of yellow and green/Towering over your head." Although the singer is telling the listener to "look for the girl/With the sun in her eyes," she is never identified explicitly as Lucy. I think this was carefully done to make the seeker's relation to Lucy ambiguous. The girl, although sought-after, is only described by her eyes. Based on her eyes and her constant movement, she is a representation of fractured being. She has kaleidoscope eyes; a kaleidoscope is defined as shifting parts constantly changing, having no one color or image. The entire spectrum of color, the sun, is in her eyes. But she is "gone" wherever you look for her.

The chorus is in a major key, following the shifting-key verse. It lets loose of all tension, into a major key, when Lucy is envisioned. She is "loose," free up in the sky, above flowers grown "high." She is up high with "diamonds." It is interesting that she is not in a sunlit sky, or a night sky with stars. She floats among glitter and false stars. It is as if the light in her eye was deracinated, shattered, and surrounds her. Her many-lensed eyes burst their confines into glittering prisms of light. Become a rainbowscopic prism herself, her eye has evolved. See a discussion of the Beatles use of the "eye" motif in Chapter Six.

I know "Lucy in the Sky With Diamonds" which can be abbreviated as L.S.D., is "supposed" to be about a child's drawing; John said that his son Julian brought home a drawing he had done and titled as such. Perhaps that event did happen; but whether or not, John certainly extended in the lyrics the symbolization of the IFP, along with providing a soundtrack or visualization for the hallucinogenic drug culture. The inner eye of the listener is set "loose" with this new way to see. (That is exactly what psychological visualization does.) John (or whatever "Pepper" persona he "picked") also provides a symbolization of, in his description of "Lucy," the new "type." This can be regarded as simply a marketing tactic. A new "type" typically helps launch a "new" product. Describing Lucy's "kaleidoscope eyes" is akin to declaring, "Be the girl with the curls" to sell permanent wave treatment, or "He would rather fight than switch" to sell cigarettes to manly men. "Lucy," floating high, is someone to desire and emulate, or "follow." However, one cannot ignore the fact that researchers at SRI and Harvard were interested in creating a new "type" of personality.

As a side note I also suggest that the lyric "rocking horse people" could have been John's way of labeling the pedophiles he was probably coming in contact with in the London scene. John would often label people as the "x"- people, the G-men and so on, by way of classifying people. The "rocking-horse people" eat "marshmallow pies." John is singing a children's song about a girl who could be an Alice in Wonderland (John said to one interviewer he was thinking of this story, by one of his favorite authors), so his Alice wanders among pedophiles. "Newspaper taxis," I suggest, refer to the situation John often found himself in, spacing out or going into a trance while reading the newspaper or watching the "telly." Viewing the random parade of daily events on the screen, perhaps not too clearly with his poor vision and after a while losing interest, John would wander into associative thinking, making odd connections and puns out of what he was seeing. The trance state he went into when looking at media such as newspapers took him "away," like a taxi might, so he coined the phrase "newspaper *taxis*." He climbs "in" to media, with his head in the clouds (possibly, high on pot) and then he is "gone," like "Lucy." Both he and this new "type" are childlike, and "gone." Both he and "Lucy"/Alice have been taken somewhere else, put way up high, and are "gone."

With the visualization comes the invitation that the listener too can be taken away—be "gone" like Lucy and the narrator (John as Pepper band member). Lucy, mute, is not a figure in therapy or sometimes breaking into schizophrenese, like Paul's characters. But, she exists in the interval of identity fracture. Existing without existing, that is, a fantasy creature, she is a kaleidoscope of fractured reflections and constantly shifting views. Lucy is there and not there. Because John, a famous rock star, is singing about such a person, she is given the stamp of approval for aspiration for the female fans and male fans; her "type" (if it can be called such, being no-one) is the new "fantasy chick." However she is a de-personalized "type" and this is the same thing that happens on LSD: de-personalization.

The show has just begun, and things are getting better, but they also can't get much worse. "**Getting Better**" continues the hidden subtext of the IFP. The song is different than "Lucy" because it comes from the standpoint of being grounded in the ordinary; however it is also framed by a therapy subtext. "I used to get mad at my school/The teachers that taught me weren't cool." But now, the singer relates that "it's getting better," to the sounds of stylized mallets hitting anvils (bright, happy-sounding anvils), as on a construction site. Paul picked this sound as appropriate for the rhythm track; it was achieved by George Martin striking piano strings with a mallet. Paul, according to Hunter Davies, worked for quite a while to find the right sound for the backing rhythm. He wanted a certain sound that he wasn't getting. Martin's idea made for a bright percussive sound of hammers as if on a (mental) construction site. Paul decided it would do.[19] Ringo didn't need to be called in, after all.

The singer relates that he is "getting better, since you've been mine." Paul puts specific chords and allusions to sentiment in, again, to clarify this is a song about romantic relationship, not just about an asocial person reforming (or even a person taking drugs to "better" his outlook). The song doesn't use phrases from therapy or psychology as clearly as do other songs of his, but it is about a rehabilitation.

"Getting Better" is followed by "**Fixing a Hole**," to continue the construction analogy. The singer is "fixing a hole, where the rain gets in," and "filling the cracks, that ran through the door." It is word-play: Cracks are running, anthropomorphized. A hole can be fixed by a junkie with a needle, a man driving a nail with a hammer, or alternatively a "hole" can be filled with a "fix." A person can be both "whole," filled, and an empty "hole." This is Paul playing around with words, but more confidently; recall the lipless kisser (which I might have overreached to see) in "All My Loving." The song comes alive, though, (Robert Lowell in his poetry seminars would jab his finger down on a poem lying on the table and say, "the poem comes to life *here*") with the phrase "and it really doesn't matter if I'm wrong I'm right/Where I belong I'm right/Where I belong." Here again is the voice of the mental patient, trying to get a statement out about his version of reality. It is the kind of poetical, a bit nonsensical phrase but with *emotional* content and a ring of truth that people would listen for and want to hear in Beatles songs. These phrases are distinctive because they were formed out of the depths of people's experience of their own mental instability and sometimes encapsulated their worldview. The phrases were picked out and used by Paul in songs, I am asserting. They could be put in almost any music genre format. But they are bits of the *real* that make the songs stand out. It is also possible Paul simply wrote in a disjointed, slightly nonsensical way; either way, the effect is the same: of encountering a character speaking "illogical logic." The song during the phrase starts to build in intensity, then: "See the people standing there/Who disagree and never win/And wonder why they don't get in my door." This is the idea of the asylum in "A World Without Love," but now the singer is decorating his "inside." In "Fixing a Hole" the asylum can also be interpreted to mean one's head, while high. He will paint his mind-room "in a colorful way, and when my mind is wandering, there I will go." He will be someone else: he will be no one at all, his thoughts a variety of "colors." He will be like Lucy, wandering through colors, floating high, and neither here nor there, but everywhere.

The people outside his door are like the world of "normals" living outside Laing's Kingsley Hall who "don't understand." The singer is content fixing a room where right or wrong don't matter or apply anymore. Hence, using the subtext of asylum, rehabilitation through therapy, and a phrase I suggest taken from a patient transcript, Paul wrote "Fixing a Hole" and gave it an Aesopian drug subtext. The "room" is akin to the Yellow Submarine clubhouse, the asylum of Penny Lane, and the shelter of the Octopus's Garden. It doesn't have the emotional force of a song like "Yesterday," but "Fixing a Hole" tells a story consistent with what people subliminally expect from the Beatles.

Both "Getting Better" and "Fixing a Hole" contain construction analogies. "Getting Better" has the mallet or hammer-like backing

rhythm, and "Fixing a Hole" talks of patching up a room and repaint-
ing it, "in a colourful way." At the time, LSD psychotherapy was
sometimes described in the literature using construction analogies:
reparative and reconstructive. Regression therapy was also called
"reparative therapy." At the Macy Conference, Dr. Malitz stated that
reparative, or restorative psychotherapy was akin to patching up a
house – working with what's there – and reconstructive therapy was
to tear down and rebuild.[20] Paul also threw in a junkie association
with the "fixing a hole," which a needle does.

Paul did an interesting harmonic on the fade-out of "Fixing a
Hole," which is the best part musically of the song, as if the singer
were already starting to go somewhere else in his mind out of the
ordinary.

So with the first songs, we have a community of friends and stablemates in The Beatles, therapists, a guided visualization, allusions
to reparative therapy, and revisit the asylum subtext in terms of an
asylum being a "room" inside one's head. There are also several allusions to drugs, namely pot, heroin and LSD.

In 1966, Paul and Jane left "home." They left the Asher residence,
Jane's childhood home and Paul's home for over three years, and
moved into the house Paul had bought in St. John's Wood. That Paul
would not admit to **"She's Leaving Home"** having an emotional
inspiration is typical of the Beatles wanting the fans to be "with
them," and not think the songs had a personal genesis. But, it is
reasonable to infer that it is about a real event. He had learned a lot
at the Asher's, become himself, actually. And Jane had grown from a
girl to a woman. Now, it was time for both of them to leave. It was a
big moment and Paul's music and words capture the cloistered, caring
nature of the parents, the details of the staircase banister, the dressing
gown, and the handkerchief held in the mother's hand. The song
evokes the homey, careful and loving surrounds of cautious people.
One is immediately drawn into this world. It is Paul's gift to tell us a
story with such economy that we picture so well. The "chorus," if one
could call it that, is more a passage, lifting the listener into heights of

emotion. And yet–the song has a lot of "and yet" in it. "She" is once again set loose, but maybe too loose. Up in the sky, like Lucy, she is floating higher and higher on that vocal line, like a balloon about to be lost from view. Meanwhile John intones the uncomprehending parents' "what did we do that was wrong/We didn't know it was wrong." The music leads up to the "point" of her escape, as it builds in intensity: "She ... is having ... fun." For this listener, that she left home to have "fun" is an anticlimax. That the young woman should want simply "fun," because "fun is the one thing that money can't buy," in a way negates all the emotion and self-chastisement of the parents that seemed real. The expected thing would have been to say *love* is the one thing that money can't buy. But John, as the "parents," sings, "Fun is the one thing that money can't buy," as if the parents themselves are muddled. Of course fun can be bought, and is every day. We were told in an early song by the Beatles, "can't buy me love," but now the girl is leaving love to have "fun," which can't be bought. This is a bit confusing. At any rate, she left it all behind, leaving a scribbled note.

One could question whether Paul and John were playing with the idea of a "TV-movie of the week" dramatization. John's voice on "bye-bye" sounds almost mocking. (Whiteley writes that John is mockingly singing "*buy, buy*.")[21] I don't want to think the song is snarky, because of the beautiful music. Both Paul and John Phillips booked Monterey Pop, which was coming up; Phillips had written songs about leaving home to go to California; so maybe this was Paul's contribution to the "runaway" theme.

A kite, also, flies high. And so the "high" theme continues, in **"Being For The Benefit of Mr. Kite!"** John could write associatively with the best of them: but the lyrics to this, one of his most imagistic songs, he took from a vintage poster he came across advertising a performance of a "Mr. Kite." The song is fantasy, but its quaint language fit with the vintage fashion of the time, young men dressing as dandies and women wearing long Victorian dresses. Stores such as Granny Takes a Trip in London sold vintage clothing to combine in inventive ways. The "High Hippie" look mixed scarves, beads, lace dresses, military jackets, boas and button-hooked boots. So, "Kite," with vintage sounds of the pipe organ and calliope, is definitely "for the benefit of" and perfect to accompany such polyglot dress-up fantasies.

The song is among the shortest on the album, 2:37, but packs a lot of atmosphere into its length. One could call it a carnival in sound, or a simulation of being "high as a kite" on pot. John used to complain that Bob Dylan used "artsy-fartsy" language in his songs, including carnival metaphors. "I thought, well, I can write this crap too," John later told an interviewer.[22] In "Kite," John went Dylan one better, creating a somatic experience of a carnival. ("What I want is some kind of swirly music," John told George Martin.[23])

Next is George's contribution, **"Within You Without You,"** the lecture portion of the album. "You are really only very small," he intones, and "the time will come when you see we're all one." This is another song about inner versus outer. George's conclusion is that it's all the same. The idea of the song is to guide identity (Western identity) loss toward Vedic mysteries and Hinduism. The song provided teaching to listeners—if one is feeling deracinated, well, look at what the Hindu mystics have to say about it. They don't think a self, or an Ego, is needed at all! So don't worry—you're right to feel "only really very small." One of the longest songs on the album at five minutes, this was the only song that made an unambiguous statement, except for the last line of "A Day In The Life."

Paul wrote **"When I'm Sixty-Four"** when he was a teenager, and it doesn't have any of the IFP hallmarks. It is an endearing song, on the surface, but compared to getting high, getting fractured, or being "gone," this swingy ditty of domestic lockstep seems to sink back into the couch while psychedelicized hippies run past it toward freedom. A life of marrying, working, saving, having children, then grandchildren, managing a holiday to the seaside if you can afford it, is made to sound quaint, limited and old-fashioned. However, it is a jaunty ditty, complemented by the droll clarinet.

"**Lovely Rita**" comes in with a bash of psychedelic sound. MacDonald wrote that Rita started out as a "hate figure," because in dishing out tickets and wearing a cap and uniform, she was an authoritarian. Paul initially planned that she would meet a bad end, but decided "it'd be better to love her."[24]

Paul started off writing this song, I intuit, based on nursery rhyme wordplay. Rita exists only in a singsong reality, her name being a variation of the "Peter Piper picked a peck of pickled peppers" rhythm. Rita, meet her, meet a maid. Rita-meter, meet her, made. "Made" is sexual slang. Also, Rita could be implied to be "meter-made." That is, her personality is a creation of the Beatles' music (which she is anyway). The very personality of people can (and was being formed, at that point in the Sixties) be shaped by their tastes in music. Thus, they are "made" by "meters."

The singer sings, "When it gets dark, I tow your heart away." What could this car-towing, dead-battery-alluding "pun" mean? He relates that he "nearly made it" with Rita and some "sisters" sitting on the sofa. Thus, for all the "wow" of meeting her, implied by the intro and the beautiful chorus harmonies, "Rita" was like Lucy, a figure of many aspects and yet nothing; the song is about a date that nearly turned into group sex. However, after the final chorus, the panting and groaning sounds in the extended coda imply that "making" it perhaps did happen after all.

At the end of the song someone is heard saying, "Leave it!" as a piano cascades down a scale. So it seems that "meet-a-Rita" was made, and then left, as an empty "it." (Peter "Pecker" picked a peck of pickled (drunk or high) "Peppers," so to speak, on "Pepper.") I intuit Paul was also thinking of the "Peter Piper" nursery rhyme also in context of writing "Fool on the Hill," which he penned at the same time, because it is Peter *Piper* who picks a peck, et cetera. The "Fool on the Hill" is a Pied Piper leading children away. This could be a stretch—but nursery rhymes were never too far from John and Paul's minds for sources of inspiration.

Paul had been quite connected to the London art and publishing scenes (both large, and large masquerading as small). He had been installed over the eggs of the literary scene—the books sitting in the Asher basement headed for the Indica Bookstore and Gallery. Now the eggs were hatched, and the chickens coming home to roost.

Portions of the music industry were preparing for Monterey Pop, in summer of 1967. In early 1967, on one leg of a tour, the Beatles stayed briefly in Los Angeles and hung out with members of The Mamas and The Papas to discuss the upcoming festival. Paul had recommended several acts for Monterey Pop, and John said they also took acid "at Doris Day's house, or wherever it was," during this visit, indicating they were with Terry Melcher, Day's son.[25] The release of "Pepper" was timed to be just at the beginning of the highly publicized "Summer of Love" and before Monterey Pop. The Beatles' music was integral to the anticipation surrounding this event, although they did not play at it, and neither would the Beach Boys. "Pepper" would be the sublime set-up for the event. The point to "Pepper," with its therapeutic subtext alongside emptiness (in Lucy, "She's Leaving Home," Lovely Rita, and George's lecture about porosity) would be, "I'd love to turn you on."

* * *

R.D. Laing, whose ideas the Beatles admired and I suggest put into practice in their songs, became during this time good friends with Timothy Leary. Leary, middle-aged in the mid-Sixties, had such strong media connections that he could stand on stage and utter "Turn on, Tune In and Drop Out," and it would be relayed around the world. Ginsberg, who stood on the "Human Be-In" stage with Leary, was friends with Paul and also connected to "baby Beats" such as Kesey at SRI, and also to Ferlinghetti and Stewart Brand. Ginsberg, Kesey, Leary and Ferlinghetti were all at the Human Be-in at Golden Gate Park in San Francisco, probably with many "researchers" in attendance. The photogenic Leary, a flower tucked behind his ear, repeated Marshall McLuhan's idea for a slogan, and became the poster-man or guru of LSD. Leary would see the inside of forty jail cells over four continents, such was his power to influence. In

1968, when Leary ran for governor of California, Richard Nixon called him "the most dangerous man in America." Lines from Leary's adaptation of the Tibetan Bardo for the Dead inspired John to write "Tomorrow Never Knows." It is worth discussing Leary's background briefly because of his influence on the Beatles, youth, and his high visibility as the "acid guru."

In 1963, Timothy Leary was asked to leave his lecturing post at Harvard. Prior to this, Leary had been chief of Clinical Psychology at Kaiser Permanente Hospital, Oakland, California. The suicide of his wife had precipitated a change of life for Leary at age forty.

Not only his wife's suicide, by carbon monoxide gas in her car, but his sense of overwhelming ordinariness spurred him to change his life. When he took his first mushroom "trip," he was overwhelmed by the sense that he was "just like millions of other middle-class liberals, with a two-car garage and home in the suburbs, and a commute."[26] As a young man enrolled at West Point military academy he had written to his mother that he wanted to be known for some grand achievement. Leary later took a doctorate in Psychology, and formulated a personality assessment questionnaire that became standard in the profession.

In 1960, Leary was living in Italy with his two children when he was asked to work as a clinician at Harvard. At Harvard, Leary was mentored by Harvard Psychology Clinic head Harry Murray, who had been doing personality research and collating psychological types since the late Twenties. Murray had in the early Sixties conducted tests on student volunteers to "de-program them" of beliefs they held (the young mathematician Ted Kaczynski, later to become the Unabomber, was one of Murray's test subjects). As we have mentioned, one of his methods was to record the subject's responses to questions about their beliefs and core opinions on film, then play them back later for the subject to view themselves responding. Recording and then playing back responses to the interviewees is identical to Burroughs's idea of using feedback as way to "hack" society's "Control."

Leary has described his "Good Friday" LSD experiments on students as benign. But he knew as well as anyone the deracinating
properties of LSD. Hence I suggest Leary was not giving LSD to
students to as he put it, "turn them into Buddhas." His research was
straddling the ethical line between cracking open the mind to study
what constituted personality and sense of self, and giving people a
drug to "open their minds."

In any event it is likely that these experiments were MK-Ultra
funded research. Similar to Savage's work, he was researching the
shattering of beliefs; or how they could be shattered. Leary administered LSD to prison populations and led studies to treat alcoholism
with LSD. After administering the drug to students, Leary was asked
to leave. Supported by siblings in the wealthy Hitchcock family, he
lived on their Millbrook estate in upstate New York,[27] publishing
Psychedelic Prayers in 1966 and *The Psychedelic Experience* with Allen
Ginsberg. Leary's idea, according to SRI director Willis Harman,
was to "give LSD to every teenager and change the world."[28]

Leary in 1967 opined that "listening to a Beatles album is half
an hour of de-programming." As a colleague of Murray's Leary
would have known exactly what de-programming entailed in terms
of psychological research. And, it is odd that that Burroughs, who
was sharing a recording studio with Paul, had the same interests and
approach as Leary used. They were working toward the same goal from
opposite directions. Of course, Burroughs and the Beats wanted to
"de-program" people—as did Leary. This begs the question—was anyone
"working" on de-programming or programming Paul? But here the
terms get fuzzy. Could it just be a matter of influence and inclination?

Leary's record, "You Can Be Anything This Time Around" was
produced by a socio-research entity linked to Harvard, Intermedia
Systems Corporation. For this recording, which featured early sampling technology, Leary also enlisted the help of musicians Jimi
Hendrix, Stephen Stills, John Sebastian and Buddy Miles.[29]

A major rock and roll producer, Paul A. Rothchild, also had
ties to Harvard and specifically the music recording archives of the

Woodberry Poetry Room. Rothchild worked with an audio engineer Stephen Fassett on recording Harvard Square protest folk singers who were just emerging.[30]

The Poetry Room was apparently an incubator of talent. Its audio library was a magnet for "folkies" such as Joan Baez, because vintage music at the archive could be mined for new songwriting inspiration. "Digging up and sharing old folk songs was an essential part of the Cambridge (in Massachusetts, where Harvard is located) scene. The more obscure the song, the better,"[31] singer Eric Von Schmidt related. Old music could be re-worked into new songs and protest anthems, in much the same way folk musicians found inspiration in the archives at the New York City public library. The budding folksingers were recorded by Fassett and Rothchild at Fassett's studio near campus, and encouraged to perform.

Rothchild, after working with Fassett, went to Los Angeles in 1964, where he would produce five out of the six Doors albums. He recorded the first demo for Crosby, Stills, Nash and Young, and worked with several other famous Sixties acts.

Sylvia Plath and Ted Hughes were both recorded by Fassett, and kept up correspondence with him after they left Boston for London. They were also in correspondence with John Sweeney, curator of the Poetry Room.[32] Sweeney was left-leaning, as was Fassett, and referred to Plath and Hughes as "a great couple of young ones."[33]

It is interesting that Harvard-connected people had such a reach—with Leary, Alpert, T.S. Eliot's family, psychologists, toward nurturing Confessional and Beat poets, into recording studios, producing successful Sixties acts (Rothchild's work), and connections to SRI (Stolaroff). And there is also a connection to Paul through Margaret Asher, as a member of one branch of the Eliot family.

I also note that the tendency to use or adapt pre-existing "texts" (or music) seems to have been in the air at the time. According to Carol Brightman, a Grateful Dead biographer, "Jerry Garcia's fondness for old-time music" grew in the early Sixties as he collected and learned songs from field recordings made by Francis James Child and Alan Lomax. These recordings, "along with folk music from the Riverside, Vanguard, and Tradition labels, offered young musicians like Garcia, Dylan, Phil Ochs and Joan Baez a range of voices ... that were dazzling in their variety."[34] Although arguably getting her career start at Harvard, Joan Baez had gone to Palo Alto High with Garcia. (Francis James Child, incidentally, was good friends with Charles Eliot Norton at Harvard, and married into the Sedgwick family of model Edie Sedgwick.)

However, I submit that Paul had an artistic and personal resonance with the subtext he would use, from before he met the Ashers. "A World Without Love" already had the asylum metaphor in it that would be used to such effectiveness in later Beatles songs. Paul had been influenced by his schooling, his drama teacher, and John; he had been swimming in so-called alternative thought and influences for several years. I feel that no one individual or group of people "converted" him to write as he did. At the Asher's, Paul found a way to write the songs that resonated with him. He was able to put alternative ideas into song, through his personal, private praxis. He wrote this way because it sold, but also for I suggest personal reasons explained in Chapter Six.

From "Revolver" onward the Beatles albums would be almost entirely *about* the IFP. The albums would be taken to be Bibles for a new personality type. The same subtext of mental asylums, mental patients, the language of therapy, and so on would be used.

* * *

Paul worked with Derek Taylor, the Beatles' publicist (at that time working for the Beach Boys) and John Phillips of The Mamas and The Papas selecting acts for the upcoming Monterey Pop Festival. It was their shared vision: a festival "that would give rock and roll the same prestige as jazz," was how Paul put it. But there was more to it than musical prestige. Monterey Pop would be a much larger version of the Trips festivals and "acid test" concerts. It would be the first large-scale outdoor rock festival. Several acts that had played at the Trips events would perform, including the Grateful Dead. The January "Be-in," "acid tests" and exponential growth of the drug distribution underground meant that a way of *thinking about* the upcoming Summer of Love was being established. The way to think about LSD was greatly helped along by Leary's promotion of it, and by John's song "Tomorrow Never Knows." To continue the momentum, Monterey Pop would be a landmark event of the new "counterculture." Thousands of hits of LSD would be distributed to youth at the festival.

Timothy Leary must have been wringing his hands with glee at that point. "All across the nation," via print publicity and radio airplay, youth were aware of the upcoming festival and of LSD, even if they could no more find "counterculture" in their town than be handed a moon rock. About forty thousand youth made the trek to San Francisco, after organizer John Phillip's song, "San Francisco (Be Sure to Wear Flowers in Your Hair)" filled the airwaves. Leary's plan to "turn on every teenager and change the world" was moving closer to reality. In 1967 Paul financed a full-page ad in the *London Times* calling for the legalization of marijuana. Paul also heavily financed Barry Miles' (along with other contributors) *International Times*, or *IT*, that was akin to an *Oracle*-type paper for the "counterculture." *IT* was published in London. One of *IT*'s first articles was a long interview with Paul, talking about pot.

* * *

By 1967 youth were being led by the Beatles into both communal and drug-taking experiences. Paul, as prince of a diffuse movement, was confident in his role. In a world where people were supposed to lose their ego, Paul began to be accused of having a lot of it; this is ironic, because his very praxis meant that he had to fracture, somewhat, his own sense of identity.

If you imagine the two-profile or vase figure-ground illustration (a graphic beloved of psychologists), instead of there being a gap between the two "profiles," imagine the vase *filled*—filled with colorful possibilities—infinite perceptions of the expanded collective mind. This new "dialectic" was possible, supposedly, if you just killed your ego.

Contrast the Beatles' frequent allusions to "deadness," their meaninglessness-mongering on such songs as "Eleanor Rigby" with the stirring of emotions by presenting new "feelings," and it can be argued that the Beatles had been setting up a need for change into this new dream of self. Cynically, they would allude to this as filling holes-wholes.

Paul's interest in acting had led him to a refined understanding of when acting is identified as such: the precise point at which someone is perceived as not sincere, but a "good actor." Acting is in itself an interesting boundary-area. It is a kind of Gaza strip people can fight over endlessly, whether or not an actor is any good, whether they are acting, or just "being themselves."

I note here that personally, I hadn't thought much about acting when I was younger; I just accepted that some people were actors. But as I got older I began to see how weird the profession of acting is. People fall in love with actors—relate to them. They believe the actor is somehow distilling reality, even though the performance is patently false. In a way, how people react to acting is a kind of litmus test for what is consensus reality.

I think that Paul's immersion in an acting household might have given him an extra insight into the more subtle gradations of acting and how actors are perceived by audiences.

That most of "Pepper" was all an "act," allowed the album some plausible deniability, in that it could be taken as satire or simply as entertainment. The songs fit in the IFP framework of sounding vaguely like drugs, ego-loss, therapy, or any combination of those. The album would be both a key statement and colorful wallpaper for the "ostensive" culture. It would also present an engaging, mind-altering statement to the uninitiated.

* * *

I am aware that these are not sympathetic interpretations of Beatles songs. I am not alone, however, in suspecting something *louche* about Rita. Sheila Whiteley in *Between the Notes* accused Rita of being a whore, "who can simply be towed off for a session on the sofa."[35] I suggest that Rita is another empty character whom we have encountered in several Beatles songs by now. Yes, on one level it is a lighthearted song about meeting a girl, but she can also be seen as empty. Paul and the other Beatles (except for possibly Ringo) were thinking about, and enacting, before the psychedelic era and during, experiments on themselves in losing identity, losing sense of self, or what was called ego-loss. They were reading and studying about loss of the self, fracture of self (I suggest in patient transcripts), and practicing Transcendental Meditation. Given all this, why would they sing about "a cute girl who writes parking tickets"? There has to be something else in it, and I submit that most of the characters the Beatles present in songs are those who depict *loss* of identity. Their interests are well documented, and I am adding them to my careful reading of lyrics and my own theory that Paul had a drive to fracture his own identity. That is why he used the texts so effectively that he found at the Asher household.

In addition, although they were becoming open about their views on pot and Paul admitted taking LSD, the Beatles had fundamental "concerns" which were effectively hidden from the public. Their views were subversive; they were against the idea of what others would call "a normal life"; they saw inequities in almost a Cooperesque fashion. John explained it later, "I have this great fear of this normal thing."[36] Their own publicist called them "anti-Christ."[37] Paul commented later that the rock and roll philosophy is to "stand things on their head."[38] They were constantly "taking the piss out" of things and people: this was expressed all through their work, including their taste for nonsense verse and wordplay.

"Good Morning Good Morning" was John's take on the banal boredoms of everyday life. I quote Beatles biographer Mark Hertsgaard:

"Foreshadowing the themes of the album's approaching finale, "A Day In The Life," "Good Morning Good Morning" cast a jaundiced eye on the banalities and everyday tragedies of modern urban life. Its first line writes off an anonymous man at death's door with stunning casualness; the next recites the tired small talk that two acquaintances—or worse, friends—have exchanged for years. This is how we look, trudging numbly through the daily grind, implies Lennon, and one can almost hear him smirking during the refrain that he adapted from an insipid breakfast cereal commercial. And yet ... the raucous opening shouts of "good morning," the pumping brass, and especially the scorching guitar solo from McCartney simultaneously animate the song, with the constant, throbbing vitality of life... Anyway, it was ever thus, so there's no point in complaining: 'I've got nothing to say, but it's okay.'"[39]

"Good Morning Good Morning" took its title from an advertisement for Kellogg's Corn Flakes.[40] John did another visualization along the lines of "picture yourself," from the point of view of a jaded observer: "Everything is closed, it's like a ruin/Everyone you see is half asleep/And you're on your own, you're in the street." McCartney's psychotic or rather psycho-cathartic burst of guitar contrasts with the desultory scenes described. The implication is that underneath the façade, there is potential for emotion, passion, noise and tumult. "It's time for tea and meet the wife" ("Meet the Wife" being a sitcom of that era)[41] is followed by a squall of abandoned guitar. This would have been a "joke" effect to put in a song in the mid-Fifties, but in 1967 it could be taken as saying something seriously in context with the Beatles' other "message-giving" songs. The idea propounded in many a psychoanalytic text and also in "Good Morning Good Morning" is that society demands mundane exchanges when there could be so much *more*. There is a whole world "within," and the guitar solo blares this into the listener's awareness.

After a cavalcade of animal noises, the implication of which is that society is a barnyard, the **Reprise** of the title tune brings the entertainment to a close. The Beatles thank the canned audience and hopes they enjoyed the show. Of course, this is a reminder of the acting motif, and it also functions to seal off one experience, and then open the door to another. This would be "**A Day In The Life**," the Beatles' masterpiece.

The show is over: the performers are gone, leaving their feathers, powder and spangles in piles on the floor. John Lennon begins singing to little accompaniment, as if he is alone under a spotlight. His song is framed as real—not just acting real. Lennon, not a "Pepper" character (if they ever were) is addressing the real audience: you. You sat through the artifice, and now comes the real. But as Lennon sings half to himself, the real seems no longer real either.

This song was the first recorded for the album (not counting the exercise of recording "When I'm Sixty-Four"). It is an example of John "summing up." I will discuss some of its motifs.

The "holes" which John reads about in the Albert Hall are "empties." They are the people he sees as holes—they think they are wholes, but they are holes. (Sheila Whiteley has the same interpretation.)[42] The "holes" settle for a clichéd piano flourish as their entertainment.

The orchestra winds up with a monstrous, tortured motion and hits a final note simultaneously: a piano chord in E is struck which is allowed to reverberate for almost a minute. I would say that the chord kills everything that has gone before it, the album, the melancholy of John, the wholes-holes, the useless pattering of Paul going to an office, the English army having won the war, and life in general as it is lived. With a touch of alchemy and much economy, John and Paul managed to sum up Western culture and then point to.... LSD, or something unspecified, as the "future."

John originally thought of having "A Day In The Life" conclude with an orchestral sound that would start out really tiny and then gradually become huge,[43] but Paul proposed the orchestra play a scale randomly up to E. Paul came back later to record the final chord (literally, since pianos use hammers, a "hammer blow"), with John, Mal Evans, George Martin, Paul and Ringo simultaneously playing it on four pianos.

Ian McDonald wrote, "The sighing tragedy of the verses is redeemed by the line, 'I'd love to turn you on.' ...which becomes the focus of the song. The message is that life is a dream and we have the power, as dreamers, to make it beautiful. In this perspective, the ... orchestral *glissandi* may be seen as symbolizing simultaneously the moment of awakening from sleep and a spiritual ascent from fragmentation to wholeness, achieved in the resolving E major chord."[44]

Lennon later commented, "It's a bit of a *2001*, you know."[45] He might have been referring to the final sequence of *2001: A Space Odyssey* where the astronaut's space-pod hurtles through a kaleidoscope of lights, as space and time are bent. The point the orchestra reaches is schematically like a triangle base which goes to the top of the triangle, and then the chord which reverberates outward is the inverse of this. Thus it is schematically like two triangles tip to tip, which is the same as the kaleidoscope "tunnel" which the astronaut travels through in *2001*.

Hertsgaard wrote that the final chord, with its fifty-three seconds of gradually dwindling reverberation, "brings to mind the eerily spreading hush of the mushroom cloud."[46] So many ideas can be overlaid on the song that it is the best example of John *and* Paul "summing-up." "Strawberry Fields Forever," which the group recorded first of all for "Pepper" but which was not included on the album, also summarizes "culture" and we shall discuss it in Chapter Nine.

The last chord of "A Day In The Life" I call a "Laingian" chord. Laing wanted opposing sides (sane and insane) to move together toward mutual understanding. Fremont-Smith of the Macy Conference also wanted something similar, apparently, when he mentioned that he had hoped researchers could form a model of personality that incorporated madness. Cohen's circle was a model of this sort, with its pie-slice of "unsanity." The last chord of the song of course could also be taken for a state one could experience on LSD, or a "new consciousness."

* * *

Some critics disliked the album: Richard Goldstein, writing for the *New York Times,* called the entire album "fraudulent"[47] except for "A Day In The Life." He was correct, but since the conceit of the album was acting, he wasn't going too far afield.

That the album was taken to be a "fun" album and a "celebration" for the Summer of Love says much more about how the music *felt* to listeners. People were impressed by the technical polish, the inventiveness, "the sheer brio of the enterprise," and many genuinely inspired musical moments (including "A Day In The Life," "Lucy," the production of "Kite," and the beauty of "She's Leaving Home"). The overall production of the album, its spangling, colored landscape, was nothing short of phenomenal.

It *was* fraudulent, and that was its insurance policy: but it also was about the inner life or counterculture that was supposedly possible. The Beatles were champions of Modernism because they presented songs that in Wassily Kandinsky's words (founder of the NKV art collective in Munich) would embody the expression of the inner life. Kandinsky, who thought form less relevant than inner expression, stated that an artist should express their inner life rather than narrowly conform to one style. "I value only those artists," Kandinsky stated, "who really are artists, that is, who consciously or unconsciously in an entirely original form, embody the expression of their inner life; who work only for this end and cannot work otherwise."[48] Art critic Richard Stratton commented that "this search for a spiritual reality in art, coupled with the wide range of nonrealistic art encouraged and achieved by the (*Blaue Reiter*) group gave it international scope and impact."[49] The work of Arp, Braque, Klee, and Picasso—Modernist painters—is thus comparable to the art of the Beatles. And it was (ostensibly) more important that the listener form his or her own inner life in *response* to it, than that the album actually express an inner life.

An inner-becoming-outer was certainly achieved in "A Day In The Life." We feel we are seeing/hearing the real deal in this prosaically titled song, and also that it is simultaneously turning reality inside out. The real is seen to be not the external at all, but the formlessness.

There is no core—no ego. So, let go. The world could be, after being "turned on," one big Laingian non-dialectic utopia.

The effect of "A Day In The Life" in 1967 on its primary audience was galvanic. "When Lennon sang, 'I'd love to turn you on,' I felt like it was a Messianic message. It was like the early Christians," Alison Kennedy recalled. "*I* wanted to turn people on."[50]

* * *

The average person in the mid-Sixties had had little to no exposure to drugs such as pot or LSD, and no experience with therapy or the mental hospital. To recognize these subtexts in songs by a pop group would have never occurred to them. But the IFP subtext helped make listeners feel a little differently about themselves. People felt differently about things they had always taken for granted. They felt there was more "inside." But paradoxically, the Beatles were often implying that a person was a "hole." It was a Vedic or Jungian idea that one must transcend the limited Ego.[51]

Books were for bookworms: Vedic philosophy, Beat poetry and radical psychology, even writers such as "Constance Newland" going on at length about her LSD psychotherapy, were not going to persuade people to change anything at all. In the Fifties, drugs were for losers or the mentally ill: psychotherapy for rich people. Not many were lining up to experience extreme visions that "Newland" said she had witnessed on LSD. Sidney Cohen commented later, "When I found (LSD) was getting out onto the street, I thought, 'it will never sell. It's too intense.'"[52] But, people were quite willing to experience different ways of thinking, a bit of identity fracture even, if John, Paul, George and Ringo took them through it. It was fine to sit back, put on a record, and "go somewhere" with the Beatles. One could question reality and one's own core or lack thereof in the comfort of home. And at the end of the album was a little bit of insane gibberish in the run-out groove.

This penultimate album of the Sixties would continue the Beatles' method of introducing the strange into the familiar and vice versa.

This Laingian-inspired path, (which was equally inspired by Lewis Carroll and books such as *The Comforts of Unreason*) fit the Beatles' concerns. For all its artifice, "Pepper" was much more than entertainment. It would be taken as a roadmap to the future.

CHAPTER IX

I Am the Walrus, Strawberry Fields Forever and "The Culture"

There is a recurring motif in Sixties and early Seventies films of an "empty swimming pool." The pool is not brimming with water, happy children and activity; rather it is vacant and gathering leaves. In the 1972 experimental film *Chao! Manhattan*, which was filmed at Leary's Millbrook mansion and also in Los Angeles, Edie Sedgwick plays an ex-model who was given ECT and is now living in the bottom of an empty pool. Her room is set up with posters of her own publicized image and other media stars affixed to the pool walls. Edie's character, rambling on the phone and rolling around in her bed, is a picture of being unmoored.

In the 1970 film *Deep End* which starred Jane Asher, the story is set around a community swimming pool. The finale takes place in the empty pool as it fills up with menacing, rushing water. Jane's younger would-be boyfriend bonks her in the back of the neck with an overhead metal light fixture and then caresses her as she numbly bleeds out. A 1973 cult horror film, *Warlock Moon*, also has an empty pool scene, where a young man and woman have a conversation which turns threatening. Interestingly, the film was shot at the then-vacant Livermore Sanitarium, where Charles Savage had conducted LSD experiments. The 1968 film *The Swimmer*, starring Burt Lancaster, has many pools. (Eleanor Perry wrote the screenplay. Perry, nee Rosenfeld, had a degree in psychiatric social work and penned several scripts, including 1970's *Diary of a Mad Housewife*.) In *The Swimmer*, the protagonist decides to take a route through his neighbor's backyards, swimming in each of their pools as he makes his way home. He knew them well; it is implied that he "swam" in their lives metaphorically as part of his search for self; but it all went awry. Crashing a pool party uninvited, he sees all his friends there. He reaches his old home to find it boarded up and deserted.

It seems that Macy-type researchers were aware that the pool as metaphor for the mind or personality, however simplistic and heavy-handed, was being used for movie purposes. At the "LSD Reunion Party," (video of this house party is available on YouTube), held in the Seventies, there was some conversation among psychiatrists about metaphors for the mind and then Timothy Leary quipped, "I thought the mind was an indoor plumbing system."[1] The other researchers laughed in recognition. So, various metaphors for the mind were going around at the time. A pool was cinematic trope, I suggest, for the mind and psyche, but it was also signified an approach to personality formation and MK-Ultra activities. The swimming pool was a motif for the mind/brain/personality: "it's all in your head."

A swimming pool, to be cleaned, must first be drained of contents. Then it will be cleaned, and filled back up with fresh treated water. This is the "psycho-catharsis" of Charles Savage's research; "psyche" is the Greek word for the breath, principle of life or soul. Catharsis is defined as "to purge, to cleanse spiritually or emotionally, to release from tension, moral or emotional." However when this process is likened to cleaning a pool, I think that is suggesting there is an intrinsic "emptiness" in people: that people are just an accumulation of sensations, images, and "programming." A pool, when emptied, is somehow even more vacant-looking than other spaces that are vacant some of the time. To be surrounded by its curved, blank walls is vertiginous, with no visual cues for homeostasis. An empty swimming pool just looks "wrong." (It is also as much of a hazard to small children when empty as it is when full.) The empty pool in these movies suggests that a person has no intrinsic core. It is usually a scene of entropy or if someone else is there with the protagonist, a place to enact sex, aggression or murder. (Earlier in *Deep End*, Jane and her "boyfriend" unsuccessfully try to have sex in the empty pool.)

* * *

This book is mainly about my theory of Paul's method of songwriting, which the other Beatles adopted. But John's songs, although they also have the concept of identity-fracture in them, are much more "heady" than Paul's. John had a different method of songwriting. He had a gift for wordplay and he would use a lot of association, even triple associations, making some of his lyrics impenetrable to listeners. However, most of John's songs after 1965 fit neatly into the IFP subtext. More than anything else, John was a great summer-upper of ideas and situations. He would often become exasperated with something or someone he observed, and this he used artistically, to craft songs that are still recognized as brilliant works of art today. John also had an attraction to, almost a love affair with or a sensual response to disintegration. I sense it in his songs and in his very process of writing them. He would go to the edge of fragmentation, and then write about it. (This is a little different than Rimbaud's edict that an artist should go to the extreme of the senses. John went toward losing self.)

I suggest that "I Am the Walrus" needed to be heard *after* the "Pepper" album to even be *accepted* as a song. Besides being a very experimental song, "Walrus" communicates a sense of madness and disillusionment. It was prescient of John to write a song about a failure of Summer of Love awareness only month or so after its main event, and the release of "Pepper." I attribute this to John's propensity for seeing the ends of things—especially things the Beatles had started themselves.

At any rate, at this point in my progress through the Beatles' albums, I could de-code John's more impenetrable songs.

John worked on "**Strawberry Fields Forever**" in an apartment in Spain, while filming *How I Won the War*.[2] Ian MacDonald writes that the song is a continuation of "sensations too confusing, intense, or personal to articulate." John uses a typical Paul way of writing lyrics, like a therapy patient stumbling to get the words out, or elsewhere as I have noted, phrases echoing schizophrenese. Since the listeners are always included "with" the Beatles, Lennon goes further with this method, and in just one phrase, the song's title, summarizes the effect of the IFP on the listeners.

"Let me take you down/'cause I'm going to (too)," John sings. This is another guided visualization like the "picture yourself" of "Lucy." He is going to take us to "Strawberry Fields/Nothing is real/Nothing to get hung about." There are no troublesome distinctions, dialectics, differences, and therefore nothing to get hung (up) on. In "Fields," John is perhaps singing as the therapist who has taken LSD along with his patient. You and he will go to the land of ego-loss together. Nothing is real there (this is similar to the idea in "Penny Lane," where the nurse is in a play "anyway.")

"Let me take *you* down," I suggest is the real intent of the phrase. This is to take a person's sense of self away: similar to how some of the MK-Ultra Macy Conference researchers would go about it. They would take away people's notions—their opinions—take all that away, and then see what was left. They would empty the swimming pool, either with cognitive feedback, or with more violent means, by administering drugs: take a person down. Of course the phrase can be assumed to mean that John is inviting us to go somewhere, "down to" the fields. But John seldom wrote with just one meaning in mind.

John thinking of his poor vision could account for the melancholy of the music in "with eyes closed, misunderstanding all you see." Then allusions to erasure of self continue with "It's getting hard to be someone, but it all works out/It doesn't matter much to me." It is hard to be a person: but who cares, let's take ourselves down and forget about having a self, for a while. ("Forget who we are for a while," as Paul said about the concept for "Pepper.")

Paul apparently sings the next lines. He can't tune in, that is, he can't find anything "there" when he "tunes in," as Leary instructed people to do—to find their inner core on LSD. "But it's all right," if he doesn't find a core to himself. "That is, I think it's not too bad," he amends. This is the idea of the empty person, the Nowhere Man, the hole in the whole, again. Also the halting speech is like a therapy session where a person is struggling to get the words out, which we have encountered several times in Beatles' songs—it was one of the Beatle "voices."

The next section has some wordplay with "know" and "no." A hole is in a whole and a no is in know. Paul (it sounds like Paul's voice to me but could have been John's varispeeded) sings: "Always, know, sometimes think it's me/But you know, I know when it's a dream/I think a "No" I mean a "Yes"/But it's all wrong/That is, I think, I disagree." This is making somewhat of a philosophical point in that when someone knows something, they also "no" other things—to make a statement about something excludes other ways of thinking about it. He concludes that he thinks, therefore he disagrees. John, ever the contrarian, "no's" when he thinks—his natural inclination is to dismiss or "take the piss out of" people, concepts and institutions.

The song, which John later described as "psychoanalysis set to music,"[3] ends with repeating the first chorus. Going where "nothing is real," I might add, is also about going into the mental space where a person makes art. But as we consider the IFP and LSD subtexts to other Beatles songs we have discussed, the final instrumental section of the song has a more dissolute meaning thrown in.

Using the scaffolding of psychology tropes as a way to write a song, John wrote "Fields" as a kind of exercise of thinking about self, or lack of interest in self, in his case. He wants "you" to be as disinterested in having a self, too. Then, there will be "nothing to get hung about."

But why call the place to "go" to Strawberry Fields? I suggest the last section of the song fills in the picture.

"There wasn't any conscious we'll-sit-down-and-remember-our-childhood," Paul remarked in 1995 about "Penny Lane" and "Fields."[4]

John's composition was initially titled, according to Steve Turner in *Beatles '66*, "Not Too Bad."[5] So, assuming that this song is not really about a landmark that was near John's house, I suggest it is about the IFP of The Beatles and the overall effect of their music upon their fans. Thinking about it as a vision of ego-death, of literally being taken down, I understand the instrumental coda to be John's vision of what happens to those who "go" with him, and are gathered together in the fields.

They have been made to "feel." They have been invited to be one of the "feeleds"—courtesy of the Beatles' art and songs like "Yellow Submarine." Brian Wilson, a colleague, had played for Paul his "feels," or pieces of melody and chord that carried emotional content into the mind of the listener.[6] The "fields" thus are full of the "feeleds." They are fans filled by Beatles music, made to feel. They are holes, but filled, as in the Albert Hall, by music.

The song is an exposition of lack of interest in having a self, and its conclusion is the gathering of the "feeleds" in the "field." The "feeleds" constitute a "field," their arms and bodies swaying like waving wheat. This is another cereal or grain reference of John's. A field of ripe wheat looks remarkably like a swaying, standing stadium audience. The wheat, the fields/feeleds of grain, become hollow straw eventually, and (as is practiced in agriculture) plowed under at the end of the season. So, these "straw men, the hollow men," (a line from T.S. Eliot's poem *The Hollow Men* is a possible association) are straw-"buries." Straw is plowed (buried) back into the field, to fertilize it. The people who gathered to feel had their egos emptied-out or made-dead (ego-dead, by LSD) and the Beatles. Thus hollowed-out, they are then "buried" back into the field. A new generation of "feeleds," (presumably children grown up on their parents' Beatles albums) will spring up again, to be in turn emptied-out and buried to fertilize the next generation. In this way, the art of The Beatles will go on forever.

If this seems ominous, after all, to John, who is giving the listener this story about the fields, being someone doesn't matter much to him.

"Let me take you down," thus, could have a harsh meaning somewhat akin to what Harry Murray and the other egg-men at Harvard personality research were doing with college students: trying to take them down. Trying to take away the "you" that you think is yourself.

"Strawberry Fields forever!" John declares. Amid the slashing cellos, marching cadence and flutters of odd recorder loops, an alarm fades to a piano on one note. The listeners march into the field. The non-self can replicate forever. This is a cybernetic vision, and the music compliments it as drums and marching up-and-down rhythms, like 1's, are interspersed with recorder tape loops (O's). Was John warning us in his lyrics about some future of cybernetic societal control, which the "egg-men" are planning for humanity? Or was he just playing with images?

As usual, John frustrates finding meaning, and he mocked those who would try. However, given my exhaustive and somewhat exhausting analysis of Paul's praxis, it seems possible that John in "Strawberry Fields Forever" summarized the entire Beatles musical enterprise. The song goes from guided visualization, to a rather convoluted therapy session where the singer analyzes himself, finds himself to be nothing, and then enters into the "field." The empty Beatles and their empty fans are one in being no one, but the existence of the *field* will go on "four-ever."

I call this a cybernetic vision for no idle reason. In cybernetic systems, no identity is assigned to individuals, but the primary reality is the resultant action as set up by certain participants or parameters. An example often given is that a man does not cut a tree down, but the combination of man plus axe plus tree leads to a cut tree – this example was given by Norbert Weiner, father of cybernetic theory. Thus, the field set up by the Beatles is a system that carries on forever and *is* the point, rather than the individuals that brought it about. Even the Beatles who helped set up the field or counterculture are "no-ones," or "nowhere men." Once the system is set up, *it* will go on replicating forever.

(With this mention of "it," it is worth mentioning that "it" itself is an idea, in that it is a neutral word, unassigned to gender or any religion. One can get hung up on "it" as some kind of signpost to cryptic revelation. Perhaps tangentially or not, Paul financed *IT* magazine.)[7]

There were enough links between cybernetic research, LSD and creativity research, and even social scientists and psychologists like Gregory Bateson that, if one was as clued-into these developments and as creatively minded as John was, one could have written a very out-there song about it all – which is what I submit "Strawberry Fields" really is. And, the song includes an enactment at the end – a musical meltdown into a cybernetic "field." One can see that John's "break down" or analysis of the culture and also "what was coming" was darker, and heavier, than Paul's: also astute and rather funny, in a dark way.

Taking things in this general context of discussing a "field" of activity, it is plausible that, as the song devolves into noise over one note, John's saying "I *buried* Paul," could be a joke meaning I "*berried*" Paul. To hear for myself what John was saying, I recorded the end of the song on tape and then sped up the tape on playback. Doing this I could hear John's normal voice clearly saying, "I buried Paul." He enunciates the words as if making an official announcement, and stresses the second word as if to show that he is making a pun: "I '*berried*' Paul." On "Paul" he drops his voice a bit in volume, as if the point of the phrase was making the pun on buried/berried.

It could mean either "berried" or buried," and John used varispeed to make that point. If you say "bare-ee" very slowly (or slow-down the audio recording), it will sound like "bury" ("bur-ee"). John was having fun with varispeed, and making a pun. He's saying he "berried" Paul because Paul became one of the field of "berries"/buries when he sang on the "I think a no" section. Paul's in the field, with the buries/berries. In any case John could make the joke that he did the "berrying" or "burying" of Paul because he is, after all, the *leader* of the band and he is joking that Paul is under his control. (Also the pun alludes to the Paul-is-dead thing they have going.)

People contend John was saying "I'm very bored," and John said he was saying "cranberry sauce." As a Beatle, John gets to have it both ways. He can encode meaning and debunk meaning, because the point of the Beatles enterprise was to erase distinctions and take away meaning where they can (It *all* can be gibberish, nonsense verse).

Also I must point out at the risk of ridicule that strawberries look a bit like little Beatles. The stem-caps of strawberries look similar to Beatle haircuts. I don't know if this image might have occurred to John in "picking" the laden-with-association phrase of "Straw-bury/berry Fields/feeleds For/Four-ever."

* * *

Strawberry Fields is the place to go to be "gone," the asylum, the interval. It is the "w/hole" where everyone can be "fixed," and every-one can be "all together now" with The Beatles. In the Beatles' asylum of Straw-bury-feeleds there are no troublesome dialectics. There are no differences to overcome: no high or low, past or future, good or bad, us or them.

John in "Fields" is inviting the listener to be in this relativist, flowing state, and indeed there is no conflict in the song. It is ironic John was preaching a unity because John was ever the contrarian. "It was always confrontational" with John, commented audio engi-neer Geoff Emerick in his memoir. In The Beatles' Utopian idea, the evisceration of identity would lead to an oceanic awareness of "love," which both understands (knows) and has no "no" in it. This is Cooper's ideal and the "total analysis" or total understanding between people which Macy researcher Harold Abramson had complained was sheer fantasy.

All You Need is Love" was the Beatles' statement to the world on a televised broadcast in June 1967, on the very doorstep to the Summer of Love. "Love" was the Beatles' reply to all the philosoph-ical and realistic conundrums. In the U.K. the verses were regarded as somewhat of a joke. "There's nothing you can do that can't be done/Nothing you can sing that can't be sung." But in the U.S. the lyrics were taken more seriously, as possible koans containing mean-ing ("Beatle" meaning). "Nothing you can make that can't be made/No-one you can save that can't be saved/Nothing you can do/But you can learn how to be you in time/It's easy." Then the simple chorus: "All you need is love." Just what the doctor ordered.

The memorable anthem reached an estimated 400 million people on the television broadcast.[8] The Beatles appeared singing in hippie haberdashery, surrounded by signs with "love" written on them in many languages.

John had to write a song in a hurry so he went for what he knew. His poor vision being his daily reality, John wrote "All You Need is Love" based on the music to the nursery rhyme song, "Three Blind Mice." He did what composers call an augmentation of the phrase, and doubled the value of each note, quarter note to half note, and so on. "Love, love, love" which goes on in back of the almost spoken-word verse uses the same three chords as the nursery song, slowed down: "Love … Love … love" is "Three … blind … mice." The biographer Albert Goldman wrote that Lennon's default songwriting idea was "Three Blind Mice."[9] I always took this for a slur or a joke, but on examining this particular song I find the statement to be true. And it is kind of hilarious that John composed a worldwide anthem using the most rudimentary materials—it is a stroke of artistic genius. The verse repeats a half-step up, and then comes to the same interval (a third) for the chorus, "all you need is love." (The next line in "Three Blind Mice" is "see how they run," which appears a few times in Beatles songs.)

John wrote "All You Need is Love" only a few days before the broadcast. Someone at Abbey Road studios reminded him that the show was in a few days and John said, "Oh God, is it that close? I suppose we'd better write something."[10] Paul had ready "Your Mother Should Know," but John trumped him although Paul might have hoped the late notice would mean that his own song would be used. John's anthem was deemed far more appropriate to the broadcast, which reached more home viewers than any television broadcast in history.

This in itself shows how "wide" the Beatles were always opened. Their message was to be taken in by as many people as possible. "All You Need is Love" is one of the most recognizable songs in the world, and at the same time one which Lennon probably had to think the least about to write. Because of this hat trick, it can be regarded as one of Lennon's masterworks.

*   *   *

John really latched onto the idea of "showing," or of doing what is in effect a guided visualization. He began this way of writing with "Tomorrow Never Knows" and continued with it on songs such as "Fields," "Lucy," and "**Rain**." "I can show you … Can you hear me/ That when it rains and shines/It's just a state of mind," John sings on "Rain," because (again, erasing differences is the goal) rain and sun are all the same. (Ringo's drumming is exceptional on "Rain.")

Even though Paul's IFP was dictating at this point almost every nuance of sound and lyric on the albums, John (fracturing his ego on LSD) was writing songs that also fit perfectly with the new "type" having a new "awareness." John's psychedelic-era method of writing was to turn out simple songs, which "became massive" in the studio. John's songs could be added to—orchestrated, made huge—in a way, they were "a tiny sound" growing larger. John commented to George Harrison that he thought of songwriting as "doing little bits which you then join up."[11] If that is so, his sense of transition between "bits" was impeccable, because listening to his psychedelic-era songs one does not get a sense of modularity but of cohesion. His songs were empowering to listen to because they seem inspired, even though Lennon made them from a place that, I suggest, was rather cynical.

*   *   *

Looking Through a "Glass Onion"

Paul created a method to write songs because of, I have suggested, personal needs for self-protection. For John, the realm where "nothing is real" was by 1968 his world, period. This is in contrast to the "normal" world where "it must be high or low." He offers listeners another place you can go, "where everything flows," John sings somewhat sarcastically to the fans in "**Glass Onion**."

John's caustic "Glass Onion" is about Paul's creative process. John finds it at fault, implying that to fix "a hole in the ocean" is a ludicrous notion. He also charts in one economical phrase, the progression of The Beatles from innocent to corrupt: "Oh yeah. Ohhhhh yeah. OH YEEEEAAAAAAH!" However, it was not sung this way on the demo. It is a humorous song, almost a brilliant song by John, analyzing his friend. Paul's fractured identity John sees as a series of layers (fractures or plates) that are also, transparent, and also there is no core. Paul enabled or drove himself to this state, artistically, and took his listeners with it, so in a sense he is transparent to them. They are looking through him, and maybe through themselves.

"I told you 'bout Strawberry Fields/You know the place where nothing is real," John sings. Now he will tell you about "another place you can go, where everything flows." Another "van" is here to take you away.

"I told you 'bout the Fool on the Hill/I tell you man he's living there still." I take this to mean John is casting aspersion on Paul's level of "new awareness." A Pied-piper-like flute comes in, sounding like coo-coo-coo (cuckoo, or crazy). Vertiginous strings rise and fall.

I suggest that the song is born out of John's exasperation that Paul, having become enlightened at least on paper, is still persisting in being anyone at all. John's complaint about Paul would go like this: there is no reason to "fix a hole," to mend one's mind if everything should be let in. There's no reason to make a Beatles song if doing so would limit consciousness.

John uses images in the song to indicate futile enterprise. "Fixing a hole in the ocean/Trying to make a dovetail joint." A dovetail joint is a fixed combination of two pieces of wood. It is rigid and not bendable. But a joint can also be bendable. (An elbow joint for example.) Trying to make the rigid bend and to patch a hole from rain getting in when you're already in the ocean is just being contrary to what really is, says John. Paul (who might be the glass onion, as well as the Walrus "speaking of many things") is just singing about niceties. "Paul writes them (songs) like novels. You can see the influence now—these stories about boring people doing boring things—being postmen and secretaries and writing home," as John put it later.[12] "I try to get to the nitty gritty, except for an occasional 'Walrus.'"[13] In "Glass Onion," John is lodging this complaint, saying Paul is being fussy, making small distinctions where one shouldn't make them. He's fractured meaning and identity into many layers, but he is see-throughable anyway (to John) and his layers are made of glass. John is upping the cosmic ante here. Why make the layers of something transparent when it shouldn't even have recognition as a thing in the first place. The Paul praxis is to fragment something that is not really a thing anyway (a glass onion is not identifiable, and its layers being glass are invisible as well, and since layers define the structure of an onion, such an onion is nothing).

John is typically exasperated. Even in his "limitless" interval that he had created, Paul was still being Paul and writing about small picture. John wanted big picture. He didn't want "granny music."[14]

I propose that "Glass Onion" was about John's beefs with Paul, but at this point the song could also be taken by a large section of Beatles fans to be about them. There is a sense of relatedness to the image of a glass onion. The listener has long felt that the Beatles see through him or her.

"I told you 'bout the fool on the hill (actually he didn't, Paul sang that song about himself)/I tell you man, he's living there still," could also imply that Paul never "returned" from his LSD trips—that he permanently fractured himself. This I think unfortunately might be true. Paul had a lot of facets, was driven to fracture his personality perhaps as a way to escape being vulnerable, or from some inner drive. But taking LSD was just a plain mistake. Now "Paul" is supposedly "understandable" to millions (since they have taken acid to be "with" the new awareness). But, John is saying, all Paul's layers are all "see-throughable": he has no core. How would it feel to be both ostensively "seen-through" and also ostensibly "loved"? John is saying it's neither here nor there: nothing – a glass onion. In light of what I have been discussing about the IFP, the meaning of "Glass Onion" is, well, transparent. John was singing about Paul.

But now we should ask ourselves, what about the idea of an internal "split" anyway? Psychologists, novelists had for at least eighty years been talking about doubles, false fronts, and split personalities. It seems that John might also suspect that all those people are talking about things that "aren't real." "You know, the place where nothing is real," is all a joke to John. A big, fat "con," as he said about the Beatles' music. This song is related to his exasperation about the ad-men and the egg-men in "Walrus." What bothers John (or at least seems to) is that the Beatles are now part of the bullshit brigade.

John had a word-shuffling, punning mind (which Geoff Emerick states was John's defense against his own insecurities).[15] John could "take the piss" out of anything with his wordplay and sometimes tone-deaf insults. If the Beatles did not even believe in what they were doing after a certain point is anyone's conjecture. I am simply pointing out the structure whereby they wrote songs. To be the Beatles they employed the many layers/fault lines of Paul's "interval" and Identity Fracture Project.

But John was also using an ordinary image of an onion, so he was aware that he too was hardly exempt from image- and meaning-less-mongering. After a while, he probably had come to realize, too much of an associative mind doesn't do you any favors.

I Am the Walrus

> "The time has come," the walrus said, "to talk of many things. Of shoes—and ships—and sealing-wax—of cabbages—and kings."
>
> –LEWIS CARROLL

This was perceived as a pivotal song of the Sixties; it was released in November of 1967, following the Summer of Love. John's imagistic rant formed an impenetrable rubric of chaos that seemed to encapsulate society. As with every Beatles song, it seemed important that people listen. The song, for all its seeming randomness, is decipherable with what we know by this time of the IFP, and of motifs the

Beatles used. But in analyzing this song, I also was able to see how John formed associations in his mind. So, it was fun to analyze this song, and unlike other songs I have analyzed in this book, I will discuss John's "I Am The Walrus" line by line. It is kind of a summation of what Paul has been doing, and also the effect Paul's IFP and the Beatles music has had on their fans and the "culture." One can assume that the walrus is Paul, and that in this song John is singing the song as Paul, i.e. from Paul's point of view (if you can call his fractionated sensibility a point of view); but one can also assume John is simply speaking of "everyone" affected by the Beatles, including himself.

First off, everyone is lacking boundaries. "I am he as you are he/ As you are me/And we are all together." I am the Walrus/Paul, you are he, and we're all together. This is just a compression of what the Beatles have been doing all along: trouncing dialectics. It is the same idea as Love is the only word, or the world will live as one, and so on. However, in "Walrus," the notion seems to be aggravating John.

This line also could have been born, again, of John's exasperation about Paul leading the Beatles, at this point. He made all the aesthetic decisions in the studio, even told George and Ringo on occasion what to play, or stepped in to play their instruments. George told Paul once, "When you write a song ... I feel as if I wrote it."[16] They were "all together" to a degree probably hard to comprehend. But the fans, too, have been enjoined all along to be "with" the Beatles and feel as if the Beatles lead them. John will really stretch his associative mind here and let out all the stops, to launch invective on the Beatles, Paul, and society. The rhythmic motif is a back-and-forth, which MacDonald wrote was inspired by an ambulance siren. "See how they run, like pigs from a gun/See how they fly." John is describing the Beatles – the Beatles in their early promo videos were always running in a row like little projectiles or specks running in lines, seen from a distance, across fields. "Pigs from a gun" might have been inspired by John's watching the TV commercials for Quaker Puffed Wheat and Quaker Puffed Rice, breakfast cereals which were "shot from guns!"[17] Of course it is also alluding to police, who were called "pigs" at the time, running from a gun. "See how they run" is also a fragment of Paul's "Lady Madonna."

"Sitting on a cornflake/Waiting for the van to come." This could have happened; John could have finished his morning cereal, and sat on a cornflake while waiting for the group's van to arrive. With this phrase he implies the listener is just waiting around, as he does. He waits to hear Paul's next album concept. In the listeners' case, the public waits for the band to say something new to them. But a "van" coming is also reminiscent of a paddy wagon coming to take a person away to either the police station, or the asylum.

"Corporation T-shirt/Stupid bloody Tuesday." The girl whom Mick Jagger sang about in the Rolling Stones song "Ruby Tuesday" was an original who could not be labeled: "Who could hang a name on you/When you change with every new day." John puns on Ruby Tuesday as "Stupid Bloody Tuesday" who wears a corporation T-shirt. The person has lost their originality and is merely a follower, wearing a corporate t-shirt, waiting for the next song from The Beatles. There are no originals, just meter-mades.

"Man you've been a naughty boy/You let your face grow long." In the meantime, Paul has grown older, and his face is thinner. He lost his baby fat. However, it could also refer to a Joker nose, which grows longer, both when telling lies, like Pinocchio, or alluding to sexual lust.

John cries out, "I am the eggman/They are the eggmen/I am the Walrus." Because of all the "feelings" and new awareness the Beatles brought to people, everybody has become their own psychologist: an "egg-man." Dr. Asher had an egg-shaped head, and John, who often came up with insulting nicknames for people, might have been inspired by that to dub him an "egg-man": one who examines heads. The expression of labeling someone a G-man, (Government man) an Ad-man, or any other –man, depending on their profession or alliance was current at the time. John says he is an "egg-man," examining his own head, and they (other people, and/or the Beatles) are egg-men.

"Mr. City p'liceman sitting pretty little p'licemen in a row." This is another pun, in that the city policemen are also "sitty," or sitting, policemen. In addition, John is slurring the word to make policemen sound like "Please" men, who were the Beatles; their debut album, "Please Please Me," made a hit with the public, pleasing fans. Thus the Beatles started out as "Please-men," (in John's view) just like advertising men are Ad-men, Government men are G-men, etc.

John is singing about the Beatles—the "Please-men." He sees them all in a row, as they often ran in little rows, in their film clips. Again it is the idea of several items in a series doing identical things. In the *Magical Mystery Tour* film sequence for this song, policemen sit in a row like Humpty Dumpty's on a wall, which compresses the policemen/please-men/egg/egg-men association.

In "Walrus," John was often burying the core word under associations, and then linking one core image to another. The core word is the Beatles, but he free-associates over that idea.

"See how they fly like Lucy in the sky/See how they run." Here he is continuing to think about the Beatles, who now are "flying." "Flying" was John's expression for being high on LSD. "See how they run" is a line from "Three Blind Mice."

"I'm crying." John was probably channeling his grief for the loss of Brian Epstein, who had died just a few days before this song was recorded.[18] But then, his phrase is backed with staccato cries, and cycles upward in a loop, as if even real grief is being turned around on top of itself.

"Yellow matter custard/Dripping from a dead dog's eye" is a line was taken from a nonsense verse Pete Shotton would say. John, thinking of the "egg-men," associates them with custard. The custard drips from a dead eye, signifying the dead mind, or baked mind, in back of it. If one is an "egg" which is "baked" (or "dead") then custard would be the result.

The "crabalocker fishwife, pornographic priestess" could be English actress Diana Dors, who was featured prominently on the "Pepper" cover. A fishwife is known for having a coarse manner and loud voice, which Dors had. Dors would hold orgies at her home.[19] The "fishwife" keeps crabs (sexual lice) in her "fish locker." A fish locker is where a fishwife stores the caught fish. "Fish" is also related to Liverpool slang for female sexual anatomy.

"Boy, you've been a naughty girl/You've let your knickers down" could be about Dors, in her role as pornographic priestess. But the expression "boy" as in "oh, boy," is mixed with girl to imply transvestitism.

The next section is "Sitting in an English garden, waiting for the sun/If the sun don't come you get a tan from standing in the English rain." In California, people can bask in the sun. But in England there is much less sun, and the only way to get "tanned" is by the beating of the rain on one's skin, he jokes.

Then John, thinking of jokes, makes a rhyme on chokes, smokes, and jokes. He returns to thinking of Ad-(advertising) men, who encourage smokers to choke. He puns on joking smokers and choking: "expert textpert, choking smokers/Don't you think the joker laughs at you?" The joking smoker he compresses into a choking smoker. A joker (flip-flopper) has the final laugh, even though the "textperts" might think they are on top.

A lot of the song is bewailing how easily people are led. They are led by corporations, by music (waiting for the van to come), by advertising. "I'm crying," displays John's distress at this, or abstract call of grief, as backup voices cycle upward in a vertiginous circle.

The backup voices cycle, like a rollercoaster looping the loop. This evokes a fun-house world, like James's "awful mixture in things" whereby no act stands by itself as having meaning; nor does any word. Any word is associable into any other word. It is a "joker" world.

"Semolina pilchard/Climbing up the Eiffel Tower" is maybe John's most obscure lyric. It is a series of compressed images. Semolina is a coarsely milled grain. "Pilchard" was the name of a character in a play John had tried to write in art school (he only wrote a page or two of it).[20] Pilchard lived in an attic and thought he was Christ. John sometimes compared himself to Jesus; he once came into an Apple meeting and told everyone that he was Jesus Christ. While growing up at his aunt Mimi's, John "had the whole run of the top floor to do as he liked," she remarked.[21] So, Pilchard was based on John. In "Walrus," the Semolina Pilchard—namely John—climbs the Eiffel Tower. "Eiffel" is "I Fell." John's song "If I Fell" was another one of their early successes; it helped their rise. So, this bran-Christ, (John) is climbing the "If I Fell" tower of fame. He is an "Exi"-speck, a tiny grain, but he broadcasts to millions from the tower. Likening himself to a grain, he is also like his fans, whose swaying bodies at concerts he would compare to waving grain in "Strawberry Fields Forever." His songs also in a sense broadcast or spray replicas of himself, similar to the specks of puffed wheat shot from guns and engulfing people on the Puffed Wheat advertisements.

The Eiffel tower in Paris was initially planned to be a temporary structure destined to be torn down; reportedly it was left standing because it was good for radio broadcasting. Radio airplay certainly helped the Beatle's climb to success.

"Elementary penguin, singing Hare Krishna/Man you should have seen them kicking Edgar Allen Poe." Penguin Books published a major translation of Eastern religion in 1966. Penguins follow each other in a row (like the P'licemen, or the Beatles). Penguin was a major textbook publisher, so John is envisioning that books on Vedic spiritualism for elementary children are next. He envisions the children marching like little penguins (or holding little Penguin editions), walking in a row singing Hare Krishna. (Earlier, an illustrator at Penguin Books had proposed drawing the Beatles-as-penguins for the cover of one of John's books, but Penguin management had nixed the idea.) The children will be told to 'kick' (get rid of) Edgar Allen Poe, because Poe in his day wrote several articles criticizing the Vedic-influenced Transcendentalists. Poe called them the "Frog-Pondians."[22]

"I am the egg man/They are the egg men/I am the walrus." He is singing of "everything," but, he is singing primarily of how people are led—how they are manipulated. But, if we are all "egg-men," as is the walrus, this points to Paul being the instigator, perhaps, or the chief egg-man.

This fits with my theory that Paul's process has delivered psychological subtexts into song, which led to people trying LSD, making each person able to "operate your own mind," as Leary put it; the idea was that we are all "egg-men," and can analyze ourselves, choose to think what we want to, and so on. However in John's vision, being an "egg-man" is not positive. It seems to be just another category of person, like the "Ad-men," or something the "corporation T-shirt" wearers are led to do.

A Shakespearean play is heard over the radio (broadcast from the Eiffel tower?) as the song dissolves into a demented miasma to chants of "Stick it up your jumper," "everybody's got one," or "everybody smoke pot."

The song argues for John using Jungian associative techniques, in order to write songs. He would go into a "trance" and write songs that way. (This is mentioned in *Revolution in the Head*, and by several biographers.) The song's basic structure is nothing very inventive—it was based on hearing a siren outside his window—but the lyrics and the production are penetratingly associative.

"Walrus" was the first song the Beatles recorded just days after Brian Epstein's death. Geoff Emerick recalled the look of utter emptiness on their faces as they were playing.[23] Maybe the moment when Brian Epstein died, was when Paul and John's impetus to create as *Beatles* started to implode. Epstein had taken a fatherly role toward them.

The youthful high spirits and irreverence which were hallmarks of 1964 Beatles songs had in only a few years become a despairing cry in "Walrus." The song paints an abstract, yet decipherable, picture of the story of the IFP, told in associative language and sound. Even though it seems to be a "madman's rant," that in itself made it fit with the IFP subtext. It was accepted and listened to as a "Beatles song," if an odd one, because it continued the subliminal story which The Beatles had been telling their listeners and, in one way or another, been taking them on all along.

More of It: Penny Lane, Only a Northern Song, and The Fool on the Hill

At this point Paul's IFP or "the interval" had widened to the point that the general public were willing to act in unconventional ways, ways that would have brought them under the treatment of the "egg-men" only a decade earlier. In 1967 homosexuality was decriminalized in Britain.[24] By 1967 state mental hospitals in the U.S. were de-funded, changing to an outpatient services system, and involuntary hospitalization was made much more difficult. The birth control Pill was made available by the mid-Sixties, and abortion legalized in the U.K. Abortion laws were being challenged in the U.S. The young were wearing motley and smoking pot, and there was strong sentiment against the Vietnam War. Censorship laws were lifted in both the U.S. and the U.K. Even just one of these changes would have had a huge impact on society, but to combine all of them in one decade made for a sense of upheaval, as if all values were being spurned.

"I Am the Walrus" seemed to criticize just about everybody in its "madman's rant." Paul's "**The Fool on the Hill**" was by contrast a gentle song about a "madman," but one who seemed to be not so bad or mad, but rather relatable. Both songs use the trope of the madman, but as usual, Paul's treatment of the Laingian idea of society-is-insane was much more commercial than John's. Paul's strong sense of melody gives us feelings for a Fool who is gentle, whimsical, and honest about "what is." He "sees the sun going down/And the eyes in his head/See the world spinning round." Of course the world does spin, so the Fool is actually seeing the truth.

There are aspects of the Fool that could be related to Paul's artistic process. He has his "head in a cloud," and is "the man of a thousand voices talking perfectly loud." Paul explored and voiced the identities of many (at first it was acting out the halting phraseology of mental patients); now Paul speaks for many, and *as* many, "perfectly loud." Paul, as the Fool, speaks for the culture of expansion (or fragmentation). (A Fool, of course, is traditionally also a Joker of inversion. High is low, good is evil, and so on.) "But nobody wants to know him/

They can see that he's just a fool." Here is the Laingian idea, again, of the insane being sane, and the sane, insane. To the listener, the Fool whom no-one likes seems harmless. The music is gentle and sensitive. If no one wants to know him, or hear what he's saying, then maybe society has the problem. Paul affirms this: "And he never listens to them/He knows that they're the fool." He is left seeing the world spinning, round and round. Inversion and the relativity of a circle, with no beginning and no end, suit the Fool fine.

Paul plays a recorder solo, reminiscent of a Pan or Pied Piper figure leading his followers off with him. Having gathered listeners together under the banner of "unsanity," the gentle, truthful Fool—Paul—leads away a generation of children to the new awareness.

Bob Dylan often used circus motifs in his songs[25] to represent the free anarchism of the new "culture." So, the circus of the newly aware, (to John, they were fellow inmates and "egg-men" fooling themselves, and stuck in a consumerist rut that maybe had a few new things about it) are in Paul's view led by a Fool—him—and they aren't *stuck* in a loop. They see the world spinning round, but then they are also led—somewhere. The irony is that the one of the main tools for supposedly expanding peaceful consciousness—LSD—had been used by both "egg-men" and by military intelligence. LSD was the Tangee lipstick of drugs; it looked different on everybody.

Only a Northern Song

The Beatles were in a sense making satire albums—just as artists like Spike Milligan and Peter Sellers had done before them with George Martin on Parlophone. It was just that nobody could see the joke. George Harrison commented later, "We weren't really serious. We could be singing a song about raspberry jam and people would not realize it." He implied that even a song like "She's Leaving Home" could be based on something completely unrelated to its dramatic, touching pathos. This comment also supports that they might have been writing songs using an associative method. George contributed his own song about this state of non-recognition of the Beatle's absence from their own material in "**Only a Northern Song**." Northern Songs was the name of the Beatles' publishing company. "If you're listening to this song/You might think the chords are going wrong/But they're not/He just wrote it like that," George intoned, as the music swirled like a psychedelic™, mind-expanding eddy or stream. "It doesn't really matter what chords I play/What words I say/Or time of day it is/'Cause it's only a Northern song." Beatles songs have their own "way," and it implies emptiness and meaninglessness on both sides. "If you think the harmony/Is a little dark and out of key/You're correct/There's nobody there/And I told you there's no-one there." This is the same emptiness-on-both-sides-of-the-mirror that we encountered in "For No One." It was "hip" to accept this, is the implication (possibly, although it seems George was a bit fed up with the Beatles' "way" of composing). Of course by the time of "Mystery Tour," the emptiness was desirable; it meant something could "come" out of it.

To a certain strata of listeners and critics, however, the avant-garde compositions on "Pepper" and "Magical Mystery Tour" *did* indicate a lack of substance. These were critics and older listeners who wanted more songs on the compositional level of "In My Life" and "She's Leaving Home." To these critics, Beatles albums were becoming less rewarding to listen to. "Magical Mystery Tour," which had more experimental songs, was the first Beatles album to receive substantially less critical adulation.[26] Critics had taken pot-shots at the group before, and Christian communities denounced their records and burned them in 1966. No one thought to accuse them of using a formula, however; that was the last thing they could be—formulaic. And yet a trademarked, patented "Beatle way" is what George implies in "Only a Northern Song." His song effectively satirizes the music and "culture" the Beatles partly created.

The Davies biography states the Beatles and George Martin were distinctly unimpressed by "Only a Northern Song." MacDonald wrote that "George had yet to recover his enthusiasm for being a Beatle" when he recorded the song.[27] Paul, taken aback, ended the recording session early, and went home, seemingly depressed. I am suggesting that the song revealed the formula of their songwriting; it partially lifted the curtain of the men-behind-the-curtain. The song in theatrical terms broke the fourth wall. At this point however, the audience were part of the theatre performance themselves. People were their own experimenters, their own "egg-men," their own test-subjects, and acting in their own play. "Operate your own brain," enthused Timothy Leary. "You have the past of thousands of centuries of people and events in your DNA. You have only to unlock it." Sex and creativity were the carrots held out to the public to try it. Leary said in *Playboy*, a publication reaching millions of readers, that a woman on LSD could have over a hundred orgasms. Other writers touted the drug's effects on creativity. Due to events like Monterey Pop, many more people had the opportunity to try LSD. The Macy Conference attendees had been stumped to try to define what LSD did that other therapies and drugs didn't already do. That very indefinability made LSD the "it" drug of the Sixties.

Songs like "Only a Northern Song," and "Walrus," however, raised the question of whether the whole "culture" was empty, misled, and the music merely décor. "Walrus" was on the "Magical Mystery Tour" album and was a B-side of the single "Hello, Goodbye" by Paul. "Only a Northern Song" was hidden away, put on the soundtrack to *Yellow Submarine*, the animated feature. I suspect this is because the Beatles and particularly Paul wanted the sunny Summer of Love to happen first, before any doubts set in.

Penny Lane

"Penny Lane" is in the vein of "Yellow Submarine." Based on real shops along the lane,[28] its character portraits are nonetheless tinged with oddness. They can be taken to be "typical British eccentrics." And yet, the lyrics include the IFP subtext. The barber of Penny Lane has a photograph "of every head he's had the pleasure to know." Are they "heads" who smoke pot, people getting haircuts, or is the "barber" an egg-man (psychiatrist) who knows/no's heads? It is ambiguous, but there are IFP tropes. Drug allusions are interchangeable with eccentric behavior, the asylum, and so on. The banker "never wears a mac, in the pouring rain/Very strange." Little children laugh at the banker behind his back. Is he a flasher? Or just forgets his raincoat? Paul does sing that it's "very strange," but his tone is indulgent. The fireman rushes in, in a hurry although it is pouring rain. This could be explained, but isn't. All the characters are doing activities that are "very strange," the singer says mildly. But they are usual, on Penny Lane. "The pretty nurse is selling poppies from a tray." Now comes the "acting" motif: "and though she feels as if she's in a play, she is anyway."

No one is normal, or they don't feel quite normal. Penny Lane is the same community of the yellow submarine. It is also much like the characters in parody songs on the later White Album. The denizens of both could just as easily be insane people acting roles in an asylum, and the barber "shaves" the heads of incoming inmates. Once again Paul is presenting Laingian ideas of sane society being insane and vice versa, blurring the two to create community around an asylum metaphor. The nurse in the roundabout could be a nurse at a station in the middle of the ward, dispensing "poppies" or medications. Paul reportedly wrote "Penny Lane" in response to John's song, "Strawberry Fields." "Fields," I submit, has a motif about burying "empty" people. Accordingly when it came time to analyze this song, I had to acknowledge that "Penny Lane" *sounds* the same as "penny lain." This would be to lay a body out, with pennies on the eyes. The chorus makes the observation that "Penny Lane is in my ears and in my eyes." One assumed of course that the singer was seeing and hearing all the color and liveliness of Penny Lane, and bringing it to the listener.

However, given the "concerns" of the Beatles to kill the ego, Paul's "penny lain" goes with John's "straw-*bury* fields." Both images are of taking people down. Putting pennies on eyes of the deceased appeared in a line in "Taxman," so Paul would have been aware of an alternate association lurking in the phrase.

The pretty nurse selling poppies from a tray (selling poppies for war veterans) "feels as if she's in a play." And though she feels that way, "she is anyway." That is, although she feels she is acting, every-thing is a play. It's similar to "all the world's a stage and men and women are only players." To put this sort of observation directly following a reference to war veterans, who fought for a *meaning*, is a rather deliberate *cynicism*.

The song is taken for a bouncy, loving homage to British soci-ety. The Beatles' image of promoting "love," the bright colors they donned, and the often-innocuous backing music allowed The Beatles to seemingly sing about almost anything. But my analysis shows some consistent threads in their work.

Meanwhile in the United States, everyone from pre-adolescents to professors was trying to figure out the meaning of Beatles lyrics. After the aesthetic triumph of "Pepper," people felt more than ever that the Beatles were saying things in code. To their followers, they were gurus of the New Age—cultural leaders.[29]

"Penny Lane" seems to suggest more than anything else that Paul was well-enclosed inside his method of writing and producing songs. Perhaps he thought his identity of "Expando-Paul" was real and that Apple would enable people who had followed the inner fool in him-self or herself, a new creativity would flower. The new "culture" was *supposed* to be real. It was supposed to grow—to be in today's slang, "a thing." However, in the meantime Paul was writing in a variety of song styles as he always did, and using the IFP subtext. In "Penny Lane," it's another asylum.

For all the seeming surface variety, he was in a state of suspension creatively. It all had to go on a little longer, seemingly, until the end of the decade. I submit that "the culture" of the Sixties was not an organic event, except for what Paul instigated back in 1963-64. It was an "ostensive" culture.

Magical Mystery Tour

By late 1967, The Beatles could sound like barkers for their trip: "Step Right Up! Join the Magical Mystery Tour! Right this way!" "Roll up/ Roll up for the Mystery Tour," their joyous voices sang in blended harmony. John's harmonies were dependable transporters to another realm. "That's an invitation!" sang Paul, as if he were a mustached man with a boater hat and baton-herding people into a carnival tent. The Beatles sang in unison: "The Magical Mystery Tour is coming to take you away/Coming to take you away!" They were satirizing the "culture," but in typical Beatles fashion they were also acknowledging and asserting their own status as leaders of the "trip" into the "mystery."

The "mystery" was whatever you wanted it to be. The Beatles enticed listeners to begin their own journey. That is what was positive about them.

But I argue, the subtext was that you were being "taken into" an asylum, and the flip side of so many of their songs was that there is no "self inside," or as George would say, "nobody there." After a certain point in my analysis I became aware of the persistence of what I can only call nothingness or emptiness in Beatles songs. The Beatles' meaningless-mongering, their insistent motifs of deadness and emptiness, became impossible for me to ignore. And again, even as they come to "take you away" (as if to the mental hospital), the Beatles sing, "The Magical Mystery tour is dying to take you away/ Dying to take you away/Take you today." To enter the "mystery," you also have to be like the Beatles, who are "gone" or "dead." One takes this to mean the concept of ego-loss that Leary was ranting on about at the time, and, to be fair, the idea of transcending the ego is in Jung's writings[30] and is a tenant of Eastern Hinduism. The idea of ego-loss was too divorced from Western thought, however, to be anything the Beatles could sing about openly in *every* song. George handled direct allusions to it in his songs.

The fade-out ending to "Magical Mystery Tour" is perhaps the most interesting Paul ever did. One could go more places than expected, was the message.

* * *

Meanwhile, the identity-merchants prospered. There was a new pluralism and sense of anything-goes in "the culture." Illegal drugs were easier for people to get. The creative state of mind that the Beatles seemingly personified inspired many to ingest them. The Sixties "culture" was a mimetic looking glass people had wandered into.

Along with access to the Pill, abortion clinics, and lifting of censorship on print books and film, alternative lifestyle ideas surged into what I am theorizing was a Paul-created "interval." Communes, nudism, meditation, vegetarianism and Yoga made the editorial pages in newspapers and were featured in mainstream magazines. Now an American raised on Post Toasties could consider these lifestyles. But the Beatles' reach was international. Only a few countries banned their music.

John's lambast in "Walrus," however, was that confusion was the result of the Beatles' enterprise rather than enlightenment. To John, people wearing "corporation T-shirts" and chanting Hare Krishna were deluded—and a new, communal level of stupidity had been reached. People had wanted to enter the door the Beatles seemingly opened upon a self heretofore repressed, one that seemingly would reveal within themselves supra-normal powers of creativity and insight. But in "Walrus," John despaired (although rather humorously) that there was really none of this happening—just more T-shirts, commercials, sex and pot smoking. However, everybody was their own "egg-man," their own psychologist. "Feed your head," Grace Slick of the Jefferson Airplane sang. "You have to go out of your mind to use your head," Leary said. Or was it the opposite?

One could answer my analyses with the observation that the Beatles were just a rock-pop group. Why bother thinking about anything they sang and why try to analyze it? But this book is to chart a process—how the IFP Paul began with developed and how it spawned the Sixties.

John said in an interview (in 1970) with *Rolling Stone* publisher Jann Wenner that if he hadn't become a Beatle, he would have wanted to be a fisherman: "It's no fun being an artist. You know what it's like—writing—it's torture." A fisherman pulls in something unexpected, a fish caught by chance or luck or skill. If John had been a fisherman, he would have had the sense of something come to him, without the effort that it took to produce art. John said it was getting harder to be an artist (someone) because the "psychiatrists … these bastards are sucking us to death; that's about all that we can do, is do it like circus animals."[31] He didn't want to make art (apparently, he implies) on demand like a "circus animal" artist and would rather be in the audience. "But, I'm not capable of it."[32]

CHAPTER X

Penny Lane is in My Ears and
in My Eyes: Beatles on Film

Paul's "interval" of new "feelings" had opened up the possibility
of a new spectrum, almost a telescoping of ways to be in society. Underneath the hopeful vision, the underlying cohesion
of his art was the words of the broken-minded and lyrics that referred
to the mental hospital, the mental patient, and therapy. By 1966,
this language from the world of psychology would be used to allude
to "expanded" awareness or drug "realities." That the interval was
expanding was proven by the seamless addition of a bevy of effects
and instrumentation into the 1967 multi-genre album, "Pepper," that,
for all its pluralism, cohered. Each Beatles album (even the early ones)
was a stepping-stone along a path. The music led listeners into the
interval by the means I have been discussing, with a fusion of lyrics
to sound.

From a psychiatric point of view, this new Beatle-led era was creating an enclosure: a new asylum. To describe the new counterculture
in the terms used by psychiatrist John Rawlings Rees, the Beatles
had created a Reesian subgroup. This "sub" group (pardon the pun),
still in its nascent form in the mid- to late-Sixties, was developing its
own passwords, uniforms, symbolism and metaphors. The Beatles and

other groups gave the counterculture songs, fashions to copy, long hair to emulate, code words and imagery. The Beatles songs were imagistic anthems: the Yellow Submariners, "Lucy" girls, Mr. Kite, were held up to "pigs" (police) who used or fled guns, "pigs" (Capitalists) who had wives and over-ate in restaurants, or even "piggy" people who gorged on bonbons. The imagery was quite diverting and diversionary, all the while remaining more or less ambiguous; it kept the underlying subtext of psychiatry, therapy, and mental patients, as I have shown, hidden from view. Keeping the subtext hidden gave people the feeling that the creation of the counterculture was an organic movement. There was no clue as to *why* they felt as they did, about the songs. One passkey to the new culture was, it was implied, LSD, but one could experience some of the disorienting effects of LSD and a lot of the "feeling" of the new culture through its music.

If we view the counterculture as a formation of a Reesian subgroup (assuming for discussion purposes that such a project existed in the Sixties, with specific sociological aims), as an experiment, then the hippie counterculture definitely looked less viable after the Manson murders. The murders have been called "the end of the Sixties," along with Altamont.[1] But the new culture's ideals, *as* ideals, still existed. Also, the Sixties had established commercial enterprises connected to the subculture.

The Reesian subgroup concept came out of Rawlings Rees's research into groups within organizational structures and the function of such groups. Rees, who was a co-founder of the Tavistock Institute of Human Relations, worked for military intelligence in WWII and was a Nazi interrogator. At Tavistock, Rees wrote about management organization. His theory was that groups formed preemptively inside an organization would forestall eventual splintering or spin-off groups. Immersed in their own goals and internal politics, the sub-groups would be too preoccupied to question the overall goals or direction of the organization/corporation. Rees' theories, developed in the Fifties, were taken up by many organizational thinkers and put into practice in corporations. His main simple but effective idea was to rather than combat the groups and discipline them, to intentionally set up sub-groups, ("task forces" for example) and then empower the sub-groups and recognize them. And once they established their own sub-cultures, the more detailed and developed they became, the better; the more to divert them from examining or thinking about broader management goals.

This is one way (I suggest, but do not insist) of viewing the seemingly spontaneous generation of a new counterculture in the mid- to late-Sixties: as a Reesian subgroup purposely and specifically set up to cordon off any concerted challenge to governmental control. This *could* be a possible reason for the hard-to-reconcile actions of the CIA and MK-Ultra.

One could describe the Beatles as agents of creating a Reesian subgroup, namely, the Sixties "counterculture;" but these are just words. I am only making the point that the main underlying subtext to their work, the cohesion, was Paul's IFP. Without it, audiences would not have responded so much to their earlier work, and would not have accepted their later work. It is interesting that in a 1970 interview with Jonathan Cott, when asked about songwriting, Yoko remarked, "we always go back to the madness."[2] The remark was not expanded upon and left open to interpretation. What I am doing in this book is hazarding to expand and interpret these artist's transmissions. John and Paul, and later John and Yoko, always did go back to the madness as the cohesion and the basic context from which to present their art.

* * *

Paul was keen to make films, and the Beatles had contractual obligations that could not be gotten out of. Their first two films, *A Hard Day's Night* and *Help!* were madcap romps, showcases for their songs and vitality. A critic commented about *Help!* that "the Beatles don't have much to say." Much of the screen time was given over to Britain's pre-eminent comic. John complained that he "felt like an extra in my own film."

The other Beatles were less "keeny" and must have viewed another film project with a sense of dread. Films are tedious, hard work, especially if shot on location: logistics need to be organized by professionals so that everyone is adequately fed and sheltered, let alone paid on time.

Paul had confidence at this point, though, that he could transfer all his IFP from recordings to film. He could use the "cut-up" technique of Burroughs, which would put on film the sense of fracture and dislocation, as well as madness, which had been in Beatles' songs. However, he was to run into problems.

Film is a different animal than other media. In most media it is easy to leave some ambiguity; words can leave out a lot; a painting can be blurry or abstract; a song can be ambiguous; even a sharp-focus photo can be interpreted various ways, usually focused with a caption underneath it. Film is perhaps the most documentary medium because it starts with what is *there*. How could the ambiguous Beatles present themselves on film?

The Beatles had reviewed over 40 film scripts by 1967 written specifically for them, but none had been approved.[3] Walter Shenson, as mentioned earlier, had commissioned a script for them about a multiple personality. Denis O'Dell had pushed along negotiations for them to star in a *Lord of the Rings* trilogy, but this had been abandoned at the eleventh hour. Cinema was changing: the studio system had broken down in the early Sixties, obscenity laws had been loosened, and a rating system for movies was being devised. Penguin Books was a key player in obscenity laws pertaining to book publishing when they went to court and won the right to publish the unexpurgated version of D.H. Lawrence's *Lady Chatterley's Lover* in 1960. William Burroughs's novel *Naked Lunch* also made history beating the obscenity laws and establishing a new allowable level of the perverse in literature.[4]

Musically, the Beatles, in Paul's words, always wanted to go "louder, further, longer."[5] They wanted to stretch the world's envelope. However the problem Paul would face was in translating what I call the Beatles' "concerns" (their fundamentally subversive views) and their metaphorical engine (the IFP) to a visual medium without giving away their game and/or alienating a good two-thirds of their audience. Psychological research and the preoccupations of Beat poets were not what one normally associated with the Beatles. How to put the Beatles' *modus operandi* and their "concerns" into a film, cunningly?

An associated problem, not a small one, was that any script would give them something to *say*, and therefore, an associated *identity*. Identity was not what the Beatles were about. They reportedly considered acting in a Western, based on a book called *A Talent For Loving*; but this would have put a permanent overlay of association over their carefully maintained Beatles image. They were already "saying" things, in songs, in subtext (while maintaining their choice of lyrics was "random").[6]

Denis O'Dell, their producer, suggested the idea of the Beatles playing in an elegant Edwardian garden to a colorfully dressed audience: certainly a pleasant idea, and relatively easy to execute.[7] But Paul had other ideas for a movie, which the Beatles called "Paul's baby."

Paul would be inspired mainly by the Beats to make *Magical Mystery Tour* what it was. The "Merry Pranksters" (sponsored by Stanford Research Institute, as I discussed in Chapter Four) had been traveling the U.S. dispensing LSD and garnering press exposure. A Beat, Neil Cassady, drove the Prankster bus with Allen Ginsberg along, who was a friend of Paul's.[8] Ginsberg, known for his poems "Howl" and "Kaddish," was with Burroughs and Kerouac the most famous of the Beats. It seems reasonable to assume Paul combined the Merry Prankster bus idea with the English convention of taking "mystery bus tours" to undisclosed locations. Most of these tours would wind up at the seaside.

Paul was enthused about the idea of a "mystery tour," which was, of course, exactly what he had been doing with his IFP all along. He had been taking people to an unknown place, to "another kind of mind, there." A bus tour was also the idea of dislocation, again.

With this idea for a movie, he then set up a fractured head as his template for the film. He drew a circle, divided it into fourths, and invited each Beatle to contribute their own segment. This was in keeping with the Beatles being, in effect, four aspects or minds of the same person—the same fractured "head" or identity. The template brings to mind Paolozzi, a favorite artist of Paul's, who entitled his large sculpture of a fractured head, "Head of Invention."[9]

The next idea in keeping with his IFP was that the people on the bus—a mixture of actors, friends, and other people the Beatles selected—would be ignorant of where they were going, or what would happen next. The mystery tour (experiment) would be filmed in "real-time." It was pretty much a given with this set-up as the "structure" that there would be no linear plot to the film. The film sequences could be presented as "cut-ups" or collage, that Beats such as Burroughs and Gysin favored.

However, each Beatle had to think up *something* for their segment. Let's look at how the IFP and the Beatles "concerns" appeared on film in *Magical Mystery Tour.*

The most obvious reference to mental illness is the 18th century madman's cap that Ian MacDonald identifies John wearing in the "I Am the Walrus" segment.[10] John, seated at the piano, wears the skullcap, making his head look egg-like. By the song's end, a string of people also wearing the caps, wrapped in what appears to be a large sheet, dance conga-line fashion, looking like a bumpy centipede behind the bus. They are the happy inmates following the bus.

Using the "cut-ups" approach, Paul directed the editing of every scene in the film. Except for the "Fool on The Hill" sequence, most of the film is disjointed. Dialogue is random, sense is left behind, and sequences inserted for apparently no reason. People sing a drinking song, Paul's eyes dart back and forth, and then we see a girl in a bra. The dwarf runs, people run lamely, then a car screams around a track. The intent behind the senseless editing would have been explained by Burroughs, if anyone had asked him, to "destabilize Control." Burroughs, the most theoretical of the Beats, maintained that any linearity including that of language was a "control system." To break out of control, one had to cut up texts, movies, newspapers, or record audio and then splice it, or use it as a kind of reverse feedback de-stabilization (at least this is how Burroughs *explained* what he was doing).

Intentionally "losing the plot" brings to my mind the ending sequence of Michelangelo Antonioni's *Blow Up*, which was released in 1966; in that film the photographer, played by David Hemmings, is so overtaken by random events that he fails to contextualize even his witnessing a murder.[11] It is clear that he was at the scene of a murder, and we even see the result, the body; but by the end of the film the photographer has no impetus anymore to even report it or judge it as something immoral amidst the senselessness of his environs.

But *Blow Up did* tell a story; *Magical Mystery Tour* did not. Many of the images and sequences in it could be taken as disturbing, depending on one's sense of humor. An unfair amount of abuse is heaped on "Ringo's aunt," played by the actress Jessie Robins. She is the subject of a romance scene on the beach, skirting ridicule, and then is humiliated in a restaurant by a waiter, acted by John, who shovels what looks like pre-digested pasta onto her plate until she cries. Behind her the bus patrons are enjoying a "naked lunch," (a nod to Burroughs) as they sit down to eat lunch semi-clothed, the men shirtless, the women in panties and bras. This sequence is explained as being a "dream," but that it is shown at all is the point. The Beatles play "warlocks" or wizards in a laboratory, deciding what they will cook up next for the unsuspecting passengers—an apt metaphor for their position in "the culture."

Other than perhaps Paul's sequence for "The Fool on the Hill," I can think of no single uplifting sequence in the film: a cello is set on fire, the fat lady cries, little children dance with blackened eyes, there is a shot of a male torso with "magical mystery boy" carved into it, while the "rocking-horse people," John and one other Beatle, move onanistically on rocking horses while they watch an ominous sequence for "Blue Jay Way" (which includes George's face morphing into a demon-animal face, a shocking visual). The sequence could be alluding to pedophilia, as there are quick frames of naked men and a naked child. The second-to-last sequence in the film features a song sung Elvis-Presley-style by an associate of the Beatles, Vivian

Stanshall. A young woman strips onstage while the song proceeds and at the end it is implied that the subject of the song will "pay her fare" with sex and/or be murdered.

The film ends with a dance sequence with very little dancing. The set was for a grand ballroom finale, and yet all that happens is well-dressed people sway side to side, as the rhythm to "Your Mother Should Know" begins to oscillate. The Beatles gingerly descend the stairs. Paul, wearing a black carnation, is handed a bouquet for his performance/production.

These are the Beats "concerns": fracture, subversion, anarchy, and darkness. Most people don't connect the Beats and their philosophies with the Beatles, but they should consider conflating the two. In *Magical Mystery Tour* the Beats are filtered through Paul. As for the official publicity, the film is supposed to be "all a bit of fun." With the "cut-ups," their dream machine, their obscenity trials, the Beats ostensibly wanted to break "old" associations up, cut them up and rearrange them. Some of them posed as heroes for the common man, but they were actually the anarchic drug-taking faction of society. Madness and dislocation was their chosen paint box. I have been suggesting the world of the unstable began Paul's artistic "praxis." As Ginsberg once put it, "make your neurosis your *style*." (He was talking to me as a fashion magazine editor, at that time.) Paul used the neuroses of others, and he was heavily influenced by the Moderns and the Beats, aesthetically and philosophically.

The Beats also favored activities found in the Middle East, in old cults and countercultures. Some of the Beats were pedophiles, based on anecdotal evidence.[12] The Beats would travel to Morocco and Leary remarked in the Nineties, "I always wondered why all my friends were raving about Morocco; I didn't know it was because of the sex." Burroughs murdered his own wife in a consensual "game" of William Tell, and then wrote his novel which broke the obscenity laws, *Naked Lunch*.

So, the "bus" which everyone took to partake of the "trippy flower power" anti-war agenda had those kinds of tires on it—of the subversive Beats. Beats such as Neil Cassady, of course, drove and Ginsberg rode in the very bus that the film idea was based on— Kesey's "Further" bus. The Beats had segued into the Hippie era with a good assist from Harvard, both in the music producer Rothchild, and in its archives being made available to folk protest singers. The Beats, nascent hippies and personality researchers confluenced at institutions like Stanford and Harvard, funded by the same sources.

Magical Mystery Tour, show on television in the U.K. intentionally on Boxing Day to garner a large youth (and child) audience, was trounced by many critics. The *Daily Mail* called it "blatant rubbish."[13] Paul defended it as "a cool little film," and that it sent a message to the youth that they would understand. He said that it was a mistake to have it debut on black and white televisions of the time, as it needed color to be enjoyed. I think this remark disingenuous. Paul would have realized television was black and white. The main thing was that it be seen by a large audience. *Magical Mystery Tour* is generally taken to be "fun" by those who just want an opportunity to see The Beatles and hear their music, or, among those who take exception to some of the imagery, passed over in silence as simply a case of "Paul McCartney Goes Too Far." (His major biographers avoid critiquing it.)[14] Yet it does contain many elements of the Beatles' "concerns" and influences.

* * *

If *Magical Mystery Tour* was more than a slight nod to the influence of the Beats, then *Yellow Submarine* was more "Beatles." It was colorful, jokey, told a story, and renditions of the lovable lads were in almost every frame. *Yellow Submarine* would be the most expensive animated feature ever made in Britain, using hundreds of animators.[15] It was a colorful animated story of the Beatles' mission to fuse opposites in "Love."

The script was co-written by Erich Segal, a Classics professor at Harvard, Yale and Princeton, who would also write the novel which was made into a film called *Love Story*. Segal co-wrote the *Submarine* script with the assistance of an experienced writer for animation. Although I could find no psychological connection directly to Segal, the film, on examination, does depict landscapes of the mind, in visual metaphor.

Holes figure prominently, as the cartoon Beatles travel in and out of them through space and time. This is in effect traveling inside the holes in yourself, the "hole" in the "whole." We recall mention of "holes" in the subconscious in Chapter Two at the Macy Conference. The sequence with fantastical creatures, snails, trains and so on moving in and out of doors in a corridor is a similar idea. The doors in the corridor-mind keep material under a lid; but when "the doors" are opened, the most unusual "material" emerges (as is supposed to happen on LSD, or in a therapy session).[16] One landscape the Beatles travel though in their submarine has inhabitants inspired by psychiatric concepts of various neurotic types. In "the land of the beasts," a sucker-faced beast vacuums up another, everything in its path, and then itself, which recalls the concept of the devouring personality. Another beast rolls over itself, sticking out its tongue each time it rolls. The art director for the film, Heinz Edelman, reportedly took the look for these creatures from another German artist, Friedrich Schroder-Sonnenstern. Sonnenstern's paintings[17] were inspired by those of a fellow inmate in a mental asylum Sonnenstern was in for a time. They are inmates, depicted as fantastical beings.

The inhabitants of Pepperland are drawn in a different style, but their "frozenness" and imprisonment inside themselves when the music is silenced is similar to the Reichian idea of "character armor."[18] Wilhelm Reich, yet another psychiatrist kicked out of Nazi Germany (he wrote *The Psychology of Fascism*), hypothesized that people form character armor around their personalities that "freezes" them into rote roles and ways of being.[19] He wanted to liberate them from their armor (which could be achieved by more sexual freedom and orgasms, for the "healthy genital character").[20] The Victorian-themed denizens of Pepperland are liberated at the end, when the Pepper music returns (of the Beatles); the thawed Pepperland population gather in a field, and out of the top of one man's head sprouts a giant lotus. The tail of a "cute" Pepperland creature grows longer and sprouts, in an allusion to enlivening of the spine and sexual energy. And of course, the eyes of the Pepperland denizens turn kaleidoscope-colored.

The Beatles, as depicted in cartoon form and voiced by actors, spend the movie joking in puns and asides. Cartoon Ringo appears in a winged helmet, alluding to the headgear of Hermes, messenger of the gods. John also appeared with a feather on either side of his cap in *Magical Mystery Tour*, so it seems the Beatles want to be associated with Hermes, divine messenger. Hermes is connected to the image of "Lucy" with kaleidoscope (rainbow) eyes, because the legend of Hermes includes both an eye and rainbow motif. Hermes took over the job of bringing divine messages to the people from the goddess Iris, who rode a rainbow.[21] From the goddess Iris we get our word for the part of the eye that is colored, the iris.

Yellow Submarine also has the psychological idea of the double in it: Beatles meet their *doubles*, which were imprisoned inside a bubble dome in Pepperland by the Meanies. This is split and identity fracture; but of course it is "all a bit of fun." The split-identities merely exchange jokes with each other. The seemingly free-associating (but, well-salted with psychological concepts), lysergic or light-hearted (depending on how "experienced" you are) movie supports the popular conception of The Beatles as messengers of peace, harmony and goodwill. The malevolence of the Blue Meanies is overcome by love; their terror campaign against Pepperland is forgiven and forgotten as everyone joins in to sing a song.

The final sequence is worth noting because it is a *tour de force* of prisms and hierarchical pyramids of color, and was what the filmmakers wanted to send the audience out of the theatre with in terms of ideas. Along with the liberation of the frozen denizens, we see the giant letters of NO turn into KNOW, and then turn into NOW. A giant NO turns into YES. The many "devil horns" hand signs, which I lost count of after the first five minutes of the film but were numerous, are flashed even more obviously during the final friezes of imagery. Outstretched-arm characters are arranged hierarchically, their arms forming "devil-horn symbols," while in the foreground dance a row of fat devil figures with tall horns/ears and extended tongues. Atop the pyramid of outstretched-arm figures is a stylized demon face, made of rainbow prisms. John and others hold their hands aloft in devil-signs. "Yes is the only word, the eu-monius word," the assistant to the (now reformed) chief Blue Meanie gushes. The little "nowhere man" smiles at the chief Blue Meanie. So it seems violence and enemies are forgiven if you just cross over to the other side, or they do, or something.

This flip-flopping with no concept of boundary or "judgment" is similar to the Laingian idea of if you understand the world of the insane, you will not think them insane. Only this time the "opposite" faction is the Blue Meanies, who merge with the Pepperlanders into the happy satanic hierarchy at the end.

The animation concluded, the four Beatles appear in the flesh, each holding a "play" prop from the movie. John, raising a spyglass, announces that he sees "Blue Meanies in the vicinity of this theater! ...What do we do? Sing a song!" The film concludes with a spirited rendition of "All Together Now," which is akin to a children's nursery rhyme: "One, two, three, four/Can I have a little more?" except that it also includes, "Can I take my friend to bed?" (this line was left out of the film rendition). It is a faux-naive ditty: "Sail the ship/Chop the tree/Skip the rope/Look at me!" (In this context one wonders what part of "me" is being displayed.)

Much more appealing than *Magical Mystery Tour*, *Yellow Submarine* has a lighter touch, and illustrates in a fanciful way the Beatles' subtexts of psychiatry, unification of people through music, and overcoming separate consciousness which is seen as loneliness (dialectics). But could they have put this message across without flashing all the devil signs? Apparently the script writers did not want the idea of "justice being served" to be in the movie. The Meanies receive no judgment, or comeuppance; they are kissed on the nose. I suggest that yet another psychological trope is at work here. Perhaps the unification of opposites at the end of the film was yet another acknowledgement of psychological research carried out at various institutions including Harvard. The taking of one over into another, or the flipping of one belief into its opposite, was a goal of mind research in certain institutions and in academe, including Harvard.

Mentor to Timothy Leary, Harry Murray was a leader in person-ality research and an advocate of global government.[22] He researched personality "types" of Harvard men and OSS personnel; his research was around both how personalities are formed, and in hopes of form-ing a global man, or "fashioning a new superego."[23] Like MacLeish, who was also at Harvard, Murray was convinced that WWII indi-cated the need for a new type of "global" individual that would make war obsolete. Murray wrote in a letter to writer Lewis Mumford, "We will create a new moral order with artists like you, checked and verified by scientists like me."[24] Murray and his researchers had been conducting tests and interviews to "type" personalities since Twenties. During WWII Murray directed OSS personality assessment test-ing for intelligence personnel selection. He also had an agenda to found a new religion: one that fused opposites. The idea was to work with dialectics, in a kind of core reality apart from all influences of society, and find "something new." This is a "nice" way of putting it, but Murray and his mistress Christiana Morgan basically flagel-lated each other in their "Tower" (built in emulation of the Jungian tower at Bollingen) toward this effort of forming a new religion, what Morgan's biographer called a "Satanic Christ."[25]

T.S. Eliot, whom we keep returning to, stated that the "project of the 20th Century is to form a humane society that is not Christian." That is a fairly broad statement, but, I am just pointing out that psy-chologists at Harvard were interested in non-Christian dialectics, and a sense of justice and punishment for evil is indeed lacking from "Yellow Submarine."

One wouldn't usually drag in all these allusions to what is a chil-dren's film, but given the other pattern we see in Paul's lyrics, and John's, and some of George's, it all seems to fit.

Although I mention the research at Harvard in this book, I do not think that the bringing-over of a person to the other side, or taking people in a loop-the-loop circle (as John referenced I suggest in "Walrus") was something *Paul* had on his mind. Paul's IFP came from his own innate drives, perhaps from a need to protect himself, and the influence of the environment he found himself in. Withal he wrote tuneful songs often with a subtext of psychological ideas.

Even though I am asserting that psychological motifs are in Paul's songs, and that there are many connections between institutions during the Sixties, I also assert that Paul's songwriting process was forged by him and him only. I do not think anyone told him write songs as he did. He already was influenced by theatre classes he had taken, the environs of the Reeperbahn, and John's drug-taking and irreverence, even before he entered the Asher residence. Then, he found material that resonated with him personally—"another kind of mind, there." The moment when he found these materials, he did commemorate in "Got To Get You Into My Life." He just wanted to hold them. To be an artist, to write songs, was all he wanted. He forged his identity based on a synthesis, and what he was doing was taken for real. The metaphor of the asylum was extended to form the ostensive counterculture.

He had expanded the interval, the asylum, greatly on "Pepper." But the public's reaction to *Magical Mystery Tour* was a disappointment to him.[26] He apparently did not realize how much the film contradicted the Beatles' image. In 1967, probably to most of the public the Beatles were still cute Paul, witty John, spiritual George and funny Ringo. Paul tried to put some of his own anti-establishment politics or "concerns" into *Magical Mystery Tour*, but its relatively cool reception among critics meant that it could only succeed where it failed. Several years passed before the film was shown on television in the U.S., and it was rented to universities and colleges for one-day screenings before becoming available on DVD.

CHAPTER XI

And I See You Again … Francie and *The Beatles* (Blank Asylum Walls)

The Beatles, or as it came to be called, the White Album, was a strange hermetic experience of potpourrism, and no one critic could sum it up. A sprawling amalgam of rock, pop, folk, Blues, ballad and noise concrete, the album nevertheless formed a cohesion of sound and mood, and many thought it to be the Beatles' best work. Jann Wenner called the double album "the history and synthesis of Western music," and wrote that in it The Beatles "not only expand the idiom but they are also able to penetrate it and take it further."[1] A *Time* magazine reviewer said the album showed "the best abilities and worst tendencies" of The Beatles, and that it "lacks a sense of taste and purpose."[2] Robert Cristagau of the *Village Voice* called it "their most consistent, and probably their worst" album,[3] but listed it among the top ten releases of the year. In this chapter I will explain why the album is the most successful and complete rendition of Paul's IFP.

Initially, Paul wanted to write hit songs—he found a formula. But the material he found resonated with him. Paul, after all, had written early on, "Please, lock me away." In a sense, The Beatles song catalogue would begin and end with that simple request. Paul and John would joke about the lyrics to "A World Without Love."

"Please, lock me away," Paul would sing.

John would reply, "Yes, okay." Song over.

They would laugh.[4] Because even if they did not realize it, those words meant a lot to them—they summarized their rise to fame. Paul found a way to write hit songs using asylum-inmate texts. John, after being a young "Pilchard" in Mimi's attic room, climbed to worldwide fame. If both of them had kept themselves entirely locked away, we never would have gotten the Beatles. But now they were subliminally putting the idea of an asylum back into society—the new "home" of the counterculture.

John often called the buying public "the Normals," although not to their face. ("Normals" to denote the general population was a term used by researchers at the Macy Conference, so it seems to have been official jargon.)[5] The Beatles wrote music tailor-made to the anti-psychiatry movement of the Sixties and Laing's assertion that the insane were the sane, and that the repressive *mores* of society needed loosening. The Beatles worked in reverse of Laing's method, but had the same philosophy. They did not tell the insane that they were sane, but rather, brought the illogical logic of the insane to the Normals. At first it was introducing lyrics culled, I assert, through patient transcripts. The voice of the muddled confessor, the ontologically insecure, Paul brought successfully into compositions. Then the language and feelings they pioneered could be segued by 1966 into psychedelic or cosmic allusions.

Although the translation of their method onto film, *Magical Mystery Tour*, had caused motion sickness in many viewers, Paul still had hopes that his new expansion could be expressed in many directions. He believed that the undefined possibilities that the Beatles stood for in the public mind were real, not simply an artistic statement—that the ostensive, new dialectic of the "interval" was real and could be explored infinitely in a flowering of ideas and possibilities. What he had tapped should be achievable by anyone, and it was only a matter of access. Apple was Paul's real-world launch of what I call his "Expando-Paul" phase. In April 1967 the Beatles set up Apple Corps as the holding company for a series of subsidiary companies. These included clothing retail, film, music, publishing, and even a school for children. Producer Denis O'Dell was appointed director of the film division, and Peter Asher director of the music label. Vaughan Evans was put in charge of the Apple school. The business model of Apple made it exempt from capital gains tax, and each Beatle was to buy a stake in the company.[6] Paul was to be by far the most involved Beatle in its day-to-day operations, and regularly came to the board meetings.

Paul wrote and took out ads in large newspapers calling for creative submissions from the public (The call was directed toward young men, picturing Alistair Taylor outfitted as a one-man band). *Forbes* interviewed Paul about Apple's business model and plans. An artist friend of the Beatles, "The Fool," was commissioned to paint a psychedelic mural on the outside of Apple headquarters, and he and his collaborators also designed the Apple clothing line.

The Beatles already owned a four-storey brick building at 94 Baker Street. The Apple boutique was put on the ground floor and administrative offices above. Paul tried to reassure local shopkeepers, many of whom were aspiring counterculture entrepreneurs, that Apple was not a big fish eating littler fish. He explained, "The idea is to have an 'underground' company above ground, as big as Shell BP or ICI but with no profit motive. The profits to go first to the combined staff, so that everyone who needs a Rolls-Royce can have one, then after that, we'll give them away to anyone who needs help."[7] Apple was hard to categorize, just like the Beatles' music resisted categorization. Apple was "something new." However, it seemed important to emphasize that it was all about sharing and creativity. The Beatles went on U.S. television and "basically asked anyone who had an idea to send it to them," wrote O'Dell. (Derek Taylor recalled the Beatles said that "anyone who had a dream could come and see them in London, and they would make it come true.")[8] Apple was consistent with the ostensive culture in more ways than one, standing for openness, freedom, expansion, ideas without constraints, lack of gatekeeping, as well as the Beatles' "concerns."

In the Apple Electronics division, people tinkered with phones that responded to voice commands and wallpaper with hidden loudspeakers that the Beatles called "loudpaper."[9] "In the Sixties there was this feeling of being modern," commented Paul, three decades later during the early Silicon Valley technology boom. "So much so that I feel like the Sixties is about to happen. It feels like a period in the future to me, rather than a period in the past." The Beatles were supposedly starting a boom—they were sponsoring research into new tech—new audio—new everything.

"The Beatles Lead Now," proclaimed *The Beatles Book* monthly in 1968, during the calls for submissions, and after the Apple retail shop opened. "Every country and sphere of activity has its leaders. The important people who start things going and show the way for everyone else to follow. The Beatles are now, without doubt, the unchallenged leaders of pop music and, for that matter, the most forward-thinking members of the new generation.

"Their influence already has been considerable. Basically, they are anti those things which stop progress, like stuffiness, pomposity, and pig-headedness. Against the whole attitude of some older people which can be summed up under the heading, 'Do what we tell you because we know best.'"

The venture was the embodiment of the hopeful vision of the Beatles—that creativity was latent in everyone, and that it was only "pig-headedness" and gatekeepers who stunted the growth of a new, better society. "The Beatles ... are doing their level best to help new talent to emerge," the article continued. "They are putting effort and money into new enterprises so that many young hopefuls who have the ability to become top stars but, at the moment, no opportunity to do so, will be able to get a chance to show what they can do ... (The Beatles) remember their early struggles very well, when it seemed as though they were never going to break through the barriers which were preventing them from climbing the ladder to stardom. And they hate to see talent go to waste."[10]

It was a big takeaway of the Sixties—that we could as Cass Elliot sang, "make your own kind of music." Of course, she added, "even if nobody else sings along," but that was in 1969.[11] In 1967 most everyone, or at least, all the youth, had higher aims. The "ostensive" culture, led by the Beatles, seemed to have so much truth and basis to it.

The reader will be aware by now of the strange situation I have described in this book, in that the culture which was supposed to transform the world (and kind of did, in a way) was created in a sense by just one man, Paul McCartney, who was working with psychological texts from a closed-off, invalidated world. He was using insights and phrases, also situations, from the world of the locked-away. Strangely, it was as if he had created a can-opener to pry open society, and now everything could come out of the can. Whether the Beatles helped create a culture based on verities, or just liberated what had been stifled for good reason, is a question people in Western culture are living out today.

But in 1967-68, a venture like Apple made perfect sense. The Beatles' accountants advised it would save the Beatles approximately three million pounds in taxes,[12] and Apple's invitation to everyone captured the cultural moment. It seemed as though young people had so much to express—new ideas, new fashions. Young women's skirts went as high as they could go, and then disappeared as models like Edie Sedgwick started to wear only huge earrings, black tights and a tunic. There was a lot of energy around fashion and art. More and more women started using the Pill for birth control. Young men were wearing long hair and flouting authority in other ways. Making a business enterprise out of all this energy was almost what Paul had to do, even if it might turn out to be a bad idea.

Paul took out ads in major newspapers asking the public to contribute scripts, stories, ideas, inventions—to write songs—to join Apple in this great endeavor, to get around the gatekeepers and those who would inhibit creativity. The nascent counterculture seemed to be, on the surface, a fertile field for such sprouts to flourish. On an intuitive level the time seemed right for Apple. Also, the Beatles had enough money to try such an enterprise.

Robert Fraser, drug dealer and manager of Indica Gallery, had gotten out of jail in early 1968, and began to promote artists again.[13]

John and Yoko did an exhibition, "You Are Here," which featured a large group of collection boxes for the blind, the spastic's society and similar charities. (This was again showing John's interest in vision and blindness.) There were many jokes about cripples and deformity that had also informed his writing. Yoko's touch was to release 365 white balloons, each attached to a tag printed with the phrase, "You are here."

George later said about Apple: "There were a lot of ideas, but when it came down to it, the only thing we could do successfully was write songs, make records, and be Beatles."[14] This was borne out by the release of "Hey Jude," which stayed at Number One longer than any Beatles single. It was released in August 1968, with a B-side of John's "Revolution," three months ahead of the White Album. Paul selected, sponsored, and produced Apple recording artists, including Mary Hopkin whose song he produced, "Those Were the Days," went to Number One. Proud of Apple's releases, he sent four Apple singles gift-packaged to the Royal family, with a card announcing "our first Four."[15]

Zapple, Apple's spoken-word label, was launched in early February 1969 and seems to have been primarily a loudspeaker for the Beats. It released material by Lawrence Ferlinghetti, Michael McClure, Allan Ginsberg and comic Lenny Bruce. Barry Miles, Paul's good friend and co-owner with Peter Asher of the Indica Gallery, supervised the Zapple program. John and Yoko recorded an album for the label, *Life with the Lions*, George composed some electronic Moog music, and Richard Brautigan recorded his own poetry. Once again, the Beats were keeping their hand in. Zapple was hand-in-glove with the Beatles' politics and "concerns," which were, as one can gather, fundamentally subversive for all the surface sunshine. In 1968, Ken Kesey and his coterie including screenwriter and novelist Robert Stone arrived to confab at Apple headquarters at George Harrison's invitation, George having met Kesey earlier on a visit to California. Stone commented later about this expedition, "We were still young enough to enjoy ourselves."[16] "There were hoarse whispers," according to Stone, "about some kind of Prankster-Apple-Beatle amalgam."[17] George Harrison also said "come on over" to a group of Hells Angels "on (their) way to straighten out Czechoslovakia," as he informed the Apple staff. "They may look as if they are going to do you in, but are very straight and do good things, so don't fear them or uptight them." George eventually had to ask the biker gang when they would be leaving, after they took over the Apple guest lounge, drank to excess and seemed to want to stay on indefinitely.[18]

Paul said later, "I wanted Apple to run; I didn't want to run Apple."[19] He had confidence in his Expando-Paul identity; it had spread into the culture, therefore a business built on it should succeed.

In the midst of all this expansion, Paul had an album to make with the other Beatles.

After "Pepper," Paul wanted to cram even more into the "interval" he had created—using Burroughsian ideas of tape loops, cut-ups, found sound, noise concrete, all manner of sound effects from the BBC sound library and anything else he might come across. John, catching Paul's wave as usual (but as he often did, making a more expansive statement) had become enamored of using random sound in compositions and experimenting with tape loops. John discovered he liked the sound of reverse speech, achieved by running tape backwards. He would do quite well with his experiments with cut-ups, or splicing tape, on the White Album track "Revolution 9."

The run-out groove at the very end of "Pepper" was also reverse speech, the fruit of many studio hours to achieve a track that had a message whichever way it was played. I suggest this again is the idea of overcoming dialectics that was the Beatles' concern perhaps since 1964, which by 1968 they could bring to a fine consistency in the studio. "Hello Goodbye" was the clean, pop version of this idea, and the run-out groove the Burroughsian-Nietschean ("We'll all be magic Supermen/Never could be any other way") "gibberish" way of saying it. From pop song to reverse speech, the Beatles strove to get their message across. John could write an anthem of unity ("All You Need Is Love") in a day or two because the smashing of any distinctions ("pig-headedness, or those who think they know better") was foremost in the Beatles' minds.

However, for all their message of unity, the Beatles still needed outside inspiration, or at least enough to make another album. As it happened, Apple was to bring John and Paul inspiration and song material in the form of Francie Schwartz, an emissary from the advertising world of New York City.

Francie is thought to be a mere fling of Paul's, his live-in lover for the spring and summer of 1968. But she had a lot in common with Paul. She believed intuitively in the messages The Beatles' music had conveyed and was in a way, acting them out in her own life.

Francie Schwartz was an independent young woman working in advertising, in her mid-twenties. She had married young and divorced, finding out that she did not want to be tied to domesticity. Launching herself into New York, she was able to support herself with her illustration skills. She led a fast lifestyle, and after watching an art movie on speed one evening, smoked a joint that seemed to be spiked with LSD. She woke up the next morning feeling terrible, and two days later was still hallucinating. After a consultation with her mother and a social worker, she took a cab to Roosevelt mental hospital in Manhattan.[20]

Francie was in the hospital for several weeks. They probably gave her an extensive "work up," or interview; she was medicated with Thorazine. Francie was not given ECT, although it was administered at that hospital. She demanded to be released after a few weeks, but her mother informed her she would have to stay for at least forty-five days, because otherwise the insurance would not cover it; she denounced her mother on the phone and told her she never wanted to see her again.

Francie knew the inner workings of the desire merchants; she also was a creation of the outpouring of Paul's creativity that he had begun with the IFP. She reflected the seed of the Beatles subtext—a "free" individual, but one who was also a mental patient. She knew about the end product of the Beatles' creativity: the marketing of stuff to people. Francie was on both the beginning and the end of the Beatles' creative "loop." Somewhere in the middle was Francie, the "psychedelic personality."

She herself felt she was the new type. "I have a psychedelic personality," she told the doctors at Roosevelt. They furrowed their brows at the special meeting called to interview her, and asked her what she meant. "I've been tripping since I was a little girl." She explained that when she was a child seeing all the bright colors in nature, "as the colors popped out and grew more intense, that was a trip." She told them, "In fact, I'm tripping right now on all of you. You're all wearing dull suits and narrow ties and horn-rimmed glasses, and you're all starting to lose your hair."[21]

After Francie left the hospital, she was promptly hired at another advertising firm in Manhattan. One evening she befriended a street musician named Richard, playing violin near Carnegie Hall. She was interested in him, "an avid reader of Einstein essays, science fiction, and dramatic theory."[22] He wanted recognition not as a violinist, but as an actor. He did not want to sleep with her, but he told her his life story, and she spent a night and morning typing up his life story in movie form. Then they took the story to his agent, but the agent refused to pay for it. She told Richard she wanted to help him, that she could fly to England and show the story to Paul McCartney. That same day, she was let go from her job for refusing to sleep with the art director; taking her severance pay and the script, she flew to London, where she met Paul at Apple headquarters.

Francie had gifts to give, and so did Paul. Paul "always did like Jewish girls from New York,"[23] Miles noted. The two could talk—she could bring him information, and he could bring her—his Beatledom. This, even though he was non-monogamous, was enough to utterly charm her.

In a way, he had created Francie, because the Beatles' "way" had formed the culture which was now being marketed to. One could argue that he was doing some reconnaissance work by choosing her as a lover. He could pick her advertising brain for what was being marketed, how marketing was changing, but also see where her blind spots were. That would tell him where he as an artist stood apart from the art-into-money "loop."

Once again, Paul was learning from his lover. He had, I suggest, learned from Jane about acting the role of a pop star, and how to portray "feelings." Now he was the lover of a woman who had spent time in a mental ward, and had worked in the center of the advertising industry in New York. Both Jane and Francie could show him dividing lines he wanted to know about. Where was the line between acting sincere and being sincere? What was the dividing line between being an artist "selling" dreams, feelings or fantasies, and doing almost the same thing in advertising? Was there any difference anymore, in the late Sixties? And this could have ramifications on youth identity as well—who was authentic and who was just an act? Was he an act? Or part of him was? Maybe hanging out with Francie could furnish him with some answers.

Paul's exposure to Dr. Asher's world, which sorted out the sick from the acting sick, and the physically ill from the mentally ill, was another case of his finding dividing lines and learning from people whose job it was to make those distinctions. Learning this type of information had enabled Paul both to hone his craft of acting emotions which would sell, and also to be able to carefully mix things together, not too little and not too much. A lot of things as a result could come under one umbrella (that of the IFP) in Beatles songs. His art had (seemingly) made a new personality "type" among youth. And Francie felt she was that type.

Paul could do reconnaissance, of a sort, by being around Francie. This is not to criticize Paul. In a sense, everybody has a bit of spy in him or her—we go out into the world, find people to be inspired by, take a bit of what is around us, and then hopefully make something of ourselves. Francie had more in common with Paul than Jane at this point. People influence us, we influence other people. Paul's IFP to my mind really soared and found completion in the White Album. And Francie inspired more than a few songs on it.

* * *

Any person working in an advertising agency has a keen interest in "what's new." Advertising people also circulate a lot, and spread information—they can do it in a natural, organic way like an animal carrying seed on its fur, or they can do it in an intentional way. Ad agency people want to know what people are thinking—and how and why they think about what they are thinking. They have to craft ads that will convince, and with the advent of a more youth-driven culture in the Sixties, it was getting harder for the older heads in the business to fathom the trends.[24] Increasingly, advertising wanted youth to guide it. Agencies began hiring younger and younger staff, trying to adapt to mercurial trends.[25] But the younger heads didn't have any basis in reality either, due to same situation.

Francie was living this upheaval: she had left her husband, taken many lovers, worked in advertising, but was hired and fired multiple times. She was promiscuous although wrote in her memoir that she always thought the next one would be the lifetime partner. She shared Paul's enthusiasm to be a trendsetter.

Francie too had an idea for an artistic, educational and retail empire, and had dictated her vision for it into a tape recorder on speed one night in Manhattan, a few months before she met Paul. She envisioned that it would be "bigger than Playboy," and called it the "New Renaissance Empire."[26] After her hospital stay she still wanted to pursue her dream, and it was partly due to this that she went to London and walked into Apple HQ, meeting Paul near the front desk.

I give this background for Francie to show how she had been both encouraged by the "culture" Paul's Identity Fracture Project had engendered, and had a vision for an artistic empire which seemed to have been similar to Apple.

Paul would write one of his most poignant songs at the beginning of his affair with Francie. It must have seemed to Paul as if he met his own creation. Francie was welcomed into the Beatles fold, and was present at the recording of much of the White Album material.

* * *

On the White Album I can ascertain that eleven songs are IFP. They use language from the world of the mental asylum, therapy, or have a mental patient subtext. Of the nineteen remaining tracks, six are satire or parody, and four I classify as "raucous." That leaves nine songs in the "other" category: "Sexy Sadie," "Long Long Long," "Julia," "Don't Pass Me By," "Honey Pie," "Cry Baby Cry," "While My Guitar Gently Weeps," "Dear Prudence" and "Mother Nature's Son." Several "other" songs and all of the parody songs, however, support the IFP. I will discuss the IFP songs on the album first. Some are transparently IFP; others took a bit of decoding. The main point is that throughout the album, John, Paul and George would again use the subtext of the mental asylum, the therapy patient, and ego-loss just as they did before.

For a few weeks John and Yoko lived in Paul's St. John's Wood home, where Francie was Paul's live-in girlfriend and cook.[27] Francie, John and Yoko would hang out together in the evenings when Paul was out "raving, getting it up for who knows who," Francie recalled.[28] Francie liked both John and Yoko, and they seemed to have felt comfortable with her. Francie liked Yoko's "sweetness."[29] One night the trio tried eating some opium cookies, but nothing happened. On other nights, they watched television or discussed the Apple empire. It seems reasonable to assume that on one of these evenings, Francie would have told John and Yoko her story—her ordeal of being incarcerated in a mental hospital in New York.

Francie's story contained disturbing things in it. There was the nightmare of staying high, of being medicated against her will, and her own mother insisting she stay in the ward. Stupefied on medication, she had watched the nurse come out with the tray of pills, and inmates being taken away for ECT treatment. The camaraderie she shared with other inmates was the flip side of the misadventure: a silver lining. Francie experienced first-hand the solidarity of the asylum which was the subtext of "Yellow Submarine." But she had also felt the powerlessness of being "fixed" by "egg-men." They could have electro-shocked her, if they had decided that was to be her treatment.

CHAPTER XI | 287

I suggest Francie's story could have inspired John's song "**Happiness is a Warm Gun**." After John wrote the song, all the Beatles worked on it with zest in the studio: it was one of their favorites on the album. Since it is about a mental patient, it fits the IFP perfectly and it also expresses Laingian sane-are-insane ideas in its final section. Although it has the structure of a song-suite, "Warm Gun" has the same "concerns" and subtext as more conventional Beatles songs.

"She's not a girl who misses much," describes Francie, a "savvy New Yorker." She is "well-acquainted with the touch of a velvet hand/Like a lizard on a windowpane."[30] This line could be an allusion to the Velvet Underground, a sado-masochism subculture in New York. Francie would have been aware of this type of thing, if not well acquainted. Paul commented later that he contributed the lizard image in the lyric. He and a friend had seen a lizard on a window, a cold-blooded creature laying on a cold surface. The image could conceivably go toward describing an S and M encounter. "The man in the crowd/ With the multi-colored mirrors on his hobnail boots" was from a news story John had read or seen on television; a man had been discovered to be using mirrored shoes to look up women's skirts.[31] John would latch onto this story, because it implies that the kaleidoscope eyes' multi-colored mirrors (the man's mirrors were probably *not* multi-col-ored, but John added that touch) are now being used simply to see up girl's skirts—this is a good compression of what happens to Feminist plans. The "man in the crowd" is also apparently "Lying with his eyes/ While his hands are busy working overtime." Francie said that this line reminded her of Paul, but it could apply to any young man taking advantage of the new, looser sexual *mores*, and who is sexually "work-ing overtime." Making a soap impression of a wife, however, is quite an odd image, let alone donating said soap bar to the National Trust (for Historic Structures). However, it might be John's way of saying that the "mold" of womanhood, formed by husbands, has become some-thing to preserve, or is somehow "eaten." The lyric is obscure though.

So, we have a picture, in abstract, of a young woman and her milieu. Then, the scene shifts: "I need a fix 'cause I'm going down/

Down to the bits that I left uptown." Francie had to go uptown to the mental hospital, to get a "brain fix." She was both going down, (falling apart mentally) and needing to go uptown, or downtown. Her mind needed to be "fixed," and "get a fix," that is, a drug to reconstitute herself.

"Mother Superior jump the gun," John sings eight times. This is describing when the head nursing sister "jumps the gun" or administers the electric current in ECT. The head nurse "jumps" the current to administer ECT to the girl's brain, and there is "fuzz" distortion on the backing guitar. Nurses who administered electric shocks were completing the circuit in the same way a stun gun or jumper cables do.

Stun guns were in the news at this time, being discussed as possible tools for crowd control.[32] "Sisters" were the name for nurses in the U.K., so the head nurse would be called the "Mother Superior." She would "jump the gun," or apply the electric shock (over and over, as the repeated phrase implies) to the head of the patient. Thus rehabilitated or become one of the Normals, John sings that a warm gun equals happiness. This was taken to be a poke at "gun-lovers" in the U.S. The phrase "Happiness is a warm gun" John supposedly found in a gun owner's publication,[33] and it also could be a pun on the title of Charles Schultz' then-popular book, *Happiness is a Warm Puppy.*[34] John punned on the phrase as part of a hidden story in coded associations. In both a hidden and overt sense, the song conveys the Laingian idea of the "madness" of society.

Listening to this one usually pictures a nun jumping over a gun, somewhat like Jack jumping over the candlestick, but this nonsensical image is explained away with an understanding that ECT works along the same principles as jumper cables, or a stun gun,[35] and that nurses in the UK were traditionally nuns, or sisters, who would have a "Mother Superior," or head nursing sister in charge of the mental ward.

So, the song, telling most of Francie's story, fit like a word puzzle most of the Beatles anti-authoritarian "concerns," and uses the scaffolding of Paul's praxis, or what I call the IFP.

"Warm Gun" is ingeniously coded so that we do not know what we have just listened to. It was intense, diverting, it made us feel, and we have no idea what it meant (until now, if you subscribe to my analysis). The music was interesting, the transitions somehow appropriate yet inexplicable. The whole thing was unprecedented in music history.

That it was one of the Beatles' favorites and they worked hard on it shows, like their enthusiastic jumping-in to work on "A Day In The Life," that songs telling a story using association were their favorites.

Next is an equally inventive song, "**Martha My Dear.**" In this song Paul sings as if writing a letter to a "silly" girl. I suggest that he is actually writing a letter to that part of himself which is creative. Paul wrote this song in October 1968,[36] probably after Francie had left, so he might have wanted to reassure himself that he still had a muse *within* him.

The title is a portmanteau of "my idea." Cleverly, he addresses Martha, my dear—*my idea*. Sing it with the soft "r" and you will hear what I mean. This is similar to when John sang "Eiffel Tower" for the "If I Fell" tower. It could be heard as either (again, this is the figure-ground illustration, but in lyrics). Martha, my deah, Martha, my idea.

"Martha" is Paul's creative muse that, like a friendly dog, is sniffing around everywhere, wagging her tail, approaching strangers and happy to interact with people. Paul is writing a letter to the "Martha" side of his fractionated personality, who is always "interested."

He tells her, "you have always been my inspiration/Please, remember me/Martha my dear/Don't forget me/Martha my dear." By 1968, maybe, Paul was more aware of how he was wrote songs— based on dislocation, even a split. Paul asks his friendly, interested "Martha" side of himself not to forget him—because "you have always been my inspiration." He tells his "idea" to "hold your hand out," and "when you find yourself in the thick of it/Help yourself to a bit of what is all around you." This is what (one side of) Paul has been doing: circulating among people, finding inspiration where he can, taking a bit of what is all around him—most fruitfully in the Asher library.

However, the song is also about the nature of his creativity: his own fracture. That is also what the song is about—a letter to himself, which he in the song split off into another character, in order to write. The *raison d'etre* for the song is *because* he has split himself and is writing a letter to an other self, asking, "Don't forget me."

This is the same muddled voice of confession that we heard in Paul's early songs after he had met the Ashers; or rather, it is the same vulnerability. The split between Paul and his "idea" is hidden in the song (until now). It is poignant to write a letter to someone asking them not to forget you, even more poignant when that person is yourself.

On the one hand, "Martha" is enjoined to go out into the world, help herself to a bit of everything—to be the new, explorative type. On the other hand, the letter-writer-from-home asks her not to forget him, and that she and the writer are meant to be for each other. But whether they will end up together, is left ambiguous.

The song also functions as a kind of reassurance to the "new type" of woman, the "psychedelic personality," that she will always have a man waiting for her. The Beatles were never going to criticize a person's choices—they were all about openness and possibility and ostensible expansion.

I am just pointing out how Paul wrote the songs, which is about his songwriting process and split-off artistic self. He tells his "idea," "you're bound to see/That you and me/Were meant to be for each other." He also encourages himself: "Hold your head up, you silly girl/ Look what you've done." Along with the hopeful, even productive tone of the chords, Paul is telling the "him" side of himself that he has much to be proud of. Look around at all you have done, Paul is saying—all those hit records, all that success.

While his split-off inspiration is out in the world helping herself to a bit of what is all around her, he spends "days in conversation." It is worth noting in this regard that the key edict of the Philadelphia Association, dedicated to increasing empathy toward mental illness, was "conversation" with patients. The Paul at home, writing a letter, is in the asylum, while his "idea" wanders around freely outside of it. This is interesting in that although Paul writes songs using the scaffolding of the IFP, this song indicates that he feels his "idea" is somewhere outside of his songwriting process. He puts in "silly girl" so we assume he is addressing a girl, as usual combining his artistic IFP with romantic allusion.

He has said that the song was addressed to Martha, his female sheepdog. But Paul, although finding perhaps an initial spark in the outside world to start a song, will then actually write a song from his own praxis. The song is consistent with, even an extension of, his IFP. At each return of the interestingly composed verse is a very defined, three-beat rhythm reminiscent of "jin-gle-bells" or "Christ-mas-tree." This imparts even more of a happy mood. It is as if he is saying to himself that his "interested" muse does deliver, like Santa, wonderful gifts. But the gift that always keeps giving is Paul's split.

"Martha My Dear" is followed by John's **"I'm So Tired."** Many can relate to this song. But the song's lyrics can be taken to be a complaint directed at a therapist, as much as a lover. "I haven't slept a wink … my mind is on the blink." "My mind is set on you/I wonder should I call you, but I know what you would do." The therapist, he imagines, would tell him that he was putting him on, "but it's no joke, it's doing me harm/You know I can't sleep/Can't stop my brain/You know it's three weeks/I'm going insane!" John begins to scream.

The building intensity of this monologue addressed to "you" was really nothing people had ever heard before in a song, in the context of a pop album. It was like listening in on a private rant of someone who confessed he had "no peace of mind." He was "feeling so upset … I can't stop my brain…. I'm going insane!" If the Beatles wrote one song like this, then people would think, what an intense song. But if you put it in context with the other songs, "I'm So Tired" is again making use of psychological tropes, the meltdown of a patient, which was taken to be "about a couple." The patient wants the therapist or psychiatrist to supply "help." John had written about a stablemate in "Help!" and a therapy session in "She Said She Said." In "I'm

So Tired," he sings like a man in near panic, almost to the brink of insanity. The tension builds until John scream-sings, "I'd give you everything I've got for a little piece of mind!" repeatedly. Then he abruptly subsides into mumbles. A great vocal performance. "I'm So Tired" anticipates John's later expressive singing on "Mother" and "Cold Turkey," during the time John took primal scream therapy with Arthur Janov.

The reason this and many other Beatles songs were so memorable is that they were delivering "voices" from the world of the therapy patient, which people (including of course children) did not recognize as such, but thought could apply to them. People just did not know the therapy world at all, compared to today. This type of meltdown had never been heard in *song* before (it had been in the theatre). It disarmed people. Somehow the alchemy of music and the attractive bard singing onstage made the lyrics harder to dismiss, and the Sixties saw the debut of the rock star bard. Like "What You're Doing," a song like "I'm So Tired" was teaching people about what was possible to *feel* in relationships. The song structures the Beatles wrote could be nursery-rhyme cadences, familiar genres, and their chord changes sometimes quite predictable—but the lyrics always had this strange element of something different and new. "I'm So Tired" is a transparent example of the IFP. The subtext of therapy or mental patient is right there in the language used. After shouting "I'd give you everything I've got for a little peace of mind!" to a cascading piano, the singer is mumbling to himself. It is as if to calm his outburst, a shot has just been administered and now he (the patient) is "calmed." This is also an allusion to a junkie wanting a fix, as John was both literally with Yoko (they were sniffing heroin) and in the sense of his wanting to get "peace of mind" from her.

John had his go-to sources for inspiration: his poor vision, nursery rhymes, and grains. Cereal. There is nothing bad about that; artists always have inspirations, and some might be quite private. He was inspired to include grains or cereal several times in songs, including the "semolina" Pilchard, an unspecified person "sitting on a cornflake," "Good Morning Good Morning" from Kellogg's Corn Flakes, allusions to grains or pigs being "shot from guns" like Quaker Puffed Wheat commercials, and John also said "...Chapter One, in which Doris gets her oats" in the introduction to "Maggie May" (an old pub song, not the Rod Stewart song). Francie recalled that "John liked his cornflakes."[37] Paul was also evidently aware that John liked cereal, according to the Letters section in one issue of the *Beatles Book Monthly*. A fan had sent Paul a care package which included a box of cornflakes; Paul replied to the fan that "John was very jealous that he didn't get a box of cornflakes, so being a good Beatle, I let him have some of mine."[38]

We have already discussed how one of John's grandest anthems, "All You Need is Love," was based on the melody for "Three Blind Mice." He combined both the nursery rhyme of "see how they run" and cereal in the line "see how they run/Like pigs from a gun," inspired, I have asserted, by the "shot from guns!" commercials for Quaker Puffed Wheat and Rice. "Three Blind Mice" might have been always somewhat at the forefront in John's mind, due to it being about blindness. He was to use the same three notes in the sad refrain "My mummy's dead" on a later Plastic Ono Band album.

John also referenced eyes or seeing quite often in his songs, as did Paul. The motif of the eye would be used again as a means of transporting-meaning in "Blackbird."

Blackbird is a very important song for Paul. It is in a sense his Beatles mission statement. But it also has emotional meaning deeper than that.

Francie's last name was Schwartz, which in Yiddish is schvartz, meaning "black." She had dark hair and eyes. It could have been his feeling for her that fueled his writing the song, which he wrote soon after they met. Paul has been giving "broken wings" and "sunken eyes" to enable among other things, the Beatles to "fly," Lucy to be up in the sky, and to make women like Francie possible. His artistic process has made it (ostensibly) possible for the counterculture to "arise." His art has lifted people; it allows them to "fly." However, they fly "into the light of the dark, black night," and the blackbird is supposed to use broken wings to fly and sunken eyes to see. It is significant that Paul wrote "sunken" and "broken." Sunken eyes are dead eyes, and broken wings cannot be used. Why is the singer giving (with tenderness, it seems) dead and broken things? Because Paul has been using the words and worldview of the mentally ill in his compositions for several years. It is even possible that by 1968 he felt a little broken, fractured, even a little "dead" (as in ego-dead, the "goal" of taking LSD). But he is able to put broken things in songs, and the songs have seemed to help others. This is why "Blackbird" is the IFP mission statement. It states the goal of his (fractured) organization—to help the "blackbird" "arise."

The song also acknowledges that Paul "gives" broken things (and tenderly). This is another inside-is-out, outside-is-in, no high or low of the Beatles' imaginings. It is not rational to suppose one can rise on broken wings, or see with dead eyes. But, as Paul once commented, "Paradoxical thinking is part of the game in our art. In rock and roll you often stand things on their head."[39] It somewhat related to the Vedic-Transcendentalist-Jungian concepts that there is always a little bit of dark in the light, and you can find light in the dark. So, the blackbird flies "into the light of the dark, black night."

That Paul wrote this soon after beginning his affair with Francie points to the song possibly being emotionally inspired by her. Francie could have been the black "bird." (In London, young women were called "birds.") He cared about her, understood where she was coming from, and hoped his art would help her "fly," even though he could see that following its message of freedom and more possibilities in life had landed her in less-than-ideal situations. There is a poignant sadness to this work, and it has more of that voice of the "vulnerable, slightly nonsensical confession" that we encountered way back in "Yesterday."

If we can hazard a guess into Paul's emotional response to Francie, he might have been wondering what would happen to the bird that flies into the night on broken wings. He also recognized that a lot of events had led up to Francie being with him at just that moment in time, events that the Beatles had put in motion. And that his and

Francie's was a meeting of kindred souls (at least at first). However, he is anticipating that sooner or later, she will have to fly away.

"Blackbird" could also be a love song to John. Paul could sense in 1968 that their long collaboration might be nearing its end. Paul wrote into the song hidden associations related to John—motifs of blindness *and* cereal. Saint Lucia (recalling "Lucy" of John's imagining) is a Catholic Saint who gives her gouged-out eyes as an offering, and she is the patron saint of the blind.[40] Saint Lucia usually offers her eyes in her hand, or on a dish. And even more pertinent to John, there is a connection to grains: Saint Lucia, after she was martyred, was prayed to during a famine in Italy and then was thought responsible for a grain shipment arriving by boat which saved the people; so her feast day is celebrated with a wheat cake or hot cereal.[41] Paul's thinking of Catholic Saints is not remarkable because his mother Mary was a Catholic.[42]

In "Blackbird," the singer is imagining giving "sunken eyes" (as does Saint Lucia) to a blackbird so it can see. Paul gave words from the world of the "broken" to the world—and his collaboration enabled John to "arise." Many people are moved by "Blackbird"; it is one of Paul's best compositions, made, Paul has said, from taking a bit of Bach. This *delicate* song of Paul's might be in its essence his truest expression of himself, and it might be an outpouring of his affection for John. Blackbirds also have an association with a nursery rhyme: "Four and twenty blackbirds, baked into a pie. When the pie is opened, the birds begin to sing. Isn't that a dainty dish, to set before the King?" In "Blackbird," a little bird *does* sing. The pie has been set before, and opened for, the King. John, like their early idol Elvis Presley, was "king" of The Beatles. Even though Paul, after 1966, *led* The Beatles, John was their *king*. Paul had a vision of John as such when they both took LSD at Paul's home in St. John's Wood: "John had been sitting around very enigmatically and I had a big vision of him as a king, the absolute Emperor of Eternity … in control of it all … just sitting there."[43]

The next IFP song is "**I Will.**" It is on the surface a romantic ballad, written and sung very soothingly by Paul. However an analysis of the lyrics reveals the hollowness at the core. The singer is in love with someone he doesn't know if he has ever seen. "For if I ever saw you/I didn't catch your name/But it never really mattered/I will always feel the same." This is not the dreamy idealization of, say, "Johnny Angel" (which was the anticipation of ideal love as sung by a young girl) but something different. It is a Valentine to the female fans, who have been "nothinged" along with the Beatles, and the song is almost absurdist. Arthur Koestler in *The Act of Creation* describes absurdist maxims such as, "never work between meals," which is ostensibly a motto about work, but the point is not to work at all.[44] Some of the same nonsense is in "I Will." There is no love where there is such a comforting feeling of absence and dislocation—some of the main motifs in Paul's songs. Also, the singer of the song is absolutely passive, even though the song refrain is "I will." The singer has no will. It is a love song written by a ghost with invisible ink. It's up to "you" (the fan) out there to sing, rather than the singer to sing—even though that is just what he is doing. The song has a wonderful soothing feeling, though, around its tropes of lack of presence, dislocation, absence, and absurdum.

Even with his method in place for writing songs, and validation of it through the success of "Pepper," Paul wanted someone to bounce ideas off of. Imagine if you had created the culture that everyone else is copying. Where would you find feedback? He couldn't relate as well to Jane, anymore; he was overseeing his Expando-Paul identity in Apple. There was so much pressure on him to come up with song material and to keep the group together. Francie observed that "Paul gave an impression of a continuous, high level of nervous energy,"[45] but also that "he seemed to have so many minds, untangling the hang-ups in each one would take all the energy in me."[46] Paul could "rap" with Francie. But as we have discussed, the situation with her (and with everyone else perhaps) was a bit of a loop, or he was afraid it was. This situation was the genesis of the song "**Helter Skelter**," I suggest.

Paul's Loop

A helter-skelter is "a spiral slide in English funfairs," according to Ian McDonald.[47] I suggest Paul selected a slide that turns a person in near-circles as his metaphor for his artistic process. He imagined going for a ride on it: "When I get to the bottom I go back/To the top of the slide/Where I stop, and I turn, and I go for a ride/Till I get to the bottom/And I see you again." He gets to the end of his process, and then he has to do it all over again—write another song. The last line is screamed, as if seeing "you again" is the last thing he wants. John said once about "Helter Skelter" that he assumed it was "about Francie." I am suggesting that in this song, Paul is complaining that his split muse, his "Martha" is not around at the moment. Francie, a person who is the embodiment of his (hidden) artistic method has shown up. She is like him (Francie said they were too alike— "a pair of unmatched shoes"). The "culture" is like him, too. He goes in circles in a feedback loop.

"Beatle Paul" is "relatable" to millions (since they have taken acid to "understand" the Beatles music, in an act of mimesis of Paul's (hidden) praxis). However John said in "Glass Onion" that Paul's layers are all "see-throughable." That's because John knows of the fracture project, and also, to John, Paul is sometimes "acting," with his fine manners. John sometimes called Paul "Faul," or faux Paul.

"Helter Skelter" seems like the crazed ravings of a madman; that in itself was enough for it to be received as a Sixties song, at that point. Paul has said The Who inspired him to record a song as loud and raucous as possible.[48] But, "Helter Skelter" is also very much a *mise en scene* of Paul's IFP, I suggest. Its singer asks, "Do you don't you want me to make you/I'm coming down fast, but don't let me break you." This is using sex and drug slang, but is also an allusion to Paul's making "meter-mades." While on his artistic "slide," he will break, and make. But the "new type" he created, which he met in Francie, does not seem to give him outside inspiration. She doesn't give him "the answer" to himself.

Paul and the Beatles are the leaders of the ostensive counterculture. But when he gets to the bottom of his artistic slide, he sees "you" again, or in his case, "him."

I suggest that Paul, in being with Francie, had gone back to his original wellspring of inspiration: the tenuous dividing line between the sane and the insane. Francie had been of several worlds: the advertising world, and of the insane. Being with her, he could see exactly again where a dividing line, in him, might be. The Beatles' statements had been picked up so successfully and marketed by the "ad-men" in various colorful, multipronged forms, that perhaps Paul felt he needed feedback from someone who could speak to both his artistic process, and the ad world. Francie in a sense was also "meter-made." She was someone who was possible because of his IFP. This made for I think quite a meeting of minds, and Francie said, "If things were tolerable, we would rap" in the afternoons, after Paul awoke from his late nights.[49] But, Francie said, they were too alike to sustain a relationship.[50] He could ask her about her past experiences, and they could talk about Apple, but it was a kind of closed system. And she was just as rebellious as he, having hated the games and hierarchies in the various ad agencies where she had worked.

This leads us to John's "**Revolution 1**," which was done in two different versions—one angry, one more soothing in tone. Both had the same lyric content, telling the would-be Marxist agitator that it is "gonna be all right, all right." "If you go carrying pictures of Chairman Mao/You ain't gonna make it with anyone anyhow." He sings about the revolution, "we'd all love to see the plan," and "we all doin' what we can." However, he sings, "You'd better free your mind instead." "Minds that hate" are not the way to bring about revolution, John sings. You have to fill people's minds with a new kind of dialectic—a mind that doesn't see differences or want them. John knows that the Beatles' music is bringing about a different state of mind. It is a "soft" revolution—not burning down buildings and smashing storefronts, but bringing about the new awareness that will cause Capitalism to atrophy over time. "Don't you know it's gonna be/All right, all right," John sings confidently. I classify this song as IFP-related because no longer seeing divisions between people would certainly need a new sense of self-identity, or less ego, or identity fracture, or total analysis, for such a mind-meld to happen. The Beatles were busy creating the "ostensive" culture, and it was a softer revolution.

The last two songs on the White Album that I categorize as IFP are "Savoy Truffle" and "Goodnight."

George's **"Savoy Truffle"** follows Paul's sugary **"Honey Pie."** What is the "savoy truffle" that everyone wants? Paul, I suggest. This song is warning the fans that Paul's sweet act will turn "so sour." Paul is the prized truffle, the one all the pigs want: the Capitalist pigs. And also, the fans who are "nothinged" by the Beatles. "What you eat, you are," George warns, "but what is sweet now, turns so sour/We all know Ob-la-di-bla-da/But can you show me where you are?" This is an accusation of emptiness leveled both at Paul and at his legions of fans, who are made "empty" by what they consume, paradoxically. However, I suggest that George is saying that the Beatles' "way" is be an ontological mirror, of which nothingness is reflected on both sides. (In fact, one can argue that the Beatles and Paul are a Boojim from Lewis Carroll's short story, *The Hunting of The Snark*. The "Snark," who is highly sought-after, sometimes turns out to be a "Boojim" instead, who has the power to make people disappear.)

George often used a motif of eating in songs, to criticize people. George got the inspiration for the song by watching a friend consume bonbons,[51] but then I intuit he thought about Paul's oppressive managing of the band: "I feel your taste, all the time we're apart." Every time George sat down and picked up his guitar, he anticipated Paul having something to say about his playing, when he got to the studio.

"Ob-Bla-Di, Ob-La-Da" was Paul's composition. Paul could write competent, memorable songs—but they were based on a split. His sweetness, or sourness, of the "savoy truffle," was consumed to such an extent that people were overdosing on it— "you'll have to have them (your teeth) all pulled out, after the savoy truffle." I suggest that here is a threatening image, like Octopus's Garden, of what might result if you stray too far into consuming, or being nonentities in the "interval." "Savoy Truffle" is coded as a song about desserts, "ginger sling with a pineapple heart.... Coconut fudge really blows down those blues." I suggest that the Savoy Truffle, (that a pig digs up) is Paul. Paul is the prized truffle, the delicacy that the pigs (consumers and industry people) want. And, nobody knows who Paul is. Like a buried truffle, he is hidden from view, but everyone wants him. However, to find him, and then "consume" him, is to be left "toothless" or dis-empowered. I suggest that George felt Paul was dis-empowering him with his "autocratic" control in the studio. Besides being controlling, and taking away people's teeth or sense of self-agency, Paul also is getting information out of people he hangs out with in order to write songs, in George's critical view.

In analyzing these songs I am aware that taken one by one, you wouldn't necessarily see this pattern. But if you accept my theory of what Paul's songwriting method was, the songs fit very neatly into it, in their subtexts. They form a subliminal story for the listener to follow.

George would get as exasperated as John would about people, but his invectives are typically less inspired than John's. George would help Ringo later with words and music to "Octopus's Garden" which describes some of the same underlying threat to self as does "Savoy Truffle."

I will now discuss the parody songs and "other" category songs before discussing the last two IFP songs on the album, "Revolution 9" and "Good Night."

Parody or Satire Songs

Like the denizens of Penny Lane, the characters in story-songs like **"Ob-La-Di, Ob-La-Da,"** **"The Continuing Story of Bungalow Bill,"** and **"Rocky Raccoon"** are people with something a little bit strange about them. In "Ob-La-Di, Ob-La-Da," "life goes on bra," which makes no sense in English, and it is revealed at the end that Desmond is a cross dresser. Bungalow Bill is mocked by children for killing, and then gets zapped by Captain Marvel "right between the eyes" while hunting for a tiger. The rural men in "Rocky Raccoon" have a gunfight over a woman whose "name was Magill, and she called herself Lil/But everyone knew her as Nancy." Francie described these ditties as "ego-music that Paul was laying down tracks for in the studio," but the point to these semi-comical-but-with-sharp-edges songs (Philip Norman describes them as "songs in smiley masks")[52] is that the character portraits in each song "fit" with the IFP as inmates do in an asylum. According to MacDonald, John's "Polythene Pam" was originally planned to go on the White Album, as another character sketch.[53] An asylum has all kinds of odd people in it: a woman who thinks that she has an opera career and is only in the hospital temporarily before she returns to the stage; a girl who gives birth to a baby every night and awakes to find it stolen in the morning; a man who every time he hears a door slam is back in a prisoner-of-war camp. Their behavior is a way they have pieced together reality in order to live in it. The character-songs, besides fitting with the IFP, were also Paul's way of using his skills to write in a wide variety of musical genres. Each little bit of music could be a "person" in its own right—the fragmentation, humor and illogic is accepted. They could all fit, as if in an asylum.

The album's coherence-in-fragmentation was taken, again, to be Beatles' "magic." Like a flying Hindu magic carpet, fabric patchworked and decorated with mirrors, every little odd musical sound effect and piece could seemingly fit onto a Beatles album. But when one looks into the little mirrors on the carpet, "nobody is there." The Beatles were, by now, promoting the idea of losing the ego, but to do this, they used the metaphor of the asylum. Of course, asylum inmates are locked away and told their minds must change. The story-songs were another way to apply the asylum idea that the Beatles invite listeners to join in with.

"Julia" seems to have been John's love song to his mother. "Yer Blues" is an over-the-top Blues screamer by John; "Don't Pass Me By" is a country-tinged ditty by Ringo. "Sexy Sadie" was said to be about the Maharishi.

A few of these songs are about concerns related to the IFP; take "Everybody's Got Something to Hide Except Me and My Monkey," for example. This song, written by John, is about dialectics, just as Paul's tamer "Hello Goodbye" is. Everybody's got something to hide, which is a condition of having a self, a soul; everyone is necessarily separate from one another. And yet to the Beatles (and Cooper), a separate "ego" was just a "construct." So, the song celebrates that "me and my monkey" can just jump over all barriers, instructing that, "the deeper you go, the higher you fly/The higher you fly, the deeper you go/So come on/Come on is such a joy." The message is that if one fuses in an orgiastic "in and out," or goes more "inner" into oneself on drugs to fly high, there will be nothing to hide, no separation. This is the same no-middle-ground idea that is the undercurrent in so many Beatles songs: of being "seen-though" or, in the obverse, "hide themselves behind a wall of illusion." The frustration of being separate, which was sung about in early Beatles songs, is now offered an antidote, which is sex and drugs.

"**Why Don't We Do It in the Road?**" is in the raucous category; it's a joke, but it's also a howl of revolt. "**Piggies**" is more openly critical of *mores*, as it sneers at men who wear white shirts, work jobs, and have wives they take out to dinner.[vi] These songs are a nod to the Beats: those who scorn all conventions. "**Birthday**" is ostensibly a rock song for one day of the year, but it is also an exhortation to let go—to dance every day as if it's your birthday. MacDonald called "**Honey Pie**" "pointless," but the charming ditty is stuck like a flower sticker

---

[vi]   Manson's deranged LSD-"family" apparently took the line in "Piggies" about forks and pigs literally; in July and August of 1969 several members of his cult killed nine people, scrawled "pig" on a wall in blood, and stuck a fork and carving knife in one of their victims. It is possible that the Manson cult followers were in a group-identity experiment that went horribly awry. Why they took Beatles lyrics for their "bible," is I think because the Beatles wanted to eliminate dialectics or gaps, similar to what is purported to happen on LSD (you become what you are looking at, as one researcher put it). Lennon alluded to the ominous loop-the-loop of conflating evil with good or Satan with God, however, in "Walrus," and the cybernetic vision of identity loss in "Strawberry Fields."

    The fusion of opposites as mentioned in Chapter Ten was a project undertaken on off-hours by at least two well-placed Harvard personality researchers. I refer the reader to the Reference Notes which cites biographies of Harry Murray and Christiana Morgan.[65] In 1969, the fusion of good with evil, or the "Satanic Christ" of the Harvard clinician's imaginings took the degraded form of Charlie Manson, who thought he was Christ, and his followers who apparently believed that good and evil were the same, and that life was the same as death.

on the album; it shows listeners that "Paul is still nice." "Honey Pie" is a companion piece with the song following it, "Savoy Truffle," which warns people off consuming Paul.

"**Cry Baby Cry**" is an enigmatic and atmospheric song by John. The whispered vocal, nursery-rhyme cadence and ominous-yet-resolute chorus are not IFP-related, but then it is followed by something that is: Paul singing, "Can you take me back, where I've been from, can you take me back?" This is another psychological reference, I suggest, to patients (given LSD) who were "taken back" which we discussed in Chapter Two.[54] Following the children's games, and "voices out of nowhere" put on "for a lark," the segue is not like being taken back to one's childhood self, but put on a slide to chaos: John's "**Revolution 9**." Sound-snippets overlap and succeed one another in ebbs and flows; meaningless montages are interrupted by words. It is a dream of fragmentation. Some critics called "Revolution 9" a scrapbook of the Sixties, others a vision of what Marxist revolution would sound like. I think it is akin to the cut-up pictures and texts of the Beats. And even more than the Beats insisted their "cut-ups" did, John's montage tries to find the "real" message. It's an experiment in the spirit of the Beats. "Revolution 9" also brings to mind F. Scott Fitzgerald's comment that before one awakes, there is a "cathartic" nightmare, which enables the dreamer to face a new day.[55]

However, what follows the nightmare of "Revolution 9" is not the light of day, but the light of the moon. The album's final song (which John also wrote) is "**Goodnight**." This is what follows the dream— more sleep. The ward is closing down for the night, and ward nurse, Ringo, comes in to lullaby the inmates to sleep. "Close your eyes, and I'll close mine," he sings. Again, John's thoughts are often on vision or eyes when he writes lyrics. At the end of the White Album everyone closes his or her own eyes. Taken in context of all the other songs of fracture, "close your eyes" takes on dislocated, even faintly sinister overtones. "Dream sweet dreams for me/Dream sweet dreams for you" is an odd line, as if again, the listener is both *inside* the singer of the song, and *outside* dreaming for their own self. In this context, "close your eyes" can be taken for closing the lids on one's own eyes, as if one was standing looking down at one's deceased face. The accompaniment is a lavish, studio-orchestra-style reassurance. The children-inmates lay themselves to rest and the music ends. The two record discs are tucked into their sleeves. The white gatefold walls close on the asylum.

* * *

The Beatles thus created the "ostensive culture" of Bateson's dream. The ground was laid and seeded, not visible to the waking mind. As I went along this journey, I still appreciate their genius and consistency of method, their method in the madness.

You can take these songs at face value, or in the manner I assert, or in any way in between; however, I am only asking the reader consider the consistent IFP (psychological) subtext that I find in their songs and which to me, is completely part of Paul's, and John's story. Francie met Paul, he and John both probably heard her sad song, and made it better. They made a Beatles™ statement. Which is to say it was a Laingian, Beat-influenced, IFP associative language-coded song.

The basic formula, if one boils it down, was this: an event, or a person tells a "sad song." Or a cereal box is read, or the newspaper: add a psychology subtext, a sense of void or emptiness, allude to drugs or the all-is-oneness or "nothing is real" of the Vedics/Beats/Transcendentalists, mix in experimental sounds and sounds of the avant-garde, and then the result is a Beatles song.

It doesn't cheer me to write these unhappy analyses of the Beatles; but one has to face facts. If one's role model is Allen Ginsberg, and Beat writers are slated to be released on one's own label, then what are one's values, after all? Of course, the Beatles were only in their twenties and easily influenced, according to their friend John Dunbar.[56] Perhaps it was a matter of influence.[vii]

[vii] While editing an "avant-garde" trend magazine in the Nineties, I was contacted by some of the same people from the Sixties, namely Burroughs, Leary and Ginsberg. To me, this underscored how small the avant-garde really is. I felt like I was in a very small Petri dish that usually would have had to have been set up.

After "Pepper," Paul was aware that he had introduced new terrain musically. His expansion into the interval worked on an artistic level, and he felt an expansion or validation of his own identity as a songwriter. And yet as Francie said, in 1968 he didn't wear the mantle well. He wanted to be recognized as who he felt the old Paul had been, while also receive acknowledgement of his success in becoming someone else. He and Francie went back home to Liverpool and he spent an evening with his old pals. But instead of a homecoming, it was a reminder of his loneliness. The party "went on around him" with Paul at the piano and everyone else circulating.[57] Then, he went to the local pub. Later, Francie found him standing at the bar surrounded by his cousins, saying angrily, "You treat me like I'm *him*, and I'm not *him*, y'know. I'm just me!" Outside, Paul cried to Francie that he just couldn't take it anymore, fell to his knees and beat his fists upon the pavement. When they got back to his father's home, Paul "sobbed helplessly on the floor."[58]

I suggest that Paul did not experience a bonding with others that he so needed at that point. He felt he had become more of the person he was inside all along, that is, Expando-Paul, but to his friends, he was "Beatle Paul." So, he must not have felt loved and understood. I think the fact that Paul broke down in tears after this visit with family and his old pals shows that he hadn't made or received any bridge over his divided self, and it was still left to him to sort things out and in a way, "carry that weight." He had created Beatle Paul—but his old pals thought that was him.

His identity fracture remained unsolved. He wanted Francie to help him sort it out. Maybe she could have some insight, some answers. Several times, she said, a drunken Paul wondered aloud to her if women actually preferred to be "treated rotten."[59] "He looked at me as if expecting a transformation," she said. But she just looked at him blankly; she didn't have any answers. Francie would be waiting at the bottom of his slide of creativity, but when he got to the bottom, he saw not another soul, but a kind of mirror of himself. They were too much alike. One, an ex-mental-patient from the advertising world, and the other a songwriter with a "desparate curiosity"[60] so that he could remain current and find new inspiration for songs.

In any case, the translation from external material the Beatles encountered, to writing and releasing songs, was happening very fast. If the translation from I-see-that to I-write-a-song to millions of people humming it and selling objects off of it happens so quickly, imagine how sucked dry one would feel. There was plenty of consuming of Paul and the Beatle's creativity going on; but not any feedback. I think what he really wanted, from Francie and from his pals in Liverpool, was feedback. But, they didn't have any answers for him. Only questions. "Do you ever think consciously of the power you have to communicate with millions of young people?" Francie asked him in the car, as they sped along. He did not answer: "His eyes stared ahead, blanks."[61]

It was as if Paul was the patient now, the mental patient whom all the psychoanalysts wanted to interview, to scoop out whatever was inside of him, and take it apart. He would have become, as a Beatle, some black box that everyone wanted to see inside. Yet to John, who knew Paul well, he was a glass onion.

That Paul felt frustrated at his old pals, and at Francie, (evidenced I think by the screams in "Helter Skelter") says to me that there is a core in Paul. There was a hurt person, who needed defenses. He had driven to split himself apart, perhaps as a way to defend himself—similar to John wanting to take refuge in wordplay. They both needed a "front." A front was a self that they could control. A divided self. One could argue they both bolstered their hiding, acting and ultimately self-damaging tendencies in each other. But Paul "had found no one," John remarked, by the White Album, which Francie was around for. Paul felt he had a core, that he wanted someone to recognize and love —something everyone wants in his or her partner in life.

Francie had her own ambitions for a "New Renaissance" art-empire. Paul put her to work at Apple, but she said later, "at a job I couldn't even define."[62] She said no more than that about her job, in her memoir.[viii]

The flip-flop of Beatles' views, the "joker" aspect, the in-is-out and out-is-in, the no high or low, all fit with the initial image of the Beatles as "irreverent"; there was no essential change *to* the Beatles. What we see as they "evolve" is the unwrapping but simultaneous concealment (as I show) of the Beatles, all the while never coming quite out in the open (although quite close in the *Magical Mystery Tour* film) with their "concerns." Their fundamentally subversive views all fit with a rock and roll perspective on life, but they were so carefully wrapped, both in the style statements of the time, and more importantly with their use of the IFP.

Paul's Split

Paul might have made an inner split in himself at about this time into Paul and "famous Paul." Over the course of many interviews over decades, he has described a way he thinks of himself, as being two Pauls. Here are some of his quotes:

> "There are two Paul McCartney's".... "It's kind of there's me, and there's him. He's very famous!".... "In a way, I think of Paul McCartney as 'him.' I do wake up some mornings and think, Jesus Christ, am I really that guy that is in the same body as I'm inhabiting?".... "I've learnt to compartmentalize. There's me and there's famous him. I don't want to sound schizophrenic, but probably I'm two people".... "I've always had this thing of him and me; He goes on stage, He's famous, and then me; I'm just some kid from Liverpool".... "I look in the mirror and just

---

viii   Is it too much of a stretch to wonder if Francie Schwartz, who lived with Paul in 1968, might be related to Loren Schwartz, who first gave Brian Wilson LSD? In Francie Schwartz' memoir *Body Count*, she wrote she met Paul in 1968, and her sister "Harrie" also met Paul that year when he visited Los Angeles.[66] It would be quite a coincidence if two sisters were able to meet Paul McCartney in separate countries in the same year without having some in-crowd connection. Loren Schwartz was a frequent visitor to Melcher's home where the Beatles sometimes stayed, and could have invited Harrie Schwartz to come over and meet Paul.

think, I, in this shell, am the guy I've read so much about. I don't know whether it's a schizo thing. I'm very proud of him, but you know, I don't imagine I am him, 'cause otherwise it would just blow my head off."[63]

I think this means that Paul chose to remain his own hidden self, locked away, to *keep* his creativity. He doesn't want to "buy himself," that is, to take the public's perception of what he does as him. He wants to give himself elbow room: "somewhere to go" and at the same time releasing himself from having to go anywhere. His IFP praxis gave him and the Beatles artistic freedom, and like Laing's books, gave "people a little more space to be." The strange thing is that they also put people into an asylum.

* * *

The songs follow one upon the other like a low-fever-dream, a state of near-torpor punctuated by agitated moments, all in another universe inside blank walls. In the White Album, Paul had recreated the asylum—the randomness, the confiding of inner thoughts, the void, the emptiness, the ego-destruction, the illogical point of view, and the administered drugs. Right down to the ward nurse wishing everyone a good night, at the end. We are listening to the medicated voice of the co-incarcerated, alternately tender, delusional, or ranting: or letting go completely to dance madly in the hallways. Dance, dance, it's your birthday every day, dance for me, dance for everyone. Close your eyes; sleep as the entire world sleeps with you. You are loved even though your beloved has never seen you, met you, or knows your name. It doesn't matter what your name is, because he will always feel the same—the same as you. There are no distinctions, nothing outside you, nothing within you. Everyone dreamt of flying acrobats, as y/our eyes broke into kaleidoscopes of every color—and no particular color. Love is all you need. Lock yourself away, within blank walls. Meet the Beatles: co-inmates of the asylum, they are together with you, they let you know you are only very small and everything is a play;

nothing is real. Even though they admit they are acting, and they tell you that everyone is acting and unreal, you see them as neither insane nor actors. They are your gurus. They are prophets, men of rare knowledge. They can never be put in one category or other. The Beatles are beyond categorization and you will be also, floating freely in the emptiness of the infinite.

"The White Album was a Paul album," John said later. Even though or because Paul reached a pinnacle of loop, or void, or IFP, he could produce and "stage" the songs on the album. He was the prince of the Nothings—the four nothings and their fans. But people didn't know this. They saw the Beatles as creative leaders, even as savants and seers. The Beatles were leaders of the "new social aristocracy" as model Twiggy's boyfriend-manager termed the "culture" springing up.[64]

The mid- to late-Sixties saw a shift in media, marketing and advertising agencies toward catering to a younger demographic. Record labels, film companies and ad agencies were no longer being run exclusively by people over forty or fifty. The Sixties were when the "inmates" would start to "run the asylum" and young people market to their own demographic. This shift in the advertising world would affect a younger person's expectations for at least the first half of their life. Francie was at the forefront of that shift in the Sixties, her mind being picked for new ideas, even after she came out of the mental asylum and after ingesting LSD.

CHAPTER XII

Nowhere to Go: Abbey Road Scraps, Patron Saint of Mental Hospitals, and That Magic Feeling

We had traveled through the holes, the secret places in our psyches: as a fad. We had found new "junk" to buy, new colors to wear, and learned new slang expressions. Some of us had taken LSD, the model-psychosis or, if you prefer, the "psyche-manifesting" drug. We had thought-ourselves-into, or in reality, traveled across boundaries of space and time, sexual morality, or of conventional behavior. All this under the leadership of the art of the Beatles, and of the Walrus (Paul). The Beatles had birthed a new culture, or at least new markets. Millions identified themselves in some part with the "counterculture" that the Beatles represented. Whether it was imaginary or real didn't necessarily affect retail sales. People were buying it.

However, in practical terms, by 1969 Apple Corporation, the Magical Bus of Paul's "Expando-Paul" identity, had nowhere to go. Apple was sinking under massive expenditure with less to show for it than anticipated.[1] The retail boutique was open for only about nine months, before it was closed and its inventory given away. The clothing, which was not mass-produced and had embroidery, bead-ing, and other embellishments, had been for sale at a price point that would not compensate its makers adequately for the time involved. To add to the problem, the clothing label affixed to each item, which its designers insisted should be woven in silk, was as or more expensive to produce than the cost of the garment.

The store ran up against practical realities. There was no way it could make a profit. The Fool's colorful mural on the outside of the building was painted over in a few weeks due to signage ordinances and complaints. If it were a mural of that size commissioned by the city it would have been all right, but what was in effect a huge paint-ing posted by a business was not legal.

Shoplifting was a problem also, since people wanted a piece of the Beatles without paying for it. The store's layout provided cover for shoplifters.[2] But hadn't the Beatles taught them that everything was for everyone?

Although Apple did not prosper, in keeping with the new spirit of populist art, some much older Modernists were able to re-fashion themselves. The Institute of Contemporary Arts (ICA) moved its headquarters and had a splashy re-opening in 1968 in a new building. Some people behind the ICA had been in the arts scene for decades, including Roland Penrose, a surrealist from the Thirties, and Sir Herbert Read, an "anarchist" poet from the Twenties. The opening exhibit was based on the work of R.L. Gregory, a military psychol-ogist who had just published *Eye and Brain, The Psychology of Seeing.*[3] Gregory had researched how the physiology of the eye affects the brain and personality—a topic which resonated with the "culture" at that time, and which was found in Beatles eye imagery in their songs. The show featured many optical illusions, including a photo of Penrose's wife Lee Miller, the WWII photojournalist, naked save for a camouflage net. The ICA had previously been based in the former home of Lord Admiral Nelson and artist Eduardo Paolozzi had remodeled a portion of the house. (Paolozzi wears many hats, including Surrealism, Pop Art collage and Brutalist sculpture. We have noted his sculptures of fractured heads.) Paolozzi had a similarly long association with the ICA.[4]

Paul had bought one of Paolozzi's cast sculptures, entitled *Solo,* and kept it in his music room. The sculpture, a tall metal "H" shape with a sort of vanity-mirror-shape in the middle, can be seen as a "divided self." When the early-Beatle-replacement Micky Dolenz of The Monkees came to visit Paul, the two posed for a picture seated at the feet of the sculpture, as if they formed two halves of one solo Beatle.

Not so coincidentally, ICA co-organizer Sir Herbert Read (an old friend of T.S. Eliot's[5]) co-edited with Jungian authority Gerhard Adler the *Collected Works of C. G. Jung*, which was re-issued in 1967 by Penguin Books[6] (its manager, Tony Godwin, closely connected to Indica Gallery's Barry Miles). Gerhard Adler is related to Alfred Adler, "father of individual psychology" who was a colleague of Freud's, and also to producer Lou Adler, who formed The Mamas and The Papas.[7]

Carl Jung passed away in 1961, just before the Beatles rose to prominence. The re-opening of the ICA was another marker of the "new culture" of the Sixties, but the artistic ideas in the ICA were not really new. The notion of populist art that the Modernists propounded had been given a shot in the arm by the Beatles. The White Album was artistic proof of the viability of Modernist fragmentation—that anything could be put into an album and it would magically cohere. The album supposedly extended the "idiom" of modern music, rather than some of it being a rather uncaring smorgasbord of withering leftovers. The White Album seemed to prove that Modernism with its associated Relativism, Surrealism, now being added to with Pop Art and Op Art, was viable. Only a few years earlier, American composer Aaron Copland wrote in *What to Listen For in Music* that Modernism, which he described as dissonance and fragmentation, had been assimilated and music remained, for the most part, diatonic and melodic.[8] In the late sixties, Modernists had been revivified—even validated, with the Beatles White Album triumph.

Tinted glasses became fashionable, famously worn by singer Janis Joplin. Optical effects were popular during the Sixties: there was a fascination with prisms, kaleidoscopes, black lights, and *trompe d'oeil* posters such as those drawn by M.C. Escher, a popular artist of the time. There were objects to hold and gaze through as one's mind wandered on drugs. Checkerboard patterns that fooled the eye with ghost shapes appearing in their interstices were akin to the omnipresent vase-face illustration. There was no basis or point of view one need hold onto. And if any signpost were offered, a joke would be made to dismiss it.

Pop art begat Op art: your brain could generate artistic images. Optical patterns could now be hung in a Modern Art gallery.

Art in the Sixties was treated even more liberally than it had been in the Twenties by Modernists, in that optic patterns, lithography reproductions of newspaper images, and so on, were sold for small fortunes. It all just depended on how you looked at things. "It's all in your mind"—as cartoon George said in "Yellow Submarine." The time was right for funders to splurge on a flashy new ICA building as a monument to Modern Art and populist–everything. An arty breakthrough and an associative free-for-all were seemingly in reach of everyone.

However, the Beatles' choice of lyrics was not as "random" as they said it was. They did use associations aplenty, especially John. The associations came together, as I have attempted to explain in this book, because of the IFP subtext.

Because of the Beatles' Mobius strips of meaning, irreverence was also king: satire flourished on television and in publishing in the later part of the Sixties.

Being that everything was in your mind, a store that wanted to charge people money for clothing was just too square. John confronted Paul when he objected to John charging personal expenses to Apple. "You're always right, aren't you?" John sneered at Paul. "To be right didn't bring any rewards, it brought scorn," Paul said later.[9] Paul's practical business side was not a value in the enterprise he had created.

Once again, Paul had tried another experiment to see where the line was, and he found out. But it was a noble experiment.

Couldn't everyone be loved and understood, in the new culture? Or would people just take "everything they could steal," as Dylan sang about a girl being robbed of everything she had psychically and physically, in "Like a Rolling Stone"? Was the world cold, was it not as John said, "If you're lonely you can talk to me"?

The Beatles' trouncing of dialectics, found in psychiatry of the time, (Laing and Cooper's books, as discussed in Chapter Three) was evidenced by the piles of cassette tapes arriving at Apple. The tapes were time-consuming to listen to. There was no way to listen to them all, after a point. There was no new artist found "in the whole lot," Peter Asher said later. The film division had to hire five full-time script readers.[10] However, in none of the submittals was a good movie script found, according to Denis O'Dell. He wrote that he had never discovered any talent in unsolicited material: "I wish that weren't true, but it is."[11]

Apple films division had a lot of interest and energy around it, but produced the flop, *The Magic Christian*. The basic premise of this movie was that "people will do anything for money." The script was written by Terry Southern, and featured bawdy, tasteless comedy with black humor. It starred Peter Sellers and Ringo Starr.

According to author Ken McNabb (*And In The End*), and producer O'Dell, most Apple divisions were by 1969 losing money.[12] O'Dell wrote that if Apple was in part an experiment in anti-materialist, creative ideals, "then one can only conclude that it failed miserably."[13]

The Beatles as a band, too, seemed to be almost *finito*. In November 1969, the month the White Album was released, John and Yoko released their first album, *Two Virgins*. George had been busy, playing with the band Cream on the song "Badge," and producing an album for Jackie Lomax, *Sour Milk Sea*. Ringo had walked out for a few weeks during the White Album sessions, although had returned. But all three Beatles were tired of being Beatles. To be a Beatle was to be mostly under the direction of Paul; they had to write "to" his concept for each album. His concept was identity fracture, the asylum, mental patient, and therapy: those were the metaphors to use, and they were fitting almost all the songs under those themes. The White Album was an even larger encapsulation of Paul's identity fracture exploration; and even including many genres of songs, the album still sounded cohesive, in a way no one could explain (until now). But to the other Beatles, who knew how Paul controlled the sound and concepts in the group, the worldwide, magic circle of inclusiveness which they had constructed was a form of confinement. To use an apt metaphor, it felt like a creative straightjacket.

After going through the process of recording the double album, the other Beatles felt they too could make their own music without being Beatles (that is, without the IFP subtext to tie things all together). John, fastening onto the tape loops and noise concrete of the Burroughsian avant-garde, would continue in this path with Yoko Ono. Yoko, far from being a complete outsider, as she was perceived, was an artistic kindred spirit to the Beatles. The blankness and emptiness, the whiteness, too, of the White Album cover was found in Yoko's art—and the idea of a fracture, in her "Half" art installations where each object in a room was both painted white, and cut in half. Her "Half" art echoed Paul's aesthetic of fracture, which by now we have seen both in Beatles songs, in the Moderns, and in the Paolozzi sculptures of fractured heads. All had managed to be right in step with the early Twentieth Century avant-garde. Ono's koans, too, could be taken as relatives to the nonsense verse John favored. Ono had also been involved in avant-garde films in Los Angeles, had worked with composer John Cage (whose work influenced Paul), befriended collector Peggy Guggenheim and exhibited with the Fluxus Group. I don't know to what extent Yoko Ono's aesthetic influenced the Beatles to choose the White Album cover, and this has been debated. But taken objectively, Yoko Ono's aesthetic was not so far from the Beatles' after all. In Yoko John would find his soul mate.

George could continue along his path of Vedic spiritualism into Eastern music, and on "Abbey Road" he emerged as a strong songwriter. Without George's songs on "Abbey Road," it would have been a much weaker statement.

The *Mourre* and the Apple

Paul knew that his innate feel for the ordinary was a factor in the Beatles' success. It pleased critics and fans that the Beatles could introduce the unusual and unexpected alongside the comforting feeling of the familiar.[14] This duality influenced Paul's taste in art, and also his own painting. In choosing the name and logo for Apple he was reportedly inspired by the Magritte painting *Le Jeu de Mourre* (The Guessing Game).[15] Magritte's huge banal green apple (The Listening Room), which has taken over a room in a home, is akin to Beatles music entering homes and becoming "huge" in the minds of listeners. Paul had done that magic trick. He had made the ordinary loom large and strange (as Magritte did, and as LSD does) in such songs as "Penny Lane." His "granny music" songs next to John's experimental ones made the old-timey normal seem stranger. He had also put surrealism in his lyrics, as part of the IFP. His IFP could encompass many minds and many genres, even music and art that was "old-fashioned." The variety would still sound like "Beatles music" because the songs shared the same underlying psychological subtext.

If Paul's expansion into Apple Corps, (which also can be a pun meaning apple core, a Paul core, or even "a Paul corpse," making the other Beatles, in their subsidiary roles, pall-bearers or "Paul-bearers") was not a financial success, it did succeed for exploratory and publicity purposes. It encouraged people, and made the news. The real financial payoff was to be in the counterculture itself, birthed in the mid-Sixties. Millions more records could be sold, censorship laws lifted, the Human Potential Movement would begin; thousands of courses in alternative medicine, body work and Yoga would be taken; millions of tickets would be sold to rock concerts, and millions of people would try pot and cocaine and whatever else. The drug market alone would be worth billions of dollars—part of a package, almost, with the Sixties "ideals." The seeming viability of all this as a "counterculture" was in many ways due to the artistic process of just one man, Paul McCartney. Not that he planned it that way, but that was how things happened.

In light of the fascination with optics, altered states, social protest and the Beatles' use of psychological subtexts, it does follow that a Surrealist (Roland Penrose) would team up with an Anarchist and authority on Jungian psychology (Sir Herbert Read) and an ex-military intelligence officer and expert in optics (R.L. Gregory) to put together the flagship exhibit of a new Modern Art center. It was an alliance that made sense in the art world of 1968. The Beatles, or at least Paul, would have been aware of the ICA's gala re-opening across the Thames.

In addition to the refashioning of the avant-garde of the early Twentieth Century, occultist ideas which had gone back centuries, and which before the Sixties been represented by disparate groups, began to enter mainstream culture. In the Sixties there began to be an agglomeration of ideas under the umbrella of counterculture. One could shop the New Age, and be one of the try-everything crowd. Since the Seventies the occultist subcultures have gone back into their corners again somewhat.

There was everything to do and to be: therefore there was no-*one* to be, and no*where* to go, but one could have "that magic feeling" about it. "You can be anyone this time around," enthused Timothy Leary. People had been made to feel de-stabilized, yet encouraged, by The Beatles, and possibly by LSD. Some had made themselves the equivalent of the "empty swimming pool." They could be filled back up with—whatever. But, it wasn't supposed to be certainties of religion, law, or parental wisdom. Youth were encharged with a sense of new frontiers. "Never trust anyone over thirty" became a slogan.[16] Many people, not just youth, rejected the advice of those who "think they know better" because that was in itself a stale sort of mind.

* * *

After closing the doors on the inmates of the White Album, it would seem like there would be nowhere to go, musically. But the Beatles went on to release two more albums, 1969's "Abbey Road," and "Let It Be" in 1970. They would contain what I call reconciliation songs.

Paul's "him" was more successful than ever after the White Album. The White Album is judged by many critics and fans to be the Beatles' ultimate achievement. Paul had let Francie go, after using her she helped him to make the album "better." It certainly had depth and atmosphere, due to the feelings he had encountered with someone so like him, and yet, not him—his "blackbird." He let her fly back to New York, and made what was perhaps his biggest decision as Paul, and not as Beatle Paul. He made the momentous decision to choose Linda Eastman to be his wife.

However, Paul knew that as Beatle Paul he needed to write some songs to comfort people, and perhaps, himself. He was embarking on his new life with Linda. He had found a home, and could see the end of The Beatles coming, but he wanted to reassure himself, acknowledge the end of the band, and comfort the fans. That was a tall order, but as it happened Paul was up to it and wrote some beautiful works. Again, they would use his IFP praxis.

Usually John had done the summing-up songs, but by this point he couldn't be bothered. For the last two albums Paul did most of the summing-up, looking at where The Beatles had been with their fans and what was in store for the future.

Fortuitously, in 1968 when things had seemed rather disjointed and dark, Paul had found a way forward, a light at the end of the tunnel. Once again, I assert that he found guidance and inspiration from psychology texts. A book by Maxwell Jones, *Social Psychiatry In Practice: The Idea of the Therapeutic Community*, I suggest gave Paul the means to frame what he and the Beatles had done in the context of helping society.[17] The book was published by Penguin in 1968 with a forward by Morris Carstairs. Maxwell's theories would give Paul a way to end the Beatles story on a positive note and reconcile what they did for their fans to a larger benign purpose—even though Paul buried the idea in a seemingly pointless song about a serial killer.

So, although 1968 was a dark year in several respects, it was a year which led Paul to both artistic reconciliation and personal growth.

His personal growth was to come from Linda and Heather; but the Beatles had been busily collapsing dialectics for years. How to write reconciliation songs if they had always eclipsed the two sides? And how could the Beatles leave their fans if they had always been "with" them? The answer was to transfer the governing of the asylum over to the listeners. The fans would become the Patron Saints of mental hospitals, and Paul would write their anthem.

The first song to hint at his reconciliation of his role in the band, and the summation of what the Beatles had done, was "**Hey Jude**" released in August of 1968. The "Hey Jude" single with B-side "Revolution" was released three months prior to the White Album.

Francie Schwartz wrote that after she returned to New York, (apparently sometime in September of 1968), "Hey Jude" was all over the airwaves: the first few chords, she said, "spooked" her "the worst," but after that she could listen to the rest.[18] I intuit she knew what the first lines were referring to—Paul's use of her own "sad song." She had told her story of the mental asylum to Paul and John, and it had found its way, made "better," in coded subtext into songs on the White Album.

"Hey Jude" would be both about his artistic process, and a celebration of it.

The song is Paul encouraging the creative side of himself, similar to the song "Martha My Dear" (my idea). He lets people in, and then will "make it better" because he will be inspired by them to make a song. "The minute you let her under your skin/Then you begin/To make it better." The creative side of Paul lets a person into his heart, or under his skin, and then he produces art—a song. He has the movement he needs on his shoulder (this could mean that the music will come to him by instinct. He is only waiting "for someone to perform with," the other Beatles). "Don't you know that it's just you, hey Jude, you will do." Paul knows that it is him that makes the song, even if he does feel like he's split, making art. All he needs to start the process is "a sad song" from somewhere or someone to get under his skin. He is both acknowledging that he makes his art, split or not, and addressing yet another song to the creative side of himself. It is interesting that although the "sad song" or other person enters into him, he perceives the creative side of himself as someone else (and often writes letters to it). "Hey Jude" is akin to "Martha My Dear," because in both songs Paul splits off his praxis, and talks to it as if it (he) were another person. In both songs, he is encouraging himself.

Paul has said that he sang the name "Jules" initially, because the song was addressed originally to Julian, John's son. Paul composed the melody on a drive to John's house, feeling sorry for the little boy being the victim of an imminent divorce.[19] His feelings for Julian could perfectly well be the inspiring emotion for the song, how he arrived at the name "Jude" ("It fit better") and what shaped the comforting melody; but after that emotional inspiration, the song moves along the by-now well-worn tracks of the IFP.

The most common associations with "Jude" are "Juden" (the German word for Jewish), and Judas Iscariot, the disciple of Christ. Both these associations carry a negative connotation: the scrawling of "Juden" by Nazis onto Jewish storefronts, and Judas betraying Christ to authorities who crucified Him. One night Paul and Francie scrawled "Hey Jude" on the white-painted windows of the closed Apple boutique, causing a disturbance among shopkeepers who feared it was slurring or threatening Jews.[20] So, Paul picking Jude as a name for "himself," that is, his muse, seems rather provocative. Francie, whom he so identified with that he screamed to see her again at the end of his artistic process, was Jewish. But Francie also came to him from a mental hospital. Out of these multiple associations, plus the IFP praxis of the Beatles, Paul sees reconciliation in art can be made. "Jude," I suggest is really referring to Saint Jude, the patron saint of hospitals, and of hopeless causes.[21]

Paul in this song includes the listener and himself in the IFP framework of mental hospital, asylum and mental patient. Saint Jude is a Catholic patron saint of hospitals, and of hopeless causes.

Combine the two, hopeless causes in hospitals, and you have—mental patients! Saint Lucia was an association Paul put into "Blackbird," inspired by Francie and written at about the same time, and "Hey Jude" also invokes a saint which relates to Francie's asylum story.

"Jude's" expansive, measured approach indicates that Paul is very comfortable with his IFP, his praxis, and the result of it, and that you should be too. The listeners are included in the reconciliation. Everything related to his songwriting, The Beatles, and the subtext of the mental asylum underneath the new awareness-counterculture is "better." The instruction he gives "Jude" is to "let it out and let it in." This is like a therapist saying to a client, "Let out your (xyz). And let in (xyz)." Breathe. (In-and-out in this context refers to inspiration.) And: "anytime you feel the pain/Hey Jude, refrain/Don't carry the world upon your shoulders." Make art out of pain and make it "better." This is the "praxis" of his IFP. He gave listeners "broken wings" and broken things, and made (in his opinion and in the opinion of many) society better. There was the Civil Rights Movement. The Feminist Movement. People were motivated to "arise."

Paul counsels himself and the listeners, "Remember to let her into your heart/Then you can start/To make it better," and "Remember to let her under your skin/Then you begin/To make it better." He works up "better, better," until he cannot contain his "pseudo-soul shrieking," as MacDonald describes it. Then comes the refrain of "Na, na, na, na na na na," which goes on for several minutes, as a large chorus of voices join in unison and one can picture a crowd of people swaying together as they sing.

"Hey Jude" is not the cataleptic negativism of John's "Strawberry Fields." Where John imagined a nightmarish march of "feeleds" into a field, "Hey Jude" gestures outward toward a future of motivated acts, which "make it better"—open-air rock concerts, dancing, communal acts of celebration—actions full of movement and *self*-motivation. John's "feeleds" by contrast were coldly plowed under—they were "berried/buried." His wheat-"feeleds" had no control over what they felt. Paul's (St. Jude's) inmates in the song video are also swaying in unison like wheat, but Paul makes a point of riffing to almost gratuitous excess over the refrain, as much as to say that one can do anything one wants to and to feel free. Thus his song is one of liberation: however, it carries the strange paradox of the IFP, as we have seen with so many Beatles songs by now. Not only is St. Jude a patron saint of, as I suggest, mental patients, but the listeners can apply Paul's advice for Jude to themselves, essentially becoming patron saint of their own mental hospital. Related to this split and quasi-anarchy, "Na" is essentially "No." The song implies defiance, but its production implies that self-motivated defiance is henceforth going to be a little more out in the open. Breaking rules won't be confined to smoking a joint at your friend's apartment or outside a nightclub. The large orchestra denotes this—one pictures a space such as a monumental amphitheater with a public chorus. The chorus sings in "Hey Jude" as a communal act of defiance, or raspberry, singing "Na, na, na, na," somewhat as little kids stick out their tongues. So while John's concertgoers are straw, Paul's are blessed by a benevolent saint of the asylum which is also themselves. Defiance of *mores* has thus been emotionally (ostensibly) "let out" into the open—into the field. You can gather with others, listen to music and smoke pot at a festival, and Bill Graham will sell you a ticket to do so.

One can't avoid considering Kurt Lewin's Field theory[22] (Lewin was a favorite at Harvard, of course)[23] as applicable to group determination of *mores* as influencing individual behavior. If the Beatles were trying to change society, as John said they set out to do, then influencing group behavior seems to have been how the Beatles went about it. However they began this process by reaching into people, via emotions and their lyric immediacy. This I have asserted was achieved by Paul's use of texts at the Ashers, psychological subtexts which worked because psychology does work (to some extent. Some would argue this point).

Paul's screams (he called them "Cary Grant on heat,"[24] because Grant was famous for saying "Judy, Judy, Judy") were a release of emotion and liberation from restraint that the Beatles music always delivered to their fans. In the video filmed for "Hey Jude," the assembled crowd of varied individuals, singing the chorus in unison, stand for a community gathered around and formed by the Beatles' music. If you're in the club you will feel liberated, and "make it better." It will be "getting better all the time," to quote another therapy-"rehabilitation" song of Paul's.

Paul could by now write about all of this, using huge chords that demanded an emotional response. "Hey Jude" was taken for another sign of musical genius, that Paul could write a song with a seemingly meaningless refrain of "Na, na, na … Hey Jude," and magically, it worked as a song and everyone wanted to sing along to it. I assert that once again, the key to this song's effect is in its subliminal subtext. As usual, Paul mixed in conventional ideas of "romance." It is interesting however that it uses an extended refrain of "na, na" which is both infantile ("Nana" being infant talk for calling mother or nanny) and a negation. The refrain goes on for about four minutes to monumental orchestral chords and a forceful piano accompaniment by Paul.

Paul thinking of himself as the patron saint of mental hospitals and his gathering many people together to sing the song with him and the other Beatles is consistent with inviting everyone to be "all together, now" in the asylum. They (and the listeners are invited to) sing a negation of vaguely defiant affirmation, while Paul screams "Jude" ecstatically. However the listeners are invited to be their own saint of their own asylum.

Critics wrote that the song came out at a time when its message was most needed, and that "Jude" reassures many as much as it reassures one male.[25] Both MacDonald and Pichaske wrote that the song alleviated male guilt over "sleeping around." The refrain suggests open defiance even as it trivializes the essential problem. No firm rejection of anything is needed; one can simply say "na, na, na." Also, you can also be the Patron Saint and do the same process that Paul does. You are still "with the Beatles."

This IFP anthem is Paul's much more soft-pedaled but still subversive implosion.

It is interesting that three reconciliation songs most associated with "the end" of The Beatles and their good-bye to their fans, "Hey Jude," "The Long and Winding Road" and "Let It Be," were actually written by Paul in 1968, at the time he was working on the White Album. Maybe Paul was intuiting in 1968 that the end of The Beatles might be near. John had penned the complaining "Glass Onion" about Paul. (John also wrote the transcendent "Across the Universe" in 1968.) "Let It Be" came to Paul from a dream he had of his mother appearing to him, telling him that things were going to be all right. Paul was beginning a huge personal transition during the White Album, in that he was deciding to commit to Linda. John was bonding with Yoko.

But it seems that Francie had something to do with these songs being written, along with the poignant "Blackbird." Carl Jung theorized that women should be the *femme inspiratrice*, (the inspiring woman)[26] and it seems that Francie might have been this for Paul. Whatever her character or personality, being around her seems to have put things in focus for Paul. Francie was aware of this or became so later, and wrote in her memoir, "I'd always been secretly glad to have been a catalyst in his life."[27] Paul wrote some of his most interesting Beatles songs in 1968, during the time he was around Francie.

Although "Let It Be" and "The Long and Winding Road" were written in 1968, these two songs will be discussed along with the rest of the "Let It Be" album in Chapter 13.

There are other reconciliation songs on "Abbey Road." Surprisingly, one is "**Maxwell's Silver Hammer.**" This is taken to be a nonsensical song about a murderer, and thus, frequently cited as one of Paul's worst songs. John "simply loathed" it, we are told.[28] It is chalked up to be an unfortunate lapse in taste—"If any single recording shows why the Beatles broke up, it is "Maxwell's Silver Hammer," MacDonald wrote.[29]

So I was surprised to find a psychological subtext to this song. In my research into influential mid-century psychologists I had come across the name Maxwell Jones. I found a strong connection between Jones and Paul's song, which I shall explain.

Maxwell Jones was a doctor of medicine and military psychiatrist, who pioneered group therapy after WWII for British soldiers suffering shellshock, among other problems.[30] Given how I understood the Beatles' art at this point, it was easy to say that group therapy was what the Beatles had been *doing*, in a sense. I thought that maybe Paul was aware of or had read Jones's books, *Social Psychiatry* published in 1954 and *The Therapeutic Community* published in 1968. Then I came across a description of Jones as the *inventor* of group therapy. That was when the connection clicked. The "inventor" would be the "Edison"— Maxwell *Edison*! People use the last name of Thomas Edison, the famous inventor, to denote "the inventor." Could it be, strangely but not so far-fetched a connection, that Paul was singing about the first group therapist? I read up more on Maxwell Jones.

In his book *Social Psychiatry: The Idea of the Therapeutic Community* published first by Tavistock Institute and subsequently by Penguin/ Pelican books, Jones describes a poll taken by the National Opinion Research Center at the University of Chicago in 1950. The poll showed that although the public in general knew that psychiatry existed, "they nevertheless viewed it with vast indifference, which for all practical purposes amounted to rejection." The poll concluded that "the acceptance of psychiatry depends on the acceptance of a particular way of thinking ... lack of public acceptance and understanding may be due to the fact that the psychiatric viewpoint is alien to and incompatible with popular thinking."[31]

Jones then describes an experiment led by E. and J. Cummings in the Fifties, which tried to educate the people of two small towns in a Canadian prairie province about the mental health profession.[32]

Over several months the townspeople were treated to news stories, radio broadcasts, panel discussions, formed study groups, and attended a film festival. The intent was that by educating people in what psychiatrists do, and aspects of mental illness, their attitudes toward the mentally ill and/or "deviants" would "change." The experiment was an "outstanding failure."[33] "In fact, in trying to modify community attitudes to mental health, the programme only succeeded in provoking anxiety and open hostility on the part of the local population ... the team managed only to destroy the community's faith in the effectiveness of its own defenses," Jones wrote. In addition, the experiment made the townspeople question the discernment of the psychologists and cast strong doubt on the mental health profession in general.

Jones had led the first group therapy sessions after WWII among repatriating soldiers. Discussing problems in a group met with some success; then Jones tested in asylums the concept of a less-hierarchical system which encouraged more communication between patients and nurses and delegated supposedly more decision-making powers to support staff. This led to more meetings between patients and nursing staff, and nursing staff and doctors.

This less-hierarchical system eventually formed a new "culture" of "group-support" in the test asylums. Jones called it "the therapeutic community." Other psychologists were encouraged: Goodwin Watson wrote in a forward to *The Therapeutic Community* that "the great contribution of Dr. Maxwell Jones is not in the results ... already achieved," but in what such a model held for the future: Watson envisioned that "in the future 'psychosanitation' will emerge, and social psychiatrists will normally protect entire communities from ways of life which are emotionally crippling, much as public health officers now save cities from epidemics caused by bacteria."[34] Jones's goal, he wrote, although acknowledging that it might be unreachable, was that society itself could become a therapeutic community. This gives one pause, because such a situation would be saying that everyone is in a sense, somewhat mentally ill and envisioning a society where we all just support each other with that understanding. Another researcher concluded vis-à-vis the Cummings failure that "we should forget mental health as perceived by the general public, and start with the concept of so-called normal human behavior and work in *that* direction."[35]

It might seem a stretch, but in looking at the lyrics to both "Hey Jude" and "Maxwell's Silver Hammer," I could see the linkage between the dreamt-of "group therapy for all," and the therapeutic community of "friends" that the Beatles sing of. Couple Jones's ideas with the Beatles' endorsement of the ego-fracturing drug LSD (which John took to "erase himself" and the hippies said "kills the head")[36] and you have the formation of the counterculture-as-therapeutic-society.

Considering actions such as these it seems reasonable to connect the dots and say that in "Maxwell's Silver Hammer," Paul is singing (playfully) about the Beatles, or more likely himself, being the hammer or the tool of Maxwell. Maxwell's hammer administers a blow to the head to make sure people are "dead"—that is, ego-dead. The Beatles' original name was the Quarrymen; quarrymen are masons who use hammers. The Beatles called themselves the Silver Beatles and the Beatals before settling on the name the Beatles. Thus, a "silver hammer" who "beats" people until they are "dead," describes the Beatles' IFP. Their purpose, at least after 1966, was to fracture or "rob" identity. To "take you down." They guided people through this process, and were the four no-ones, the Nowhere Men along with their fans. The "killing" of the head was caused supposedly by LSD. But the music of the Sixties, liberalization of laws, and the mind-expanding effect of Beatles songs formulated, as I have discussed, the "new" type. This new type of person would be for the world (a global individual, such as psychologist Harry Murray wrote about to Lewis Mumford).[37] Everyone will benefit from the Beatles' blow to the "head" and the therapeutic, more tolerant society Watson and Jones theorized will have been achieved.

It is a distinction of Maxwell's hammer that it comes down upon the *head*. Drugs and music affect the head. In the song, "Maxwell Edison, majoring in medicine" (Jones was a doctor) kills people from varied levels of society: a woman studying Pataphysical science, a policeman and a judge. Maxwell makes no distinctions when he brings his silver hammer (Paul) down on people's heads.

Jones noted in 1950 that "the average American adult had never known anyone who had been helped by seeing a psychiatrist, and he had no interest, however remote, or of whatever kind, in seeing a psychiatrist himself."[38] But by 1969, Paul and the Beatles had been putting psychiatric subtexts into songs (to a beat) for years. Plus, they had encouraged the mainstream public to consider trying a major de-stabilizing drug, LSD, which had been used in psychotherapy. The Beatles definitely had hit the normals on the "head," and had worked in the other "direction" that the researcher noted above.

Jones also wrote that "it is not too much to hope that society's *mores* would become more tolerant of deviant behavior," in order for there to be a "therapeutic society."[39] Psychologist and anthropologist G.M. Carstairs, President from 1968 to 1972 of the World Mental Health Organization, wrote in the foreword to Maxwell's *Social Psychiatry* that "sensitivity to feelings and to the human interactions in the daily life are just as important to a therapeutic community as traditional medicine." I submit that Paul is connecting what the Beatles did in their music to these theories: first we have the sensitive Beatles delivering "news" about feelings, then a relaxation of *mores* amidst the new idea of the "helping" community of "friends."

I suggest that the "Maxwell Edison, majoring in medicine" of Paul's song is based on Maxwell Jones, the "Edison" or inventor of the idea of the therapeutic community. In this perverse song, Paul is linking the Beatles' job of killing-the-ego to a psychiatrist researcher who had therapeutic aims. The Beatles are a hammer to kill the ego[40] and make for more tolerance in society. So, the song's hidden message is that Paul himself is the "silver hammer." Paul sings "Silver Hammer Man!" in the last line and punctuates it with two hammer blows.

The "dink, dink" of the hammer recalls the "happy hammers" on "Getting Better" from "Pepper," a song about rehabilitation. That a song about a serial murderer could be coded in this way to mean a therapeutic society must "strike" my readers as absurd, but, I had to admit, the song's reason for being can be explained by my theory. What else could "Maxwell's Silver Hammer" mean, if it means anything? Paul could be as clever as John with the psychological subtexts.

"Oh! Darling" was written by Paul. Paul gives the simple Fifties-style song a rendition that fits with the IFP. It sounds as if the singer will go over the edge and lose all control, "if you leave me/I'll never make it alone." He sings like a madman and screams, "I'll never do you no harm!" with the barest shred of self-control. The fact that it sounds like the singer is coming unhinged makes the song fit with the IFP subtext.

Ringo's "**Octopus's Garden**" is thought to be another "children's song" sung by the lovable Ringo. Ringo wrote this song while on a seaside holiday, and presented it for inclusion on "Abbey Road." George Harrison reportedly helped him with the lyrics.[41] Although it seems a song of levity, a harmless ditty, when one examines the lyrics in light of what one now knows about the IFP, its becomes less and less benign until it seems outright hostile.

The song describes a setting we encountered before in "Yellow Submarine," on which Ringo also sang—that of a refuge or an asylum. The octopus's garden is underwater, "our little hideaway beneath the waves." "We would be so happy, you and me," Ringo sings. "We would shout, and swim about" and there would be "no-one there to tell us what to do." This lack of any governing authority is again, a picture of an asylum like Villa 21, where the inmates ran things. People were free to do what they liked—as are the denizens in the octopus's garden. Ringo says he'd like to be there, "with you." It is an invitation. You are invited to join the Beatles, be "with" the Beatles. Live on the submarine, come underwater.

Now consider the octopus. An octopus (octo-) has eight arms, as do the four Beatles in *toto*. The original title for the film *Help!* was *Eight Arms to Hold You*, a title suggested by Ringo; again in "Octopus" he was thinking of the eight arms of the Beatles "holding" their fans. But the octopus's garden is near a cave, and in the shade. To be in an octopus's arms (the Beatles' arms) is not intrinsically positive. The song is describing a situation where one would be enfolded and dragged down to one's death. It is played for cute: "Underwater" voices are heard singing on the middle eight (achieved by feeding the vocals through a compressor and a Moog synthesizer combination).[42] As a demented guitar solos, the fantasized denizens gargle along, in their airless environment. To be "with" the Beatles in the asylum is to participate in identity-fracture, to lose one's sense of what is right and what is wrong—to lose all bearings—to lose homeostasis. It is the ultimate takeover of the individual where there is no high or low, but who cares, because "nobody's home." This is the ultimate invalidation of the mental hospital environment and by metaphorical placement the listener is put in Beatles songs where the goal is to extirpate the ego. Thus, the Beatles' "garden" is another fantasy of self-negation where those who participate have lost any shred of *self*-preservation. (The "Garden" is also another planting-people idea such as John wrote about in "Fields.") Ringo "wishes" or "would like" "you" to be there. This is the most inimical song I think the Beatles ever produced. The Octopus's Garden is where people are senselessly buried, and they are buried alive underwater.

Although giving few specifics about the denizen's activities other than "we would sing and dance around," and "we would shout, and swim about," "Garden" is similar to other Beatles songs such as "Yellow Submarine," and "Penny Lane." Each describes a place of freedom from constraint, within an asylum. The asylum can include implied drug-taking (submarines were slang for a pill at the time), sex, and a bit of ego-death mixed in. (In the "Garden," we "can't be found" and we will also be "resting our head.") The underlying concept of the song is Paul's and the Beatles' praxis of the IFP. "Garden" is another asylum, but it is also something worse. I am not saying Ringo wrote it to mean all this to *listeners*—because no-one (it seems) did think of it that way. It was taken to be another fun and somewhat nonsensical Beatles song, consumed as easily as ice cream. The song does *feel* like fun. But I suggest that in it Ringo and George used Paul's method of songwriting full-bore and painted a picture of a typical Beatle environment, an asylum, in terms as threatening as any other treatment of the subtext.

"**Golden Slumbers/Carry That Weight**" by Paul also enjoins someone to "sleep." It opens with a kind of assumption that the listener has self-transformed, been through a process, and can't get back to how they were. "Once there was a way/To get back homeward," sings Paul. This implies that now there is not a way to get metaphorically back home. "Sleep pretty darling, do not cry/And I will sing a lullaby." The song told fans that they had changed—even if they hadn't particularly. The song was a bit of Beatles' myth-making, alluding to a trajectory of development that the Beatles and the fans shared (that is, as if that were so). It is a dramatic song, but then resolves to "Boy, you're gonna carry that weight/Carry that weight/A long time." It has been suggested that Paul was anticipating the burden of fame, lawsuits, and other problems of being an ex-Beatle.

"**She Came in Through the Bathroom Window**" was written by Paul in May 1968, soon after Francie arrived in April. The first line was inspired by a groupie who reportedly did come in through Paul's bathroom window. The lyrics then extend the story-song to cover some aspects of his time with Francie. He and Francie would go out to dance, so he had the line "she said she'd always been a dancer." "And though she thought I knew the answer/Well I knew/What I could not say." His answer, his secret way of writing songs, he knew he couldn't tell anyone. "And so I quit the police department/And got myself a steady job." This is alluding to the pun John made earlier, of the "p'licemen" who are the Beatles, the "Please-men." Paul quit the "Please department" in 1966, and would no longer "please" fans with upbeat pop songs about romance. "And though she tried her best to help me/She could steal, but she could not rob." Francie had ideas for the Apple empire. She wanted to help, she worked there and she and Paul would "rap" about it. But, "she could not rob." The line might be alluding to T.S. Eliot's observation, "the immature artist copies. The mature artist steals."[43] Paul takes it one hierarchy further in that he, as a Beatle, robs. And this is (gloomily) the action of a band which "takes you down" as their mission—to take away "ego," to "de-program," as Leary put it. Francie could not "rob," Paul jokes wryly about his requirements for someone to help him. But no-one can, anyway and he wouldn't possibly want them to, is the implication.

"Didn't anybody tell her/Didn't anybody see/Sunday's on the phone to Monday/Tuesday's on the phone to me." I take this to mean that Paul is disavowing having supra-normal knowledge, "knowing the answer." But again he puts in a split: in the expression he is using in the song, Monday should be "on the phone to me" but there is a gap; *Tuesday* is on the phone to him.

It's a shrug of a statement from both sides, in that "she" makes her grand entrance though a bathroom window, and the singer says he doesn't have any answers. This is a far cry from the effortless bliss of early Beatles songs like "Do You Want To Know a Secret," "Hold Me Tight" or "This Boy." MacDonald called the Beatles "self-debunking"[44] and this song shows Paul doing just that, deflating his own image. But the Beatles did more debunking of self than just their own.

George's two songs on "Abbey Road" were the life-affirming "Something" and "Here Comes the Sun." On side two, leftover song scraps by John and Paul, put together in a song-suite, moved along briskly and resolved in "The End." It was a fracture-suite that worked.

Non-IFP songs were appealing: the "**Sun King**" had a magisterial quality and blissfulness-skirting-near-ridicule as John launched into fake Spanish that sounded like a magic benediction. "**Because**" had nearly the same feeling as its spectrum harmonies dazzled, and then there was "**Here Comes the Sun**" by George. The sun shone on all—Beatles and their fans. "The sun songs contributed to the warmth of the album," according to biographer Miles. Emerick also noted that a new mixing board at the studio made for a richer and warmer sound.

"Abbey Road" was to be one of the fullest statements by the Beatles and it did the usual Beatle trick. It took you somewhere, but you end up slightly to the left of where you began. It delivers a (empty) full circle to listeners, and you are left slightly—just slightly—different than you were before. This almost-but-not-quite-completing-the-circle Laing called "elusion."

"**The End**" points to itself as the capper statement for the entire trajectory of the Beatles and their fans: the statement that sums it all up. Where or what has it been to, this journey with the Beatles? The band ought to know, after all. What could their final statement be? Paul commented much later that he wanted to end with a "meaningful couplet" like Shakespeare did, "so I followed the Bard."[45] "And in the end/The love you take/Is equal to the love you make," the Beatles reassure us, to a swell of affirmative strings, harmonies and guitar that resolve sloppily to a major chord. Their vocal harmonies cascade over the line, "the love you take." This is another circular motif, but not the ouroboros of John's "walrus" loops. "The End" is hope: it is expiation, hinting at an absolution of sexual guilt, more, that there was never any guilt to begin with. It was all equal. This is another reconciliation song by Paul. "The End" presents Beatles fans with a completed balance sheet. It reassures the listener that at the end of the day, everything is in balance when one makes or takes love.

Lest we think this summing-up pretentious, Paul followed it with the fragment, "**Her Majesty**." He denies the song a last note. It is a joke song, cheeky enough to fantasize about the Queen of England, saying, "Her Majesty's a pretty nice girl/But she doesn't have a lot to say … I want to tell her that I love her a lot/But I gotta get a belly full of wine… Someday I'm gonna make her mine, oh yeah."

"Abbey Road" was the final album recorded by the Beatles. "Let It Be," although released after "Abbey Road," was actually recorded earlier. Songs for both albums were recorded in 1969.

And so the long and winding road of the Beatles is winding down, with a few more reconciliation songs of Paul's to appear on "Let It Be." John seems to have had less interest in coddling Beatles fans, having mentally moved on, but Paul, who had always been more personally connected to his fans and assorted public (even literally, through his IFP) would pen several of these "testimonial pictures." He did not want to leave the fans high and dry, so to speak. Most fans were probably in a different frame of mind than when they began "with" the Beatles way back in 1963. Paul's songs like "Hey Jude" and "Let It Be" would end things on a positive note.

* * *

"Hey Jude" was the most positive reconciliation song; it was presented as a communal celebration. The Sixties had been creatively chaotic at best and bad-faith, even murderous, at worst. How to wrap things up, wrap the Beatles up, put a bow on them and go out on a good note? The answer for Paul was again, to write about his own process. Because, I am asserting, the "Beatles" were always about his own process—of identity fracture, the evisceration of core identity. If Paul had not spent time at the Asher's, the Beatles would have been a different group.

How to resolve everything for the fans? The answer was inspired, in a way. He would write an anthem of absolution to himself, as Saint Jude, the patron saint of mental hospitals. This is also resolving the "problem" of the Munchausen patient. But, it is also a lessening of expectations on a profound level. We are all our own "egg-men," all together in the asylum, and patron saint of our own hopeless case.

As usual, he mixed in the idea of "romance" in, "You were made to go out and get her." But he is talking about his own process. He takes a "sad song, and makes it better." Paul is again reassuring himself that he is all right.

Paul's songs on the last two albums are reconciliation songs for the fans. They have been so drawn-into the Beatles' process that they too feel the affirmation in "Hey Jude" and "Let It Be." They can say those affirmations to themselves. "Go out and get her." "Let it be." "Hey, Jude, don't be afraid." If you felt like a Judas betraying your Christian upbringing to have sex before marriage, then get over it. Everything's okay.

MacDonald also wrote that the song gave permission to men wanting to take advantage of the new more sexually permissive climate of the times—they were made to "go out and get her." The song can be interpreted in a myriad of ways, as can most Beatles songs. However, once again, I find the IFP subtext.

Paul has a fascination with mixing, and this is part of what made his song production so effective. How a song is mixed is a crucial step, after all the work of recording is done. Paul also had fantasies of mixing things in art—dumping an egg into a really big bowl of ashes, for example. For a music video, Paul once had white foam layered all over the manicured lawn of a grand estate, which killed the grass.[46] But Paul, or a side of him, was always drawn to going too far. He, and many people, went too far in the Sixties, but to measure what was due to his IFP and what was due to other influences is impossible. However, the "culture" is traceable to Paul's own process.

Paul did not set out intentionally to produce "the culture." I think his artistic process was a way for him to put out varied material, because he knew a bunch of different musical styles. The psychological subtext was a way for it all to cohere and be "Beatles." But then, the psychological research, the words of broken minds, also resonated with him—otherwise, he couldn't have written the artful songs he did.

Paul seems to have continued using the idea of doubles or splits in his artistic process. In his music videos post-Beatles, Paul often appears with a double, and even as multiple Pauls.

During the Sixties, the Beatles were ascribed powers, cosmic knowledge—but they were canny enough to include their fans in the free-to-do-anything "artist" identity. Using the hidden subtext of Paul's identity fracture project, they created a do-anything sense of freedom. They in effect refused to diagnose themselves. They were in a sense, not Munchausen people acting "ill" on purpose (as in, "You're not really an artist; you're just acting like one!"). They were posing as Modern artists: Modern art is less about skill and more about what one sees in it.

The Beatles did not base the ultimate judgment (diagnosis) on behavior. All behavior was in theory permissible. They put all their listeners sonically in the mental asylum, as fellow inmates—and there was no diagnosis on offer. There would be no judgment of whether a behavior was injurious, or good, or bad. There would supposedly only be love and understanding and increased knowledge.

There was no physical diagnosis either—no warnings of hazards around drug-taking. Reality was "all in the mind." So, the Beatles' art bypassed the Dr. Asher's of the world. The people who "thought they knew better." The Beatles opened up a supposed "new terrain" of emotional feeling and expressiveness. It was as if they access to some secret knowledge. They did. The world of psychological research and therapy, asylums and so on were unknown to the public.

Such was the "culture" the Beatles created, that no one could gainsay another. This fit well with many Modernist activities: "Happenings" could happen. Sitting in a garden in the rain, not wearing a "mac," any eccentricity was no longer eccentric. There was also a disconnect: If everything was potentially an "act," then, that was fracture. A counterculture that valued authenticity was also saying there is no true north, no moral basis, no compass. In a culture that valued authenticity and creativity, these became paradoxically in the shortest supply.

"I've got a feeling," Paul sang, in a bubbling-over, barely controlled tone of euphoria. John sang a mantra of "everybody": "Everybody had a hard time/Everybody had a wet dream … Everybody let their hair down."

In the Beatleverse, there's feeling which leads to action.[47] There's no ratiocination in between.

* * *

Maybe Paul had a bit of conscience at this point at how he had driven the Beatles, especially John, to be caught up in his own Identity Fracture Project. By the time of the White Album, the other Beatles were itching to get out. In "Hey Jude," Paul is (perhaps) confronting himself with his role in all this, not in the contentious, almost hilarious way John did in "Walrus," but in a consoling tone. Paul has a lot more of society's support now, for "making it better"; perhaps all, in their own way, will "make it better" like he did, and become "Judes," patron saints of (mental) hospitals, liberating each other onto some unspecified terrain of free-everything. (Plath's title for one of her stories was *This Earth Our Hospital*.) Thus, a chorus and orchestra back him, repeating "Na, na … hey Jude," while he free-forms ecstatic screams. "Hey Jude" is Paul's grand fireworks-and-balloon-drop-celebration for his Identity Fracture Project and its acceptance by not only the record-buying public, but by society.

And yet nobody knew what the song meant, really, except that Paul said it was written to comfort John's son Julian. It was about comforting someone—but whom? Paul had to provide at least an answer to that question, and he said it was written on a drive to Julian's home and he wanted to comfort the little boy over John and Cynthia's impending divorce; so that his compassion, his emotions inspired the initial melody. This is very likely, because strong emotions inspire songs to come to songwriters. But after that inspiration, the song, I submit, was completed based on his own IFP. The listener felt like there was something else behind the rapturous hymn, or anthem; it seemed pregnant with meaning, like the usual Beatles song. You could even extend the "pregnant with meaning" aspect and say each Beatles song based on the IFP (and most of them were) was like a baby that was "never been born," lay eternally in the womb and never got out into the world, into the light of day. The songs and the men themselves making them, hiding in a sense behind their photos and jokey interviews, seemed, after 1964, pregnant with meaning. However the hidden body of the songs, instigated by Paul's discoveries at the Asher's, was based on psychology texts that initially he found in Dr. Asher's library, and Paul's own drive toward an identity fracture.

However effectively Paul produced "Hey Jude," he may not have felt entirely reconciled to his entire artistic process. Francie wrote that when they sat listening to the final mix of the song, Paul kept saying, "I still can't hear it." "As if he was telling me he couldn't hear his own messages to himself," she commented.[48]

* * *

"With" the Beatles, the fans had telescoped themselves into infinitely expanding realities. Within that "interval" Paul had created, of the insane-being-sane, always "right," (even if I'm wrong, I'm right), and the constant thread of the mental hospital being a community, the Beatles had made it okay to do so many things. Motley was worn—colors splashed on murals—new tone colors and expression entered into music and poetry—it was a stream-of-consciousness like that of the Early Moderns, but where Virginia Woolf had her drab dress and T.S. Eliot his three-piece-suit, the Beatles had set up colorful symbols on the board game of consciousness. It was "a play," a "game." "You should play the whole game of consciousness, but be aware of it while you are doing it," said Leary. "Life is a game, which one should play the best he can," George told the *Beatle Book Monthly*.[49] These comments signaled a new split between the individual consciousness and "consensus reality." The new counterculture was saying that if you are a healthy person, you will see society is false or an "act;" and in becoming your true self, you might be regarded as somewhat insane by "straight" society. That was exactly Laing's view, as we discussed in Chapter Three.

There was a bit of pent-up demand for rebellion after the homogenous Fifties. And youth can always be encouraged to experiment; but the Beatles made experimentation the norm. People would feel that they were smarter by having listened to the Beatles; they were certainly prepared to listen to long guitar jams and acid rock. Nothing would be real; therefore no standard or diagnosis was possible. It is no wonder that in the late Sixties, Dr. Asher fell into a depression; in 1969 he was found dead, hung in the basement of the Asher home, the very same room where John and Paul had written many of their songs. It was ruled a suicide. There was no suicide note found.

"It was about the evisceration of one's core identity. That was always what it was about," said a woman who lived through LSD and the Sixties counterculture.[50]

* * *

Once there was a way to get back homeward. Sleep pretty darling, do not cry. I will sing a lullaby. Just sleep with your eyes closed. Living is easy when your eyes are closed, with pennies on your eyes. Listen to me. I will show you rain is the same as sun. Golden slumbers fill your eyes. You can't get back home. She's leaving home. You can do it in the road. Fly with my broken wings into the dark night. I will always make my way to your door. The nowhere man has nowhere plans for nobody. He is a bit like you and me. We feel. Our inside is out and we are really only very small. We are all buried, in the feeled. In the asylum every behavior is permitted. The pretty nurse will give us poppies from her tray. We are all acting, anyway. Even she is. She is a kaleidoscope-eyed girl who floats high above. Let us all sing together, on the submarine, in the asylum. Did you feel like you'd never been born? Now it's your birthday. We will turn on and turn each other on. We will become empty—naked. We will all get on the "bus" to somewhere we can't guess. Maxwell's hammer is on our head, and we are dead. We will be taken away, and leave it up to the bus driver to decide, the Beatles-warlocks-wizards to decide. Remember, there is no high or low, and the word is Yes. Yes is the universal word, the eu-monics word that works for everyone.

CHAPTER XIII

How To Conclude?
Reconciliation Songs

"We're all trying to say nice things ... but unfortunately,
we're human, you know."

–JOHN LENNON[1]

After finishing the White Album, the Beatles scattered in different directions for fourteen weeks off:[2] when they reconvened in the studio, the group took a much different approach toward making their next album. "Let It Be" (its working title was "Get Back"[3]) was originally conceived as a "real" album—"an honest album," as John put it.[4] The general story around these recording sessions, begun in January 1969, is that the Beatles wanted to "get real" and forego studio production gloss to present a grittier, more immediate performance. The Beatles' production was so part-and-parcel of the experience offered listeners that it was a bold step to even contemplate under-producing an album. The rule was to be "no overdubs and no editing." They also asked George Martin not to produce, but to simply record all their takes until they captured the essence of each song as they wanted it to be.

The idea to film the recording sessions was Denis O'Dell's, according to biographer Barry Miles.[5] This would make sense, considering O'Dell was the head of the Apple Film division; he would be aware that there would be interest in a documentary of the Beatles "at work." However, as Paul had always interacted with O'Dell the most, discussing film ideas, it is possible Paul thought of this idea as much as O'Dell did. Paul offered Yoko the job of filming the recording sessions—another indicator that Paul was a hidden instigator of the plan. Besides including her, this would also have ensured that Yoko would stay behind the camera, and not appear in front of it. But Yoko refused Paul's offer and reportedly felt "insulted" to be asked, feeling that she would be relegated to a mere assistant.[6] "Yoko sees men as assistants," according to John.[7] The perception among the Apple staff was that Yoko "might have thought the Beatles would advance *her* career," noted Miles.[8] Yoko was at the sessions, and sometimes sang. Naively, she thought that since she shared many of the same aesthetic concerns, she would be accepted; but how could this happen, when Paul's IFP had been running the show and the "Get Back" sessions were a Beatles-Petri-dish.

The sessions were filmed at Twickenham sound stage. The idea was to document the group making an album, and then conclude the documentary with footage of them in concert; one proposal was to have them play at an ancient Roman amphitheater in the Tunisian desert, surrounded by thousands of fans waving their torches (flashlights)—a kaleidoscope in the flesh.[9] There were many debates over possible venues, however. Ringo didn't want to travel. Paul proposed they play locally at small clubs, but the other Beatles didn't want to—they were way beyond that. Security would also be an issue, as their tours in 1966 had required a massive police presence. John at one point quipped, "I'm warming to doing it in an asylum."[10] Eventually plans dwindled to their playing a few songs on the roof of Abbey Road Studios, filmed by Lindsay-Hogg and witnessed by a few Apple and EMI personnel.

Their process of creation at Twickenham studios sounded much like a typical rock band rehearsal. It is a conversational mode, familiar to musicians. For instance during one session, after some aimless twanging, a bit of bass from Paul launches the band into a lounge version of "Blowing in the Wind." The impromptu fun halts, followed by more instrumental aimlessness, and then a discussion about John's new song, "Don't Let Me Down." Paul offers comments as to what he hears in the song and how it could sound. Paul and John discuss the song rapidly, their voices sometimes overlapping each other. It gives a display of how quickly they could communicate. "I just want to sing it," John says after much discussion. "Just sing it through. I have only sung it once or twice. To see what is there."[11]

Playing songs through with no edits or overdubs made for many abortive attempts. As soon as they made a mistake they would have to stop and start over again; some songs took over sixty takes. "John would be asking me if take sixty-seven was better than take thirty-nine," George Martin commented later.[12]

Thus, their method was entirely different during the "Get Back" sessions. They also made up on the spot several of the one hundred songs they worked on.[13] They tried to spontaneously make up music and words. Usually they would create in solitude. According to Miles, both Paul and John were experienced at going into a half-trance state, which enabled them to access material from their unconscious.[14] I have been asserting that they often used the IFP subtext to write their song lyrics. During the "Get Back" sessions they tried to write songs in front of each other with the camera as witness. John later said he found it dreadful,[15] but the fact is he had agreed beforehand to try it. Even though one could say this was just trying a different way of working, it is interesting that they also felt the need to document the "act of creation." Could it be that the sessions were a creative experiment?

The Beatles arrived at Twickenham studios at nine[16] (there are differing accounts as to what time; some biographers say nine, others say eight-thirty or eight) in the morning, an hour which is normally for showing up to work; they must have been groggy. Were they intending to access a half-awake state where associative language could burble from the subconscious (as Plath did with her pre-dawn poetry writing sessions)? The Beatles had put in a long stint as communicators and creators who were shaped to no little extent by Paul. Increasingly, their lyrics and entire presentation was confined to working in the "interval" that Paul had created. "Get Back" I suggest was an attempt to throw out all of this and just be themselves in the studio and see what happened.

At this point, too, it could be that they thought they might channel the new zeitgeist (spirit of the times) which they had supposedly helped create. They had expanded the "crack in the cosmic egg," as one writer put it (or rather, they had seemed to). With each album seemingly came a new expansion. The White Album had seemed to prove the new (fragmented) vision for consciousness. The Beatles might have been putting their chips down on this being so, that they could channel a beam of the new age that they had tapped into, either that or had created and which now existed outside themselves. Either means could bring them some music. Paul just "let it happen" in the studio, according to Philip Norman, in that he didn't manage the sessions and seemingly was as open as possible.[17] But he also prudently had a few songs in his pocket in case things did not spontaneously form: two he had written in 1968, "Let It Be" and "The Long and Winding Road,"[18] and a newer song, "Two of Us." These songs would fill out the last two albums and as John put it, "preserve the myth."[19]

After the recording sessions were abandoned, John pronounced the effort "the shittiest load of badly recorded shit, with a lousy feeling toward it, ever."[20] On listening to sessions uploaded to YouTube, I find no evidence of "shittiness." Several songs later made it onto acetate and were well received. But if the sessions were an experiment in creativity *al fresco*, they failed. Rather than being a case of not playing well, I suggest the sessions were a failed experiment to try to "ride bare back" through the IFP. This was what they might have really wanted, to have come to them beams from the new awareness which they had seemingly created. I know this sounds rather esoteric, but artists do have notions like that (and so do egg-men who want to test them). The Beatles were not able to create songs among themselves, as a group mind—at least none that were deemed any good. None of their spontaneous creations passed muster to land on "Let It Be." I am just suggesting that rather than being filmed "for posterity" or "for the fans," the "Let It Be" or "Get Back" sessions could have been a test to see if they could document Beatle creativity in the wild, as it were, through mutual free association.

To many psychologists of the time, creativity was "the great white whale." It was a quest Jung wrote about in *Ailon*, published in 1967.[21] The Harvardians were also much interested in Melville's whale-hunting tale *Moby Dick* as emblematic of the depth of man's repressed desire and the X-factor of creativity.[22] During the Sixties, creativity became a quest of the culture at large—it was also supposedly accessible to everyone. Not only had creativity been proffered as a side benefit of taking LSD, but it was publicly acknowledged that the Beatles had helped foster, both in the spirit of their music and ostensibly through Apple, an explosion (Francie would have called it a Renaissance) in the creative arts and self-expression. I have explained that this notion was due to the careful inclusion of Paul's IFP over time into the bands' output. The "interval" Paul created put creativity seemingly in the reach of more people. Psychologists, too were interested—quite interested, and had funding—to test where creativity came from. Experiments were conducted at Villa 21 and the Philadelphia House to find out if an insane person could be made into an artist, and supposedly this happened—with Mary Barnes.

Creating artists was not only a quest of Jungians and psychologists, but was also I suggest swirling around the intersection of psychology with music and acting. To be able to make an artist would be a perfect situation for companies whose business it was to promote art, because then they could have everything in-house. Psychologists and researchers associated with campuses and mental hospitals (SRI, Harvard, the Menninger Clinic to name a few) were also conducting tests *on* artists in order to study creativity. Sidney Cohen described that he gave LSD to artists to see how fast they decayed.[23] I infer this means that after a certain point whatever made a person an artist—to take just one aspect, their creative "editor"—would absent them and their art would no longer have that "certain something." Cohen also gave LSD to people who wanted to become creative. He found that although they subsequently had subjective feelings of being creative, they did not go on to create works of art. He explained this result as "Creativity is ten percent inspiration and ninety percent perspiration. LSD gives the feeling of inspiration, but not the desire to perspire."[24] He also found that their subsequent actions did not show that LSD had given them greater powers of perception and self-knowledge.

The reader is aware that I keep bringing Sylvia Plath into my discussions of creativity. I would never have imagined Plath would figure at all in this book, but I kept noticing connections between her situation and my theory about the Beatles. An original voice is sought-after by many artists, including Sylvia Plath—a new voice which people find compelling enough to buy, or try, for themselves. The Beatles found it, and not in any cosmic beam.

But if after all in 1969 the Beatles were sick of using the IFP subtext, and wanted to write songs in some *other* way, then they might have performed such a test as the "Get Back" sessions. Because otherwise, John's remark about trying to make a "real" album does not make entire sense. The Beatles' songs were always real—weren't they? I do not doubt each Beatle wrote the songs attributed to him. Was John using "real" as a synonym for "as-is" without Martin's production? No overdubs? But what was so bad about overdubbing? As usual, John told half the truth. I suggest what they sought was either to create without the IFP, in their "old" way, or have inspiration come to them spontaneously from the ether.

Of the approximately one hundred songs they worked on, I counted over forty (from the list on the Beatles Bible website) that were never released and were made up during the sessions.[25] These were in essence free-associations. This wasn't a typical thing at all for musicians to do in the Sixties, unless they were jazz musicians. It was even less common in an expensive studio setting. This suggests the sessions were, in part, a creativity experiment. None of the session-generated songs was deemed good enough to release. Whatever the Beatles free-associated or whatever came to them, it wasn't apparently from a "Beatles" space.

The session tapes, including Paul's recording of "The Long and Winding Road," were shunted aside, given to other producers to finish (Glyn Johns and then Phil Spector). After the Beatles reclaimed their usual method of doing things, with the addition of George's emergence as a songwriter and Martin's return as producer, "Abbey Road" saw them roaring back and shaped up to be one of the best Beatles albums of all time. It was recorded in August 1969 and released in September of 1969.

They hid the under-performing brain-children and went back to their usual method. "Abbey Road," a work of near-mastery, was the result. It had all the Beatles ingredients—dislocation, songs about Paul's praxis, all the IFP flavor that listeners had come to expect, plus a "fractured" song-suite as a new version of the IFP to add to the mix. The album preserved and reinstated everything I suggest that the Beatles had come to mean, albeit subliminally, in the listener's mind. Once again, all the tropes would be hidden, yet supported by the surface gloss and aural mastery of the recording.

The interval did not exist outside the circle, to put it in schematic terms. The Beatles had not really found "somewhere to go." They did not find something coming to them unconnected to what Paul had already established as the means by which the Beatles songs were perceived as art. Of course, *percepe es essere*, in art, and as long as the Beatles still seemed "like the Beatles" to the public, everything was fine. The Beatles I suggest wanted to go somewhere else, but didn't, and so went back to their usual method.

By 1969, although the Beatles' songs were masterful on "Abbey Road," Paul was in a different "kind of mind." He still knew his "way" of writing songs, his IFP and to "take a little bit from all around him," served him well. But his own psyche was not heading toward group-mind, pluralism and self-dissolution anymore. He had Linda and Heather as a center and as ballast. Linda's family was also helpful to him; her father Lee Eastman and her brother John, both entertainment lawyers,[26] were integral in enabling Paul to both extricate himself from the group and save whatever was left of its fortune. After an uncomfortable period "suing" the Beatles enterprise, Paul was able to dissolve the legal ties the Beatles had to each other, Apple, and Allen Klein and his company, ABKCO. This was an important, even dangerous, transition for him. Paul had ways to define himself suddenly in people outside the Beatles' circle whereas previously the Beatles, the fans and after a while, almost everyone Paul came in contact with had been almost like an extension of himself. He might have thought he was "taking a little bit of what was all around him," but by using what was all around him in the manner he did, in reality he was fairly well entangled (one might even say looped) as much as any artist could be with his band mates, his producer, and his public.

The Big Breakup

Paul may have had an intuition that separation was imminent when he wrote "Hey Jude" back in 1968; but this impetus to reconcile increased after John delivered the bombshell announcement at a meeting that he wanted to leave the group.

The Beatles, as I have attempted to show throughout this book, had used a subtext of mental hospitals, therapy and mental patients. So it is amusing that John used this very metaphor of insanity as a way to break the news to the group that he was leaving.

Paul said in a meeting on September 20, 1969, "I think we should get back to our basics. I think we've got out of hand, we've overwhelmed ourselves, and I think what we need is to re-establish our musical identity and find out who we are again, and so we should go back to little gigs."

John replied, "Well, I think you're daft! I wasn't going to tell you, till after we signed the Capitol contract ... but seeing as you asked me, I'm leaving the group."[27]

This floored everyone. Paul recalled that "everyone blanched except John, who coloured a little."[28] George or Ringo might possibly be replaceable. But everyone knew that without John, there would be no Beatles.

Since 1966, John had been by his own admission been taking LSD, "eating it," and said he had taken "thousands" of trips.[29] His love for Yoko, and a new heroin-sniffing habit, served to bring him back down to earth. For the Beatles he had written LSD-schizophrenic-madman nightmares with brilliant associative language—if the Jungians had been watching, John had placed best-in-show with his efforts. Since the Beatles had been using ideas from psychology, therapy, the asylum, and so on as a template to write songs, I find it funny that John said "you're daft" to Paul and pulled the plug that way. Paul then got dibs to be the first in the press to say he was leaving the group.[30] This annoyed John, because it made it look like he wanted to stay. It was a case of, "I'm quitting!"—"No you're not, you're fired!"

John had realized "we're human, you know." He realized that he didn't have to be "everybody." He did continue with Yoko to make semi-activist statements or "universal" statements.

After the break-up, Paul wondered for some months if he could do anything without the group.[31] One morning lying abed, he almost smothered himself inadvertently while lying face-down in his pillow. He couldn't find the will to move his head to get air. He related to Miles that with a great effort, he rolled onto his back and thought, "that was a bit near!"[32] It stands to reason that after all the within-you-without-you, I-am-he-as-you-are-me, Helter Skelter loop-the-loop, each Beatle must have felt somewhat dislocated, not quite inside themselves but no longer inside each other, either. The four had been in the band since they were young teens. They hadn't individuated like normal men would have. They had musically and personally shared so much, and had "lived out of each other's pockets."[33] Ending the band was like ending all contact with a family—John and Paul had to have new families lined up to even think about it. Separation anxiety was going to be a big thing. John grounded himself with

Yoko and heroin (allowing for one brick-throwing episode at Paul's bay windows, while Ringo and George looked on).[34] Paul had Linda, Heather, and then, a new baby; but Paul still felt very demobbed. "I exhibited all the classic symptoms of the unemployed, the redundant man,"[35] he said later, which included a "deep anger." It took him a while to get a sense of self apart from being a "Beatle." Recording songs on his own and with Linda began the process. But he had been so connected to fans as a Beatle. What if nobody cared about him as Paul McCartney?

John had a similar encounter with suddenly being a songwriter who wrote personal songs. He commented later tellingly that the critics hated his and Yoko's music because it was personal. "It's about *ourselves*, you see, and not about Ziggy Stardust or Tommy."[36] The Beatles' music, for all its accessibility, had been impersonal to an extreme—it was self-debunking in a *universal* way. Now that John was writing songs like anyone else would, from a point of view of being a person, critics didn't like it. He could have easily said that critics didn't like the songs because some featured Yoko, who had always been a hate-figure in the press and although a vocalist, was admittedly not a singer. John as usual told the truth, just half of it. He and Yoko were writing personal songs now, and not using Paul's IFP (although, as we have mentioned, Yoko did let slip in an interview, "We always go back to the madness.")[37]

To return to the last Beatles releases. Almost every song Paul wrote for "Abbey Road" and "Let It Be" was either about his artistic process, or had an IFP subtext in it. The songs generally have a more serious tone, and several are what I call "reconciliation songs." Of the dozen songs Paul wrote for these two albums, seven of them were about his artistic process. This is counting the fragments Paul composed in the song-suite as songs, although he produced the suite to be modular. The suite can be taken as a "song of fracture." Thus the IFP subtext could be in very broad form, but was it still definitely evident on examination. Of Paul's songs, only "Get Back" and "Her Majesty" seem to be entirely absent it. "Get Back" apparently started out as collaboration with pianist-songwriter Billy Preston, whom George Harrison invited to the sessions.[38]

Let It Be

The album "Let It Be" is keynoted by its first track, "**Two of Us**." The album is all about going home, but in typical Beatles fashion, "going home" with an IFP subtext. An asylum is also called a home, and thus "going home" can mean going to the asylum, or alternately leaving an asylum for home. Paul writes allusions to an asylum into the lyrics: inmates writing messages to each other on a wall ("Two of us sending postcards/Writing letters on my wall"), setting fires or trying to escape ("You and me burning matches/Lifting latches/On our way back home"). The two also do eccentric things such as inmates might: "wearing raincoats/Standing solo in the sun." It is fitting that a song about the end of the Beatles and of Paul's creative partnership with John has the subtext of mental patients and an asylum in it. "Chasing paper" probably alludes to all the legal battles the Beatles were going through at this time, but a paper chase is also an expression meaning a futile activity, or a circular activity that leads nowhere.

This is the idea of "nowhere to go" again, because of the double meaning of "home." "Two of Us" is another ouroboros-loop of a Beatles song. But it is also interesting that this Paul song is not quite a Beatles song, even though it has all the IFP motifs. It sounds like a classic folk song that someone else could cover, and many have. It is one of Paul's most grounded and likeable songs, and accordingly it had emotional inspiration. Paul was telling John that they were leaving the asylum of The Beatles for their new homes. The music has a palpable sense of hope and purpose. They are headed to *real* homes, leaving the one they constructed in art.

"**The Long and Winding Road**" is another song about finding one's way home. I find it confirms Paul's capacity for feeling. It is as strong as "Yesterday," a song that makes you want to hold your breath all the way through it. But it is a truly sad song. I suggest that "Winding Road" might have been inspired by Paul's love for John and including in his sense of loss, the fans' sense of loss. There was sometimes bad feeling among the Beatles, and turmoil signified by "the wild and windy night." Then the rain of tears washed away the anger. Now, a pool of tears is crying for "the day," some ray of hope to shine on the situation (another surreal image.) "Why leave me standing here/Let me know the way," Paul plead. "Many times I've been alone/And many times I've cried/Anyway, you'll never know/The many ways I've tried." Paul was of many minds to write songs to keep The Beatles and his partnership with John together. But all the minds he's been in, all the ways he's tried, still lead him back to what was The Beatles and its connection with its fans. This is a reconciliation song. "You left me standing here/A long, long, time ago," he almost cries. I think this might be referring to John's emotionally separating from the band somewhat after Brian Epstein died in 1967. John left Paul (and his IFP "praxis") "standing" to keep the band going. "Don't keep me waiting here/Lead me to your door!" Paul implores. He then finishes off with an affirmation for (perhaps) what The Beatles were: (fill in the blank). "Yeah yeah yeah, yeah," Paul sings as the strings (which he didn't authorize) and horns bring it all to a close.

This is an emotional song, about a relationship and real feelings. It was arguably taken to Oscar-night-level pathos by the arrangement, but it seems obviously inspired by Paul realizing The Beatles' end was imminent along with the possible end of the whole Beatles "dream." He is trying to reassure the fans that the latter won't happen.

Because of the IFP asylum, the lyrics are interchangeable with how Paul or the Beatles feel about their fans and vice versa. "Winding Road" can be read as a Valentine to the fans. Paul is crying for more connection with them: the long and winding road of album distribution always brought Beatles albums to the listener's ears. The Beatles will never end, as long as Paul and the industry know the way to "your door." Similarly the fans and the Beatles were always a concatenation—it was *always* "you, you, you" *with* the Beatles (as they put it in "Hold Me Tight"). The communication between the Beatles and the fans will always be there, "Winding Road" implies.

Their songs do bring happy feelings to millions of people: as one older fan recently wrote in a post online, "I didn't have a happy childhood, but I had The Beatles."

The rather surreal image of a pool of tears crying for the day connects with Paul's interest in surrealist painters. Paul would go on to incorporate surrealist elements into his paintings.

"**I've Got A Feeling**" was John and Paul's first collaborative effort, we are told, since "A Day In The Life" (although I strongly suspect they collaborated on "Happiness is a Warm Gun"). "I've Got A Feeling" describes their process. Paul typically gets a feeling, and then a song ensues. It is released, and millions are influenced by it. John wrote the second part of the song, "a sort of 1968 yearbook," as MacDonald calls it, of people's activities.[39] They are the ripple effect of Paul's getting a feeling. I suggest John was once again noting the progression from Paul's feelings (and the Beatles' promulgation of "feelings" amongst listeners) to a subsequent flurry of activity, some of it consumerist. "Everybody got a new coat," John said in one version of the song. Because everybody could spin off the Beatles' creativity, the "yearbook" of activities happened. This was another song about the Beatles' process although nowhere near the caustic symphony of "Walrus" or of "Glass Onion," which were about John's beefs with Paul. During the writing of those songs, John was much more involved in what was going on with The Beatles and its public – John's contribution to "I've Got a Feeling" is by comparison a bland recital of B follows A.

"**Let it Be**," the title track, is another spiritual of Paul's in the same vein as "Hey Jude." "Let it Be" recounts an experience that sometimes happened to him—"I wake up to the sound of music." A song would come to him in a dream—a sensation familiar to some songwriters. He wouldn't have to sit down and work at it—a song just popped into his mind, shortly before awaking. Songs can arrive that way, with zero effort. John described his trance method of writing songs as, "You come out of a thing (a trance) and you know 'I've been there' and it was nothing—it was pure. And that's what we're all looking for, actually."[40] Again, John was telling more truth than he realized. Does everybody want to be songwriters and go somewhere to get a message from somewhere? No. But the "we" John referred to could be an in-group of influential songwriters whom I suggest wanted to create a new collective subconscious. Those songwriters would indeed want to "go there." Where it was, is anyone's guess. Brian Wilson called it tapping into "the great source."[41]

Whether this was planned is open to conjecture and is outside the scope of this book. It is just interesting that John often tells the truth, but only half of it.

To continue with "Let It Be," "mother Mary" comes to the singer (Paul), and speaking words of wisdom, apparently says "let it be." This perhaps means let the song happen, let the message come, make a song out of it, which will be an answer to others. "There will be an answer/Let it be."

The song then repeats the "IFP mission statement," but in somewhat more rosy-coated terms than "Blackbird." "And when the broken-hearted people (schizo-phrenic in its linguistic roots means broken-hearted) living in the world agree (that is, perhaps, when they are all schizophrenic, and no-one anywhere sets a boundary whatsoever, as Cooper would have it) then "there will be an answer/ Let it be." He repeats the broken/fractured motif: "For though they may be parted, there is still a chance that they will see/There will be an answer, let it be/And when the light is cloudy, there is still a light that shines on me/Shine until tomorrow/Let it be." The image of a fractured "diamond eye" is a consistent motif in psychedelic-era Beatles songs, and here is implied a fractured (or faceted) individual who sees things in many colors and pieces and does not value one thing over another. They "shine"; but they are also "indifferent," as Leary's verse said ("Jewelled Indifference" in *Psychedelic Prayers*), as this indicates a lack of censuring judgment. Have hope that you can wait for the day when all will "see," sings Paul. Thus the motif of the eye again appears, that the kaleidoscope eye can be retained towards the day when everyone has one. It's interesting that where a church has stained glass to filter the light of God, the kaleidoscope eye has its own stained glass intrinsic to it, and needs no external structure such as the Church to filter light or knowledge. Thus, "no," the proscription of the Christian Church, in the Beatleverse turns to "know." This is the concept of spiritual Gnosis.[42]

"Mother Mary" is both a Christian allusion, of course, to the Madonna, and an allusion to Paul's mother, whose name was Mary (and as we have mentioned, was a Catholic). Paul has said that he did have a dream once in which his mother appeared, to comfort him.

The song is generally taken as affirmation both that the Beatles' songs are benign, and that the listener should not be hard on him or herself. Everyone should just "let it be."

The Beatles had seeded a culture or mindset that would sprout and grow steadily in society for many generations to come. Sidney Cohen, talking at a house party among colleagues, said, "in x amount of years," there might be a recrudescence of use of LSD. His comment indicated he was aware that young children might have been affected enough by The Beatles and LSD publicity to take the drug when they got older. This way the "strawburies" could keep on fertilizing the next field.

* * *

So, that's the end of the Beatles story. They ate acid; particularly John and George did, and made a psychedelic culture whose passkey was a model schizophrenia drug. They used some mental patient language, "doing an F. Scott Fitzgerald," writing songs based on Paul's interest in fractured identity. Psychology formed a subtext and framework to their songs. When they could take no more, they called it quits. But for a while, The Beatles were a shared "dream" and the fans could feel they were "with" The Beatles.

In this book I have set out my theory about The Beatles subtext, and from what I intuited what was going on in Paul when he wrote many of his songs. My theory is just that, a theory. This book has been an exercise in literary criticism of the Beatles' lyrics, and an artistic biography of Paul. All the facts I carefully checked from multiple verified sources: and the lyrics support my theory. The rest is feelings.

How to conclude? One could say that the Beatles forced youth to acknowledge its own jadedness. That there was a disconnect between consuming revolution and actually doing something about it.

What if they held a war and no-body came? Indeed: but what if they held a life and nobody came? Were the Beatles trying to undermine youth? Taking away self-identity is akin to surrender, nihilism. Were the Beatles nihilists to the core? I do not think so: Paul believed at least on paper in the therapeutic community; it is there in his last Beatles songs.

John had largely given up any Beatles-related enterprise at that point and was just jabbing The Beatles and their fans in his song "Come Together." He had found a kindred spirit to his concerns and aesthetic in Yoko. Paul's subsequent paintings indicate some of what I have been covering in this book: his attraction to fracturing identity or losing sense of self.

Today, half a century after The Beatles, the rainbow keeps on forming more layers. The prism-of-isms begun in the Sixties reveals ever-new divisions of self and meaning. Mystery trucks bring an influx of street drugs across the border. Unstable people, precariously medicated, camp out on the streets. Abortion is commonplace and thought to be above criticism. Sex before marriage is expected. Child drag queens appear to applause before television audiences. Yoga, once thought highly suspect, particularly in the American South in the Seventies, is a multimillion-dollar business.

People arguably feel freer to live the way they want to. Women work outside the home and marriage is not certain. Day care centers allow women to have careers. New drugs help people with depression and schizophrenia. Babies born outside of wedlock are not a point of shame. Women are encouraged to work out a combination of family life and career. Laws are on the books forbidding discrimination in employment and workplace sexual harassment.

The Beatles "ushered in a less deferential society," according to author Salman Rushdie.[43] They expressed with other rock-and-rollers an attitude of rejection of authority in all its forms, of "people who think they know better." A different perception toward one's sense of self was brought about by Sixties bands, but primarily by the Beatles. The Sixties "stirred people up," according to Sidney Cohen.[44] The Beatles were guides during this process, "gentle subversives," according to Denis O'Dell.[45] They challenged boundaries—they reversed them—they atomized them. They burned cellos and eviscerated pianos. They turned the tables on professional musicians. They said it was "all a bit of fun." But there was always an edge and their songs had far-reaching influence.

This book has attempted to explain my theory of how the Sixties came about, and Paul's artistic process. My theory is that his highly personal process which was carried out in his songwriting was latched onto by the other Beatles and enacted a shake-up in society which had far-reaching ramifications. It was not just a fad, but a new "mind."

The sheer scale of the Beatles' publicity meant that their songs had an influence far beyond what should have been. The Beatles were inescapable and unassailable. They were taken to be leaders, even orchestrators of reality by the young. Even if their impact was planned and calculated to some extent, it was too much to ask of one band, and of one drug with random effects. There were many casualties of the Sixties attitude that people and society should change all at once.

Paul's inspiration was pragmatic—the words of mentally ill people. His application of them was inspired. The Beatles possibly did create a new "type," taken from a bit of all these elements, which expressed itself in a new look, clothing, and expressive songs. Then the mental hospital-mental patient subtext dovetailed into the LSD loss-of-ego experience, and as it happened, the same vocabulary could be used. The Yellow Submarine was also the psychedelic (model psychosis) submarine. It ran into problems when it became the psychedelic-painted Rolls-Royce.

LSD was a solution in search of a problem. The way that people such as Timothy Leary approached it was to, in film terms, "open wide" with it. LSD would solve the "problems" of ownership, dialectics, and inequality and usher in a new era of love to end all conflict and war. The Beatles were naive enough to promote it as such. And, fusing it with Paul's IFP, they sold millions of records.

John said, "We're human, you know," to an interviewer in response to why, if he had written "Hey Bulldog," inviting anyone who is lonely to come over and talk to him, did he not practice what he preached? Why did he not welcome anyone onto his property? He did give one wandering visitor, a young man, some toast and tea.[46] But John and also George had a problem with invasive fans, and the outcome would be tragic for them both. Promoter Bill Graham is said to have remarked on closing the Fillmore Events, "At this time, I feel I can no longer refuse myself the time and the leisure and the privacy to which any man is rightfully entitled."[47] Lennon also found that he didn't have to be "in" everybody, or "here, there and everywhere."

Fragmentation and fracture into a shared kaleidoscope eye was just too much. LSD might have been, some thought, Aldous Huxley's dreamt-of "soma," a drug that would make the world peaceful,[48] but the entire world could not be convinced to take it—only several million youth at rock concerts. The Beatles suspended their listeners in magic for a time, but then it had to evaporate, burnt off by the sun. The effect of that time has lingered long in Western culture.

Appendices
Reference Notes
Index

Appendix I

Excerpts from a videotape of an "LSD Reunion" party
held at the home of Dr. Oscar Janiger in February
1976, in Los Angeles, California. Guests included
Sidney Cohen, John Lilly, Willis Harman, Humphry
Osmond, Laura Huxley, Nick Bercel, Timothy Leary,
Barbara Leary, Al Hubbard and Myron Stolaroff

Timothy Leary: I used to say to Sidney all the time that I felt I was
much more conservative than *you*, Sidney, because I didn't want the
government involved in any of our business. I thought that was a
pretty free-enterprise, staunch –

Sidney Cohen: We seemed to have followed our own paths. You
yours, me mine.

Myron Stolaroff: Fortunately they didn't go in the same directions;
a great deal of ground was covered.

Cohen: I guess one of the things Oscar (Janiger) might be interested
in is what does it all mean and how is it all going to work out. I know
I couldn't possibly evaluate, anybody want to try?

Stolaroff: I'm really interested in *your* opinion.

Cohen: I think that as you heard, it stirred people up, it cracked their
frame of reference, by the thousands, millions perhaps, and anything
that does that is pretty good, I think. Anything that shakes people
up a little. Not too much. Some people it maybe shook up a little too
much. That was unfortunate. But in the totality, it may have been a
desirable thing at that point in time. The next question will be, well,

what's going to happen. And there I think we will see, not soon, but in X number of years, a recrudescence of similar usage; here, there and everywhere. It's happened throughout history, hasn't it?

Humphrey Osmond: Sidney, don't you think the actual time is very important. It's very good for people to be shaken up a certain amount. So far on the whole our ways of shaking ourselves up have usually been to have real cataclysms. For instance the Iranians are being shaken up at the moment, but it would appear that many of them might prefer not to be in this kind of way. Because the difficulty with having the great cataclysms is that you end up worse than you began. If one could be able to have a sort of controlled cataclysm, from time-to-time, we'd be much better off. Because every society gets set in its ways, and a society with a vast technology is always likely to get to the point where it's simpler and easier and comfier to let the technology take over. And one of the things it seems to me that these substances and the attitudes they generate very well is that one becomes less willing to do that. Because it's not necessary. You don't have to look upon your technology as your idol. And it's easy to do this. It's particularly easy to do this if you've got no way out. If you sort of separate yourself from...

Cohen: So you think in days to come as we become more constricted and homogenized, it will be even more important.

Osmond: Much more necessary. But I think it's still necessary because we are still so clever at making all these strange and remarkable things. But when we stop being clever, then we start making things in our own image. The mind described by Thomas Willis in 1670 was a kind of mirror. Then the mind as Freud described it was a magic lantern. That's where projection comes from. That was the latest thing.

Leary: I thought the mind was an indoor plumbing system. (laughter)

* * *

Oscar Janiger (to Timothy Leary and Al Hubbard): When did you two meet?

Myron Stolaroff (chiming in): At Harvard, in 1960-1961.

Al Hubbard (to the room): I gave him a bottle of 500 tablets.

Timothy Leary: I remember that. (hilarity)

Leary: ... I'm taking LSD at least once a week, now; it's working better than ever.

Unidentified guest: You look very well. (The other guests are all smiling at Leary.)

(A man with a Russian accent who is coming in the front door. All the guests turn to look at him.): I just wanted to get some attention. (hilarity)

Janiger (to Leary): So what has it done for you, through all the years? A great clarity of vision? A great clarity of mind?

Hubbard: If he had never seen me he'd have been better off.

Leary: Oh Al, don't say that. I owe everything to you. Galactic center sent you down just at the right moment.

Janiger: Well, when you started with it all, Al, you had some kind of a purpose or a vision in mind, didn't you?

Hubbard: I've still got it. I haven't changed my mind.

Janiger: You were the Johnny Appleseed—you know, planting it everywhere you got a chance.

Hubbard: I sure did, but I don't think it's a credit thing. It should've been done, and I tried to do it. And I'm still trying to do it. I never quit.

Janiger: Why? Why Al, why are you trying to do it? What are you doing it for?

Hubbard: I don't know. Just, I think it's the thing to do. What else can an old guy my age do that's worth anything?

Janiger: Hm.

Leary: You're looking for some sort of motives I gather ... Freudian motives, economic motives...

Janiger: No, no, no, I thought he had some personal reason...

Hubbard: Well, I put up a hundred thousand dollars ... (unintelligible)

Leary (interrupting): What do you think its best use is for now?

Hubbard: I don't know, just keep on doing it. Let people see themselves for what they are.

* * *

Humphry Osmond (addressing Leary): Remembering the first time we met at Cambridge on the night of the Kennedy election in 1960... As we left, I thought it's very nice to think he would do this for us, at Harvard. And then I said to Aldous, isn't he just a little bit square? (hilarity) Aldous said, "After all, isn't that what we *want*?" (hilarity)... We thought you might be too unadventurous.

Hubbard (to Leary): Well, you sure as heck contributed your part.

Leary: I always consider myself as very square. I always try to hang around the hippest person in the area and I continue to do that. 'Cause I feel that, I really basically feel that I'm square. I have very little sense of aesthetics, so I try to hang around the most sophisticated, beautiful people in the world, so I hope some of it will radiate off on me.

* * *

Oscar Janiger: Everybody was finding their own way...

Timothy Leary: Does anyone here feel that mistakes were made?

Voice off-camera: What's a mistake? (hilarity)

Humphry Osmond: Leary, estimations in retrospect are really like the chaps, you know, who when the generals of WWII have large numbers of fellows who were not born at the time, who write about how the Battle of the Bulge could have been better fought.

Leary: That's wonderful. Everybody is going to write their own cosmology! The world was made in seven days, but where and when?

Osmond: But I think those sorts of things, one could ... I don't say mistakes ... what I say, you could have seen other ways of doing it.

Leary: My God! Quantum physics now tells us that any second can go in how many different ways. Yeah, that's one of the lessons.

Russian-accented man with beard: So that was a mistake made. Nobody gave it to Nixon! (hilarity)

Sidney Cohen: Well, in order to know if mistakes were made, you have to know what the goal is. And if you can define the goal, I can tell you whether mistakes were made. I think mistakes were made. But that's my own personal goal.

Leary (gesturing frequently): Well, I'll say one of the goals was to make American people smarter. Raise their intelligence. And I think the American people are today quantum jumps more sophisticated in exactly the general directions in which we all hoped they would become more sophisticated: about consciousness, about the nervous system, about the brain, about the options people have in creating in their own reality, about self-actualization, self-indulgence, about pleasure being self-reward instead of hive-reward. My God! Pleasure is now the number one industry in this country—recreational travel, entertainment, sensory indulgence—my God! There's no question now, they're number one. Now, that was *my* goal. (laughter, applause).

Osmond: In those days you certainly made advancements. However, let me put this out in a contrary point of view. The awkward thing that we now we have chaps like the Ayatollah Khomeini appearing on the scene, who have the potential of rather different goals. And certainly where I've been, which you know very well, in the South East, these other different goals are always potential.

Leary: All right, Pakistan is now going back to where they're going to cut off hands for the first robbery and a foot for the second. Iran is now going back to...

Osmond: A very interesting point. No no, Tim. Pakistan is going to do this, but they haven't been able to get the doctors to do it, which I think is extremely interesting ... (laughter)

Leary: One thing I've learned from criminal justice is there'll always be someone to lop the hands off.

Cohen: What was your point, Tim?

Leary: About the Ayatollah and I was saying ... (Leary, gesturing, knocks a plastic cup off the coffee table and sets it back on the table)

Cohen: You still haven't been able to levitate that, have you?

Janiger: Tim said that he was quite successful in achieving his goals, Sid.

Cohen: Well I think he's a little presumptuous.

Leary: My goals, I was talking about my goals, I'm totally...

Cohen: That's right, I forgot. Destroy the presumptuousness.

Leary: Everything they say that's dangerous...

Osmond: He's optimistic, not presumptuous. And he ought to be optimistic, I mean, it's his natural bend. (room agrees)

Leary: But since we all live in these bubbles we create, we can only basically give ourselves our own report cards at the end of every, and so forth...

Cohen: —Take credit for that which we didn't do?

Leary: Credit, I take no credit or blame. But if we're talking about goals, see that's different. Isn't it? Credit and blame, that's another interesting topic.

Osmond: Sidney, how would you liked to have seen, I suppose, this scenario have played, as you liked?

Cohen: Well, I don't put as high a stock on pleasure, although I enjoy it, as Tim does. I would hope that increased human wisdom might have been an appropriate goal. Increased human humaneness—this I don't quite see as occurring. I don't think we're any wiser. Some of us may be. And maybe if only a few of us are wiser, that's enough, that's sufficient unto the end.

* * *

Myron Stolaroff: Tim, you and I had an agreement, last time I saw you. You know we had our differences of view. We were a little disturbed that some of the things you were doing was making it more difficult to carry on legitimate research. And we agreed, if you remember that, well Myron you stay in there, and you do the legitimate research. But you need somebody to kind of shake them up a bit. You said, "I'll shake them up, and then you can take them and show them where they can learn and what the right path is." But I didn't know that when you're going to shake them up, you're going to hit 'em on the head with a ball bat!

Leary (after a pause): Well, I don't accept that metaphor. I was one of the younger members of that incredible revolution of Benjamin Spock, Abraham Maslow … somehow giving consciousness back, taking it back from experts – a totally American point of view in psychiatry – (he mentions role reversals at Harvard) – and I had several conversations with Sidney, and with you (Oscar Janiger) and with Al, with everyone, saying, "Let us be the far-out explorers, and the farther out we go, the more ground it gives the people at Spring Grove to denounce us. So we were the flanker-backs or whatever it is, and I never felt, the *hundreds* of times we debated, anything less than wise affection from you, Sidney, that we were somehow working for human freedom…

* * *

Sidney Cohen: I have to confess, that when I heard it was getting out on the street, I said, this will never sell. It's too intense; people will be too shook up. But it didn't work that way at all. I'm not quite sure I know why, but apparently people were able to sustain it – this intense of a response.

Myron Stolaroff: But it's not a popular street drug that it once was.

Al Hubbard: That stuff that's not on the street now, that's not LSD.

Barbara Leary: Wait a minute! (laughter)

Unidentified person: How would you know?

Hubbard: I had four thousand bottles of it to begin with!

Stolaroff: Do you think the hippie movement wouldn't come about without LSD, or had its impact?

Humphry Osmond: It would be a totally different impact. I don't think ... it would be much less.

Stolaroff: I think it was a necessary condition for it, really.

* * *

Man with glasses on sofa: Al, (Hubbard), you had a check on you for one million dollars ... whatever happened to that check?

Al Hubbard: Well, I finally got down to about a hundred thousand dollars.... All of it cost a lot of money...

Myron Stolaroff: About the check that Al was waving around ... It's taken a long time, but it was just a few days ago, that the last steps were taken to see that all the money was repaid. It was a long battle, but all the money went back to where it belonged.

Hubbard: Is that right?

Stolaroff: That's right.

Hubbard: Which money was that, Myron?

Stolaroff: Don't you remember? Oh, you had several of them? (Big laugh from Leary when the rest of the room is silent.)

Janiger: I must say that he (Hubbard) doesn't make much money selling that stuff at all. He was a great trader, though. (Tells story of Hubbard trading one drug for another. Laughter.)

Hubbard: How do you figure this 'belonged' business, Myron? Went back to where it belonged?

Stolaroff: From the source. The person who furnished the money got it back.

Hubbard: How?

Stolaroff: Well, you know how. But it's not a matter for public record.

Cohen (changes subject): One other change in life, in connection with LSD, or at least LSD contributed vitally I think, was the whole upsurge in the study of the chemistry of the brain. I think that had a lot to do with it.

Janiger: Yes, the clinicians, if not disdain, it is not an area of terrible concern to them, but accelerating the entire notion of the neurochemistry of the brain, and how the brain processes emotion. And so we're trying to include that (in a book he and his colleagues are writing), but as you say I think that chapter is most importantly well worth writing … I think it was LSD and serotonin which in turn gave rise to the early hypotheses of the brain amines in relation to affective disorders.

Man with glasses on sofa (addressed as Bill): I think it had the most effect on the larger population that had never even taken it. The marginal participation in the counterculture movement, is what I attribute largely to LSD.

Janiger: Well, Bill, when we were running our subjects—about the third or fourth subject was an artist. And he saw a Kachina doll that was sitting on a shelf, and said, "I must draw something." So we took the doll off the shelf, and he began to draw it in a haphazard way, and when he was through with the experience, he said, "This is the most important artistic experience that I've ever had. Do you mind if I tell other artists about it?" Well, we weren't quite prepared for this. I had no idea that the artist would be any more affected than anyone else. And he began to bring in his friends, and before long, it was like the entire project would be inundated with artists. That's how completely eager and absolutely interested they were in taking it. And we had to really limit the number of artists. So at least from their point of view… And we had a very elaborate record of what the artist had said, and the follow-up, as you know, because you used some of that data. And the artists seemed to derive an enormous amount of interest and of help from LSD, among all the others. The worst reactors we had were the psychiatrists, and the second were the ministers. There was nothing gravely serious, but they didn't have good reactions, very often. Two or three Rabbis, and I think we had two Catholic priests.

Leary: In general, artists have more fun than ministers, don't they?

Janiger: Well, they may have more fun, but … then we'd be going back to the original thesis! (laughter)

Leary: They do more good. They move the race farther ahead.

Janiger: Well, psychedelic art is still something that has to be evaluated. It's an unproven thing in a way. But we do know that we have a hundred pairs, and so we are now processing these pairs of art (painted before and during), to see how the people handle being under the drug. If the subjects took (LSD) a number of times, they developed a facility so they could paint fairly decently on it.

Stolaroff: I'd like to understand that a little better, with the doll. You first had them paint it before they'd taken LSD and then during. And how about—did you do any after?

Janiger: Yes. There were some we did after.

Stolaroff: I would be interested whether they felt that they had some enhanced ability afterwards.

Janiger: What was improved wasn't their artistic ability, by no means; but there was just this whole sense of opening up and having more choices, and being able to see things—many more permutations and ideas. Would you all like to have something to eat? (Everybody gets up.)

Appendix II

List of Participants to the Conference on d-Lysergic Acid Diethylamide (LSD-25) and Psychotherapy, April 22, 23 and 24, 1959, Princeton, New Jersey, Sponsored by the Josiah Macy, Jr. Foundation

Paul H. Hoch, Conference Chairman – Department of Psychiatry, Columbia University, College of Physicians and Surgeons, New York, NY

Harold A. Abramson, Conference Transactions Editor – The Biological Laboratory, Cold Spring Harbor, and the State Hospital, Central Islip, NY

Gregory Bateson – Ethnology Section, Veterans Administration Hospital, Palo Alto, CA

Arthur L. Chandler – Psychiatric Institute of Beverly Hills, Beverly Hills, CA

Sidney Cohen – Neuropsychiatric Hospital, Veterans Administration Center, Los Angeles, CA

Jonathan O. Cole – Psychopharmacology Service Center, National Institute of Mental Health, National Institutes of Health, Bethesda, MD

Herman C.B. Denber – Research Division, Manhattan State Hospital, and Columbia University, College of Physicians and Surgeons, New York, NY

Keith S. Ditman – Department of Psychiatry, School of Medicine, University of California Medical Center, Los Angeles, CA

Betty Eisner – 1334 Westwood Boulevard, Beverly Hills, CA

Mortimer A. Hartman – Psychiatric Institute of Beverly Hills, Beverly Hills, CA

Mollie P. Hewitt – The Biological Laboratory, Cold Spring Harbor, NY

Abram Hoffer – Psychiatric Services Branch, Department of Public Health, Regina, Sask., Canada

Cecelia E. Jett-Jackson – Medical Department, Sandoz Pharmaceuticals, Hanover, NJ

Solomon Katzenelbogen – 5312 Pooks Hill Road, Bethesda, MD

Gerald D. Klee – Department of Psychiatry, Psychiatric Institute, University of Maryland School of Medicine, Baltimore, MD

Henry L. Lennard – Bureau of Applied Social Research, Columbia University, New York, NY

Sidney Malitz – Department of Experimental Psychiatry, New York State Psychiatric Institute, New York, NY

Robert C. Murphy, Jr. – Waverly, PA

Gwendolyn J. Neviackas – The Biological Laboratory, Cold Spring Harbor, NY

T. T. Peck, Jr. – Psychiatric and Public Health Departments, San Jacinto Memorial Hospital, Baytown, TX

Ronald A. Sandison – Powick Hospital, Near Worcester, England

Charles Savage – Center for Advanced Study in Behavioral Sciences, Stanford, CA

C. H. Van Rhijn – Men's Department, Mental Hospitals "Brinkgreven" and "St. Elizabeths Gasthuis," Deventer, Netherlands

John R. B. Whittlesey – Alcoholism Research Clinic, Department of Psychiatry, UCLA Medical Center, Los Angeles, CA

Louis J. West – Department of Psychiatry, Neurology, and Behavioral Sciences, University of Oklahoma School of Medicine, Oklahoma City, OK

* * *

Reference Notes

Principal sources are abbreviated thus:

Miles – Miles, Barry, *Paul McCartney: Many Years From Now* (Henry Holt & Co./Secker & Warburg in UK, 1997)

Norman – Norman, Philip, *Paul McCartney: A Life* (Little, Brown, 2016)

MacDonald – MacDonald, Ian, *Revolution in the Head* (1994/2005, Chicago Review Press)

Davies – Davies, Hunter, *The Beatles* (W.W. Norton & Company, 1968)

Macy Conference on LSD-25 – The Use of LSD in Psychotherapy: Transactions of a Conference on d-Lysergic Acid Diethylamide (LSD-25), April 22, 23 and 24, 1959, Harold A. Abramson, Editor (Josiah Macy Foundation, 1960)

Chapter I: Days In Conversation

1. Paul was born ... primary breadwinner: Miles, pp. 4-5
2. sing-alongs: Miles, p. 22
3. could be an excellent student: Norman, p. 34 and Miles, p. 19
4. a brilliant mimic: Norman, p. 42
5. She had surgery, but the cancer had spread: Miles, p. 20
6. the right time: Miles, p. 21
7. had almost invented: MacDonald, pp. 92-93: "The most influential performer/songwriter of the Fifties, (Chuck) Berry effectively created the genre of rock-and-roll by the simple stratagem of constantly invoking it in his clever, quickfire lyrics."
8. "make them up": Norman, p. 35
9. "to put a shell around me": Norman, p. 48
10. "hated being told what to do": Norman, p. 42
11. not set to advance: Miles, p. 606
12. looked the part of an art school: Miles, p. 49

13. after Paul picked up: Miles, p. 25
14. a high school anthem: Norman, p. 69
15. seemed more driven: Norman, p. 114, p. 120
16. art student's cut: Norman, p. 134
17. "relationship with the Ashers was": Miles, p. 116
18. Each of the children acted: Norman, p. 192
19. president of the Clinical section: from the Royal College of Physicians website
20. back to the reign of King James: Norman, p. 243
21. "have the capacity for creative": Back cover blurb, Koestler, Arthur, *The Act of Creation* (Hutchinson & Co., 1964) Koestler discussed what he termed "bisociative" thinking in dreams. p. 178
22. "It was kind of perfect!": Miles, p. 104
23. "peep, antennae out": Miles, p. 130
24. "her can of catfood": Miles, p. 282
25. supervising physician ... *Nerves Explained*: Miles, pp. 109-110 and Royal College of Physicians website
26. would lie down: Miles, p. 110
27. instituted talk therapy: Beam, Alex, *Gracefully Insane: The Rise and Fall of America's Premier Mental Hospital* (BBS Public Affairs New York) pp. 124-125
28. "a bit of a stage mum": Miles, p. 104
29. "all smooth and in command": Davies, p. 302
30. written the main melody: Miles, p. 111
31. to Number One: Miles, p. 112
32. Peter Asher wrote a middle-eight: Norman, p. 196
33. Edward Lear and Lewis Carroll: Goldman, Albert, *The Lives of John Lennon* (William Morrow and Company, 1988) p.46 mentions John's interest in nonsense verse and Carroll.
34. not intended to be a single: MacDonald, p. 94
35. "explosive pop records ever": MacDonald, p. 83
36. "confidence in all but a few": MacDonald, p. 77
37. popularity was slumping: Norman, p. 182
38. "put a third thing": Lennon put it this way in an interview; in MacDonald, p. 83 and Miles, p. 149 it is referred to as a "third party."
39. "instantly communicative": MacDonald, p. 84
40. "Beyond doubt, the record's ... Isley Brothers": MacDonald, p. 84

41. reassured U.S. radio programmers: MacDonald, p. 64
42. Jane and Paul attended the theatre: Paul: "And by the time you got to like six o'clock, a meal and then the theatre! The *evening*, the real big thing, starts then." Miles, p. 115
43. 'quite a good trick': Miles, p. 122
44. it was a "puzzle": MacDonald, p. 128
45. "half an ear": Art Kane would use this phrase in Life magazine. See Chapter Six.
46. Every medium-sized to large: Jones, Maxwell, *Social Psychiatry in Practice: The Idea of the Therapeutic Community* (Pelican/Penguin, 1968) p. 21, pp. 63-67 Jones states that in 1959 the U.S. the mental health care system was a combination of private mental hospitals; public mental hospitals or State hospitals (277 public hospitals with a total of 542,721 beds); inpatient mental hospital care; and Veteran's Administration mental hospitals. In England and Wales in 1958 there were 158 mental hospitals with a total of 149,548 beds. Also see Article, Rufallo, Mark, "The American Mental Asylum: A Remnant of History" *Psychology Today* July 13, 2018.
47. "Don't see that boy": Article, "It Became The Ultimate Told-You-So Song" in "Facts About Yesterday," *Telegraph UK* online
48. "You've got no heart": Norman, p. 151
49. He loved practical jokes: Article, O'Mahoney, Seamus, "Brimful of Asher" British Medical Journal online
50. to fix a meal: Norman, p. 196. Norman also states that in addition to cooking whatever he wanted, Margaret did Paul's laundry and ironed all his shirts.
51. riots had been "faked": Hertsgaard, Mark, *A Day In The Life: The Music and Artistry of The Beatles* (Delacorte Press, 1995) p. 358: "The allegation that the crowds outside the Palladium were in fact quite small was made by photographer Dezo Hoffman in Norman's Shout! (on) page 238... 'There were no riots. I was there. Eight girls we saw ... even less than eight.' Norman concluded that the riots were 'faked.'"
52. estimated 73 million people: O'Dell, Denis with Bob Neaverson, *At The Apple's Core: The Beatles From the Inside* (Peter Owen Ltd. Publishers, 2002) p. 29
53. almost gave away: McNab, Ken, *And In the End: The Last Days of the Beatles* (Polygon, 2019) p. 23
54. some say written on the spot: MacDonald, p. 133

55. "sense of completeness": Goldman, Albert, *The Lives of John Lennon* (William Morrow and Company, 1988) p. 375

56. "adorable runt": Norman, p. 172

57. "like an orchid in a hothouse": Rolling Stone Special Edition, *The Beatles: The Ultimate Album-by-Album Guide* (2019) p. 16

58. "I was learning ... an awful lot": Miles, p. 116

Chapter II: Backdrop: The 1959 Macy Conference

1. "in line with": Frontispiece, Macy Conference on LSD-25

2. over 2,000 ... 12,000 LSD sessions: Table IV, p. 148, Macy Conference on LSD-25

3. "quasi-Freudian" psychoanalysis: ibid p. 25

4. Siamese fighting fish: ibid p. 238

5. friends from college: ibid p. 8 Abramson: "About 30 years ago, Dr. Fremont-Smith and I were tutors together at Harvard in the division of Biochemical Sciences ... I was ... really very concerned about the lack of contact between psychiatry, as I knew it then, and the laboratory. I began to work with LSD in 1951, work which has given me great satisfaction, because it involves my interests in psychoanalysis, psychotherapy, enzyme reactions, and surface chemistry, as well as biochemistry and pharmacology."

6. "In 1949 ... Livermore Sanitarium": ibid, p. 9

7. "was surprised ... never used LSD in psychotherapy": ibid, p. 12

8. tested LSD's specific effects: ibid, p. 12

9. elephant named Tusko: O'Neill, Tom and Piepenbring, Dan *CHAOS: Charles Manson, the CIA, and the Secret History of the Sixties* (Little, Brown, 2019) pp. 374-376

10. fake "hippie pad": O'Neill, ibid, pp. 344-350

11. This type of experimentation: Macy Conference on LSD-25, pp. 48-49. Bateson comments that the 'rearranged' material (as a result of Abramson's reconstructive approach to LSD psychotherapy) is "part of (the patient's) personality structure to begin with, surely, or he couldn't have produced it?" Abramson replies, "It is reconstruction," and adds, "We had better not define reconstructive therapy now." Fremont asks, "Doesn't it mean putting parts of it (the personality) in a different opposition?" Dr. Malitz then explains: "As a student of Rado, I might mention briefly what he meant by reconstructive therapy. He used the terms reconstructive and reparative to indicate the two major forms

of psychotherapy. To describe what is meant by reparative, Rado used the analogy of a house—you patch it up. If the plaster falls down, or if a few bricks are missing, you put them back. Reconstructive therapy (on the other hand) implies a change from the foundation up (and) has as its goal the development of fundamental and lasting changes in the basic character structure."

12. given LSD to Clare and Henry Luce: Article, Shafer, Jack, "The Time and Life Acid Trip: How Henry R. Luce and Clare Boothe Luce Helped Turn America on to LSD," *Slate* magazine, June 21, 2010

13. "interested in physical diseases ... quite different": Macy Conference on LSD-25, p. 11

14. effect on creativity: Cohen, Sidney and Alpert, Richard, *LSD* (New American Library, 1966) p. 67 Cohen: "William and Marsella McGlothlin and I have been working on the first bit of controlled research into this matter. The best possible tests of original thinking and creative problem-solving were selected and given before, then two weeks after and six months after three 200 microgram LSD sessions a month apart."

15. five suicides: ibid, p. 228

16. "prolonged psychotic reactions": ibid, p. 228

17. increase in "symbolization": ibid, p. 171

18. hallucinations: ibid, p. 108

19. depersonalization: ibid, p. 114, p. 131

20. "exquisite suggestibility": ibid, p. 117

21. "massive increase in association": ibid, p. 223. Dr. Murphy's statement.

22. lack of homeostasis: ibid, p. 135. Also Hoch's statement, ibid, p. 103: "the inner experience of the patient (is) that he is not a whole ... he feels fragmented ... the disintegrative effect of this drug is one of its very important features."

23. "Dialectics are altered": ibid, p. 188

24. "you can't tell the difference": ibid, p. 30

25. "another notion of itself": ibid, p. 171

26. "neuronal rearrangement": ibid, pp. 143-144

27. tap water: ibid, p. 28

28. "related compounds": ibid, Table I p. 72

29. Insulin comas ... improvement: Beam, Alex, *Gracefully Insane: The Rise and Fall of America's Premier Mental Hospital* (BBS Public Affairs New York) pp. 78-79

30. "remit rapidly": Macy Conference on LSD-25, p. 213, p. 234. Psychotics remit: p. 127
31. "nail soup": ibid, p. 185
32. "enthusiasm of the therapist": ibid, p. 227
33. "vision … of mass therapy": ibid, p. 14
34. "that includes psychotic reaction": ibid, p. 239
35. "examining socio-dynamics": ibid, p. 207
36. "among more sophisticated … rearrangement": ibid, p. 194
37. "blanket waivers": ibid, p. 61
38. "life and soul away": ibid, p. 61
39. "it was just LSD": ibid, p. 62
40. the "murkiness": ibid, p. 21, 161, 167. See also Leary, Timothy *Flashbacks: A Personal and Cultural History of an Era* (G.P. Putnam's Sons, 1983, Forward by William Burroughs) p. 16
41. an attempt to chart: Macy Conference on LSD-25, pp. 118-123 and Table II
42. could be just making up: ibid, pp. 96-97
43. "besieged" with people: ibid, p. 33
44. lecture about LSD: Cohen lectured twice on LSD at the University of California at Los Angeles.
45. "the schizophrenic knows … very unsuited": Macy Conference on LSD-25, p. 234
46. "it is very tender … fragile, friable material … discussion we are having": ibid, p. 189
47. "the perfect situation": ibid, p. 158
48. "understand psychoses": ibid, pp. 190-191
49. if you want to subvert: John Lennon in interview, *The Beatles: In Their Own Words* Barry Miles, Editor (Larchwood & Weir, 2013) Location 1147, Kindle Edition. Lennon states that the original Communist revolutionaries "coordinated themselves a bit better and didn't go around shouting about it," whereas to stand up and protest this is who-we-are and then get killed, is "unsubtle."
50. "total analysis is dreaming": Abramson, Macy Conference on LSD-25, pp. 68-70
51. floating things … ready for them: ibid, p. 156
52. "widens the holes": ibid, p. 160
53. "He can't say to his mother … be made": ibid, p. 192

54. "use symbolic language ... talking about": ibid, p. 33
55. "Despite all our charts ... by our activities": ibid, p. 11
56. a person "over": ibid, p. 114
57. "exquisitely suggestible": ibid, p. 117
58. by themselves to sort it out: ibid, pp. 172-173
59. "It (has) a glamorous appeal": ibid, p. 33
60. "I wouldn't completely agree ... had the drug": ibid, p. 30
61. "The patient was taken back ... No": ibid, p. 49
62. "We have not communicated": ibid, p. 225
63. "Symbolysis": ibid, pp. 151-197 Paper, Hewitt, Mollie and Lennard, Henry, *Symbolysis: Psychotherapy by Symbolic Presentation*
64. "In the auto-analytic procedure ... reassuring man": ibid, p. 151
65. "a very quiet person": ibid, p. 172. Also ibid, p. 211 and p. 80, References an article by Abramson, et al., "The Stablemate Concept of Therapy as Affected by LSD in Schizophrenia," published in the *Journal of Psychology*, 1958
66. calmer horse in the stable: ibid, p. 199, Hewitt: "in 1959, we started on a project which we called a "stablemate experiment"... The second member of the group is called the "stablemate," or running mate, and is generally of the same sex and age as the patient. This person, though normal and from the outside, is generally placed in the same position vis-a-vis authority as the third member, the patient." Also p. 201 Hewitt: "The horse, by having in the race a familiar partner to whom he is conditioned, is motivated to overcome the stresses of the strange competition because of adaptation to a familiar and safe object, the stablemate ... in subsequent experiments concerned with the question of tolerance to LSD, we felt we should structure the experiment in the same manner, with the stablemate concept."

Chapter III: Contemporaries: Laing, Cooper

1. Dr. Asher's consultation room: Miles, "On the ground floor was Dr. Asher's reception room ... on the first floor was Dr. Asher's parlour where he would play piano." The ground floor was over the basement. p. 108
2. managed the paperback section: Miles, p. 224
3. Tony Godwin: Miles, p. 224. Also the following description of an exhibit on Better Books held at ZKM Center for Art and Media, Karlsruhe, Germany, from November 2012-January 2013:

"In the 1950s and 1960s, the small English bookshop Better Books of Charing Cross Road became the center of the London avant-garde movement. Situated across from Saint Martins School of Art, this humble bookstore developed into a den of discontent and cradle for creativity, catalyzing a new breed of 'angry young men.' United in their distrust of the cultural norms, the postwar generation of artists, poets and writers found new ways to distance themselves from the previous generation. Many of these artists first met one another and took refuge at Tony Godwin's Charing Cross bookstore, Better Books. Under the management of Bill Butler, Barry Miles and Bob Cobbing, Better Books became not only a haven but also the platform and 'voice' of the explosively radical spirit within London. Some came to meet writers, to hear a poetry reading, catch an underground film screening, or find a publisher; some came for a publication that would not be found elsewhere. Others came in search of a fix or a party, or to find a kindred spirit or temporary bed. The bookshop enabled and initiated meetings, gave room for ideas, and became a sanctuary for numerous avant-garde artists, poets, filmmakers, musicians and writers."

4. "The Beatles, Jim Morrison of The Doors.... Leary": Article, Paton, Maureen, "R.D. Laing: Was the Counterculture's Favorite Psychiatrist a Dangerous Renegade or a True Visionary?" *UK Independent*, November 2015

5. society's "insanity": Some of R.D. Laing's books include *The Divided Self* (Tavistock Publications, 1960, subsequently published on Pantheon in 1962 and on Pelican/Penguin in 1965); *Self and Others* (Tavistock Publications, 1961); *Sanity, Madness and the Family* with Aaron Esterson (Tavistock Publications, 1964); and *The Politics of Experience* (Pantheon Books/Random House, 1967)

6. child had been driven insane: Laing, R.D., *The Politics of Experience* (Pantheon Books/Random House, 1967) p. 114. According to Laing, similar research was conducted at Palo Alto, California, Yale University, the Pennsylvania Psychiatric Institute and the National Institute of Mental Health, among other places.

7. "In the street, nobody": Laing, *The Divided Self* (Pelican edition) pp. 55-56

8. self-conscious Peter: Laing, *The Divided Self* (Pantheon edition) p. 132

9. "not simply eccentric": Laing, *The Divided Self* (Pelican edition) p. 70

10. playing "a part": Laing, *The Divided Self* (Pelican edition) p. 71

11. "made of glass": Laing, ibid p. 37

12. "I'm thousands": Laing, *The Divided Self,* (Pantheon edition) "She could be anyone, anywhere, anytime… Since she was anyone she cared to mention, she was no *one.*" p. 221

13. "gist of her reproaches": Laing, ibid p.187

14. "only a cork": Laing, The Divided Self (Pelican edition) p. 48

15. around people who understood them: Laing, David, *The Politics of Experience* (Pantheon Books, Random House, 1967) Laing designates schizophrenics as the misunderstood and hence the broken-hearted: "Perhaps we can still retain the now old name, and read into it its etymological meaning: *schiz-*'broken,' *phrenos-*'soul' or 'heart.'" p. 130

16. W. Winnicot, who wrote its: Laing, *The Divided Self* (Pelican edition) p. 10

17. inmate-run asylums: Article, Paton, Maureen, "R.D. Laing: Was the Counterculture's Favorite Psychiatrist a Dangerous Renegade or a True Visionary?" *UK Independent,* November 2015

18. "spiritual laxative": Article, O'Hagan, Sean, "Kingsley Hall: R.D. Laing's Experiment in Anti-Psychiatry" The Guardian, September 2, 2012

19. "patients, who were all female": Article, "R.D. Laing: the Abominable Family Man" *UK Times* online

20. was given regression therapy … nothing to lose: Article, Paton, Maureen, "R.D. Laing: Was the Counterculture's Favorite Psychiatrist a Dangerous Renegade or a True Visionary?" *UK Independent,* November 2015

21. "Winnicot proposes that … is being done": Laing, R.D. *The Facts of Life: An Essay in Feelings, Facts and Fantasy* (Pantheon, 1976) p. 115-116

22. remote coast … drive: O'Brien, Edna, *Country Girl: a Memoir* (Faber & Faber Ltd./Little, Brown and Company, 2012) p. 310

23. "unhinged": O'Brien, Edna, ibid pp. 203-205

24. live more "inner": nterview with Willis Harman in *Beyond the Mechanical Mind,* Long, Malcolm and Fry, Peter (Australian Broadcasting Commission, 1976)

25. "unsanity" slice: Sidney Cohen – Unsane YouTube video

26. "wanted to get to know me": Laing, *The Facts of Life,* ibid p. 111

27. "cover the … and conception": Cooper, David, *The Death of the Family* (Penguin, 1971) Introduction

28. "the ideal end … by their children?" Cooper, David, ibid

29. "the fur-lined bear trap": Cooper, David, ibid

30. "abolish the traditional hierarchy": Article, Ticktin, Stephen, "Brother Beast: A Personal Memoir of David Cooper" *Asylum Magazine For Democratic Psychiatry,* Vol 1. No. 3

31. "control that lies in the spaces between": Cooper, David, *The Language of Madness* (Penguin Books Ltd./Allen Lane 1978) "Power is pure otherness … the recovery of our potency (author's note: Cooper means by this the ending of all forms of sexual repression – see ibid, p.132) is the precondition for the destruction of the impotent power of the bourgeoisie state – the Eunuch power – the control that lies in the spaces between us and receives substance only through our submission." p. 179

32. "fluctuations between two people": Macy Conference on LSD-25. Frank Fremont-Smith comments, "We need to remind ourselves that our most refined methods appear gross when measured by the subtleties of human interaction, even between only two people and over a period of only fifteen seconds. You spoke, Dr. Hoch, about a patient's fluctuations under LSD, and the difficulty of keeping track of them. But we are just unable even to produce an accurate description of the fluctuations between two people exchanging 'Good mornings' at the breakfast table. This should not discourage us, but we should be aware of it." pp. 40-41.

33. "As the medical attitude … method of madness": Cooper, David, *The Language of Madness* (Penguin Books Ltd./Allen Lane 1978) p. 157

34. "Non-psychiatry means": Cooper, ibid p. 117

35. magic reversal charm: Wilson, Terry and Gysin, Brion, *Here To Go: Brion Gysin* (Creation Books, 2001) p. 167

36. was tape loops: Miles, Barry, *Paul McCartney: Many Years From Now* (Henry Holt and Company, 1997) Loops, p. 240. Also refer to Wilson, Terry and Gysin, Brion, ibid, p. 171 and p. 173: "William's texts became spells." Gysin related how Burroughs apparently put a "hex" on an old woman. Gysin and Burroughs did a collaborative show entitled *Let the Mice In* at the ICA in London in 1960.

37. sharing a small recording studio: "Aside from Paul himself, William Burroughs probably used the studio more than anyone else, conducting a series of stereo experiments…" Miles, p. 240

38. "gentle subversives": O'Dell, Denis with Bob Neaverson, *At The Apple's Core: The Beatles From the Inside* (Peter Owen Ltd. Publishers, 2002) p. 80

39. used his wife Zelda's letters: Milford, Nancy, *Zelda: A Biography* (Harper & Row, 1970) pp. 299-300

40. "believe in lunacy?… healthy": Article, Aronowitz, Al, "Beatlemania in 1964: This Has Gotten Entirely Out of Control" *Saturday Evening Post* March 1964

Chapter IV: "Yesterday" and "Rubber Soul": Paul's IFP Gels

1. his "praxis": R.D. Laing uses the word "praxis" frequently in his writing for "process." I use the word to denote Paul's IFP which produced music, so "praxis" in this book means artistic process.
2. unsuspectingly with LSD: MacDonald, p. 143
3. Around the same time: I take all recording dates from MacDonald.
4. Browsing through medical texts: Miles, p. 27
5. It is a fact that John's: MacDonald, p.188
6. "quite happy to stay": Norman, p. 226
7. doing comedy songs: MacDonald, p. 162 and p. 156
8. brand might be fading: Turner, Steve, *Beatles '66: The Revolutionary Year* (Ecco/Harper Collins, 2016) p. 16
9. "scrambled eggs": Miles, p. 203 and MacDonald, p. 157
10. castigated himself: Norman, p. 569
11. "and then tell me": "It Became The Ultimate Told-You-So Song" in "Facts About Yesterday," *Telegraph UK* online
12. "really got going": *Rolling Stone Collector's Edition, John Lennon: The Ultimate Guide to His Life, Music & Legend* (Rolling Stone/Time Inc. 2018) p. 18
13. "when we still believed": Milford, Nancy, *Zelda: A Biography* (Harper & Row, 1970) p. 315
14. suddenly had a voice: Philip Priestley Documentary, *Twiggy: The Face of the Sixties* Program 33 & Arte Geie/Avro
15. "been made up"…which they're basically not": Both comments are from the 2004 BBC Documentary, *Why I Hate the Sixties*. The second comment was made by columnist Peter Oborne.
16. Paul's "Michelle": Miles, pp. 273-275
17. 'esse is percipi': Laing, *The Divided Self* (Pantheon Edition) p. 60
18. distinguished relative: Lowell, Delmar R., *The Historic Genealogy of the Lowells of America from 1639 to 1899* (Tuttle Co, 1899) p. 121-122
19. poet Robert Lowell: Mariani, Paul, *Lost Puritan: A Life of Robert Lowell* (W.W. Norton, 1994) p. 29
20. the critical debate: Middlebrook, Diane Wood, *Anne Sexton: A Biography* (Houghton Mifflin Co, Boston, a Peter Davison Book, 1991) p. 126
21. "this kind of stuff": Stevenson, Anne, *Bitter Fame: a Life of Sylvia Plath* (Houghton Mifflin Boston, a Peter Davison Book, 1989) p. 154

22. "mad stories": Plath, Sylvia, *The Unabridged Journals of Sylvia Plath* (Anchor Books, 2000) p. 512

23. "madhouse poems": Plath, Sylvia, *The Unabridged Journals of Sylvia Plath* (Anchor Books, 2000) p. 521

24. "I had my wish: Stevenson, Anne, *Bitter Fame: a Life of Sylvia Plath* (Houghton Mifflin Boston, a Peter Davison Book, 1989) p.141

25. "gotten some of myself": Stevenson, ibid p. 142

26. worked as a secretary: Stevenson, ibid p. 144

27. who gave her comp: Plath, *Letters Home* (Harper & Row, 1975) p. 399

28. any plays in verse Hughes wrote: Plath, Sylvia, *Letters Home*, ibid p. 389.

29. "fantastic market": Plath, *Letters Home*, ibid p. 392

30. did not handle her material well: Stevenson, Anne, *Bitter Fame: a Life of Sylvia Plath* (Houghton Mifflin Boston, a Peter Davison Book, 1989) p. 285

31. "patted on the head": Stevenson, ibid p. 286

32. "une oeuvre": Laing, R.D, *The Divided Self*, ibid Frontispiece

33. "terrible, but very wise": Plath, Sylvia, *The Bell Jar* (Harper Perennial, 2006) p. 39

34. strangling: Plath, ibid pg. 123

35. Sexton had an affair: Middlebrook, Diane Wood, *Anne Sexton: A Biography* (Houghton Mifflin, Boston, a Peter Davison Book, 1991) p. 108, p. 118

36. Archibald MacLeish: Biographical information from Donaldson, Scott, *Archibald MacLeish: An American Life* (Houghton Mifflin, a Peter Davison book, 1992)

37. Henry (Harry) Murray ... personality research: Biographical information from Robinson, Forrest, *Love's Story Told: A Life of Henry A. Murray* (Harvard University Press/Cambridge, Massachusetts and London, England, 1992)

38. testing fifty college men: Robinson, Forrest, *Love's Story Told*, ibid p. 172. Henry Murray and the Workers at the Harvard Psychological Clinic, *Explorations in Personality: A Clinical and Experimental Study of Fifty Men of College Age* (Oxford University Press, 1938)

39. reading several books on ... psychology including Jung's: Stevenson, Anne, *Bitter Fame*, ibid. Plath mentioning Jungian archetypes: p. 151, Plath reading Jung's *Symbols of Transformation*: p.163, Plath mentions Jungian "chessboard": p. 165

40. the unmoored perspective: Article on Eliot, Thomas Stearns by Bush, Ronald, *Oxford Dictionary of National Biography*, (online) January 7, 2016: A discussion of interests and material which "conditioned some of the poetic and intellectual preoccupations of the next part of his life. Among these was a fascination with insanity and unmoored perspective like that in a suppressed section of 'Prufrock' called 'Prufrock's Pervigilium.'"

41. Herbert Read: Seymour-Jones, Carole, *Painted Shadow* (Doubleday, 2002) p. 337

42. "the savvy rival": Middlebrook, Diane Wood, *Anne Sexton: A Biography* (Houghton Mifflin, Boston, a Peter Davison Book, 1991) p. 201

43. Critic David Holbrook: 1968 Essay, Holbrook, David, *R.D. Laing and the Death Circuit* and Holbrook, David, *Sylvia Plath: Poetry and Existence* (Bloomsbury Press, 1976) Holbrook's biographical and psychoanalytical approach to Plath's poetry as pertaining to examples in *The Divided Self* p. 152

44. the work of a "schizophrenic": Holbrook, David, *Sylvia Plath: Poetry and Existence* (Bloomsbury Press, 1976) p. 239

45. In rebuttal, critic Judith Kroll: *Chapters in a Mythology: The Poetry of Sylvia Plath* (1978) Kroll attempts to explore in depth Plath's academic research for her undergraduate thesis, *The Magic Mirror: A Study of the Double in Two of Dostoevsky's Novels*, to clarify much of Plath's poetic imagery. Kroll asserts that a profound knowledge of folk-tales, psychology and myth enabled Plath to create a personal system of poetic symbols based on mythical archetypes into which autobiographical or confessional details [were] shaped and absorbed. p. 2

46. "anyone who is sensitive": Middlebrook, Diane Wood, *Anne Sexton: A Biography* (Houghton Mifflin Co, Boston, A Peter Davison Book, 1991) p. 265

47. inmate at McLean: Beam, Alex, *Gracefully Insane: The Rise and Fall of America's Premier Mental Hospital* (BBS Public Affairs New York). Also see singer James Taylor's website, which at the time of this writing posts this text regarding McLean: "Shrink-wrapped drugs and rock 'n' roll were regular features of life at McLean's Psychiatric hospital in Belmont. For James Taylor and many other affluent young people, it was a combination of progressive music school and country club, with barred windows."

48. "feeling very Faustian": Zelda Fitzgerald, letter to the Turnbulls, Milford, Nancy, *Zelda: A Biography* (Harper & Row, 1970). p. 272 "Don't ever fall into the hands of brain and nerve specialists unless you are feeling very Faustian."

49. "be carried off … shrieking": Cline, Sally, *Zelda Fitzgerald* (Arcade Publishing, 2002, 2012) F. Scott Fitzgerald to Dr. Meyer p. 323

50. President of Harvard: Gordon, Lyndall, *Eliot's Early Years* (Oxford University Press, 1977) Charles William Eliot was president of Harvard for forty years from 1869 to 1909. p. 17

51. treated for a mental breakdown: Seymour-Jones, Carole, *Painted Shadow* ibid pp. 296-297

52. inspiration for … die in an asylum: Seymour-Jones, Carole, *Painted Shadow* ibid p. 582

53. "Earlier in the year, 75": UltimateBeatlesExperience website

54. did a photo-shoot: Pictures of the 1965 photo shoot of Paul taken by Jane Asher are viewable online.

Chapter V: Here, There, and Everywhere: Paul's IFP Expands

1. late 1965 … Paul took LSD: Turner, Steve, *Beatles '66: The Revolutionary Year* pp. 32-33 states that Paul first took LSD on December 14, 1965 at Tara Browne's home.

2. "demon drug": Norman, p. 225

3. build the bookshelves: Norman, pp. 230-231

4. "neuronal rearrangement": Macy Conference on LSD-25, pp. 143-144

5. first-hand accounts: Cohen, Sidney, *The Beyond Within: The LSD Story* (First printing, 1964; Atheneum fourth printing, 1966) Forward by Gardner Murphy, Menninger Clinic

6. account of her LSD: Newland, Constance, *Myself and I: LSD 25* (Frederick Muller Ltd., 1963)

7. being interviewed: Frank, Thomas, *The Conquest of Cool: Business Culture, Counterculture, and the Rise of Hip Consumerism* (University of Chicago Press, 1997) "A symptomatic document is "The Gap" (1967)… Ernest Fladell, the ad-man, is strangely candid and seems genuinely interested in the life of the mysterious young." p. 107

8. "search for new magic": Macy Conference on LSD-25, p. 33

9. "Aesthetically, the image … of meaning": Whiteley, Sheila, *The Space Between the Notes: Rock and the Counterculture* (Routledge, 1992) p. 105

10. "montage … an experience of madness": Whiteley, ibid, pp. 105-106

11. "peer pressure": Norman, p. 239

12. long-lasting standards: Miles, p. 284

13. increased associative language: Macy Conference on LSD-25, p. 93, pp. 223-224

14. "executive's special": Macy Conference on LSD-25, p. 176
15. his own house: Norman describes the house in St. John's Wood as "a substantial family home ... screened by a stout brick wall." Norman, p. 234
16. "had changed so much": Miles, p. 434
17. "There were fifteen ... know about": Davies, p. 309
18. "I used to think that ... a better one": *The Beatles Book, The Beatles' Own Monthly Magazine* November 1966 No. 40 p. 10
19. "the automatic routines": Koestler, Arthur, *The Act of Creation* (Hutchinson & Co., 1964) Back cover blurb
20. who observed: information on Arthur Koestler from Scammell, Michael, *Koestler: The Literary and Political Odyssey of a Twentieth Century Skeptic* (Random House, 2009) and Koestlerarts.org
21. "the elastic-sided boot": Norman, p. 226
22. take over production: Davies, p. 270, p. 272, p. 274; Emerick, Geoff, and Massey, Howard: *Here, There and Everywhere: My Life Recording the Music of The Beatles* (Penguin Random House/Avery, 2007) p. 130, pp. 135-136, p. 138, p. 143, p. 144, p. 163
23. had a theory about creativity: Cohen explains his theory in the video clip, "Sidney Cohen-Unsanity" on YouTube.
24. Number One: Number One hits in the U.S. in 1966 taken from Billboard Hot 100.
25. "a muddy wash": "No harmonic movement at all—a muddy wash made from a pair of simple loops. If this was Lennon's first attempt at realising what was in his mind, it suggests that McCartney's role in clarifying harmony and texture was crucial." MacDonald, p. 189
26. Paul's production of the song: Emerick, Geoff, and Massey, Howard: *Here, There and Everywhere: My Life Recording the Music of The Beatles* (Penguin Random House/Avery, 2007) pp. 111-112
27. played by Paul, actually: Emerick, ibid p. 126
28. "Eleanor Rigby ... quite what: Miles, pp. 281-284
29. Wilson's "feels": Wilson, Brian, *Wouldn't It Be Nice* (Harper Collins, 1991) p. 131
30. final verse "brutal": MacDonald, p. 203
31. Orange Sunshine ... Brotherhood of Eternal Love: Lee, Martin and Shlain, Bruce, *Acid Dreams: The Complete Social History of LSD, the CIA, the Sixties, and Beyond* (Grove Press, 1985) pp. 236-248

32. "suitcase full of pot": Article, Goldstein, Richard, "Drugs on Campus: A Coast-to-Coast Survey" *Saturday Evening Post Magazine* May 21, 1966 pp. 40-62

33. whoever else crossed: Leary, Timothy *Flashbacks: A Personal and Cultural History of an Era* (G.P. Putnam's Sons, 1983, Forward by William Burroughs) pp. 67-70, pp. 202-206 Ginsberg and Leary give psilocybin to poet Robert Lowell, ibid, p. 67

34. colored their lyric sheets: MacDonald, p. 179

35. tape loops: Miles, pp. 219-220

36. "take a note and": Turner, Steve, *Beatles '66: The Revolutionary Year* (Ecco/Harper Collins, 2016) p. 116. Also ibid, p. 144: The loops were inspired both by Stockhausen and the experimental "cut-up" work of Burroughs and Gysin, who "had been randomly chopping up texts from books and newspapers and reassembling the pieces to create new and unexpected meanings."

37. "rub out the word": Wilson, Terry and Gysin, Brion, *Here To Go: Brion Gysin* (Creation Books, 2001) p. 17

38. Janiger, Allen Ginsberg's cousin … study creativity: at the "LSD Reunion Party" (Video on YouTube) held at his home in 1976, Janiger states that he gave the drug to about one hundred artists and influencers, "who also had their own audiences," implying he could have also supplied the drug for those sessions.

39. in this area: Cohen, Sidney and Albert, Richard, *LSD* (New American Library, 1966)

40. Rockefellers funded … Murray: Robinson, Forrest, *Love's Story Told: A Life of Henry A Murray* (Harvard University Press/Cambridge, Massachusetts and London, England, 1992) in the Thirties, p. 226; in the Fifties, p. 332, "a Thematic Apperception Test (TAT) study of prominent American poets and writers"; in the late Fifties "a new Federal grant" of "self-image under stress" p. 337 (included Kaczynski). Also see Douglas, Claire, *Translate This Darkness: The Life of Christiana Morgan* (Simon & Schuster, 1993): Rockefeller funding in the Forties, p. 276-277 and p. 285 in the Fifties, "Morgan's new version of the TAT was intended to help measure creativity for the clinic's new project on that subject … also whether or not a patient had the capacity for introspection and was ready to withstand probing into archetypal depths." Murray was working on a "typology of the dramatic imagination." Also "a comprehensive, though unpublished, study of the creative process." p. 298

41. Gene Tierney observed: Tierney, Gene and Herskowitz, Mickey, *Self-Portrait* (Wyden Books/Simon and Schuster, 1979) p. 200, p. 203. Tierney underwent dozens of shock treatments at the Hartford Institute of Living until she felt she had "no history" and "couldn't remember what foods I liked."

42. hipsters visited Laing's asylums: Article, *UK Independent*, R.D. Laing: Was the Counterculture's Favorite Psychiatrist a Dangerous Renegade or a True Visionary? Paton, Maureen, November 2015

43. She Said She Said: Macy Conference on LSD-25 contains several mentions of LSD psychotherapy where the therapist has also taken the drug: Katzenelbogen: "I am speaking, in general, about the many statements made here that the therapist should take LSD." p. 218

44. "a muddy wash" ... role in clarifying: MacDonald, p. 189

45. "a collection of bizarre sounds": Emerick, Geoff, and Massey, Howard: *Here, There and Everywhere: My Life Recording the Music of The Beatles* (Penguin Random House/Avery, 2007) p. 111

46. one-of-a-kind: Miles, p. 292

47. the poem: Leary, Timothy, "Jewelled Indifference," in *Psychedelic Prayers after the Tao Te Ching* (New York University Books, 1966)

48. "embarrassing then, because we wanted": *Rolling Stone* Collector's Edition, *John Lennon: The Ultimate Guide to His Life, Music & Legend* (Rolling Stone/Time Inc. 2018) pp. 15-16

49. "We knew what we": Article, Gilmore, Mikal, "Inside the Making of "Sgt. Pepper'" *Rolling Stone* Magazine, June 1, 2017

50. The pilot programs: Lee, Martin and Shlain, Bruce, *Acid Dreams: The Complete Social History of LSD, the CIA, the Sixties, and Beyond* (Grove Press, 1985) p. 142

51. "to make people "live more 'inner'... impressed with ... can't really separate them": Interview with Willis Harman in *Beyond the Mechanical Mind*, Long, Malcolm and Fry, Peter (Australian Broadcasting Commission, 1976)

52. Connected to Stewart Brand ... Portola Institute: Brightman, Carol, *Sweet Chaos: The Grateful Dead's American Adventure* (Pocket Books, 1998) p. 53: "Working with Brand on the Trips Festival's sideshows—the God Box, the Congress of Wonders, among them—were some of the pioneers of the personal computer revolution, including Apple's co-founder Steve Jobs." See also Article, Dremann, Sue, "Palo Alto's Magical Mystery Trip: Historical Association Lecture to Focus on LSD's Impact on Silicon Valley," *Palo Alto Weekly* November 3, 2018

53. Savage ... VA Hospital: Macy Conference on LSD-25, List of Participants, held in 1959, Savage is listed as being at the Center for Advanced Study of Behavioral Sciences (CASBS) at Stanford and on p. 10 Savage states that he is also at this time "consultant to the Palo Alto Mental Research Institute." Ken Kesey, according to Brightman, ibid p. 20 took psilocybin, mescaline, and LSD, "interspersed with other psychotropic drugs" at the VA hospital in Palo Alto, Menlo Park, from 1959-1960. Gregory Bateson was at the VA Hospital in Menlo Park in 1959, according to the List of Macy Conference participants in Appendix.

54. worked for Navy intelligence: Macy Conference on LSD-25, p. 9

55. Bateson was at Stanford: Macy Conference on LSD-25, Participants lists Gregory Bateson as working at the Palo Alto VA Hospital, "Ethnology Section." See List of Participants to the 1959 Macy Conference in Appendices.

56. Visiting Fellow ... accompanied by his son, Alan: Brightman, Carol, *Sweet Chaos: The Grateful Dead's American Adventure* (Pocket Books, 1998) p. 79

57. guinea-pigged on LSD and other: Lee, Martin and Shlain, Bruce, *Acid Dreams: The Complete Social History of LSD, the CIA, the Sixties, and Beyond* (Grove Press, 1985) Volunteers were "paid $75 a day ... (to take) "an array of psychedelics—LSD, mescaline, Ditran, and a mysterious substance known only as IT-290." Kesey related that after he took the drugs, "I saw that what the insane were saying and doing was not so crazy after all": Slowly his first novel, *One Flew Over the Cuckoo's Nest*, came to him."

58. "What we were interested in": Brightman, Carol, *Sweet Chaos: The Grateful Dead's American Adventure* (Pocket Books, 1998) Brightman writes: "Curiously, for such dissimilar folk, (art) is what united the founders of the Grateful Dead. 'What we were interested in was art,' recalls Alan Trist, who was nineteen when he and his father, Eric Trist, a Visiting Fellow at Stanford who founded the Tavistock Institute in London, arrived in Palo Alto in 1960. 'It was the business of being an artist that totally captured Jerry and Hunter,' he states, pointing out to me, when we meet at a bagel shop near the Dead's office in San Rafael, that it was 'art in the sense in which art is free of the political frame of reference.'" p. 79

59. "was a heavy prime mover": Brightman, ibid p. 79

60. invitation for the first Trips Festival: January 1966, Longshoreman's Hall, San Francisco. "Stewart Brand came up with the original concept along with a musician and visual artist named Ramon Sender." Kesey

and Owsley hosted the events. Greenfield, Robert, *Bear: The Life and Times of Augustus Stanley Owsley III* (St. Martin's Press, 2016), p. 57

61. partially funded by the Rockefellers: Gottlieb, Lou, *A History of Two Open-Door California Communes, Chapter 1, Beginnings* (from The Digger Archives, Diggers.org)

62. a young Steve Jobs: Brightman, Carol, *Sweet Chaos: The Grateful Dead's American Adventure* (Pocket Books, 1998) p. 53

63. City Lights sold tickets: this information was printed at the bottom of first Trips Festival invite.

64. entrepreneur Charles Sullivan: Article, Carr, Gary on Charles Sullivan, the "Mayor of Fillmore" in Local History section of the *Fillmore Times*: "On August 2, 1966, the "Mayor of Fillmore" was found shot to death in the area south of Market Street ... Sullivan booked some of the biggest names in jazz ... Sullivan also owned the master lease to the Fillmore Auditorium. In 1965, Sullivan began subletting the Fillmore to Bill Graham when he wasn't using the venue himself for blockbusters like the Ike and Tina Turner Revue. Soon after (Sullivan's death) Bill Graham took over booking acts into the Fillmore."

65. Plath's former lover: "(The Oracle) featured such Beat writers as Allen Ginsberg, Gary Snyder, Lawrence Ferlinghetti and Michael McClure. "The initial impetus for the paper came from Allen Cohen and head shop owners Ron and Jay Thelin, who offered to put up the seed money to found an underground paper. In the summer of 1966 a number of meetings were held in the Haight-Ashbury district to discuss the idea of starting a paper, attracting an eclectic group of interested people. The result of these meetings was a paper called *P.O. Frisco*, which lasted for a single 12-page tabloid issue dated September 2, 1966, under the editorship of Dan Elliot and Richard Sassoon (a 31-year-old Yale-educated poet who had once been *Sylvia Plath's* boyfriend). *P.O. Frisco* was a compromise ... which wound up satisfying no one, and the Thelin brothers threatened to terminate their financial support unless the paper was completely reinvented. "A second attempt began ... under new editors George Tsongas and John Bronson. The new paper, The *San Francisco Oracle*, started with issue #1.... Bronson and Tsongas edited the first two issues of the new *Oracle* and then left after a fight with Cohen and Gabe Katz, who became the paper's new art editor starting with issue #3 while Cohen took over as editor, a role he maintained until the end." – Wikipedia entry on The *Oracle*

66. Bowen's mother: Abrahamsson, Carl, *Olika Manniskor* (Different People) (Haftad Svenska, 2007) p. 143

67. "Love Pageant": Goffman, Ken and Joy, Dan, *Counterculture Through the Ages* (Villard, 2004) pp. 266-267

68. the Diggers provided free food: MacDonald, p. 16

69. Kesey's novel: Kesey, Ken, *One Flew Over the Cuckoo's Nest* (Viking Press, 1962)

70. Kesey, Jerry Garcia … were given LSD: Lee, Martin and Shlain, Bruce, *Acid Dreams: The Complete Social History of LSD, the CIA, the Sixties, and Beyond* (Grove Press, 1985) p. 119

71. Stewart Brand received … by Richard Alpert: Article, Dremann, Sue, "Palo Alto's Magical Mystery Trip: Historical Association Lecture to Focus on LSD's Impact on Silicon Valley," *Palo Alto Weekly*, November 3, 2018

72. "the daughters in particular … IT-290": Author interview with publisher Alison Kennedy, Berkeley, California 2019

73. "grand pooh-bah": Author interview with publisher Alison Kennedy, Berkeley, California 2019

74. "were *really* free": Author interview with publisher Alison Kennedy, Berkeley, California 2019

75. "of every stripe … important": Author interview with publisher Alison Kennedy, Berkeley, California 2019

76. lectured … corresponded with her: Author interview with publisher Alison Kennedy, Berkeley, California 2019

77. Alan Trist was present: Brightman, Carol, *Sweet Chaos: The Grateful Dead's American Adventure* (Pocket Books, 1998) p. 79

78. picked at random: from Dead.net website

79. also an LSD manufacturer: Greenfield, Robert, *Bear: The Life and Times of Augustus Stanley Owsley III* (St. Martin's Press, 2016) In their early days, Owsley designed a public address (PA) and monitor system for them. Owsley was the Grateful Dead's soundman for many years; he was one of the largest suppliers of LSD (supplying LSD for the Monterey Pop festival). He was arrested in December 1967.

80. set up a fake "crash pad": O'Neill, Tom and Piepenbring, Dan *CHAOS: Charles Manson, the CIA, and the Secret History of the Sixties* (Little, Brown, 2019) West set up a fake hippie crash pad which opened in June of 1967. pp. 344-345

81. regarded as role models: Author interview with publisher Alison Kennedy, Berkeley, California 2019

82. "Beatles' transition ... complex maturity": Miles, p. 268

83. "neuronal rearrangement": Macy Conference on LSD-25, pp. 143-144

84. was replaced: information on the Paul Is Dead theory is searchable online

85. In late 1964, Brian Wilson met ... by fall of 1965-1966..."feels"... worked with Tony Asher: Wilson, Brian, *Wouldn't It Be Nice* (Harper Collins, 1991) pp. 131-140

86. Schwartz's father ... a psychiatrist: Wilson, Brian, *Wouldn't It Be Nice* (Harper Collins, 1991) A Dr. Steve Schwartz, psychiatrist, treated Wilson for a brief period before dying in a hiking accident. p. 246

87. introduced Wilson to pot: Wilson, Brian, *Wouldn't It Be Nice* (Harper Collins, 1991) p. 104

88. from Stanley Owsley ... up to music": Wilson, Brian, ibid pp. 116-117

89. had written advertising copy for: Interview with Tony Asher on AlbumLinerNotes.com

90. Wilson took LSD again: Wilson, Brian, ibid p. 122

91. son of Irving Asher: From producer Irving Asher's Wikipedia entry online.

92. Paul McCartney was given LSD for the first time: Turner, Steve, *Beatles '66: The Revolutionary Year* (Ecco/Harper Collins, 2016) p. 7, p. 33

93. Van Dyke Parks ... psychologist: Article, "The Seldom Seen Kid," *Mojo* magazine, August 2012 states that Parks' father was a doctor and military psychologist. Singer David Crosby introduced Wilson to Parks according to Wilson in *I Am Brian Wilson* (Da Capo/Hachette, 2016) p. 185

94. McCartney dropped by: Wilson, Brian, ibid (Harper Collins, 1991) pp. 164-165

95. "began to lose it": Wilson, Brian, ibid p. 165

96. "something that is intensely": Wilson, Brian, ibid p. 162

97. "teenage symphony to God": Wilson, Brian, ibid p. 148

98. "found a new sound": Wilson, Brian, ibid p. 153 quoting review in *The Sunday Express* (UK) November, 1966

99. still on the charts: On the U.S. Cash Box Year-End chart for 1966, "California Dreaming" was tied for #1 with "The Ballad of the Green Berets." The U.S. Billboard Hot 100 chart ranks "California Dreaming" at #10 at year-end 1966.

Chapter VI: Identity Fracture as Self-Protection: Henry James

1. "When you hear ... abandonment": Editor's Column, *Life* Magazine, September 20, 1968

2. Kane took pictures ... innocence of childhood: "Photographic Impressions of Beatles Songs by Art Kane" *Life* Magazine, September 20, 1968 p. 63-70

3. *Psycho-Cybernetics*: Photograph appears in Wilson, Brian, *Wouldn't It Be Nice* (Harper Collins, 1991)

4. "a terrific novel ... have time": Plath, Sylvia, *The Unabridged Journals of Sylvia Plath* (Anchor Books, 2000) pp. 274-275

5. "I will imitate until I can": Plath, Sylvia, *The Unabridged Journals of Sylvia Plath* (Anchor Books, 2000) p. 544 on Kindle version

6. "limited, folksy, vivid style": Plath, Sylvia, *The Unabridged Journals of Sylvia Plath* (Anchor Books, 2000) pp. 334-335 on Kindle version

7. women's stories: Plath, Sylvia, *Letters Home* (Harper and Row, 1975) p. 277 Also Plath, Sylvia, *The Unabridged Journals of Sylvia Plath* (Anchor Books, 2000) p. 496 Kindle Edition

8. "mad stories": Plath, Sylvia, *The Unabridged Journals of Sylvia Plath* (Anchor Books, 2000) pp. 613 on Kindle version

9. "read them deep": Stevenson, Anne, *Bitter Fame: a Life of Sylvia Plath* (Houghton Mifflin Boston, a Peter Davison Book, 1989) p. 141

10. lifted from a poem: Eliot, T.S., "East Coker," *The Complete Poems and Plays, 1909-1950* (Harcourt Brace & Co, 1952)

11. "psychological fantasia": Plath, ibid, p. 624 Kindle

12. "a potboiler": Plath, Sylvia, *Letters Home* (Harper and Row, 1975) p. 472

13. befriended dramatist Alan Sillitoe: Plath became friends with Sillitoe and his wife, poet Ruth Fainlight. Plath, Sylvia, *The Letters of Sylvia Plath, Vol 2: 1956-1963* (Faber & Faber, 2018) pp. 761-762, p. 766, p. 915

14. The character Peter Sherringham ... polish": Schneider, Daniel J, *The Crystal Cage: Adventures of the Imagination in the Fiction of Henry James* (The Regents Press of Kansas, 1978) p. 104-105

15. eyesight was so weak: Goldman, Albert, *The Lives of John Lennon* p. 47. "Without his glasses, Lennon was legally blind." Also see Emerick, Geoff and Massey Howard, *Here, There and Everywhere: My Life Recording the Music of the Beatles* (Avery/Penguin Random House, 2007) p. 99

16. to let a car pass: McNab, Ken, *And In the End: The Last Days of the Beatles* (Polygon, 2019) p. 150

17. confrontational: Emerick, Geoff and Massey Howard, *Here, There and Everywhere: My Life Recording the Music of the Beatles* (Avery/Penguin Random House, 2007) "everything always ended up with agitation of some kind; he was very confrontational ... (but) even if he was being nasty, you could see that he genuinely enjoyed talking with people." p. 100

18. a puny ego: Leary, Timothy, *Psychedelic Prayers* (New York University Press, 1966) poem, "Jewelled Indifference" page II-3

19. something "theatrical ... a play": Schneider, op cit p.109

20. the sexually repressed: James, Henry, *The Turn of the Screw & The Aspern Papers*, Dr. Claire Seymour, Editor (Wordsworth Classics, 2000), p. x and Wilson, Edmund, "The Ambiguity in Henry James" in *The Triple Thinkers* (Oxford University Press, 1948) p. 88

21. "fascination with the supernatural": Seymour, ibid. On the same page, "James's brother William was an active psychical researcher ... and also an influential psychologist." p. xi

22. "We're a con": Davies, Hunter, *The Beatles* (W.W. Norton & Company, 1968) p. 284

23. "silence at the centre": Seymour, op cit p. ix

24. "mixture in things": Schneider, ibid p. 153

25. "equation between": Epstein, Brian *A Cellarful of Noise* (Pocket Books/ Simon & Shuster, 1967) p. 212

26. "not be ourselves": Gilmore, Mikal, "Inside the Making of "Sgt. Pepper" *Rolling Stone* Magazine June 1, 2017. Also see MacDonald, p. 232 and Miles, p. 303, "to lose our identities" as "a freeing element."

27. veered into this territory: O'Dell, Denis with Bob Neaverson, *At The Apple's Core: The Beatles From the Inside* (Peter Owen Ltd. Publishers, 2002) p. 168: "I think (Sellers') main problem was that he didn't seem to have any clear sense of his own identity."

28. "can never relax": Davies, p. 302

29. "the perfume I used": Milford, Nancy, Zelda: A Biography (Harper & Row, 1970) p. 112

30. saw the latest: Turner, Steve, *Beatles '66: The Revolutionary Year* (Ecco/ Harper Collins, 2016) and states they were 'early adopters' rather than innovators. p. 5 and p. 407

31. "lives the largest ... as possible": Schneider, p. 152

32. "way of resisting": Schneider, p. 153
33. beans on toast: Schwartz, Francie, *Body Count* (Selfpub.com, 1999) p. 87 describes it using "and."
34. "same world as the rest of us": O'Dell, Denis with Bob Neaverson, *At The Apple's Core: The Beatles From the Inside* (Peter Owen Ltd. Publishers, 2002) p. 114
35. "could be good": Schneider, p. 98
36. "that's got them": Davies, p. 24
37. "He's all right, really": Miles, p. 33
38. "leave myself completely": Davies, pp. 295
39. "than you need them": Davies, p. 298
40. Henry James's rivalry: Schneider, op cit, pp. 38-39
41. early scripts: Turner, Steve, *Beatles '66: The Revolutionary Year* (Ecco/Harper Collins, 2016) pp. 351-352. The film's working title was *Beatle 3*, the script by Owen Holder commissioned by producer Walter Shenson. The project was referred to as *Shades of a Personality*. Shenson asked playwright Joe Orton to improve the script, and Orton developed a screenplay he called "Up Against It," which was rejected. In 1967 Michelangelo Antonioni, director of *Blow Up*, was announced as the director. In 1965 a script of the Western novel *A Talent For Loving* was commissioned from its American author Richard Condon, also author of *The Manchurian Candidate* (Turner, ibid, p. 18)
42. "a pristine wholeness": David Cooper lecture, ibid (Verso/New Left Books edition, 2015) p. 201
43. society that will be a "work of art": Bateson, Gregory; Carmichael, Stokely; Cooper, David; Laing, R.D.; Marcuse, Herbert, et al., *To Free A Generation! The Dialectics of Liberation* (Collier Books, 1969, Originally published by Penguin Books, 1968) p. 185. Marcuse: "It would mean the emergence of a form of reality which is the work and the medium of the developing sensibility and sensitivity of man …. It would mean an 'aesthetic' reality – society as a work of art. This is the most Utopian, the most radical possibility of liberation today."
44. "nature's child": Schneider, p. 40
45. "stay interested": *The Beatles Book, The Beatles' Own Monthly Magazine* November 1966, No. 40 p. 10
46. "desperate curiosity": Schwartz, Francie, *Body Count* (Selfpub.com, 1999) p. 85
47. "a life of its own": Schneider, p.4 and p.70

48. "mimetic culture": Goffman, Ken and Joy, Dan, *Counterculture Through the Ages* (Villard, 2004) p. 242, p. 269

49. "replacement of reality": BBC Documentary, *Why I Hate the Sixties,* 2004. Author and journalist Simon Heffer commented, "It was a decade of … the replacement of reality by illusion."

50. "selfless motive is": Dorothea Krook as quoted by Schneider, p. 52. (Krook was Sylvia Plath's academic mentor at Cambridge.)

51. terror and dread: Cohen, Sidney, *The Beyond Within: The LSD Story*, Forward by Gardner Murphy of the Menninger Foundation (Atheneum, 1964) pp. 233-235

52. "permit him to render … inner worlds": Schneider, pp. 70-71

53. "televisual vividness": MacDonald, p. 204

54. "erase himself": MacDonald, p. 173 and p. 192 and Miles, p. 542. See also Lee, Martin and Shlain, Bruce, *Acid Dreams: The Complete Social History of LSD, the CIA, the Sixties, and Beyond* (Grove Press, 1985) p. 183, and Goldman, Albert, *The Lives of John Lennon* (William Morrow and Company, 1988) p. 248

55. under Harry Murray: Article, Chase, Alston, "Harvard and The Making of The Unabomber" *The Atlantic Monthly* June 2000: As a sophomore, Kaczynski participated in a study described by author Alston Chase as a "purposely brutalizing psychological experiment" led by Harvard psychologist Henry (Harry) Murray. Subjects were told they would be debating personal philosophy with a fellow student, and were asked to write essays detailing their personal beliefs and aspirations. The essays were turned over to an anonymous attorney, who in a later session would confront and belittle the subject—making "vehement, sweeping, and personally abusive" attacks—using the content of the essays as ammunition, while electrodes monitored the subject's physiological reactions. These encounters were filmed, and subjects' expressions of anger and rage were later played back to them repeatedly. The experiment lasted three years, with someone verbally abusing and humiliating Kaczynski each week. Kaczynski spent 200 hours as part of the study.

56. "But it is fake … effort involved: Leary, Timothy *Flashbacks: A Personal and Cultural History of an Era* (G.P. Putnam's Sons, 1983, Forward by William Burroughs) p. 59

57. sponsors art-making in prisons: Koestlerarts.org.uk.

58. *Nightmare Alley*: 1947 film directed by Edmund Goulding. Released by 20th Century Fox

59. "rubbed off": Guiles, Fred Lawrence *Tyrone Power: The Last Idol* (Berkley, 1980) pp. 185-187

60. "Cripples!": Davies, p. 325

61. "come across as being so good ... an image": Davies, p. 260

62. "fraudulent": Richard Goldstein writing for the *New York Times*, June 1967

63. "any more war": Interview with Paul McCartney in *Queen* magazine, March 31, 1967, reprinted in Life magazine, June 16, 1967 issue

64. "a good PR man": *Rolling Stone* Collector's Edition, *John Lennon: The Ultimate Guide to His Life, Music & Legend* (Rolling Stone/Time Inc. 2018) p. 35

Chapter VII: The Beatles' Look and Sound: "All a Bit of Fun"

1. "We stopped being a band": Babiuk, Andy, *Beatles Gear* (Backbeat/ Hal Leonard, 2015) p. 488

2. "quiffs": Norman, p. 85, p. 139

3. A columnist in *Teen*: Column, Persons, Ted, "Short Notes on Long Plays" *Teen* Magazine, May 1964, p. 18

4. "Some Fun Tonight": The Beatles – Sweden 1963 video on YouTube

5. cropped around eight girls: Hertsgaard, Mark, *A Day In The Life: The Music and Artistry of The Beatles* (Delacorte Press, 1995) p. 358

6. "Rachmaninoff the 2nd": 2012 BBC/Arena documentary, *Produced by George Martin*

7. sound of an orange: MacDonald, p. 238

8. "wracking my brains": Emerick, Geoff and Massey Howard, *Here, There and Everywhere: My Life Recording the Music of the Beatles* (Avery/ Penguin Random House, 2007) p. 189

9. "the same thing once": Miles, p. 482

10. close-miced: Emerick, Geoff and Massey Howard, *Here, There and Everywhere: My Life Recording the Music of the Beatles* (Avery/Penguin Random House, 2007) p. 127

11. Allen Toussaint: "Southern Nights," performed by songwriter Allen Toussaint. Video on YouTube

12. piano into a sandbox: Wilson, Brian, *Wouldn't It Be Nice* (Harper Collins, 1991) p. 161

13. Yardley London to sponsor: blurb above print advertisement for Yardley Slicker lipsticks: "You'll say 'Thank you, Yardley,' when you watch The Monkees on NBC-TV every Monday night at 7:30."

14. "fuzz" distortion: Babiuk, Andy, *Beatles Gear* (Backbeat/Hal Leonard, 2015) p. 161, p. 322, p. 342

15. "Fractured Sound": Babiuk, Andy, ibid p. 342

Chapter VIII: Brian Epstein Cried, and Lucy Would Be in the Sky With Her Eyes, Scattered Diamonds

1. "juvenile psychologists": Davies, p. 340

2. Brian Epstein cried: Turner, Steve, *Beatles '66: The Revolutionary Year* (Ecco/Harper Collins, 2016) p. 211

3. "What do I do now": Davies, p. 211

4. flowers and a note: Miles, p. 562

5. "producing the album": Paul McCartney in 2012 BBC/Arena documentary, *Produced by George Martin*

6. "he's still the keeny": Davies, p. 274

7. "were a little model": Turner, Steve, *Beatles '66: The Revolutionary Year* (Ecco/Harper Collins, 2016) p. 309

8. "Forget the inmates": Paul McCartney in 2012 BBC/Arena documentary, *Produced by George Martin*

9. insisted ... poetry was impersonal: Essay, Eliot, T.S., *The Sacred Wood* (Dover, 1998) pp. 30-32. Eliot writes that what the poet experiences "is the continual surrender of himself as he is at the moment to something more valuable. The progress of an artist is a continual extinction of personality."

10. "about my identity": Print advertisement for Yardley Slicker lipsticks

11. photo triptych: The photographs for the Beatles 1966 "triptych" are searchable online

12. inspired by "floral clocks": Miles, p. 305

13. any subliminal words: (Author's note: An interesting thing about the cover is that it is possible to glimpse "LOVE" subliminally across the front of the group's uniforms, and another word on the back cover. On the cover, Paul's chest trim, elbow angles and instrument all vaguely suggest a V, Ringo's swag of trim along with the curve of his shoulders suggest an O, George's chest trim is more obviously an E. John's swag trim and bell of the horn only vaguely suggest an L; but it doesn't have to do much because the mind interpolates L based on the other suggestion of letters. On the back cover, George again has E, Paul's trim on the back of his uniform is a V, John's strip of black undershirt suggests an I, and Ringo suggests L with the opening of his jacket

forming a long vertical line. Note that the shadow under Paul's right elbow has been retouched so as not to interfere with the vertical line of John's black undershirt, which also looks retouched.)

14. "Let's not be ourselves": Article, Gilmore, Mikal, "Inside the Making of Sgt. Pepper," *Rolling Stone* Magazine, June 1, 2017. Also see Note 26 to Chapter Six.

15. "He would go off and write ten songs": Video on YouTube, *John Lennon Interview: Lennon at His Most Candid – "I don't know how much of this I wanna put out!"* Audio only.

16. hands of the same Beatles: Whiteley, Sheila, *The Space Between the Notes: Rock and the Counterculture* (Routledge, 1992) pp. 40-41

17. Morris Carstairs gave: Carstairs, G.M., *This Island Now: The 1962 Reith Lectures* (First published by Hogarth Press, 1963/Published by Penguin Books, 1964) Reith lectures are juried and sponsored by the BBC.

18. multimedia shows with: Goffman, Ken and Joy, Dan, *Counterculture Through the Ages* (Villard, 2004) p. 264

19. stylized mallets … It would do: Davies, Hunter, *The Beatles* (W.W. Norton & Company, 1968) p. 270

20. construction analogy … self-identity: See Note 11 to Chapter Two for this analogy given at the Macy Conference on LSD-25 pp. 49-50 also p. 80. Also see the "de-patterning" experiments conducted by Dr. Ewen Cameron, President of the Canadian, American, and World Psychiatric Associations as described in Lee, Martin and Shlain, Bruce, *Acid Dreams: The Complete Social History of LSD, the CIA, the Sixties, and Beyond* (Grove Press, 1985) p. 23

21. "buy, buy": Whiteley, Sheila, *The Space Between the Notes: Rock and the Counterculture* (Routledge, 1992) p. 49

22. "can write this crap too": Turner, Steve, *Beatles '66: The Revolutionary Year* (Ecco/Harper Collins, 2016) p. 191

23. "swirly music": Emerick, Geoff and Massey Howard, *Here, There and Everywhere: My Life Recording the Music of the Beatles* (Avery/Penguin Random House, 2007) p. 167

24. "hate figure … to love her": MacDonald, p. 239

25. "At Doris Day's house": *Rolling Stone* Collector's Edition, *John Lennon: The Ultimate Guide to His Life, Music & Legend* (Rolling Stone/Time Inc. 2018) p. 28

26. "like millions of other": Monogram, *Apologia for Timothy Leary* (Fitz Hugh Ludlow Memorial Library, 1974) p. 27

27. supported by siblings: Lee, Martin and Shlain, Bruce, *Acid Dreams: The Complete Social History of LSD, the CIA, the Sixties, and Beyond* (Grove Press, 1985) p. 97 Robin and Peggy Hitchcock, heirs to the Gulf Oil and Mellon fortune, gave the 64-room mansion set in 4,000 acres over for use by Leary and a group of approximately thirty men and women, "including many acid veterans from the early days at Harvard" in 1963.

28. "give LSD to every teenager": Harman interviewed in *Beyond the Mechanical Mind* (Australian Broadcasting Commission, 1976). See Excerpt in Appendices.

29. "anyone this time around": 1970, Timothy Leary spoken word, accompanied by musicians Stephen Stills, Jimi Hendrix, and others. Produced by Michael Callahan and Gerd Stern of Intermedia System Corporation. Intermedia handled some administrative and technical details for Woodstock festival. Gerd Stern was brought to Harvard by George Litwin, a management and organizational systems theorist.

30. Paul A. Rothchild … emerging: Article, Davis, Christina, "Archive of the Mouth: Tracing Baez, Plath, Sun Ra, Sexton, Et Al. Back to a Single Pivotal Recording Studio" from *Stylus* magazine published on the Harvard Woodbury Poetry Room website May 2, 2017: "Tom Rush, '63, had the unique experience of recording with Steve. In a recent email exchange, Rush recalled his experiences with Fassett very enthusiastically:

"I remember Steve—I recorded my second album, my first for a 'real' label, Prestige. Paul Rothchild was the producer and we did it in Steve's home studio on Beacon Hill … The one wire ran down the stairs to the kitchen where it plugged directly into the tape recorder, an Ampex 601." – (Author's note: The first model of the Ampex reel-to-reel tape recorder was co-designed by audio engineer Myron Stolaroff, who was at Harvard. Paul Rothchild subsequently left Harvard for Los Angeles and produced the band The Doors. In 1960 engineer Stolaroff founded the International Foundation for Advanced Studies (IFAS) at Stanford, and conducted LSD-and-creativity testing of over 300 subjects.)

31. "sharing old folk songs was part of the culture": Davis, Christina, *Stylus* magazine article, ibid. "Harvard professor and pioneering ballad collector Francis James Child (who aggregated and transcribed over 300 ballads in the 1880s) has often been cited by Eric Von Schmidt and Joan Baez as one of the early print resources for the ballads they performed.

"But the second step in that transmission was through discs themselves, when field recordings (and commercial records) began to be made of these songs in the late 1920s/early 1930s. Von Schmidt—like Pete Seeger before him—had benefited immensely from immersing himself in the extensive folk music collection housed at the Library of Congress. It's possible that with his arrival in Cambridge in 1958, he encouraged others to do so in their own nearby libraries and record stores. 'Digging up and sharing old folk songs was an essential part of the Cambridge scene. The more obscure the song, the better.'

"Whether the (Harvard) Poetry Room played a local Library-of-Congress-style role in this additional dimension of transmission is uncertain …. From the late Fifties throughout the Sixties, music and poetry recordings 'continued in earnest' at Harvard with recordings by Joan Baez, Ted Hughes, Sylvia Plath, Anne Sexton, Denise Levertov, Robert Lowell, Yvegeny Yevtushenko, Allen Ginsberg, Robert Creeley, Louis Zukofsky, Jean Valentine, Stephen Jonas and Audre Lorde, among many others."

32. correspondence with John Sweeney … great couple of young ones": Davis, Christina, *Stylus* magazine article, ibid.

33. "who can simply": Whiteley, Sheila, *The Space Between the Notes: Rock and the Counterculture* (Routledge, 1992) p. 53

34. "this normal thing": *Rolling Stone* Collector's Edition, *John Lennon: The Ultimate Guide to His Life, Music & Legend* (Rolling Stone/Time Inc. 2018) p. 51

35. "anti-Christ": "They're completely anti-Christ. I mean, I'm anti-Christ as well, but they're so anti-Christ they shock me, which isn't an easy thing." *Saturday Evening Post* August 8, 1964

36. "stand things on their head": Miles, pp. 544-545: "Paradoxical thinking is part of the game in our art," Paul explained. "Rock 'n' roll specializes in that kind of, 'This guy's a twerp. We've gotta have him on our team!' In rock 'n' roll you often stand things on their head."

37. "Foreshadowing the … okay": Hertsgaard, Mark, *A Day In The Life: The Music and Artistry of The Beatles* (Delacorte Press, 1995) p. 220

38. for Kellogg's Corn Flakes: MacDonald, p. 235

39. "Meet the Wife": MacDonald, p. 235

40. has the same interpretation): Whiteley, Sheila, *The Space Between the Notes: Rock and the Counterculture* (Routledge, 1992) p. 57

41. gradually become huge: Hertsgaard, Mark, *A Day In The Life: The Music and Artistry of The Beatles* (Delacorte Press, 1995) p. 7

42. "tragedy of the verses … E major chord": MacDonald, p. 230

43. "bit of a 2001": *Rolling Stone* Collector's Edition, *John Lennon: The Ultimate Guide to His Life, Music & Legend* (Rolling Stone/Time Inc. 2018), p. 15

44. "mushroom cloud": Hertsgaard, Mark, *A Day In The Life: The Music and Artistry of The Beatles* (Delacorte Press, 1995) p. 9

45. "fraudulent": Goldstein, Richard, *New York Times* review

46. "expression of their inner life": Kandinsky, Wassily, *Concerning the Spiritual in Art* (Dover Publications, 1977) p. vii

47. "international scope": Stratton, Richard in Introduction to *Concerning the Spiritual in Art*, ibid p. vii

48. "Messianic message": Author interview with publisher Alison Kennedy, Berkeley, California 2019

49. It was a Vedic or Jungian idea: *The Practice of Psychotherapy/The Collected Works of C.G. Jung*, Volume 16, Herbert Read, Gerhard Adler, et al., Editors (Princeton University Press, 1966) pp. 101-102. Jung writes about ego-loss in analysis as being similar to ego-loss in Vedic disciplines.

50. "it's too intense": Sidney Cohen at the "LSD Reunion Party." See Excerpt in Appendices.

Chapter IX: I Am the Walrus, Strawberry Fields Forever and "the Culture"

1. "indoor plumbing system": Timothy Leary at the "LSD Reunion Party." See Excerpt in Appendices.

2. "Strawberry Fields Forever" in an apartment: Turner, Steve, *Beatles '66: The Revolutionary Year* (Ecco/Harper Collins, 2016) p. 332

3. "psychoanalysis set to music": Turner, Steve, ibid, p. 333

4. "There wasn't any conscious…": Paul as quoted in *Mojo* magazine, November 1995, as reprinted in MacDonald, ibid p. 215, footnote.

5. was initially titled: Turner, ibid, pp. 333-334 states that when John initially wrote the song, its provisional title was "Not Too Bad," that the song was "a description of confusion that effectively used disjointed thinking to make its point… At this stage, there was no mention of Strawberry Fields in either the title or the lyric."

6. for Paul his "feels": Wilson, Brian, *Wouldn't It Be Nice* (Harper Collins, 1991) Paul McCartney visited Wilson in April 1967 during the time Wilson was working on *Smile*. p. 164

7. financed IT magazine: Turner, Steve, *Beatles '66: The Revolutionary Year* (Ecco/Harper Collins, 2016) pp. 330-331

8. 400 million people: Epstein, Brian, *A Cellarful of Noise* (Pocket Books/ Simon & Shuster, 1967) p. 6

9. idea was "Three Blind Mice": Goldman, Albert, *The Lives of John Lennon* (William Morrow and Company, 1988) p. 47

10. "I suppose we'd": Hertsgaard, p. 224

11. "doing little bits": MacDonald, p. 111

12. "boring people doing boring": MacDonald, p. 239

13. "the nitty gritty": *Rolling Stone* Collector's Edition, *John Lennon: The Ultimate Guide to His Life, Music & Legend* (Rolling Stone/Time Inc. 2018) p. 74

14. "granny music": Emerick, p. 246

15. his own insecurities: Emerick, p. 99

16. "feel as if I wrote it": Hertsgaard, p. 267

17. Puffed Wheat … shot from guns: television advertisements for Quaker Puffed Wheat and Quaker Puffed Rice are on YouTube

18. died just a few days before: Emerick, pp. 211-214

19. would hold orgies: Article, Adams, Guy, "So What Did Max Clifford Witness at Diana Dors' Libidinous Parties?" *Daily Mail* March 28, 2014

20. a play John tried to write: Miles, p. 39

21. "had the whole run of the top floor": Miles, p. 39

22. "Frog-Pondians": Article, Ulin, David L. "Looking Back at Edgar Allen Poe on the Anniversary of His Death" *Los Angeles Times* October 7, 2014

23. emptiness on their faces: Emerick, ibid, p. 214

24. in 1969 homosexuality: MacDonald, p. 268, footnote

25. often used circus: Turner, Steve, *Beatles '66: The Revolutionary Year* (Ecco/Harper Collins, 2016) p. 177

26. first Beatles album to … less critical adulation: Miles, p. 368

27. "to recover his enthusiasm": MacDonald, p. 237

28. real shops along the lane: Miles, p. 307

29. cultural leaders: Article, "Beatles Lead Now," *The Beatles Book, The Beatles' Own Monthly Magazine* May 1968, No. 58 p. 25

30. transcending the ego is in Jung's: *The Practice of Psychotherapy/The Collected Works of C.G. Jung*, Volume 16, Herbert Read, Gerhard Adler, et al., Editors (Princeton University Press, 1966) pp. 101-102, p. 292

31. "sucking us to death": *Rolling Stone* Collector's Edition, *John Lennon*, ibid p. 38

32. "not capable of it": *Rolling Stone* Collector's Edition, *John Lennon*, ibid p. 38

Chapter X: In My Ears and In My Eyes: Beatles on Film

1. along with Altamont: information from *Rolling Stone*, January 21ˢᵗ 1970 issue, Article, "The Rolling Stones Disaster at Altamont: Let It Bleed" Eleven contributing writers. The free concert was held at Altamont Speedway in Northern California, due east of the Bay Area, on December 6, 1969. The Grateful Dead "were prime organizers, but didn't even get to play" because the violence got out of hand. One man was stabbed to death in front of the stage after he drew a revolver, two people died from hit-and-run car accidents, and one person drowned on LSD in an irrigation ditch. There were scores of injuries, numerous cars stolen and abandoned, and property damage.

2. "back to the madness": Cott, Jonathan, *Days That I'll Remember: Spending Time with John Lennon and Yoko Ono* (Doubleday, 2013) p. 119

3. 40 film scripts: *The Beatles Book, The Beatles' Own Monthly Magazine* May 1968, No. 58 p. 21

4. Naked Lunch also made: The 1959 novel was banned in Boston in 1962. A Los Angeles court cleared it of obscenity charges in 1965 and the Massachusetts Supreme Court reversed the Boston court decision in 1966.

5. "louder, further, longer": Hertsgaard, p. 167

6. choice of lyrics was "random": MacDonald, p. 262

7. in an elegant Edwardian garden: O'Dell, Denis with Bob Neaverson, *At The Apple's Core: The Beatles From the Inside* (Peter Owen Ltd. Publishers, 2002) p. 118

8. a friend of Paul's: Goffman, Ken and Joy, Dan, *Counterculture Through the Ages* (Villard, 2004) p. 262 states that Ginsberg met Paul in 1965. Ginsberg was a close friend of William Burroughs, and also Timothy Leary; he met Leary at Harvard and the two traveled together giving LSD to influencers. Ginsberg and Paul were introduced in May 1965, when Ginsberg accompanied Harvard singer Joan Baez and singer Bob Dylan on a tour through England.

9. fractured head: Davies, p. 235 calls it a "clock-face"

10. madman's cap: MacDonald, p. 268, footnote 2

11. Blow Up: *Blow Up*, released December 18, 1966 (USA) directed by Michelangelo Antonioni

12. were pedophiles: The pedophilia of the Beats is supported by anecdotal evidence. Timothy Leary, friend to William Burroughs and Allen Ginsberg, said to the author in the early Nineties, "I always

wondered why my friends were raving about Morocco; I didn't know it was because of the sex." In the mid-Nineties, Ginsberg was featured in a photograph on the cover of the NAMBLA (North American Man Boy Love Association) Newsletter, speaking at its annual picnic.

13. "blatant rubbish": Davies, pp. 235-236

14. avoid critiquing: Probably understandably, I found only partial description and no critique of *Magical Mystery Tour* in the Miles, Norman, and Davies biographies.

15. most expensive animated: O'Dell, Denis with Bob Neaverson, *At The Apple's Core: The Beatles From the Inside* (Peter Owen Ltd. Publishers, 2002) pp. 84-85

16. "material" emerges: Macy LSD-25 Conference ibid. Sandison observed of mental patients given LSD: "most of these patients produce a good deal of material, but which fails to integrate, and the results were poor." p. 13

17. inspired by: Frederich Schroder-Sonnenstern's artwork is viewable online.

18. "character armor": Article, Elkin, David, "Wilhelm Reich: The Psychoanalyst As Revolutionary" New York Times, April 18, 1971

19. Reich: Reich, Wilhelm *Funktion des Orgasmus*, 1927 published in English in 1946. *Massenpsychologie des Faschismus*, 1933, published in English in 1946. Reich left Germany to escape the Nazis. Also see Elkin, David, "Wilhelm Reich: The Psychoanalyst As Revolutionary," *New York Times* April 18, 1971. Elkin notes that in the 1968 student uprising in Berlin, students threw Reich's books at police, that Reich was popular with the Beats, and seems to be popular now with youth.

20. "genital character": Wilhemreich.gr site

21. Hermes: Information on Hermes and Iris from Burkert, Walter, *Greek Religion* (Harvard University Press, 1985)

22. leader in personality research: Books on Harry Murray's life and research at Harvard include Robinson, Forrest, *Love's Story Told: A Life of Henry A Murray* (Harvard University Press, 1992) and Douglas, Claire, *Translate This Darkness: The Life of Christiana Morgan* (Simon & Schuster, 1993).

23. "a new superego": Robinson, Forrest, ibid p. 267

24. "by scientists like me": Robinson, Forrest, ibid p. 267

25. "Satanic Christ": Douglas, Claire, ibid p. 172. Synthesis of antithetical ideas: Robinson, Forrest, ibid pp. 379-380. As a new religion: Robinson, Forrest, ibid p. 170

26. a disappointment: Davies, ibid p. 236
27. rented to universities: O'Dell, ibid p. 72

Chapter XI: And I See You Again ... Francie and *The Beatles* (Blank Asylum Walls)

1. "history and synthesis": Wenner, Jann, review, *Rolling Stone* December 21, 1968
2. "best abilities and worst": *Time* Magazine review, December 1968
3. "their most consistent": Article, Christgau, Robert, "Living Without The Beatles" *The Village Voice* September 1971.
4. "Please, lock me away": Miles, p. 111-112 "The funny first line always used to please John."
5. used by researchers: Macy Conference on LSD-25, p. 39, p. 207; definition on p. 152
6. Beatles set up Apple Corps: Information on Apple from Miles, pp. 440-446
7. "'underground' company above ground": Miles, p. 441
8. "make it come true": McNab, Ken, *And In the End: The Last Days of the Beatles* (Polygon, 2019) p. 11
9. Apple Electronics ... loudpaper: Miles, p. 443
10. Beatles Lead Now ... pig-headedness ... go to waste": Article, "The Beatles Lead Now" *The Beatles Book, The Beatles' Own Monthly Magazine* May 1968, No. 58 p. 25
11. make your: "Make Your Own Kind of Music," Cass Elliot, released 1969 on Dunhill Records
12. three million pounds: Miles, p. 440
13. had gotten out of jail: Miles, pp. 464
14. "There were a lot of ideas ... and be Beatles": Babiuk, Andy, *Beatles Gear* (Backbeat/Hal Leonard, 2015) p. 428
15. "our first Four": The singles were "Hey Jude," "Those Were the Days," "Thingumybob" and "Sour Milk Sea." O'Dell, Denis, ibid p. 130
16. "to enjoy ourselves": Stone, Robert, *Prime Green: Remembering the Sixties* (Ecco/Harper Collins, 2007) pp. 174-175
17. "There were hoarse whispers": Stone, Robert, ibid p. 174
18. "don't fear them": Miles, p. 476
19. "Apple to run": Miles, p. 479
20. still hallucinating: Schwartz, Francie, *Body Count* (Selfpub.com, 1999) pp. 56-63

21. "I have a psychedelic personality ... lose your hair": Schwartz, ibid p. 64

22. "dramatic theory": Schwartz, ibid p. 71

23. "girls from New York": Norman, p. 316, quoting Barry Miles.

24. fathom the trends: Frank, Thomas, *The Conquest of Cool: Business Culture, Counterculture, and the Rise of Hip Consumerism* (University of Chicago Press, 1997) p. 107

25. hiring younger: Frank, ibid, p. 111 "By 1968, the notion that only rebellious young people could make good copywriters and art directors was so prevalent that..."

26. "New Renaissance Empire": Schwartz, ibid p. 55

27. John and Yoko lived: Schwartz, ibid p. 85

28. "for who knows": Schwartz, ibid p. 85

29. Yoko's "sweetness": Schwartz, ibid p. 76

30. "touch of a velvet hand": Lennon, Neil Aspinall, and Derek Taylor reportedly thought up the "velvet hand" lyric inspired by a fetishist they had met. – from BeatlesBible.com

31. "on his hobnail boots": a U.K. newspaper reported the arrest of a man who had put mirrors on his shoes to look up women's skirts at football matches. – from BeatlesBible.com

32. Stun guns were in the news: Article, Engber, Daniel, "Who Made That Stun Gun?" *New York Times*, May 9, 2014. According to Engber, stun guns were discussed in the media in the mid-Sixties as nonlethal crowd control.

33. gun owner's publication: Miles, p. 496

34. Schultz's then-popular book: *Happiness is a Warm Puppy* by Charles Schultz was first published in 1962.

35. ECT works along the same: Article, Engber, Daniel, "Who Made That Stun Gun?" *New York Times*, May 9, 2014. Also see Wikipedia entry for history of electroshock weapon: "Electroshock weapons are a relative of cattle prods, which have been around for over 100 years and are the precursor of stun guns ... Essential to the operation of electroshock, stun guns, and cattle prods is sufficient current to allow the weapon to stun."

36. wrote this song in October 1968: Miles, p. 498

37. John "liked his cornflakes": Norman, p. 335

38. "being a good Beatle": *The Beatles Book, The Beatles' Own Monthly Magazine* November 1966, #40 p. 19

39. "on their head": Miles, p. 545

40. Saint Lucia: McBrien, Richard P., *Lives of the Saints* (Harper San Francisco, 2001) pp. 501-502

41. a large grain shipment: ThePracticingCatholic.com

42. a Catholic: Miles, p. 4

43. "in control of it all": Miles, p. 383

44. "never work between meals": Koestler, Arthur, *The Act of Creation* (Hutchinson & Co., 1964) "The homey, admonitory structure lulls the mind into bored acquiescence until the preposterous subterfuge is discovered. Oscar Wilde was a master of this form." p. 79

45. "nervous energy": Schwartz, ibid p. 89

46. "so many minds": Schwartz, ibid p. 79

47. "a spiral slide": MacDonald, p. 298

48. raucous as possible: Miles, pp. 487-488

49. "we would rap": Schwartz, ibid p. 79

50. too alike: Schwartz, ibid p. 85

51. consume bonbons: MacDonald, p. 321

52. "smiley masks": Norman, p. 349: "The result, for the most part, are songs in smiley masks ... only in "Blackbird" does his talent fully show its glossy wings and golden beak ..."

53. "Polythene Pam" was originally planned: MacDonald, p. 364

54. who were "taken back": Macy Conference on LSD-25, p. 49

55. "cathartic" nightmare: Fitzgerald, F. Scott, *The Crack Up*, first published in *Esquire* magazine. "I slept on the heart side now because I knew the sooner I could tire that out, even a little, the sooner would come that blessed hour of nightmare, which, like a catharsis, would enable me to better meet the new day."

56. easily influenced: John Dunbar as quoted by Neil Aspinall in Whiteley, ibid p. 44

57. "went on around him": Schwartz, ibid p. 84

58. "like I'm *him* ... on the floor": Schwartz, ibid p. 84

59. "treated rotten": Schwartz, ibid p. 87

60. "desperate curiosity": Schwartz, ibid p. 85

61. "the power you have ... blanks": Schwartz, ibid p. 84

62. "couldn't even define": Schwartz, ibid p. 85

63. "two Paul McCartney's": this string of quotes is excerpted from Devlin, Mark, *Musical Truth Volume 1* (aSys Publishing, 2016) pp. 97-98

64. "new social aristocracy": 2004 BBC Documentary, *Why I Hate the Sixties*

65. fusion of opposites ... a project undertaken: Douglas, Claire, *Translate This Darkness: The Life of Christiana Morgan* (Simon & Schuster, 1993) p. 172 and Robinson, ibid, pp. 379-380. Morgan saw it as a fusion, while Murray preferred to think of it as a synthesis.

66. sister "Harrie" also met Paul: Schwartz, ibid p. 76

Chapter XII: Nowhere to Go: Abbey Road Scraps, Patron Saint of Mental Hospitals, and That Magic Feeling

1. Apple was sinking: McNab, Ken, *And In the End: The Last Days of the Beatles* (Polygon, 2019) p. 4-5

2. clothing label ... shoplifting: Miles pp. 444-446

3. The opening exhibit: *Eye and Brain: The Psychology of Seeing* Gregory, Richard L. (Weidenfeld & Nicholson, London, 1966)

4. wears many hats: Turner, Steve, *Beatles '66: The Revolutionary Year* (Ecco/Harper Collins, 2016) p. 97 and Wikipedia entry on Eduardo Paolozzi. Examples of Paolozzi's art are found online including on Sir Paul McCartney's website.

5. old friend: Seymour-Jones, Carole, *Painted Shadow* (Doubleday, 2002) p. 337

6. Jungian authority: *The Collected Works of C.G. Jung, Vol 1* (Bollingen Series, Princeton University Press, 1959) Sir Herbert Read, Michael Fordham and Gerhard Adler, Editors

7. Gerhard Adler ... Lou Adler: an IMBD entry for Nathan Adler lists his relations including Lou Adler, Stella Adler, Albert Alder, and Stephen Spielberg.

8. Aaron Copland wrote: Copland, Aaron, *What To Listen For In Music* (Mentor/New American Library/McGraw-Hill, 1939/1957) p. 55: "The harmonic revolution of the first half of the twentieth century is now definitely at an end." Copland re-affirmed that "the prime consideration in all form is the creation of a sense of the long line ... (to) give us a sense of direction ... whatever the means employed, the net result must produce in the listener a satisfying feeling of coherence born out of the psychological necessity of the musical ideas with which the composer began." p. 77

9. "You're always right ... brought scorn": Miles, p. 480

10. five full-time script readers: O'Dell, Denis, ibid p. 116

11. "wish that weren't true": O'Dell, Denis ibid p. 157

12. losing money: McNab, Ken, ibid pp. 4-5. Also see O'Dell, ibid pp. 156-157.

13. "failed miserably": O'Dell, ibid p. 157

14. comforting feeling: Article, Pareles, Jon, "The Beatles' 'Sgt. Pepper's Lonely Hearts Club Band' at 50: Still Full of Joy and Whimsy," *New York Times* May 30, 2017

15. *Le Jeu de Mourre*: Miles, p. 440

16. "anyone over thirty": This quote is attributed variously to Jack Weinburg, Abbie Hoffman and Jerry Rubin.

17. gave Paul the means to frame: Jones, Maxwell, *Social Psychiatry In Practice: The Idea of the Therapeutic Community* (Penguin, 1968)

18. "spooked" her: Schwartz, ibid p. 90

19. drive to John's: Miles, p. 465

20. scrawled "Hey Jude": Schwartz, ibid p. 90

21. Saint Jude: McBrien, Richard P., *Lives of the Saints* (Harper San Francisco, 2001) pp. 441-442

22. Kurt Lewin's Field theory: "Lewin (1947) believed that in order to make sense of the world, we should see our present situation–the status quo–as being maintained by certain conditions or forces. An approach to understanding group behaviour by trying to map out the totality and complexity of the field in which the behaviour takes place. It is one of the four elements of Lewin's planned approach to change. (Burnes, 2009). See also Burnes, Bernard and Cooke, Bill, "Kurt Lewin's Field Theory: A Review and Re-evaluation," International Journal of Management Reviews, 2013: "Field theory is a psychological theory (more precisely: Topological and vector psychology) which examines patterns of interaction between the individual and the total field, or environment. The concept first made its appearance in psychology with roots to the holistic perspective of Gestalt theories. It was developed by Kurt Lewin, a Gestalt psychologist, in the 1940s. "Lewin's field theory can be expressed by a formula: $B = f(p,e)$, meaning that behavior (B) is a function of the person (p) and their environment (e)." Kurt Lewin's books include A Dynamic Theory of Personality (McGraw-Hill, 1935), Principles of Topological Psychology (McGraw-Hill, 1936), The Conceptual Representation and Measurement of Psychological Forces (Duke University Press, 1938) and Field Theory in Social Science (Harper, 1951).

23. Lewin was a favorite: Robinson, Forrest, ibid p. 218: Just after Christmas in 1936, Harry Murray was host at Harvard Psychological Clinic to "a gathering of prominent American and European psychologists at a

conference honoring Kurt Lewin." Also see Robinson, Forrest, ibid p. 221: Murray "was influenced by Lewin's views on the psychological environment or 'field.'"

24. "Cary Grant on heat": Miles, p. 466 (Incidentally, actor Cary Grant was given LSD many times by therapist Oscar Janiger. Janiger's cousin was poet Allen Ginsberg.)

25. "Jude" reassures: MacDonald concurs, p. 304

26. *femme inspiratrice*: Douglas, Claire, ibid pp. 150-152

27. "I'd always been secretly glad": Schwartz, p. 115

28. "simply loathed" it: McNab, Ken *And In the End: The Last Days of the Beatles* (Polygon, 2019) p. 6

29. "If any single recording": MacDonald, p. 357

30. pioneered group therapy: Jones, Maxwell, *The Therapeutic Community: A New Treatment Method in Psychiatry* (Basic Books, Inc. 1953) Foreword by Goodwin Watson. First published by Tavistock Publications in 1952. Discusses group therapy for repatriating solders and "chronically unemployed neurotics."

31. "Although the public in general ... himself": ibid, pp. 44-45. Jones references Star, Shirley A., "The Place of Psychiatry in Popular Thinking," a paper presented to the meeting of the American Association for Public Opinion Research, Washington DC, May 1957

32. an experiment led by: Jones, Maxwell, *Social Psychiatry In Practice: The Idea of the Therapeutic Community* (Penguin, 1968, Foreword by G.M. Carstairs) p. 47-50. On p. 50 Jones states that E. and J. Cummings' community experiment in mental illness education was published as Closed Ranks by Harvard University Press in 1957.

33. "an outstanding failure ... its own defenses": Jones, *Social Psychiatry in Practice* ibid p. 49

34. protect entire communities: In the Foreword to Jones's *The Therapeutic Community* (1953) ibid p. x, Goodwin Watson writes that perhaps out of Jones's work, "'psychosanitation' will emerge, and social psychiatrists will normally protect entire communities from ways of life which are emotionally crippling, much as public health officers now save cities from epidemics caused by bacteria."

35. "in *that* direction": Jones, *Social Psychiatry in Practice* ibid p. 47

36. 'kills" the head: MacDonald, p. 192 describes the hippie philosophy.

37. global individual: Harry Murray to Lewis Mumford, Robinson, Forrest, ibid pp. 266-267. Also see Robinson, ibid p. 287, Murray to

Mumford: "The kind of behavior that is required ... involves transfor-
mations of personality ... one transformation being that of National
Man into World Man."

38. "known anyone who had been helped": Jones, Maxwell, *Social Psychiatry
in Practice*, ibid p. 45

39. "more tolerant of deviant behavior": Jones, Maxwell, *Social Psychiatry
in Practice*, ibid p. 53

40. to kill the ego: Goldman, Albert, *The Lives of John Lennon* (William
Morrow and Company, 1988) p. 248; see also McNab, "Lennon's abandonment of his own sense of self," p. 17; and Miles, "systematically
destroying his ego with LSD" p. 542

41. helped him with the lyrics: McNab, Ken, ibid p. 94

42. compressor ... Moog: Emerick p. 283

43. T.S. Eliot's observation: Essay, Eliot, T.S., *Phillip Massinger* (1920)

44. "self-debunking": MacDonald, p. 373

45. "meaningful couplet": Miles, p. 558

46. foam ... manicured lawn: Doyle, Tom, *Man on the Run: Paul McCartney
in the 1970s* (Ballantine, 2013) p. 179

47. feeling which leads to action: Ian MacDonald comments that "The
Beatles *felt* their way through life." MacDonald, p. 22

48. "I still can't hear it ... to himself": Schwartz, p. 90

49. "Life is a game": The Beatles Book, *The Beatles' Own Monthly Magazine*
November 1966, No. 40 p. 7

50. "evisceration of": Author interview with Alison Kennedy, Berkeley,
California 2019. Kennedy went on to be co-founder and publisher of
Mondo 2000 magazine.

Chapter XIII: How To Conclude? Reconciliation Songs

1. "trying to say nice things": Cott, Jonathan, *Days That I'll Remember:
Spending Time with John Lennon and Yoko Ono* (Doubleday, 2013)
p.76-77

2. fourteen weeks off: Referring to MacDonald's dates for when the
Beatles were out of the studio, October 15th to January 21st, I count
fourteen weeks. The Beatles began the "Get Back" sessions on January
22nd, 1969. Miles writes that it was "eleven weeks respite" (Miles,
p. 529) so perhaps he subtracted days that the Beatles were working on recording non-Beatles-related projects to arrive at that figure.
MacDonald states they were in the studio working on "What's the

New Mary Jane" for one day in November, but the song did not make it onto the White Album.

3. working title: McNab, Ken, *And In the End: The Last Days of the Beatles* (Polygon, 2019) pp. 3-4

4. "honest" album: Norman, pp. 362-363

5. idea to film: Miles, pp. 529-530

6. Yoko refused: Norman, p. 357

7. "as assistants": Miles, p. 531

8. advance *her* career: Miles, p. 531

9. amphitheatre in the Tunisian desert: McNab, ibid p.9

10. "an asylum": MacDonald, p. 329: "I'm warming to doing it in an asylum." McNab, ibid p. 9: "I'm warming to the idea of an asylum." Goldman, p. 323: "I'm warming to the idea of asylum."

11. "To see what is there": Session dated January 2, 1969 on YouTube

12. "take sixty-seven": Miles, p. 534

13. made up on the spot: BeatlesBible.com

14. half-trance state: Miles, p. 467

15. he found it dreadful: McNab, Ken, ibid p. 3

16. differing accounts: "Nine sharp" according to Norman, p. 358

17. let it happen: Norman, p. 363, "Paul gave up all attempts to maintain discipline and focus and went along with the others."

18. written in 1968: Miles, p. 539

19. "preserve the myth": *Rolling Stone* Collector's Edition, *John Lennon: The Ultimate Guide to His Life, Music & Legend* (Rolling Stone/Time Inc. 2018) p. 34

20. "shittiest load" *Rolling Stone*, ibid, p. 33

21. a quest Jung wrote about: *Ailon: Vol II of Collected Writings of C.G. Jung* Herbert Read, Gerhard Adler, et al., Editors (Penguin, 1967) p. 158

22. Harvardians … interested … creativity: Douglas, Claire, *Translate this Darkness: The Life of Christiana Morgan* (Simon & Schuster, 1993) p. 285. Morgan, Murray's colleague at Harvard, in a 1958 letter writes of student-subjects that "offer themselves for our experiments." This was the period of time when Murray and "an anonymous lawyer" performed interrogation experiments on student volunteers such as mathematician Ted Kaczynski. Morgan in this letter also mentions "the myth of static matter" and that she felt her revised Thematic Apperception (TAT) cards would be helpful in "testing not only creativity, but also whether or not a patient had the capacity for introspection and was ready to

withstand probing into archetypal depths." Two years later Timothy Leary would arrive at Harvard, and after giving LSD to Henry Murray and Arthur Koestler would begin administering LSD to students.

23. they decayed: Blurb for Cohen, Sidney and Albert, Richard, *LSD* (New American Library, 1966)

24. "subjective feeling … to perspire": documentary short, *Why People Take LSD*. Sidney Cohen: "We gave a series of fifty tests to people …. We found at the end of six months, that they were no more creative when we measured them, than they were from before they took LSD. However, their inner feeling, subjective feeling of creativity, was there. This means, perhaps, that they may have an impression of creativity but not creativity itself. Creativity is ninety percent perspiration and ten percent inspiration. And LSD doesn't enhance one's desire to perspire."

25. I counted over forty: List of "Get Back" session songs from BeatlesBible.com

26. both entertainment lawyers: Miles, p. 545

27. "to our basics … leaving the group": Miles, p. 561

28. "coloured a little": Miles, p. 561

29. "eating" it: MacDonald, p. 144

30. Paul then got dibs: Miles, p. 574

31. Paul wondered: Miles, p. 569

32. "That was a bit near!": Miles, p. 570

33. "out of each other's pockets": Miles, pp. 582 quoting Paul.

34. brick-throwing: Goldman, Albert, *The Lives of John Lennon* (William Morrow and Company, 1988) p. 395

35. "all the classic": Miles, p. 568

36. "about *ourselves*, you see": *Rolling Stone* Collector's Edition, ibid p. 67

37. "to the madness": Cott, p. 119

38. whom George Harrison invited: O'Dell, p. 150

39. "1968 yearbook": MacDonald, p. 332

40. "You come out of … all looking for, actually": *Rolling Stone* Collector's Edition, ibid, p. 13

41. "great source": Wilson, Brian, *Wouldn't It Be Nice* (Harper Collins, 1991) p. 192. "Listening to (Elton John's) songs, I knew he was hot, that he was tapped into the great source. I'd been there myself."

42. spiritual Gnosis: Jung, C.J. *Aiion*, ibid p. 158

43. "less deferential society": Salman Rushdie on YouTube video

44. "stirred people up": Sidney Cohen at the "LSD Reunion Party," video on YouTube. See Excerpt in Appendices.

45. "gentle subversives": O'Dell, Denis with Bob Neaverson, *At The Apple's Core: The Beatles From the Inside* (Peter Owen Ltd. Publishers, 2002) p. 80

46. toast and tea: Video of the visitor to Tittenhurst is on YouTube

47. on closing the Fillmore Events: Pichaske, David, *A Generation in Motion: Popular Music and Culture in the Sixties* (Schirmer Books/ Macmillan, 1979) p.224: Graham remarked, "At this time, I feel I can no longer refuse myself the time and the leisure and the privacy to which any man is rightfully entitled."

48. "soma": Huxley, Aldous, *Brave New World* (Chatto & Windus, 1932)

About the Author

Ilse Niccolini is a composer and former San Francisco Bay Area journalist. She has a degree in English Literature with Honors from the University of California at Berkeley and is a former Editor-in-Chief of an award-winning trends and arts magazine. Her work has also appeared in *Film/Tape World*, *The City* and the *Boston Herald*, writing for Associated Press.

If you enjoyed this book, please consider leaving a review on Amazon, Barnes and Noble, or GoodReads.

Index